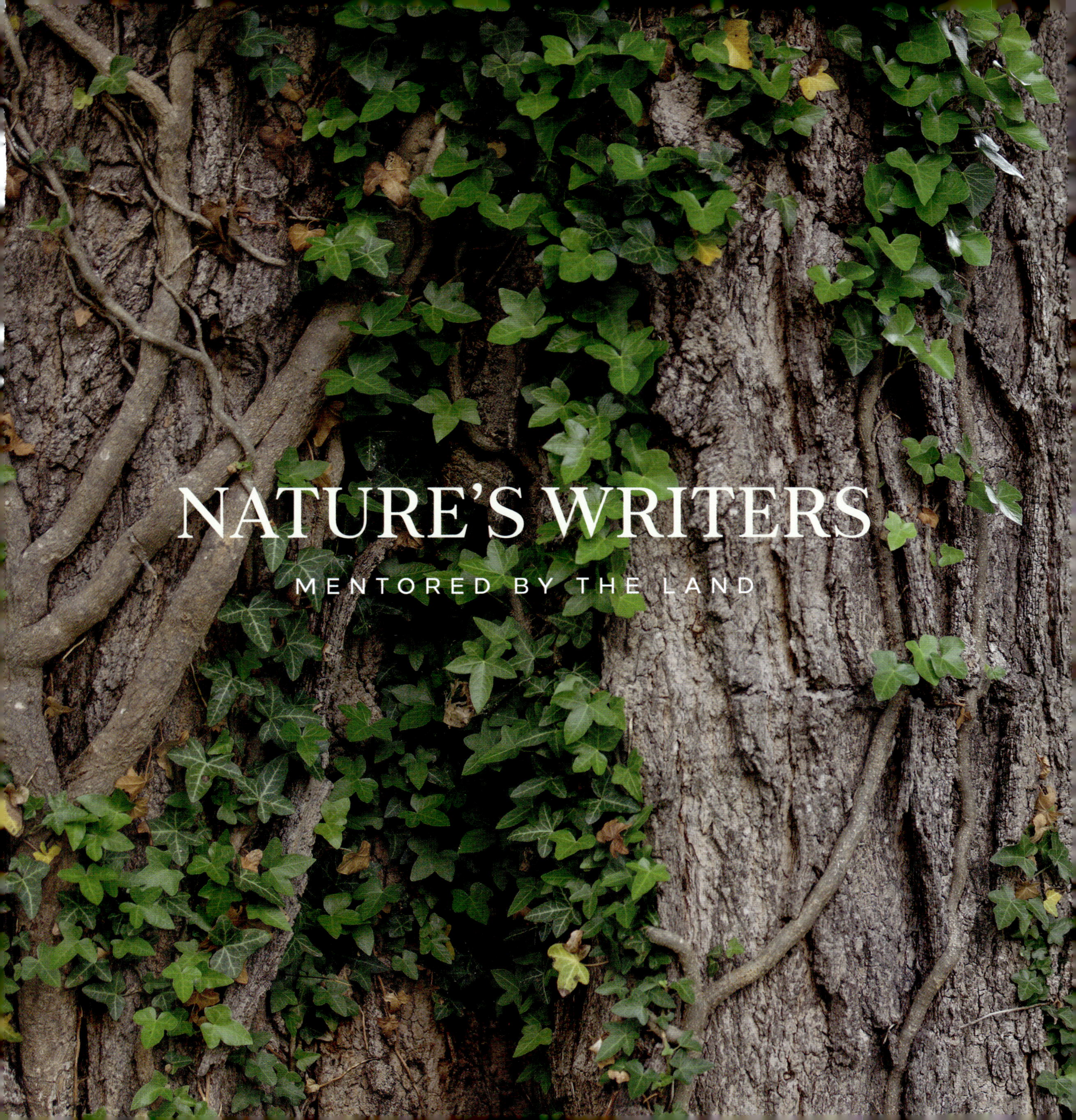

NATURE'S WRITERS
MENTORED BY THE LAND

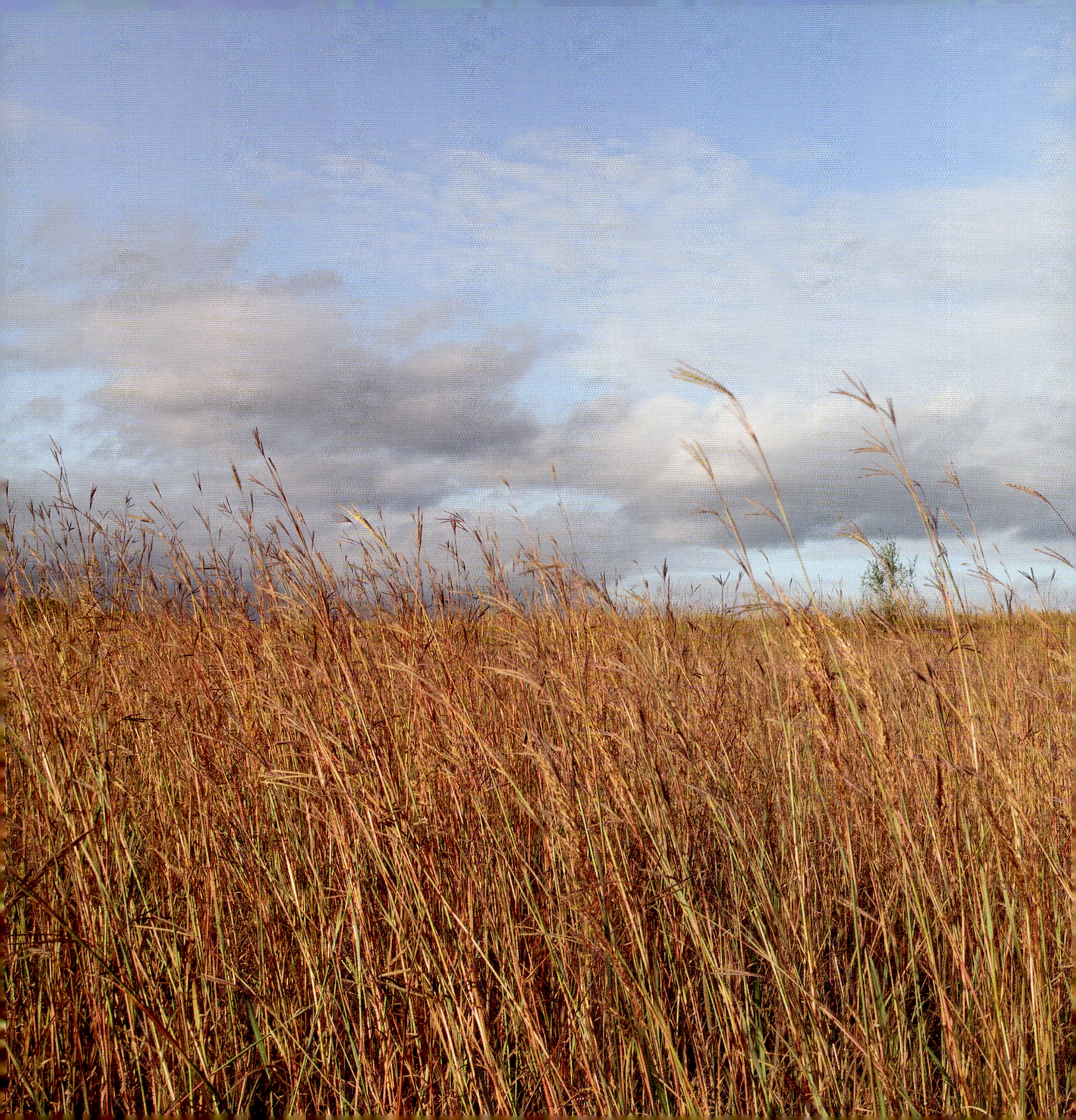

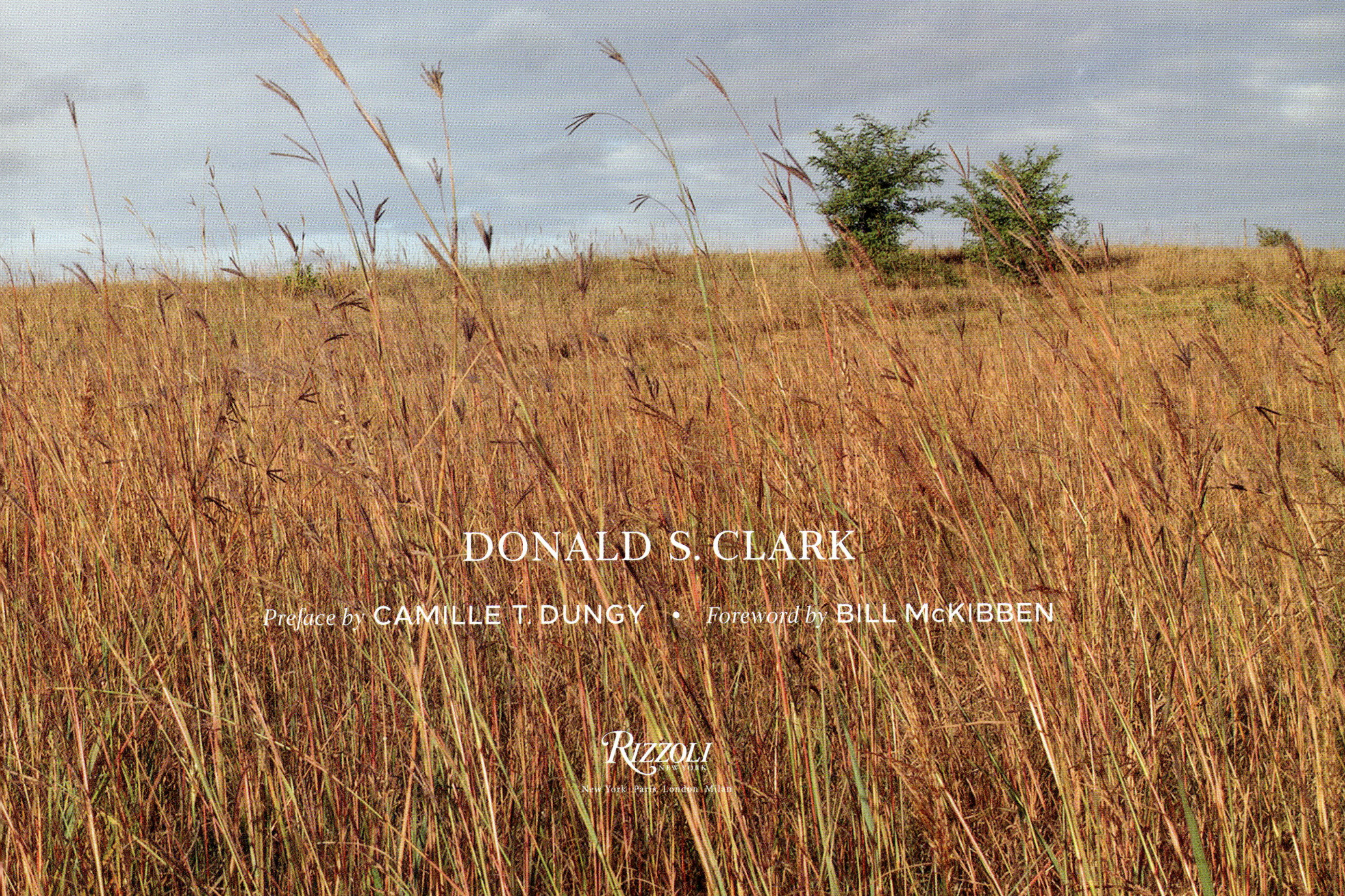

Authors and Poets Who Celebrate the Earth

NATURE'S WRITERS

MENTORED BY THE LAND

DONALD S. CLARK

Preface by CAMILLE T. DUNGY • Foreword by BILL McKIBBEN

RIZZOLI
NEW YORK

New York · Paris · London · Milan

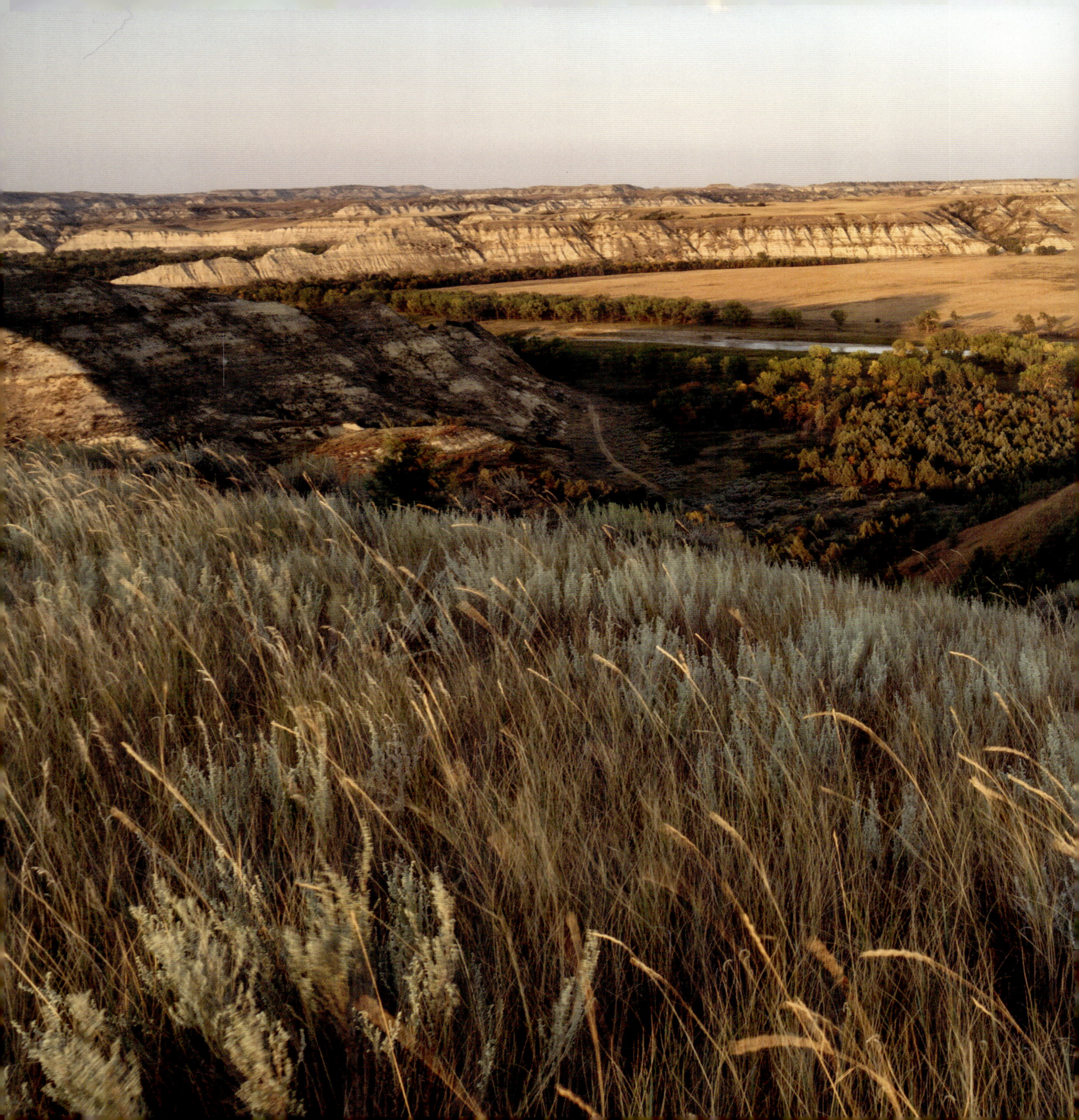

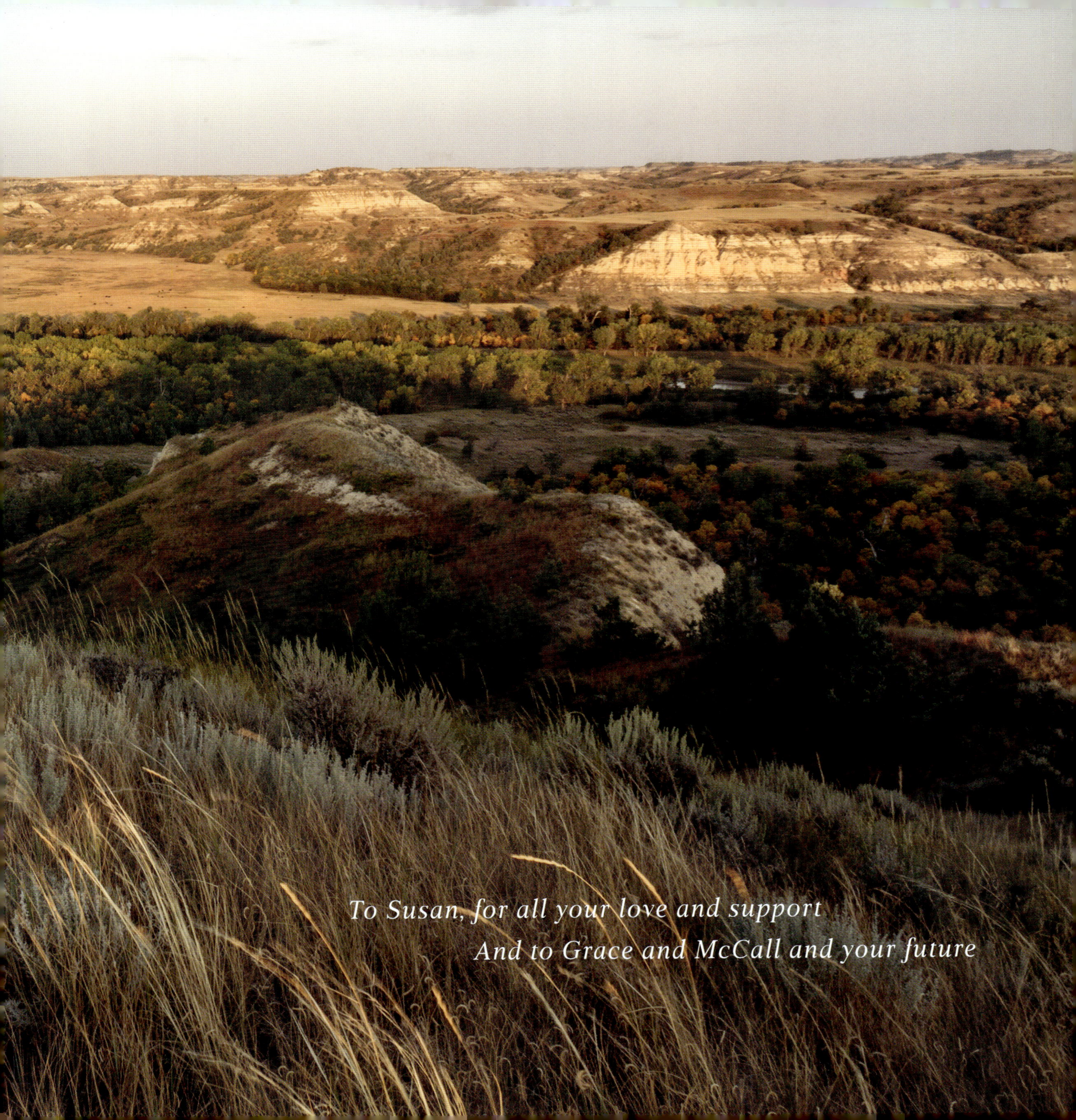
To Susan, for all your love and support
And to Grace and McCall and your future

CONTENTS

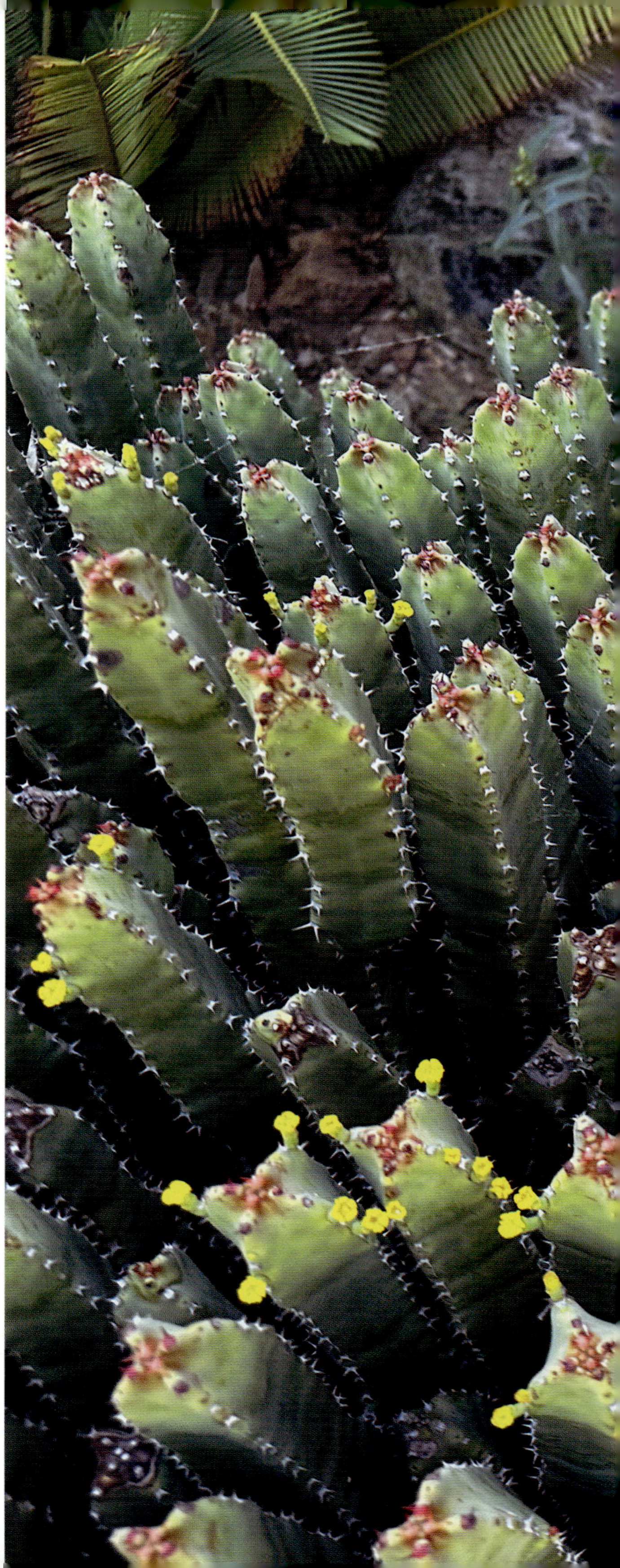

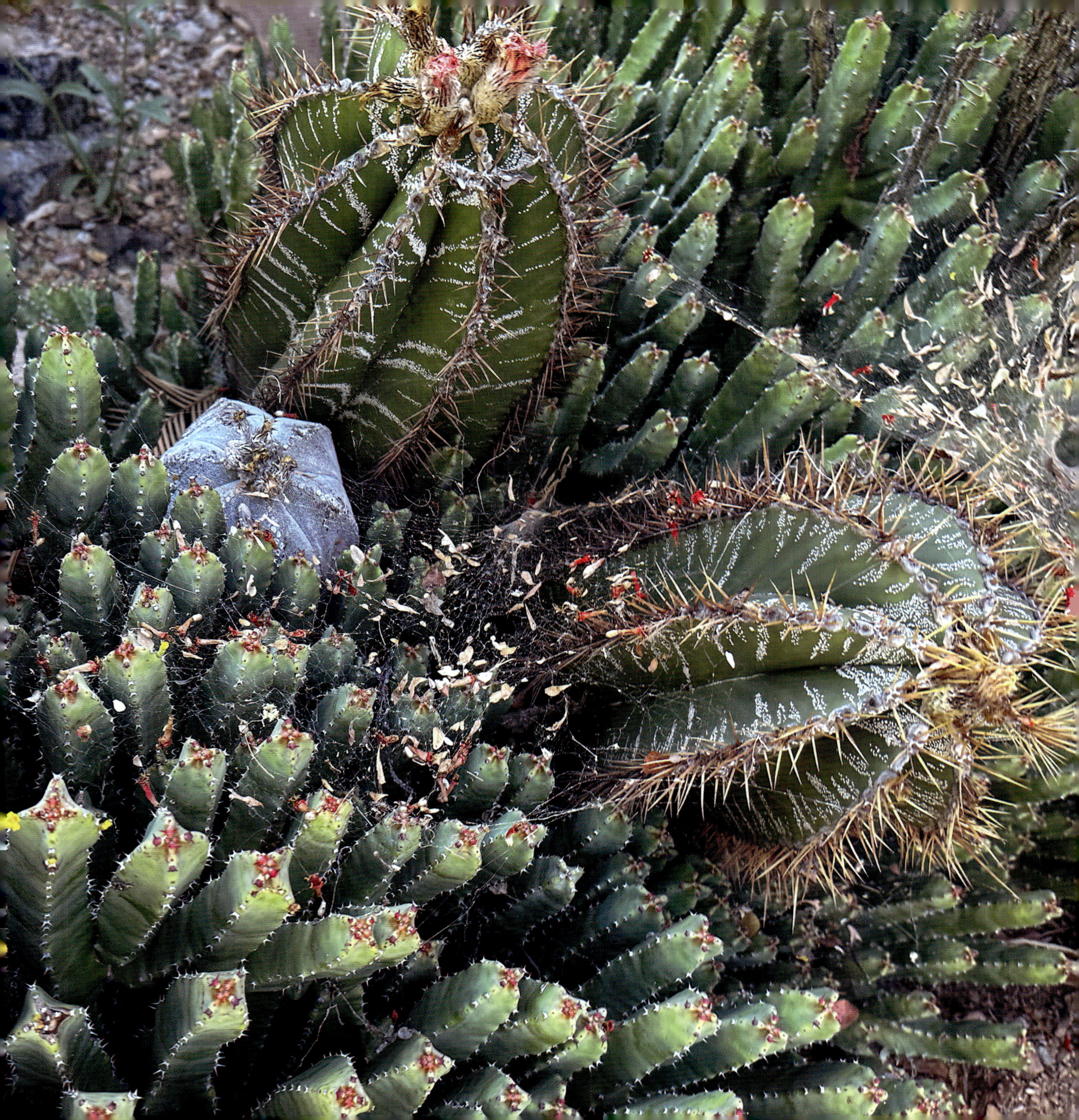

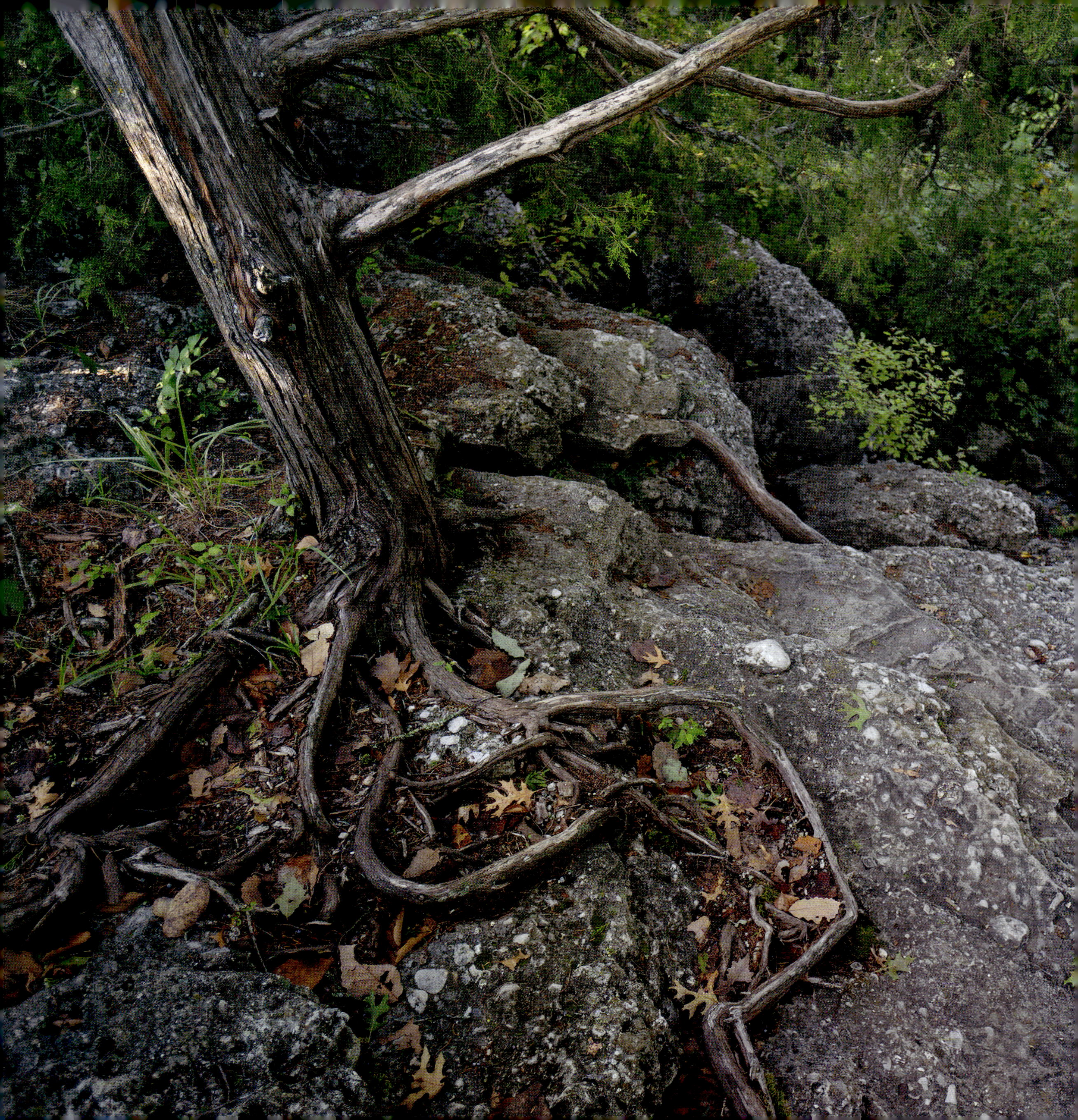

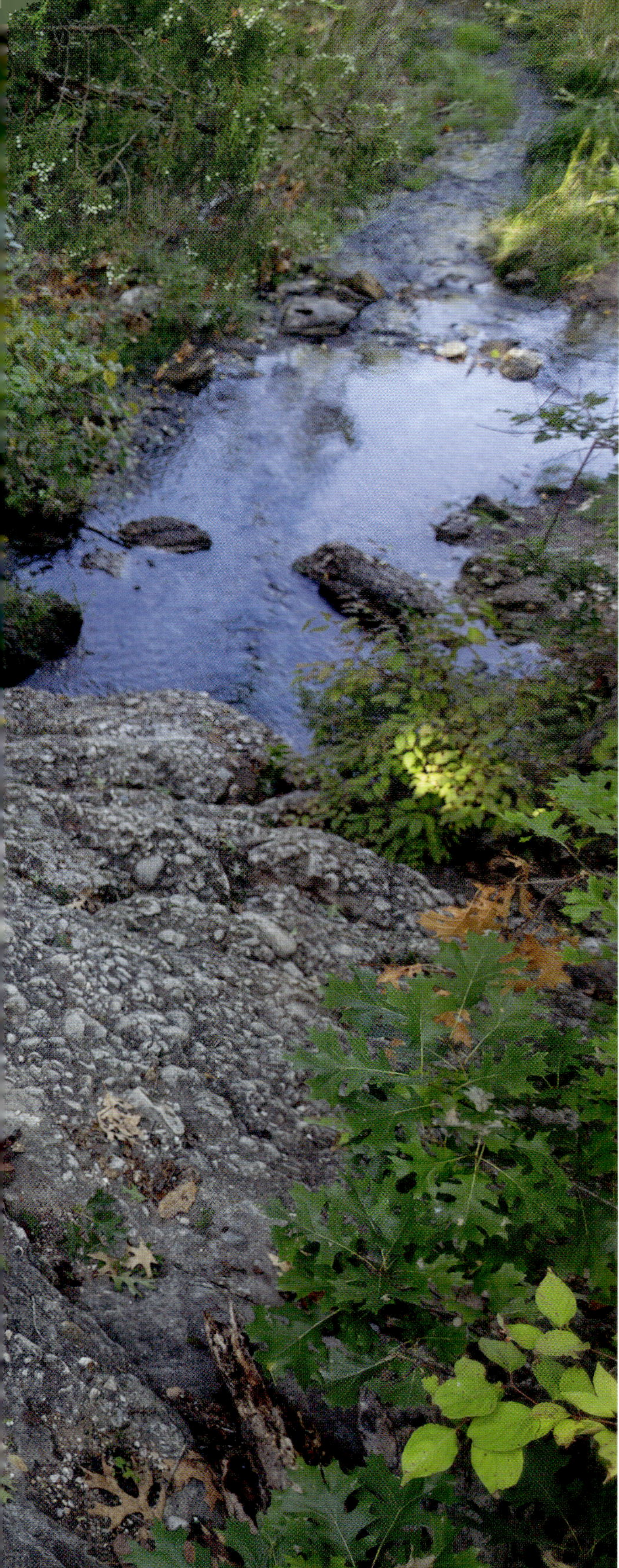

PREFACE 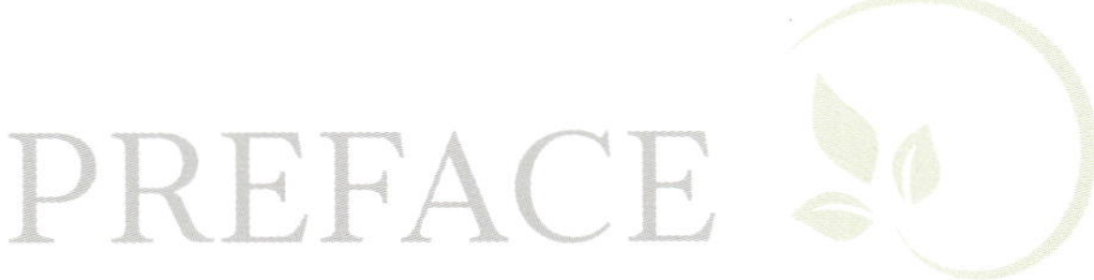

CAMILLE T. DUNGY

When Don Clark first contacted me to ask if he could photograph the places I love, I wasn't so sure I wanted to say yes. This world doesn't lend itself to such openness. But Clark convinced me to allow him into some of my favorite spaces, and seeing these beloved locations through his eyes felt immensely rewarding.

For one thing, Clark's images convey the kind of patience that lots of people don't seem to possess these days. His lens caught smiling prairie dogs and flitting damselflies and even seemed to catch Lewis flax blossoms mid-bow in an early spring breeze. And when I protested that my own space wasn't particularly large, just a small suburban plot, he assured me that he meant this idea more broadly than just my backyard and hoped that the project more clearly conveyed the parts of the world that we writers love. So I sent him all around the county, to paths and streambeds and prairie dog towns I regularly visit. The result of these excursions was a series of photos I will cherish for a long time to come.

Some of the subjects of Clark's lens, the spaces and plants and creatures his photographs capture, are in jeopardy. Construction projects and other habitat encroachment, climate change, fires, and floods: all of these and much more imperil many of the spaces I suggested Clark visit. I know the same is true for the places that other writers featured in this book shared with Clark. And so I am grateful for this book's documentary project—the way it helps us know a world too many of us have already lost or are losing, and the way it helps us see a world so many of us deeply love.

   Camille T. Dungy • Colorado

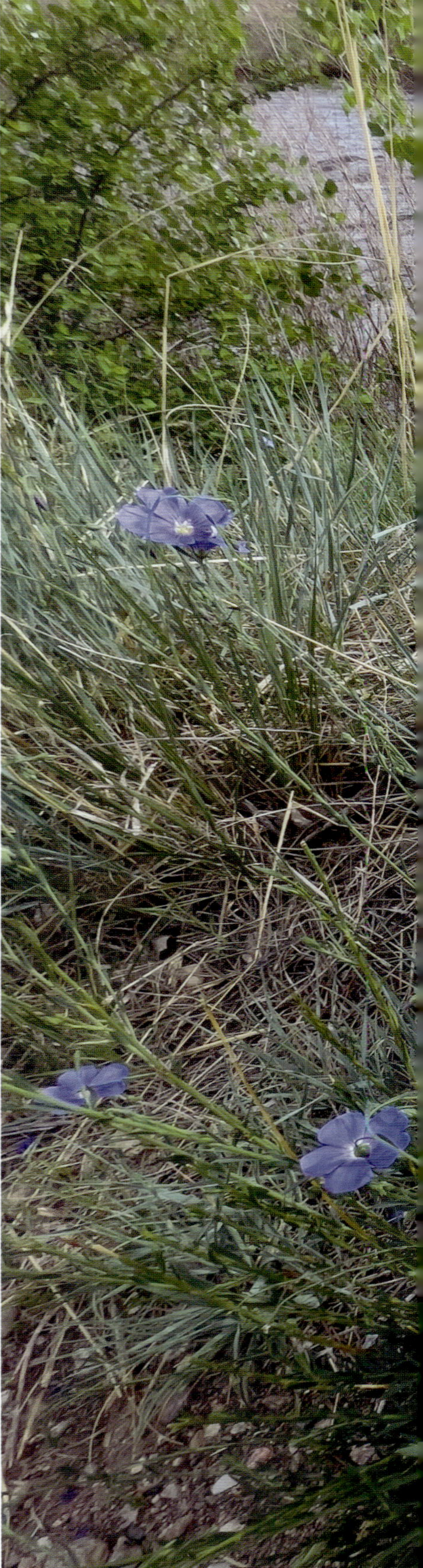

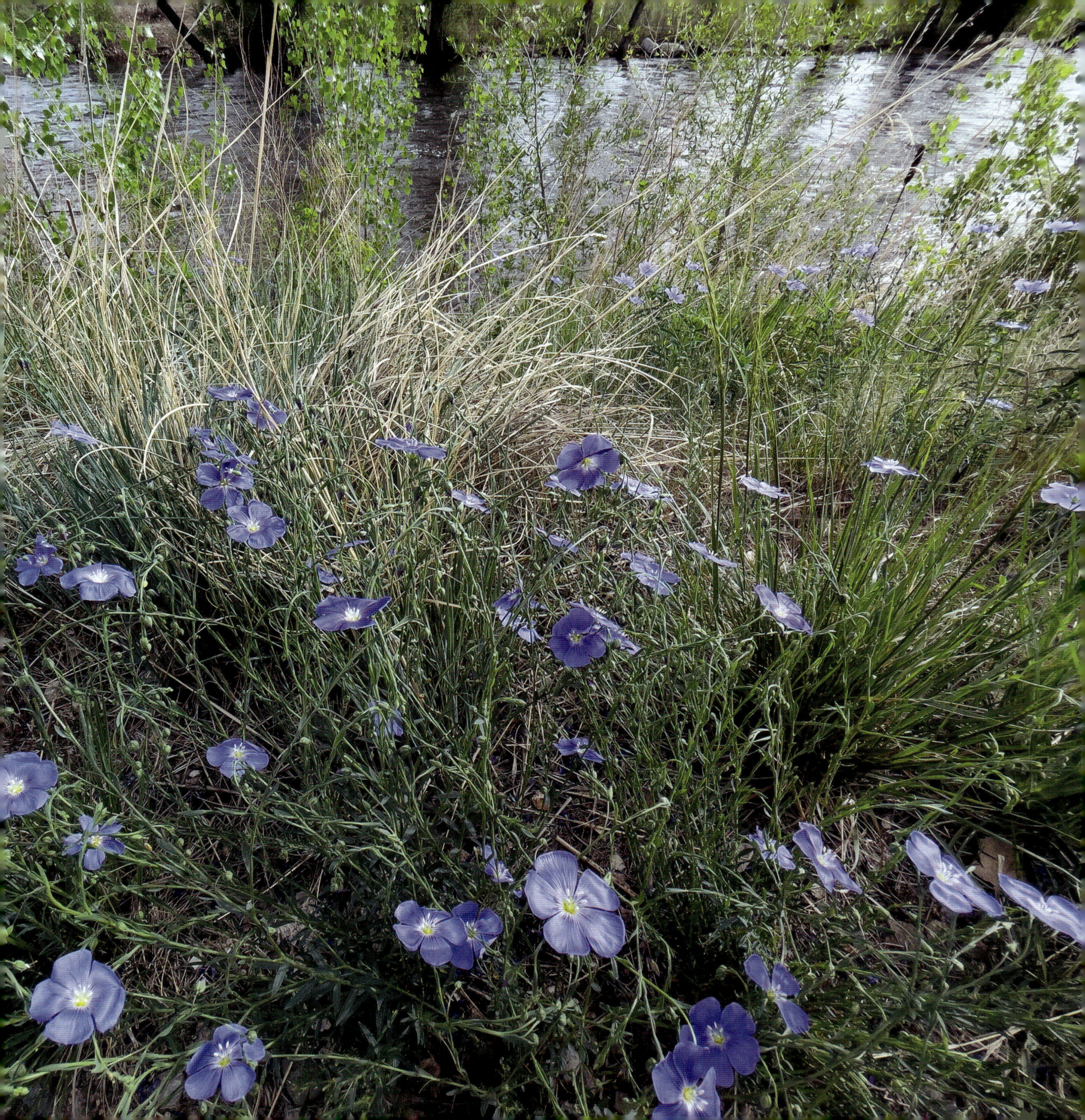

FOREWORD

BILL McKIBBEN

I have a theory—almost certainly wrong—that each of us has a landscape for which we are particularly suited, and that if we are lucky enough to stumble across it, and game enough to make it our home, then it will provide endless challenges and solace. (It is, of course, akin to the idea that somewhere in the world our soulmate waits, and that too is surely wrong, except that after four decades of a talk-filled and joyful marriage you couldn't prove it by me.) I hold this theory, of course, because that's how it worked for me.

When I was a young writer, I had perhaps the most city job imaginable. At age 21, a few weeks out of college, I moved to Manhattan to write the "Talk of the Town" column for the *New Yorker*. I knew the city from the Yonkers tip of the Bronx to the far parts of Far Rockaway, and if I imagined my future, I imagined it there. In fact, when I occasionally left the city it was only to understand it better—the first really long story I worked on for the magazine involved following every pipe and wire in my sublet apartment to its origin or destination. I visited oil wells in the Brazilian jungle because Con Ed was buying oil from them, and I traced the city's miraculous water supply network to the headwaters of the Delaware River. And then the time came to write up that report, to produce 30,000 words of copy from my year's worth of far-flung notes. Just as I was about to begin, one of my colleagues—the joyfully curious Lawrence Weschler—stuck his head into my office and said, "Do you want to go to the Adirondacks for six weeks?" As it happens, he'd been planning to spend the winter at a writer's retreat called Blue Mountain Center, but a family emergency had intervened; if I wanted to head up the next day, I could take his place. I rented a car and headed north.

     Bill McKibben • New York

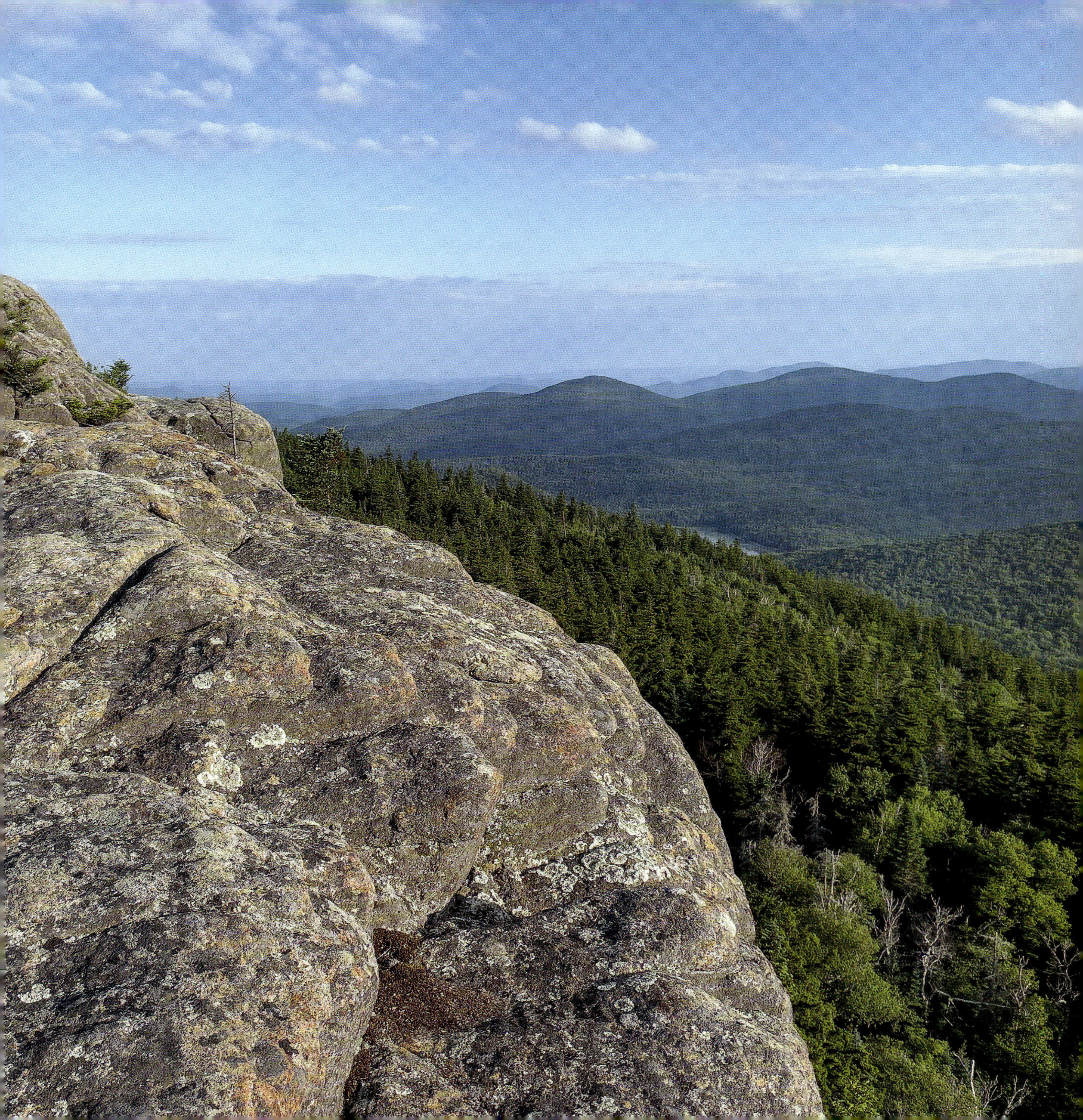

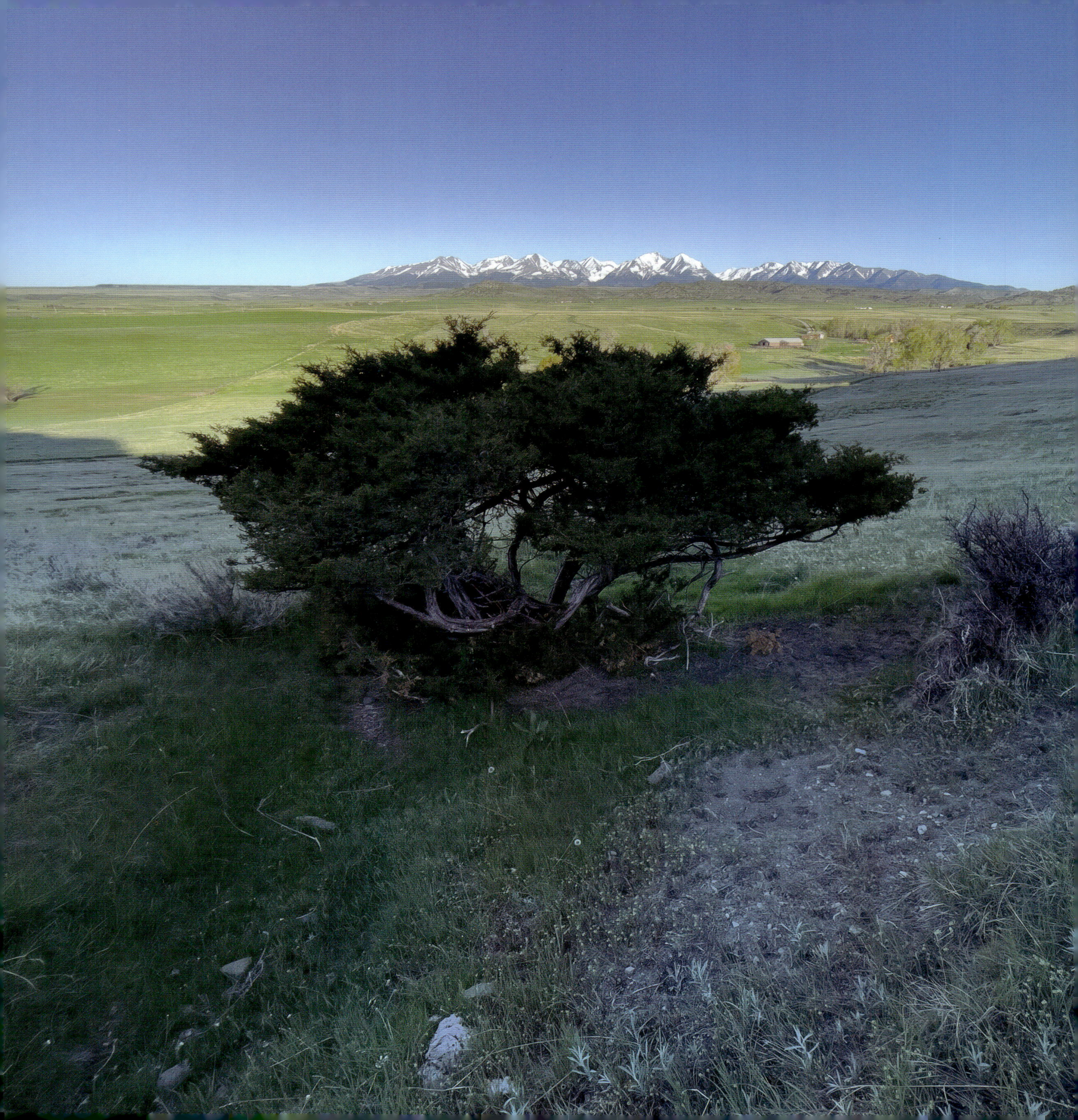

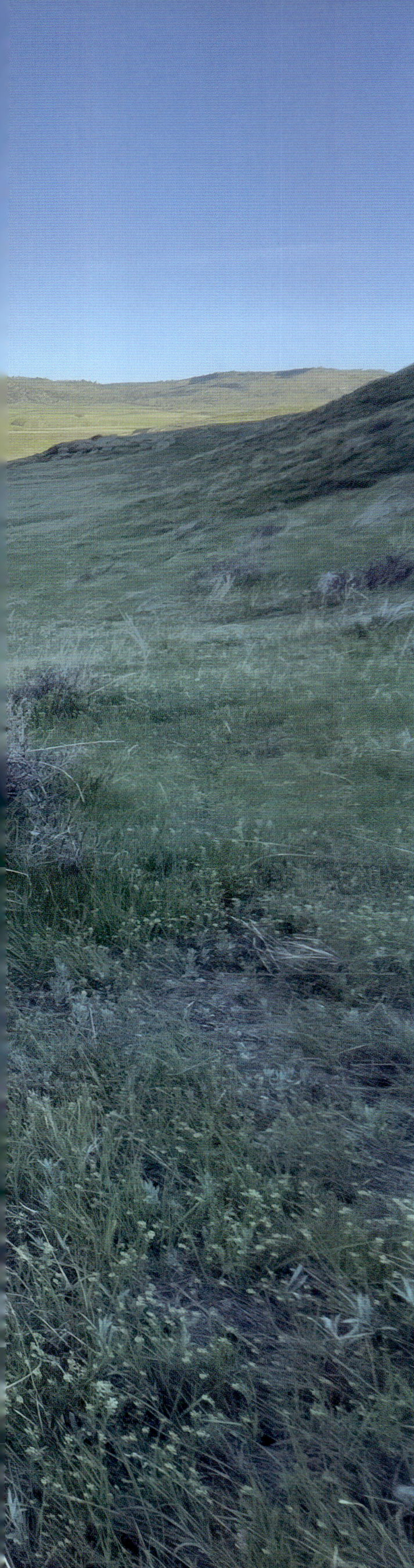

Though the Adirondacks are the largest wilderness by far in the American East—a state park larger than Yellowstone, Yosemite, Glacier, and Grand Canyon National Parks combined—I knew nothing about them. The Hudson was the great river of the great city; I'd ridden it on the Circle Line, and braved passage on a homemade hovercraft, but it had never occurred to me to wonder where it came from (a swampy pond on the shoulder of the state's highest peak), and in this I was not alone. When we think about nature, the American gaze instinctively jerks west. What could there be in upstate New York?

What there could be—as I found out when the sun rose on my first morning there—was a place meant for me. I fell in love, simple as that, with the same outsized emotions that accompany any crush. Everything about this place did it for me, especially in the locked-in cold of deep winter. (This was in the mid-1980s; the greenhouse effect hadn't yet seized control of the weather.) I couldn't get enough of the blue-sky middays, but I liked the snowstorms even better. With the leaves down, I felt an almost erotic connection to the revealed shape of the hills and ridges as the dropping sun shone from behind. I kept working on my New York opus, a few hours each morning, but I always found my way outside by noon, ready for another round of cross-country skiing. When my residency ended, I returned to the city, but I went back north every chance I got and learned that I loved these mountains almost as much in the spring and summer and fall. And just in time—over the next year or two, the *New Yorker* entered a turbulent phase, and eventually I quit. With my willing wife, I left the city at 25 and headed for the hills, where I've spent my life ever since.

The land where we settled, which you can see in Don Clark's photographs, was in an unglamorous, remote, thinly settled, and poor part of the Adirondacks, dominated by a singularly noble peak. Crane Mountain is only 3,251 feet tall, but it is broad-shouldered and spreading, with two summits and a high-altitude pond nestled in between. On its flanks, if you know where to look, are caves and cascades, beaver ponds and berry patches. I've wandered it almost my whole life now. We gave my daughter–born in its shadow–Crane as a middle name; when she married (again in its shadow), she and her husband took Crane as their married name. For me, this mountain–and its surrounding lakes and peaks and marshes and woods–is the uncontested navel of the universe. I understand the world through it; when I wrote *The End of Nature*, the first book about what we now call climate change, I was already under its spell, and so the emotion of that book is less fear than sadness about what we were doing to erode the sweet wildness of this place.

And every place. Because of course I understood that not everyone thought about the mountains of the American East like I did. I'd already visited Edward Abbey in Tucson, Arizona, and Moab, Utah, and I knew that he did not care for the "fuzzy hills" of his Appalachian youth; he didn't come fully alive until he reached the giant and austere red-rock country that made his heart sing. With the success of that first book of mine, I was welcomed into the lovely company of this country's nature writers and soon came to know many of their places firsthand. Terry Tempest Williams and her husband, Brooke, showed me the mountains above Salt Lake City and then the sere lands around Castle Valley. I spent a few happy days at Barbara Kingsolver's house in the southern Appalachian Mountains, and her husband, Steven, hiked me through the wide forest gulf where it was nestled. I saw Barry Lopez's mighty Pacific Northwest rainforest through his eyes. W. S. Merwin, over and over again, led me through the unspeakably beautiful palm forest he'd raised from nothing in a few Maui acres, and Rick Bass was my guide to the primeval high wild of Montana's Yaak country. Longleaf pine means Janisse Ray to me; I see it through her kind and savvy eyes.

It was always a deep pleasure to witness the deep pleasure each writer took in their surroundings–I cannot really imagine any of them in any other place; they found where

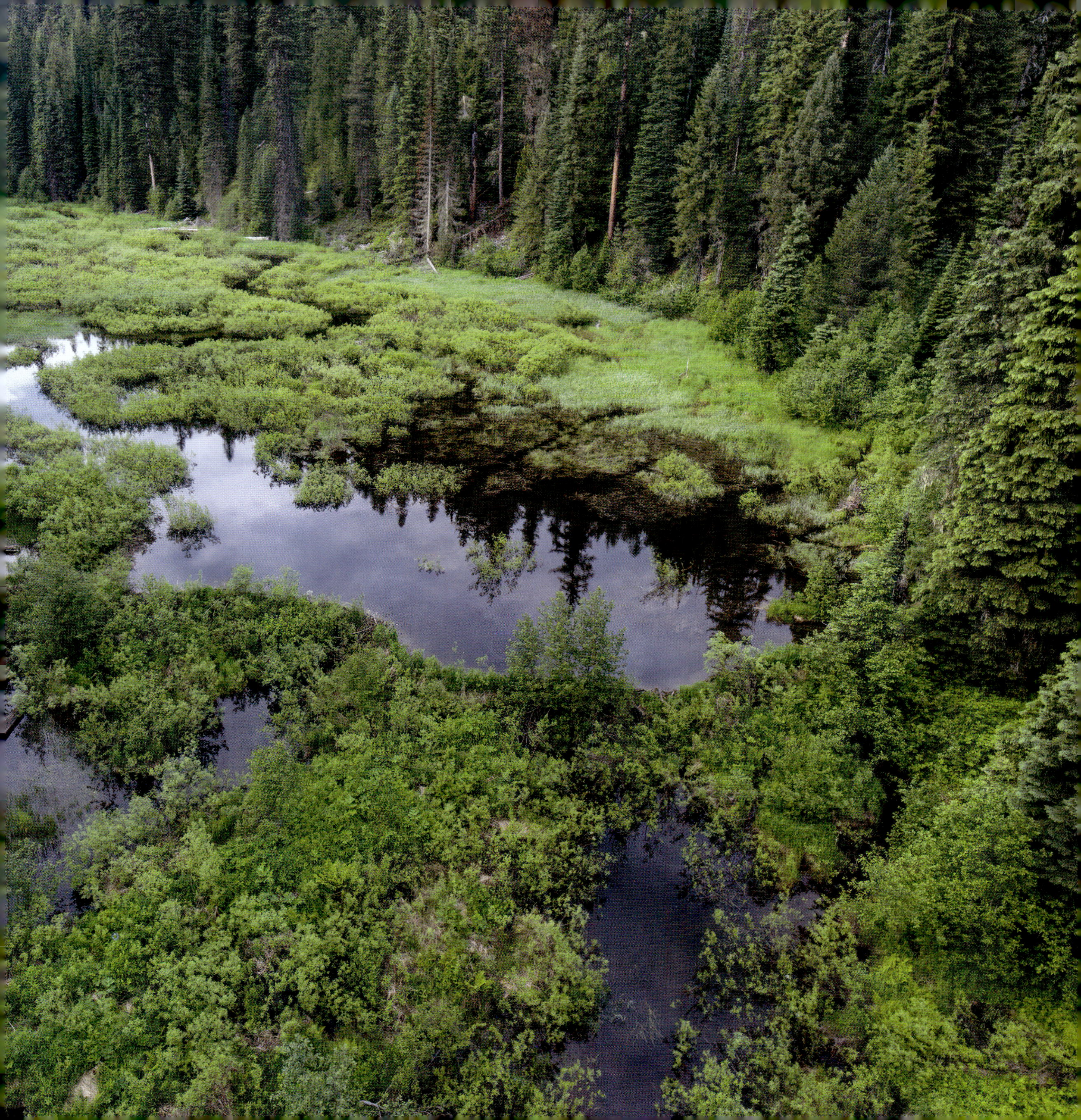

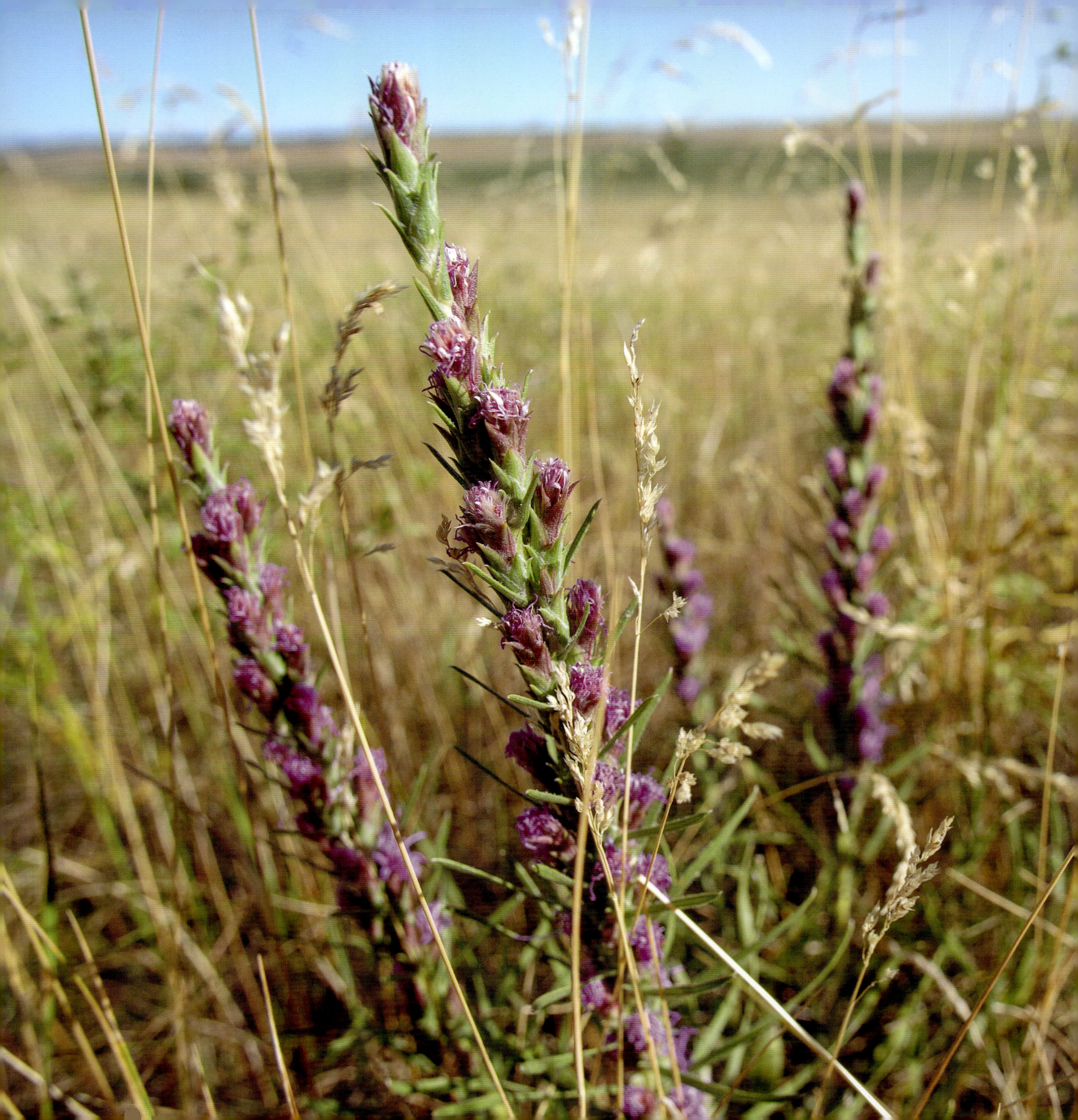

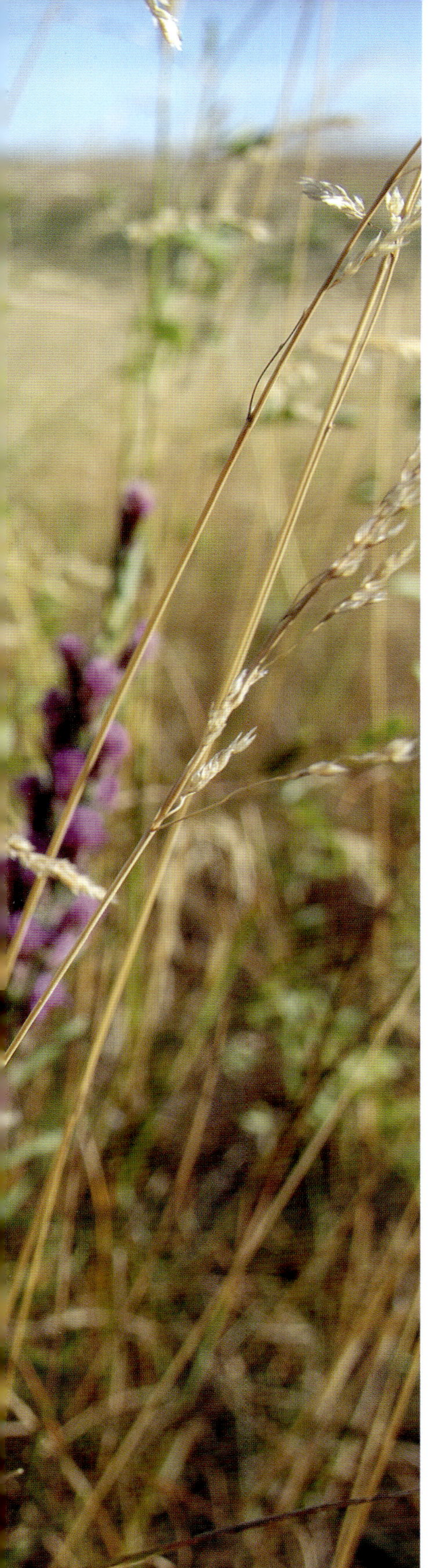

their heart clicked and settled in. And the same is true for the historical writers I've come to know. I wrote the foreword to an edition of John Burroughs's writings, so I wandered the pastoral Catskills with a particular eye to their calm beauty. Doing the same for John Muir, I came to know his High Sierra—it is no wonder that he invented our modern grammar and vocabulary of wildness in that uniquely charmed place, where humidity and mosquitoes are distant rumors and the clean granite stretches on in endless waves. I'd grown up in suburban Boston, five miles from Walden Pond, and I was in charge of a new edition of that classic, too, so I wandered its shores anew and understood how its seasons had opened up Henry David Thoreau to insights that changed the world.

It's always and forever a delight to be shown these places by the people who love them, no matter the circumstance. There is a particular joy in showing off one's own place. I remember the first time Terry Tempest Williams came to climb Crane Mountain with me. We'd hardly climbed 300 feet in elevation before she stopped for a half hour to commune with a red eft, a tiny newt that was sitting on the trail. In her dry country, she said, such a membraneous creature was almost inconceivable. My Alaskan writer friend Hank Lentfer came to visit the Adirondacks last autumn, and the day before he landed, a rainstorm swept through. I feared mightily it would knock down the leaves before he could see October's orgasmic moment in these parts, but there were plenty left to knock his hiking socks askew. Still, I know Terry wouldn't be happy here year-round and Hank needs the salt water of Glacier Bay as badly as I need the bracing fresh water of Crane Mountain Pond.

I've found, over the years, that the community of nature writers is far closer and far more supportive than any other literary community I know, and I think that has something to do with place. Almost without exception, every one of the writers I've mentioned has found themselves fighting to protect the particular landscape they love, and they've been able to broaden that love to the planet as a whole. It did not surprise me for a second (though it did gladden my heart) to approach Columbus Circle in New York during a huge climate march I'd helped organize in 2014 and see both Terry Tempest Williams and Rick Bass standing there with signs. There's not a living writer in these pages who hasn't pitched in on the climate fight.

I think that's in part because falling in love with any one place requires a groundedness that doesn't come so easily to Americans anymore. These writers know the stories of their place, stretching back to Indigenous inhabitants and even prehuman times. And they know the human communities that inhabit them at present. Their knowledge tends to be deep, ranging from names of wildflowers to names of local county commissioners. But paradoxically that groundedness is freeing; just as falling in love with one other person makes you feel happier toward the species as a whole, knowing and caring about one landscape makes it easier to see the worth of them all. At the same time, simply by virtue of being outside often in a place they care about, they have a grace denied most Americans—they're allowed to feel small against the sprawling backdrop of the natural world. Our culture—which, by now, involves staring at smartphones for constant updates—is a recipe for self-absorption. By contrast, it is impossible to wander any wild place and not be reminded that you are a fairly minor element in the great opera of space and time that whirls by unstopping.

All of which is to say that I think Don has conducted one of the most potent literary critiques I can imagine, almost certainly more useful than many of the more formal investigations carried out in university English departments, where all of these writers are put under the microscope. The wide-angle lens, it turns out, is a better tool. If you really want to understand these wonderful writers, you need to know where they're coming from. And now you do.

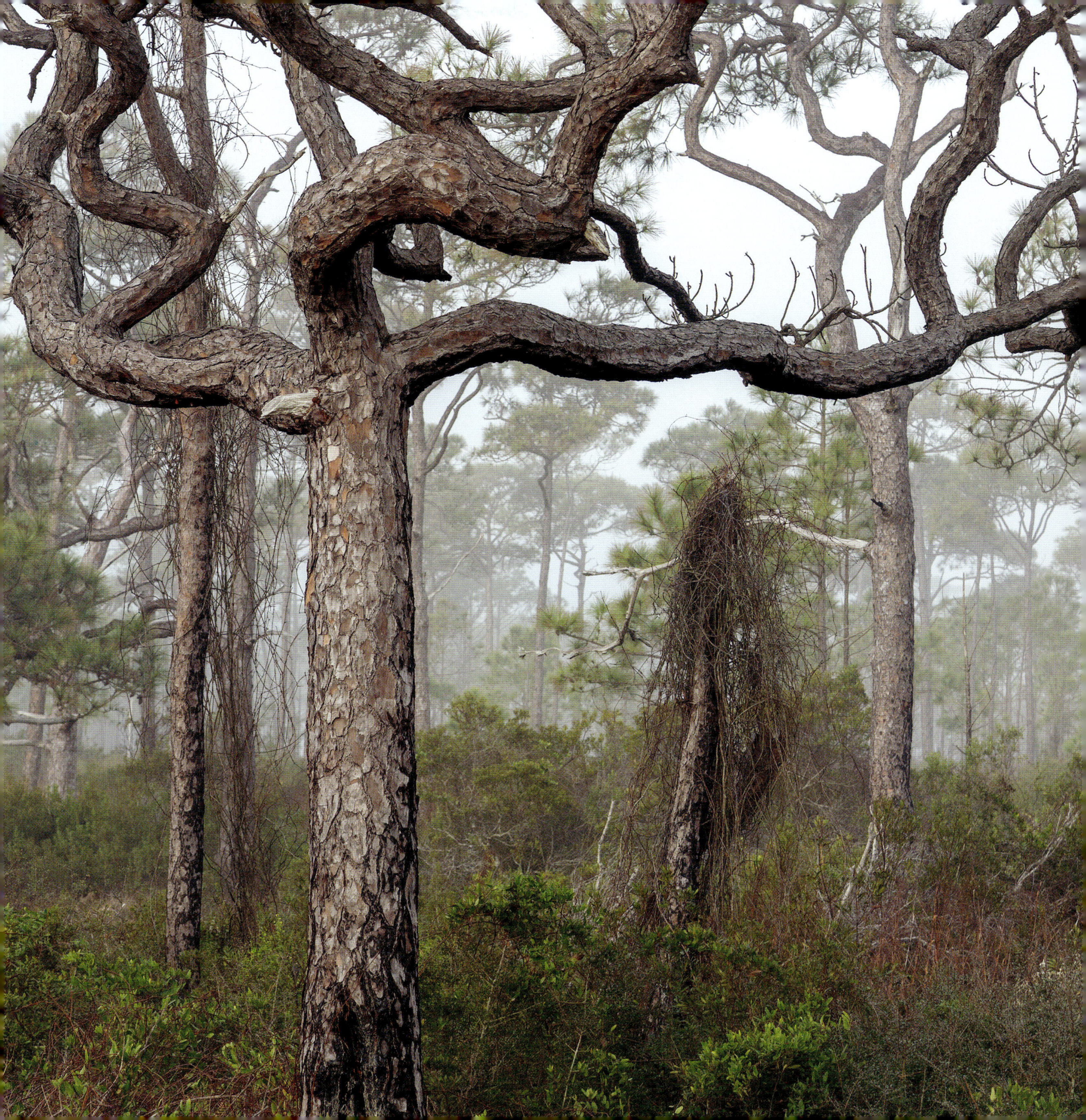

INTRODUCTION

DONALD S. CLARK

As a child, my family led a nomadic life. My father was in and out of the Army, which led to constant moves to places as far west as Texas and as far east as Germany. These moves were often disruptive and hard to take as a child. Just as I started to feel like I was getting used to a place, making friends, and getting comfortable with my surroundings, it would be time to pack up and move somewhere new. While I would have preferred to move less frequently, especially in my adolescence, I did love seeing new places, meeting new people, and experiencing diverse cultures.

I think what I missed most from my childhood experience was a sense of home, of feeling grounded to a specific place. While I never felt that kind of connection as a child, I did feel a connection with the natural environment and an affinity for the beauty of nature no matter where we lived. I loved to be outside, always playing in the nearby woods and fields. I believe my broader connection with the landscape came about from a visit to my school library around the age of 13. I discovered a National Geographic book on national parks and became enamored with their beauty.

This led me to find other books on national parks and various landscapes of the American West, with photographic images by the likes of Ansel Adams, Edward Weston, and David Muench. Images of these places had me in awe of all the beauty that our country has to offer. But perhaps even more influential were the writings that usually accompanied the imagery. Essays, quotations, and excerpts from writers such as John Muir, Aldo Leopold, Rachel Carson, and Barry Lopez helped me gain a better understanding of the

John Muir • California

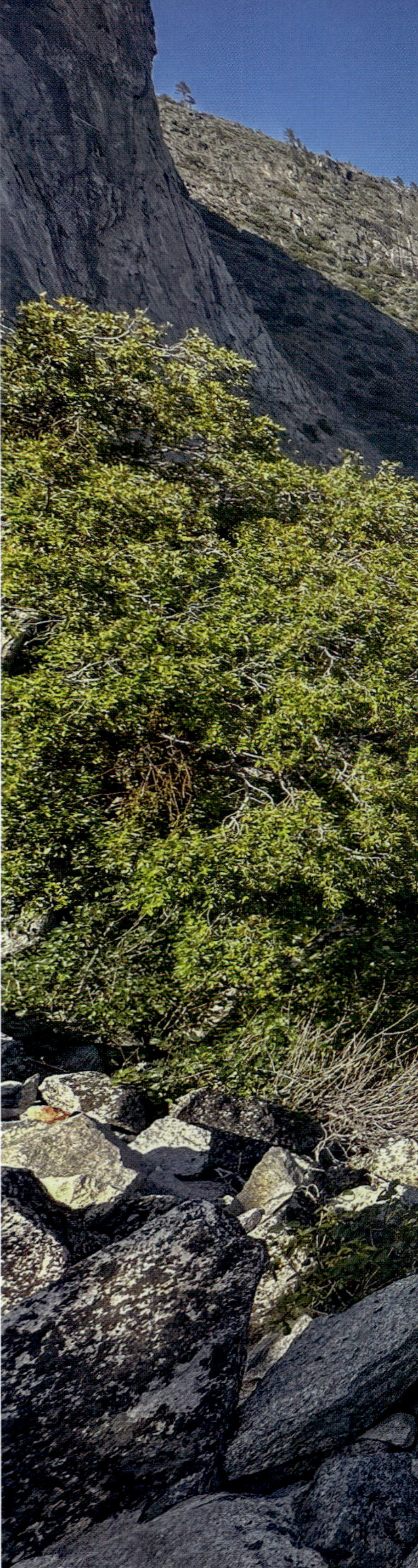

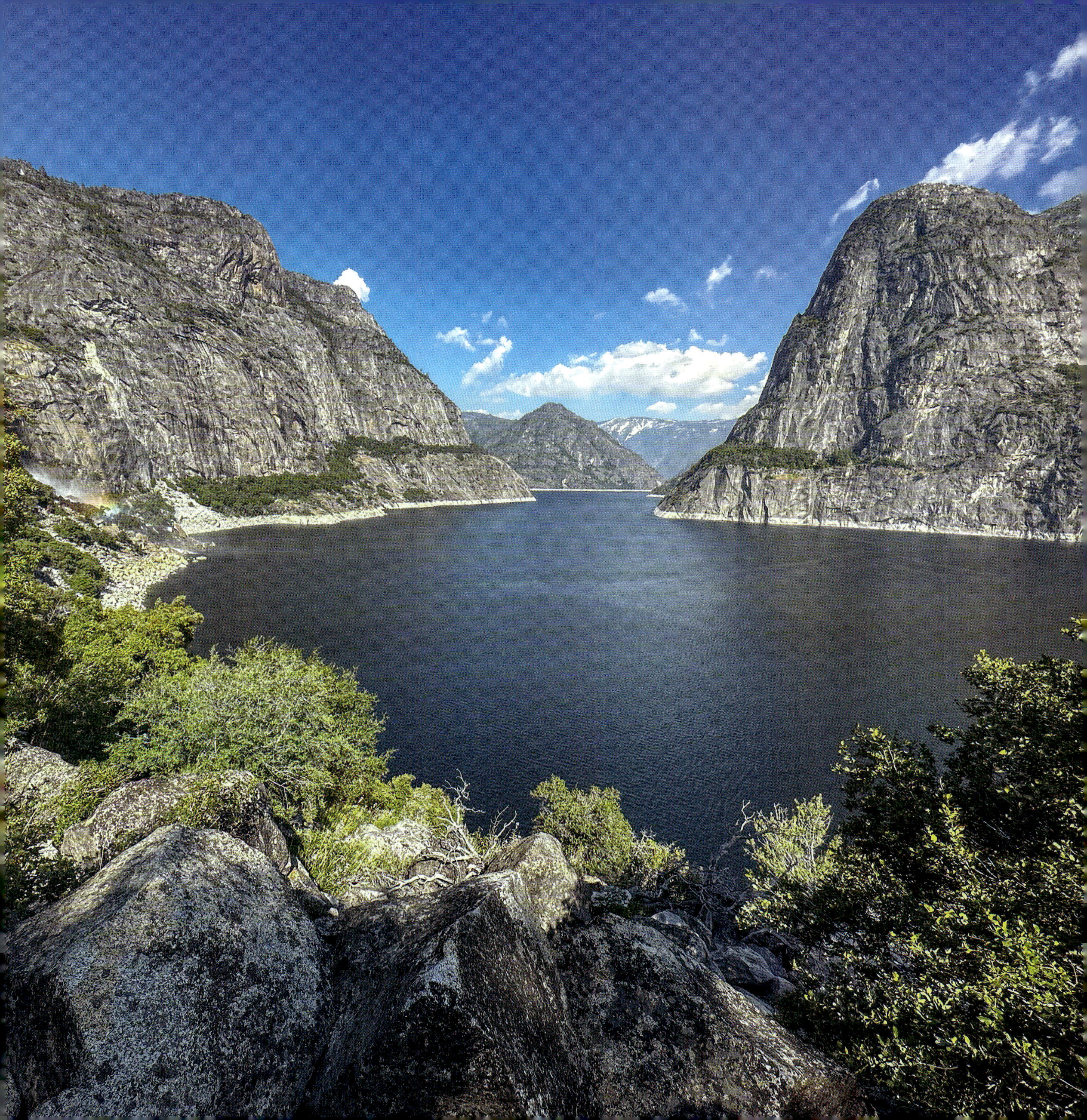

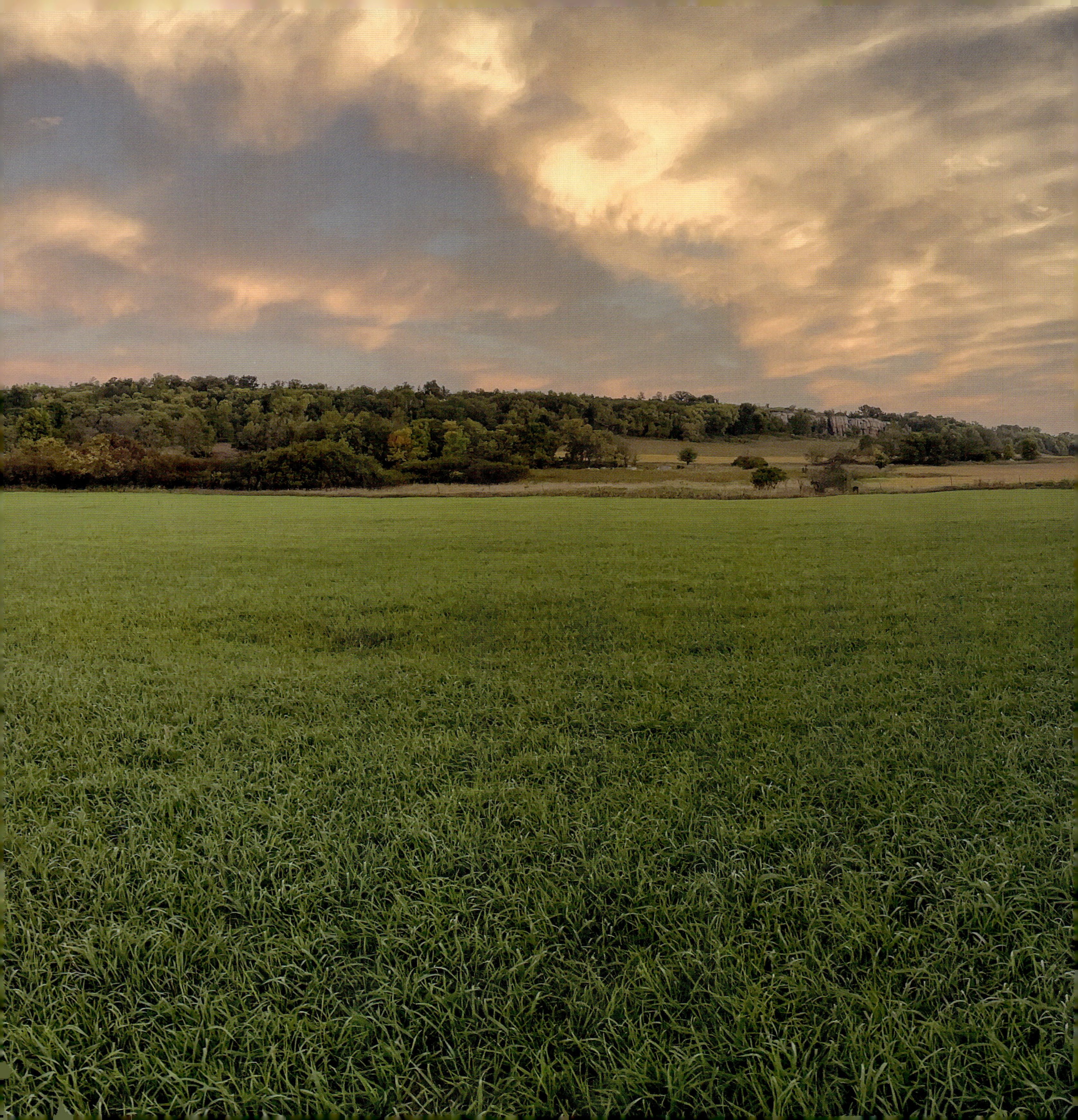

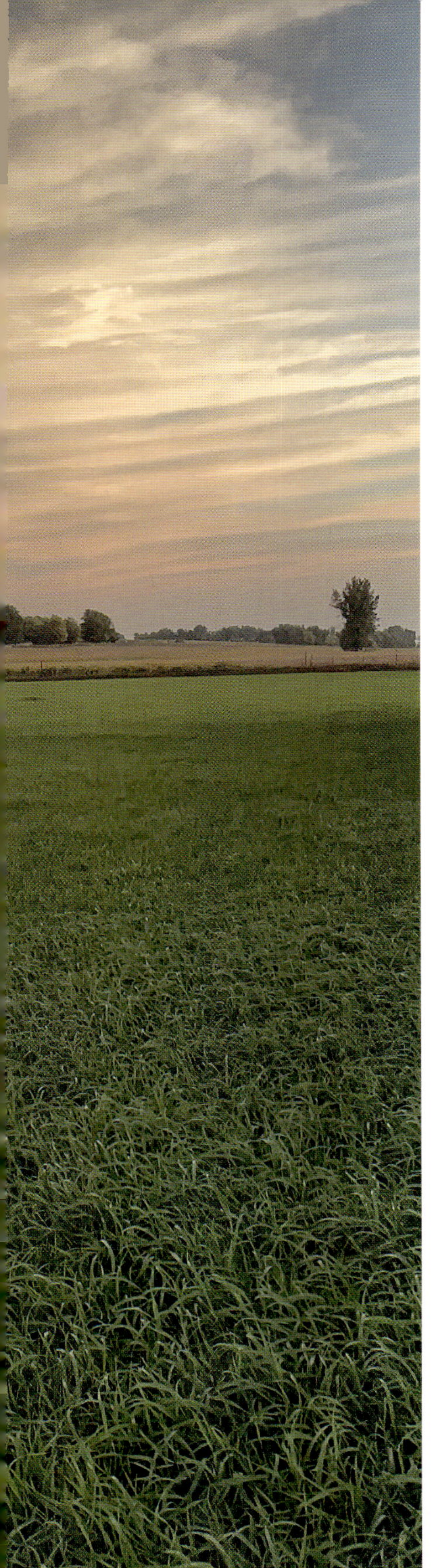

ecological, cultural, and aesthetic significance of not only these places but also other places around the world, both big and small, which led to me having a more empathetic approach to living on our planet. Reading these snippets from various writers made me seek out more of their work and helped build upon the foundation that those earlier photographic books had established.

These books influenced me so much that I decided I wanted to study to become a park ranger specializing in interpretation. I had visited many state parks and canoed most of the rivers in Central Florida, but I had never visited a national park. So, after graduating from high school in 1982, I packed my bags to study at Utah State University, which at the time had one of the best programs in natural resources. After my first year, I purchased a 35mm camera and decided I wanted to learn how to use it, so I registered for a basic photography class. I continued taking coursework in natural resources, but I also began taking classes in art and photography. Eventually, I had enough credits accumulated to graduate with a Bachelor of Fine Arts degree with an emphasis in photography. I did not finish my studies in natural resources and never became a park ranger, but throughout my career I have integrated my concern for the environment and landscape into my photography.

As an adult, I have become more grounded—not necessarily to a specific place (I'm still searching), but in general. I have come to understand that, for me, being grounded is about relationships and experiences. I believe this project is also about those two things. The writers included in this book have a strong connection to not only the land that envelops their lives but also their friends, families, and local communities. In addition, there is an interconnectedness among many of the writers in this book. They are a community, often influenced by and influencing one another. These relationships, and the writers' experiences with their respective environments, are the bedrock for much of their work.

This project came about because of my love of the natural world and the people who help make and inspire those connections to the land. I knew it would be important to include both historic and contemporary writers and to include a diverse offering in terms of the writers' geography, gender, ethnicity, and writing style. I also wanted to feel like I had an understanding of each writer's work, so I made it a point to read as much of it as possible prior to contacting them (or, in the case of deceased writers, contacting their family members, trusts, or others responsible for maintaining their legacies).

As I began reaching out to people to gauge their interest in being included in the book, I was amazed by two things. First, the vast majority of those I contacted replied back to me. I must admit I was a bit surprised they were so receptive. It turns out they thought the project had merit and would serve well as a historic record of the importance of place in their writings and, as a body of work, would add a unique collective point of view to their cause. Second, I was struck by how willing they were to give their time, especially during the pandemic. I was able to sit down with most of the writers included to discuss their place and its significance, often over dinner, a beer, some wine, or a lemonade.

Occasionally, I was able to spend an extended period of time with these writers. I hiked up and spent a few nights with Philip Connors and his wife, Mónica, at the summit of the peak in New Mexico where he keeps an eye out for fires and, in his spare time, writes of his relationship to the land and people of the Gila Wilderness. I walked barefoot in Lincoln Park in Seattle with Lyanda Lynn Haupt, who celebrates and writes of finding wildness in one's urban backyard. It was a joy walking the trails with Scott Freeman and his wife, Susan Leopold Freeman, on land that they and their family have worked hard to rehabilitate. Scott writes about the land passionately and Susan illustrates it beautifully to benefit the salmon population on a little stream called Tarboo Creek—with the same dedication that

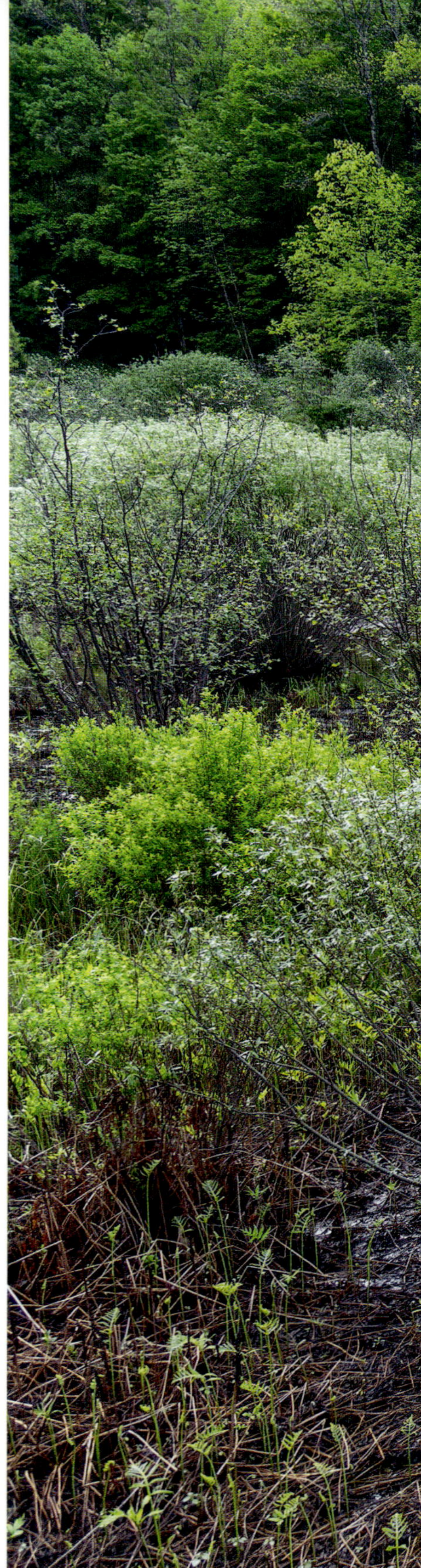

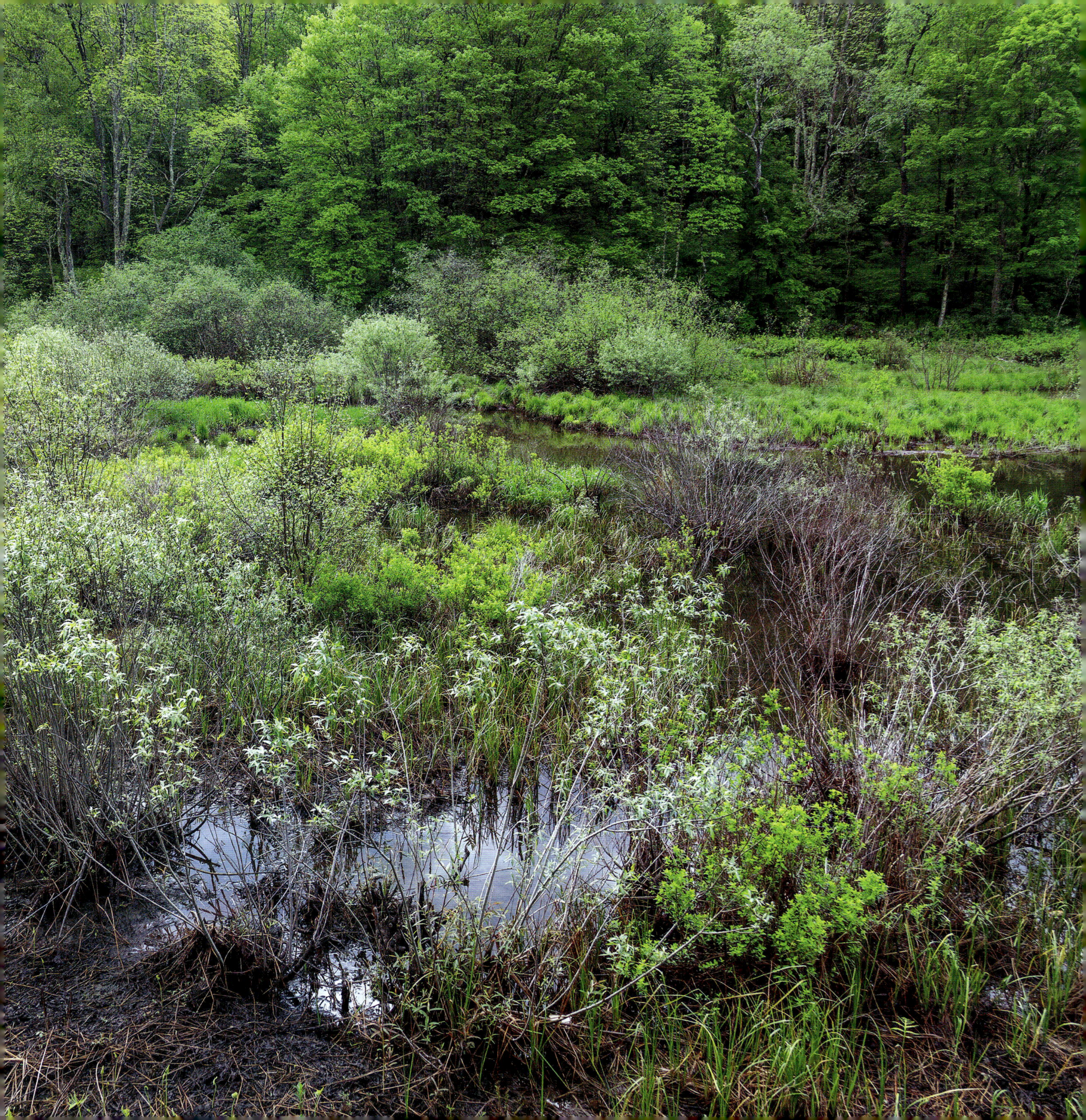

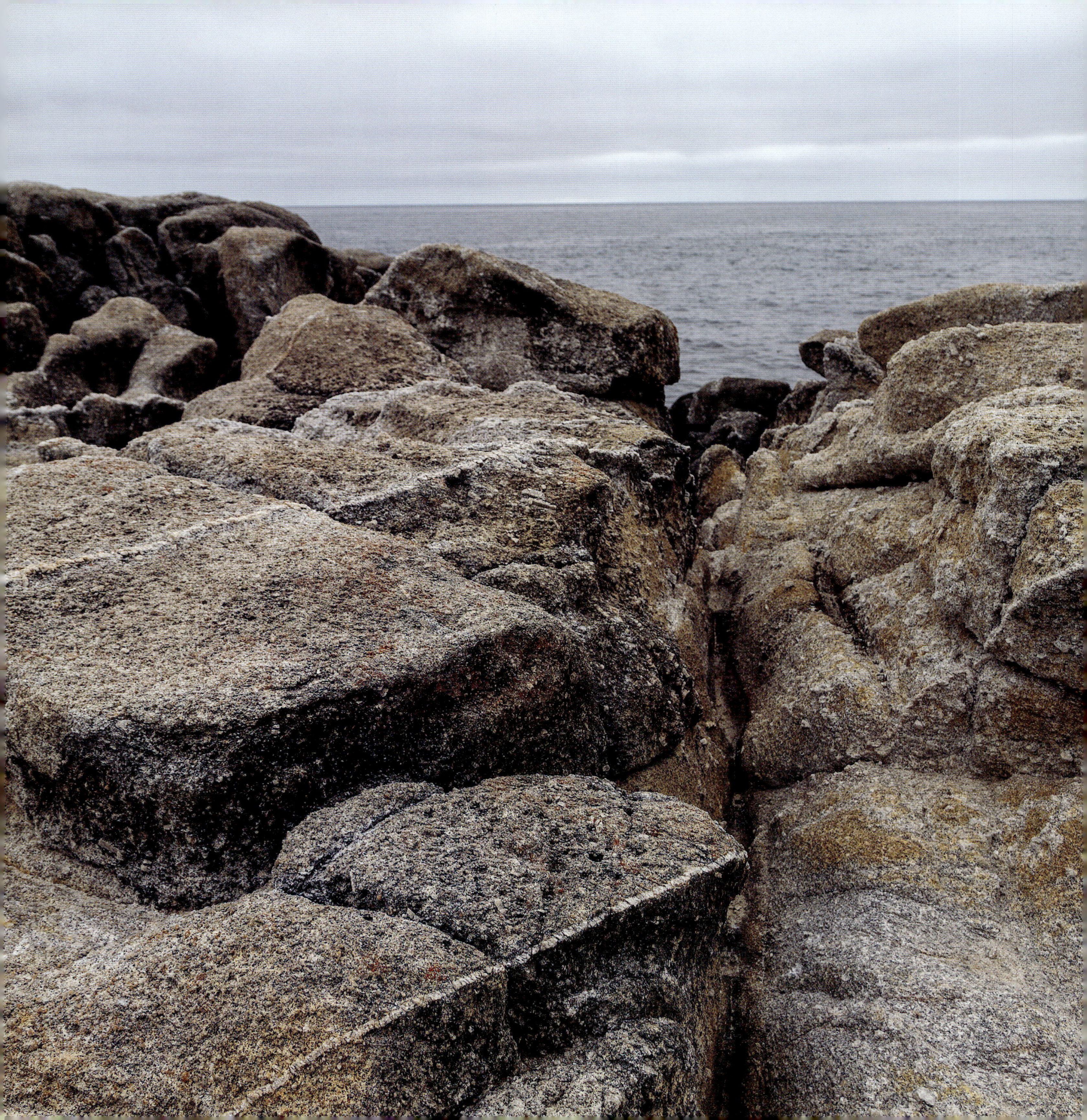

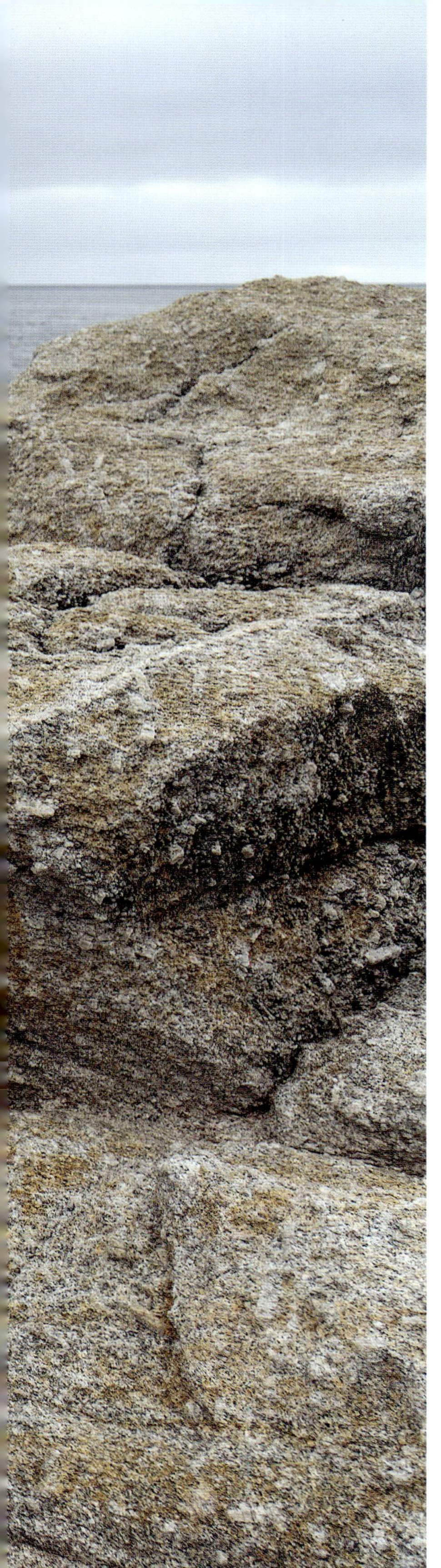

Susan's grandfather, Aldo Leopold, had in Wisconsin. And it was great to spend time with David Gessner kayaking on his 60th birthday in the marshlands and islands of coastal North Carolina. David writes of broad environmental issues and about historic figures in the environmental movement, and he does so with a sense of humor like no other.

These are but a few of my experiences with the writers included in this book; there are far too many to mention by name in a brief introduction. These adventures with each writer, and their willingness to allow me to intrude briefly into their lives, have enriched my life immensely, contributing to my feeling of being grounded.

It has been my goal to discover and document the draw that these places had or have on these individuals. I hope you enjoy my attempts to make connections between my images of their places and the words of these talented writers. Included in the back of this book is a suggested reading list containing selected works from each writer. If you already know someone's work, there is a good chance you will have read some, if not all, of their books. That's great, but I also hope you will consider reading the work of other writers you may be less familiar with. All of these individuals have chosen to dedicate their lives to drawing attention to the beauty and health of our planet.

Edward Abbey

"But the love of wilderness is more than a hunger

for what is always beyond reach; it is also an

expression of loyalty to the earth, the earth which

bore us and sustains us, the only home we shall

ever know, the only paradise we ever need—if only

we had the eyes to see."

From *Desert Solitaire: A Season in the Wilderness*

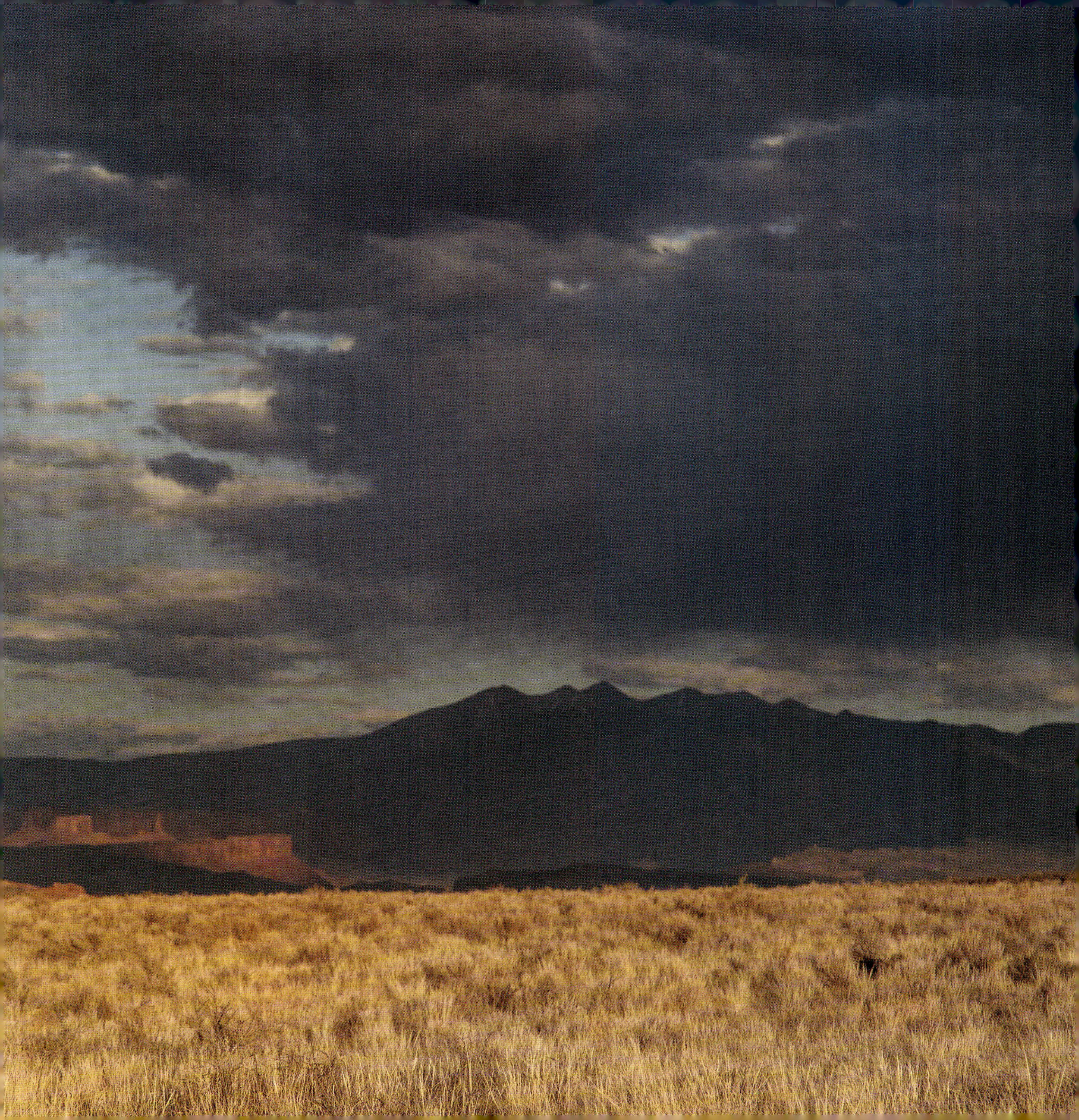

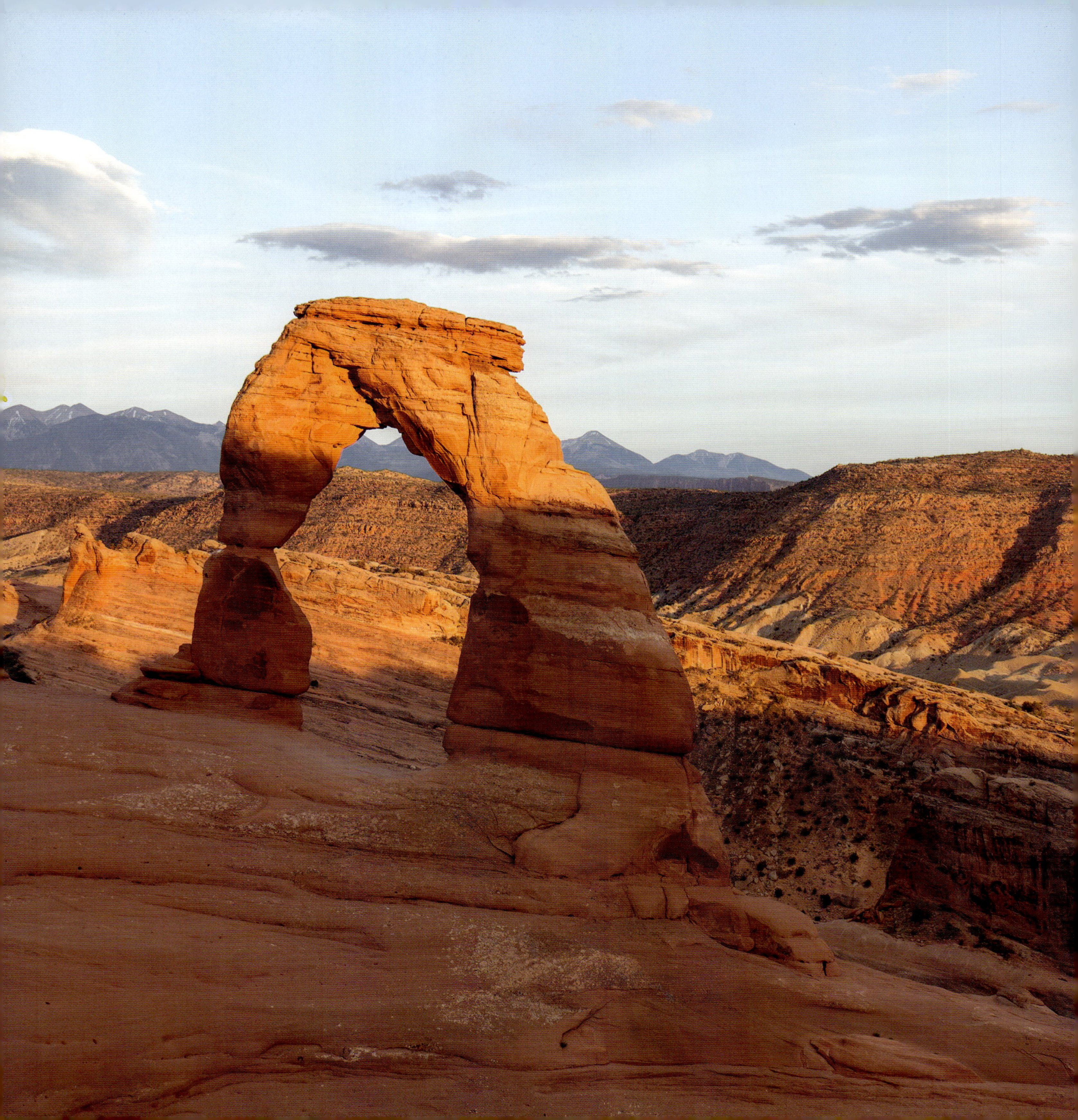

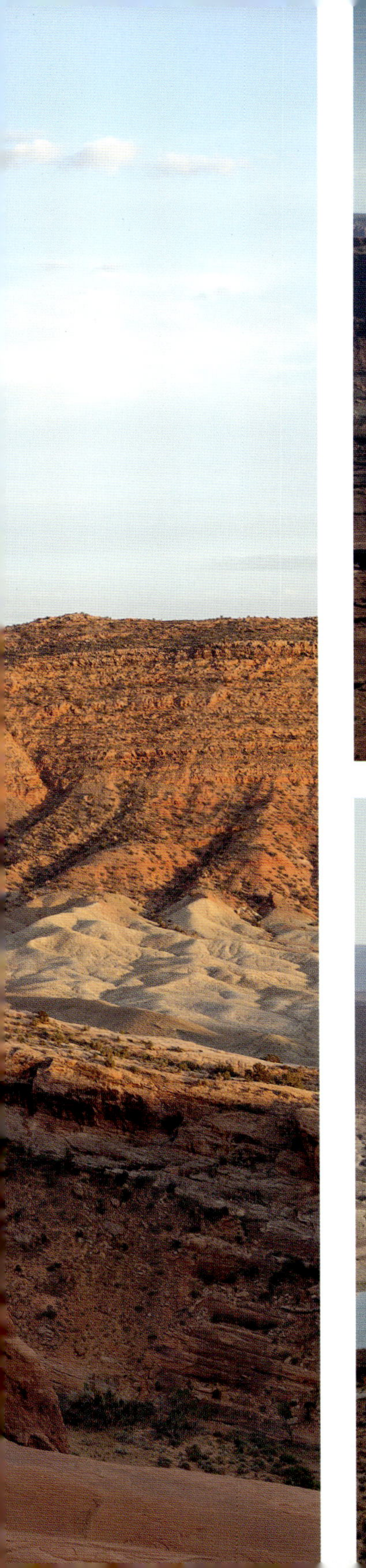

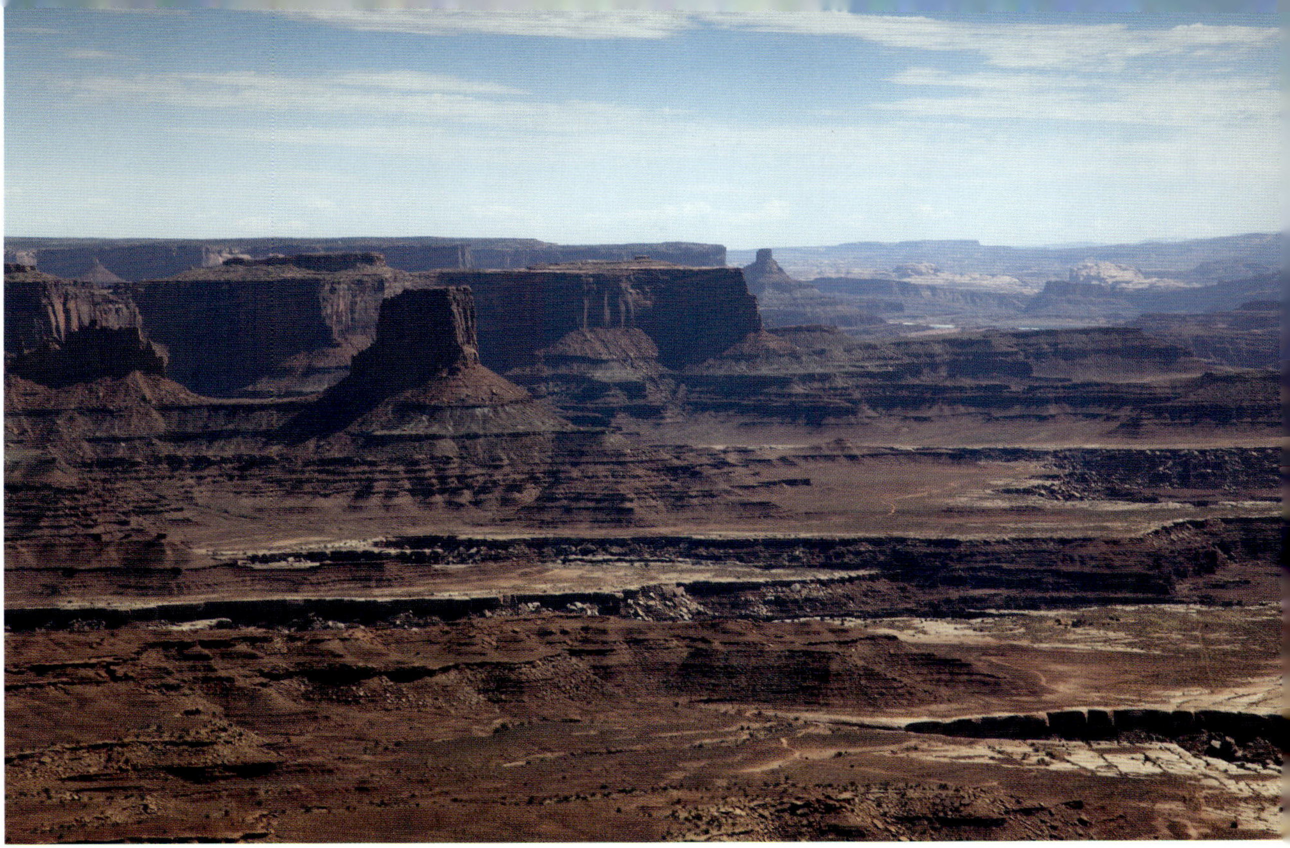

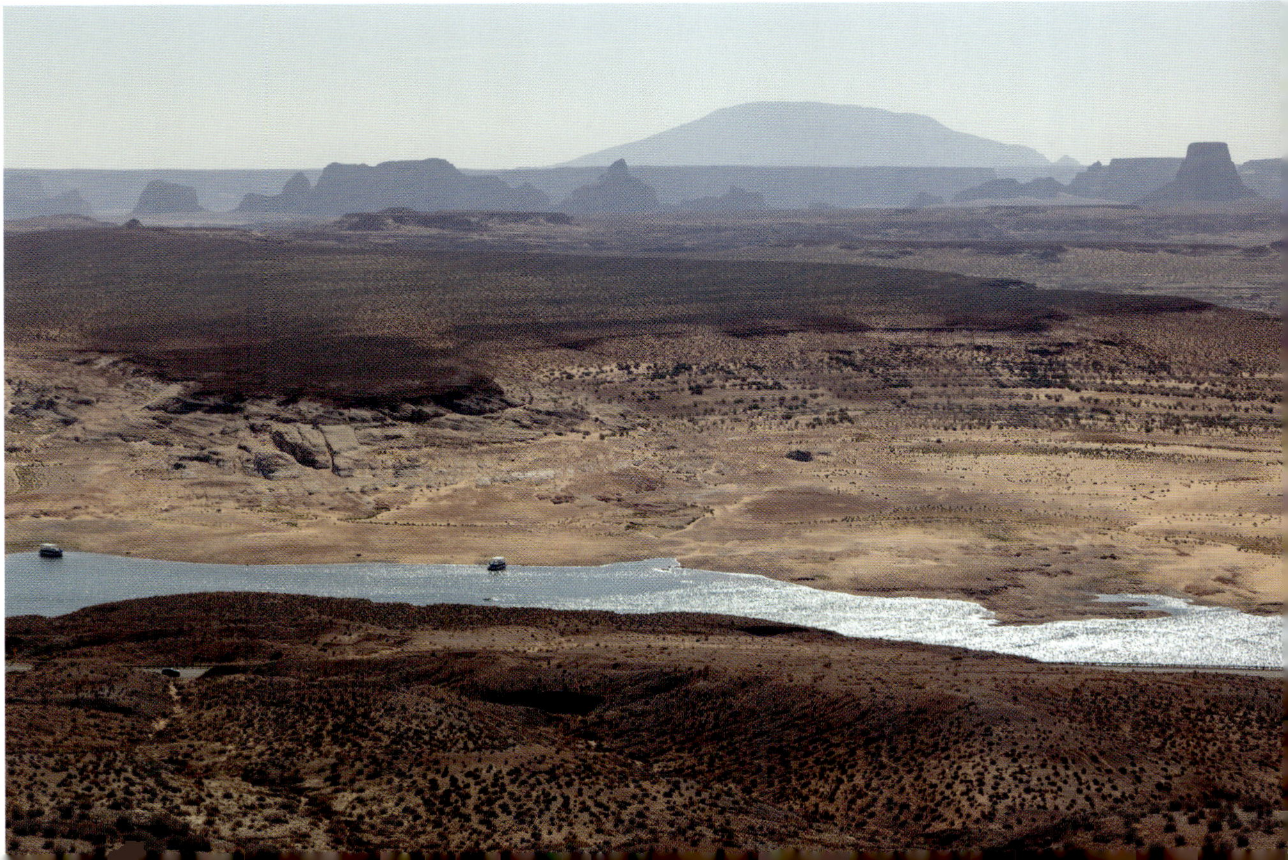

Mary Hunter Austin

CALIFORNIA

"This is the sense of the desert hills, that there

is room enough and time enough."

From *The Land of Little Rain*

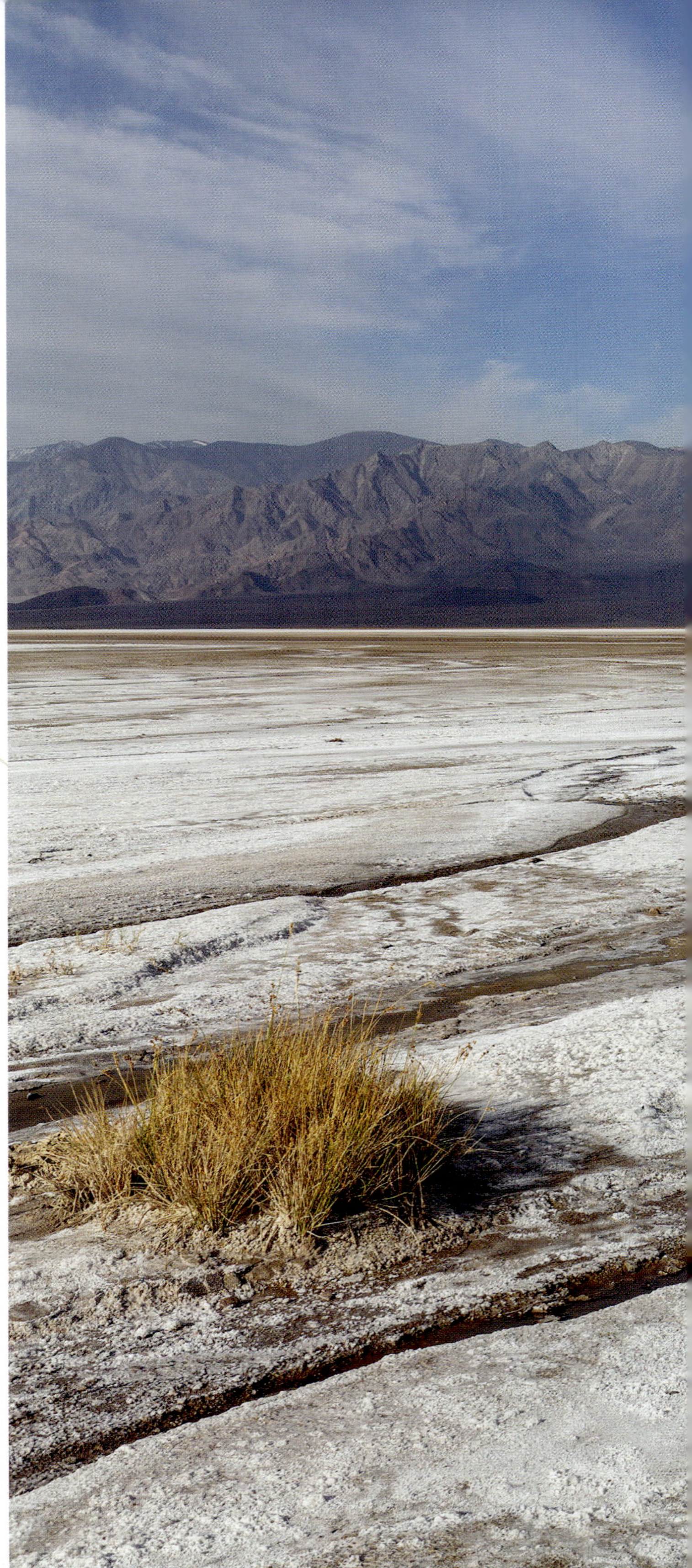

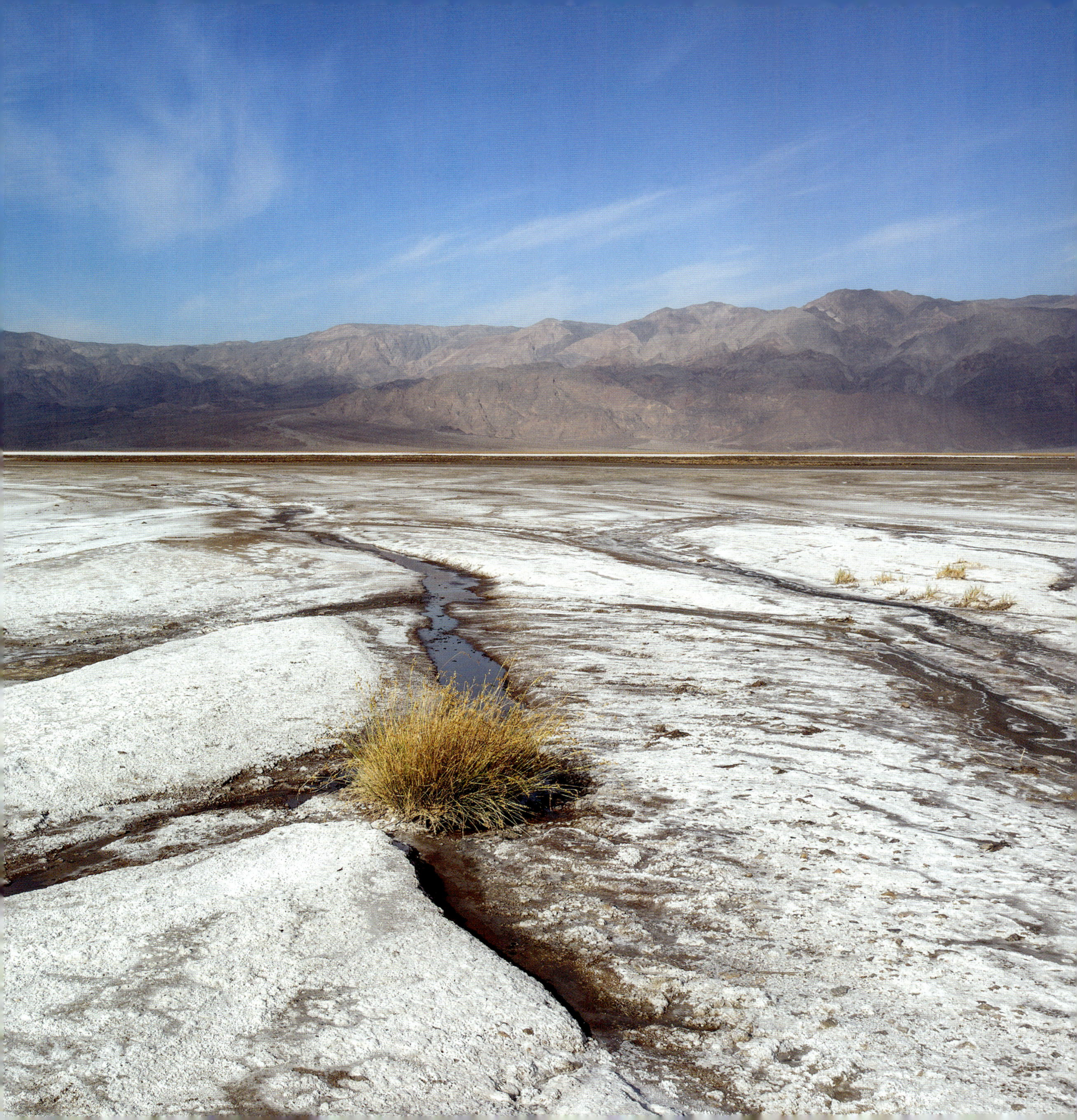

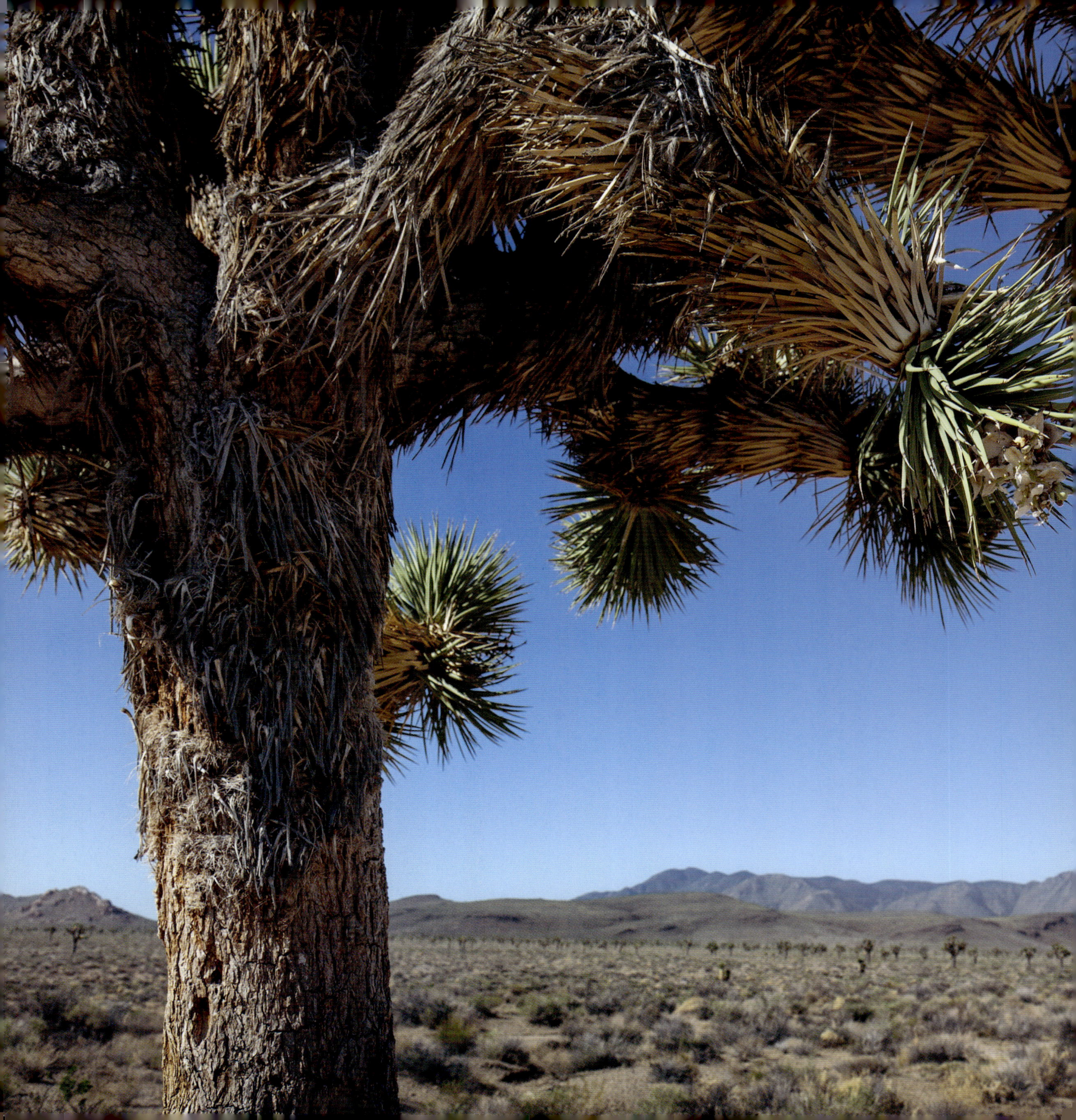

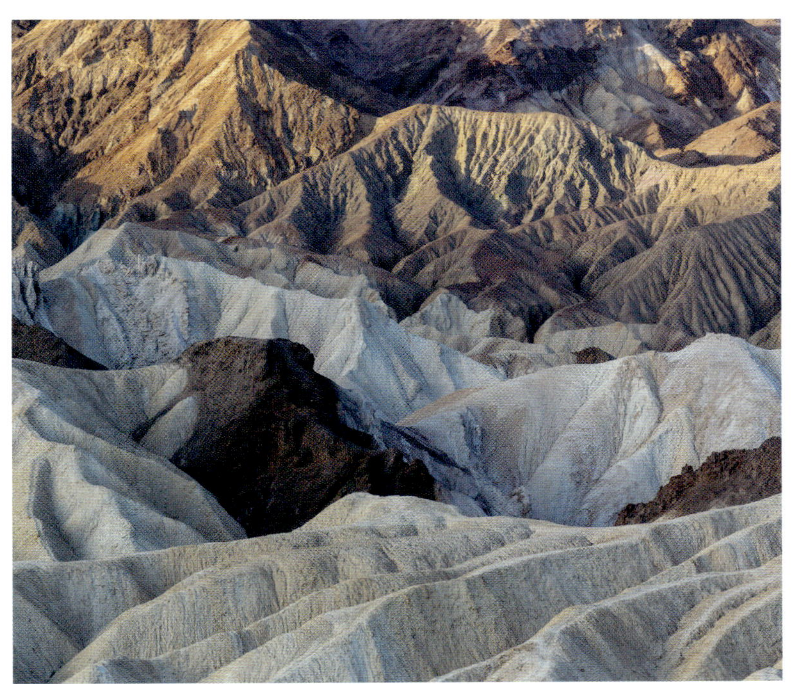
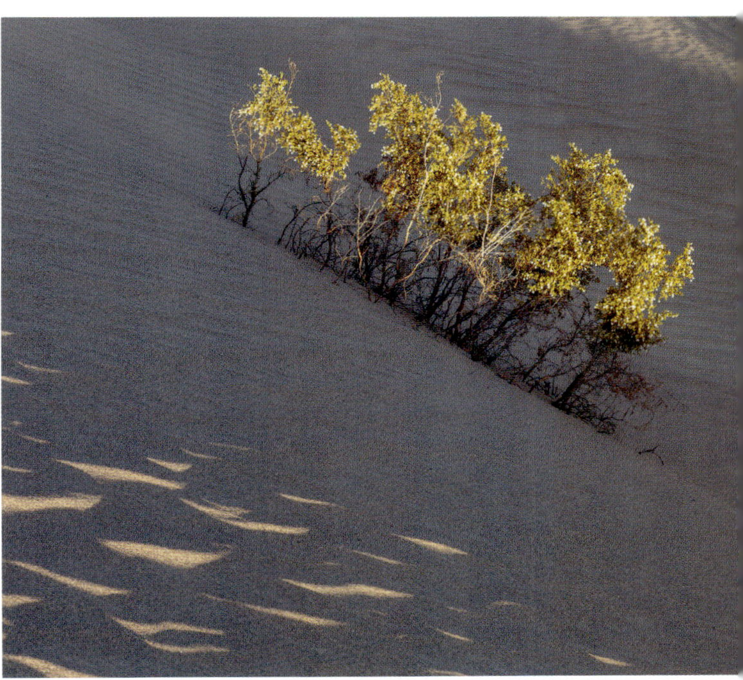

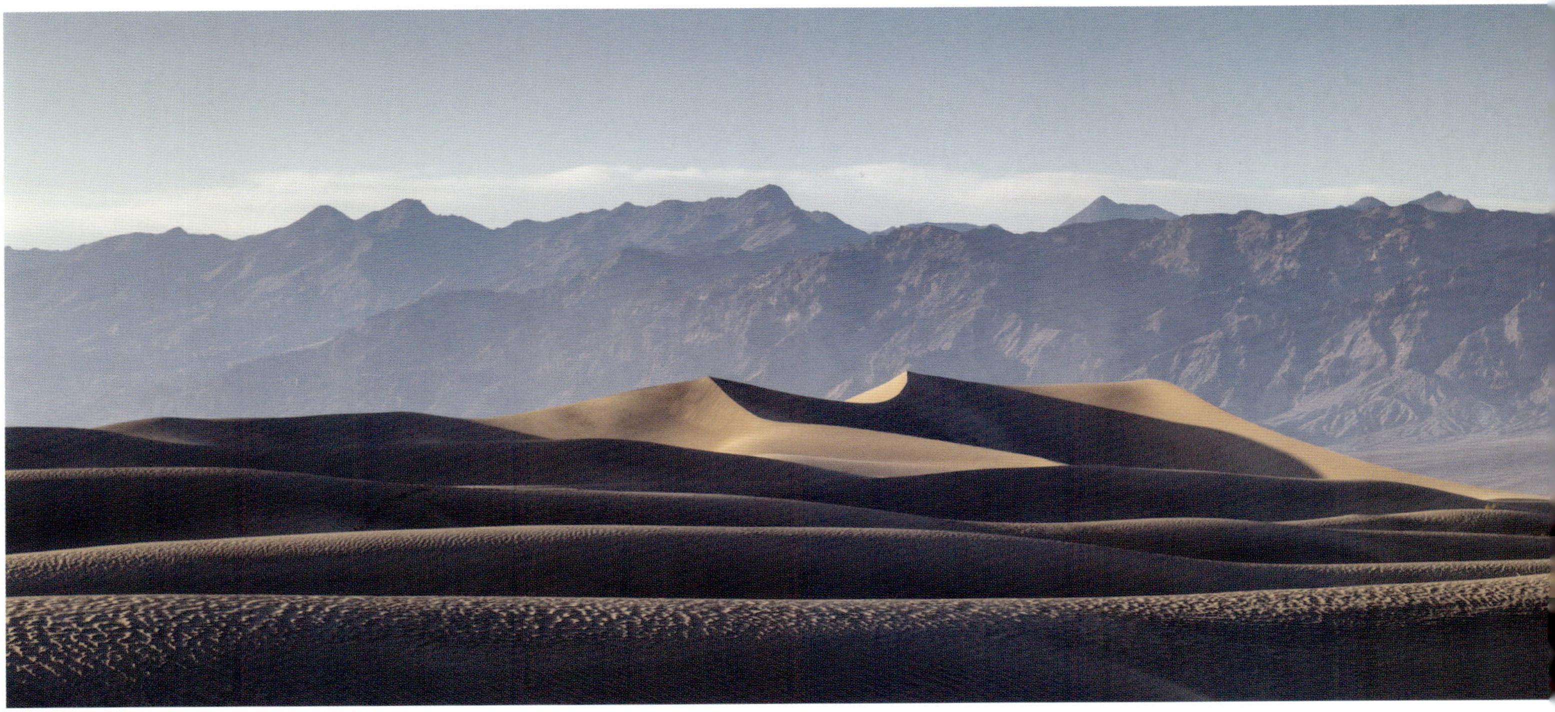

Rick Bass

MONTANA

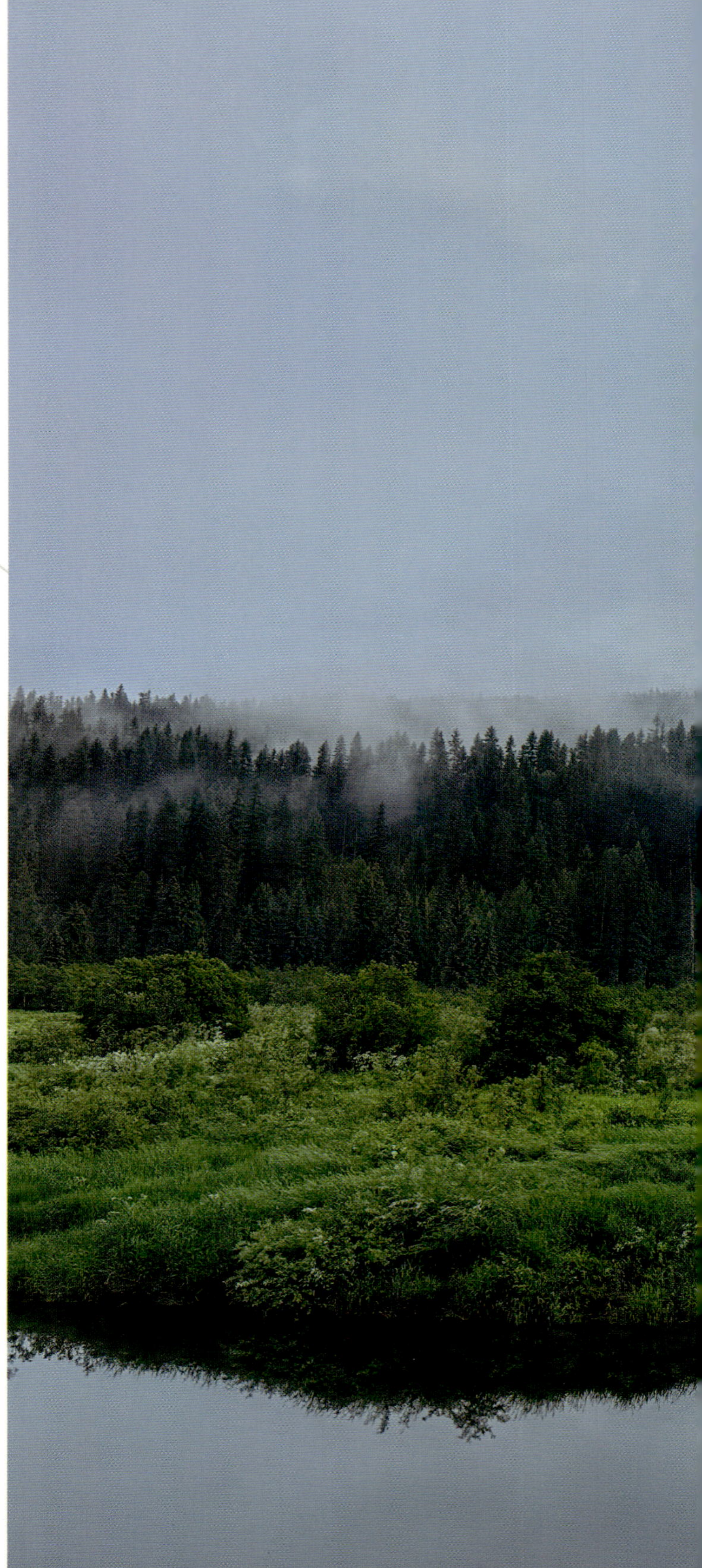

"If it's wild to your own heart, protect it. Preserve it. Love it. And fight for it, and dedicate yourself to it, whether it's a mountain range, your wife, your husband, or even (heaven forbid) your job. It doesn't matter if it's wild to anyone else: if it's what makes your heart sing, if it's what makes your days soar like a hawk in the summertime, then focus on it. Because for sure, it's wild, and if it's wild, it'll mean you're still free. No matter where you are."

From the essay "River People," from *Wild to the Heart*

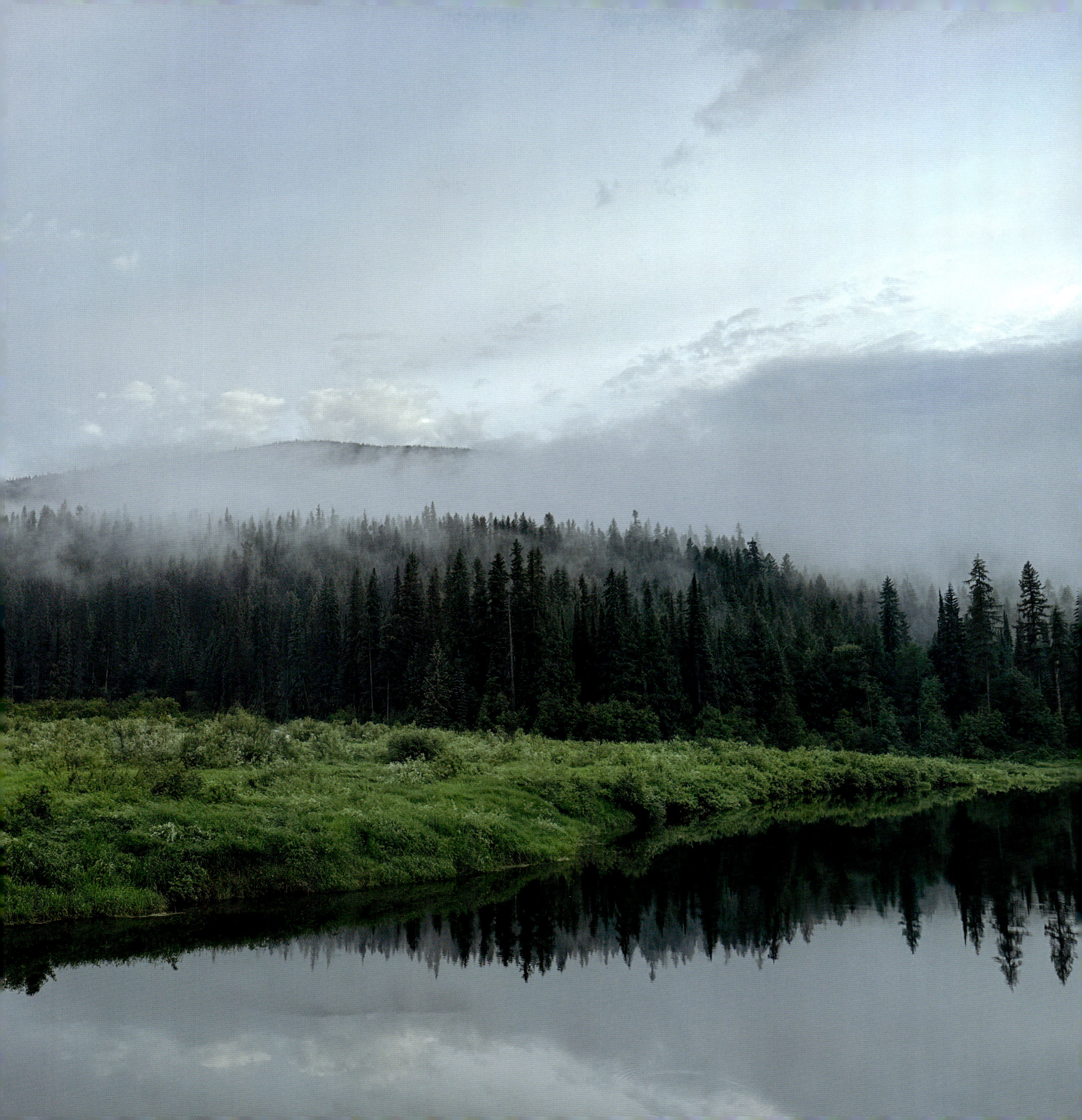

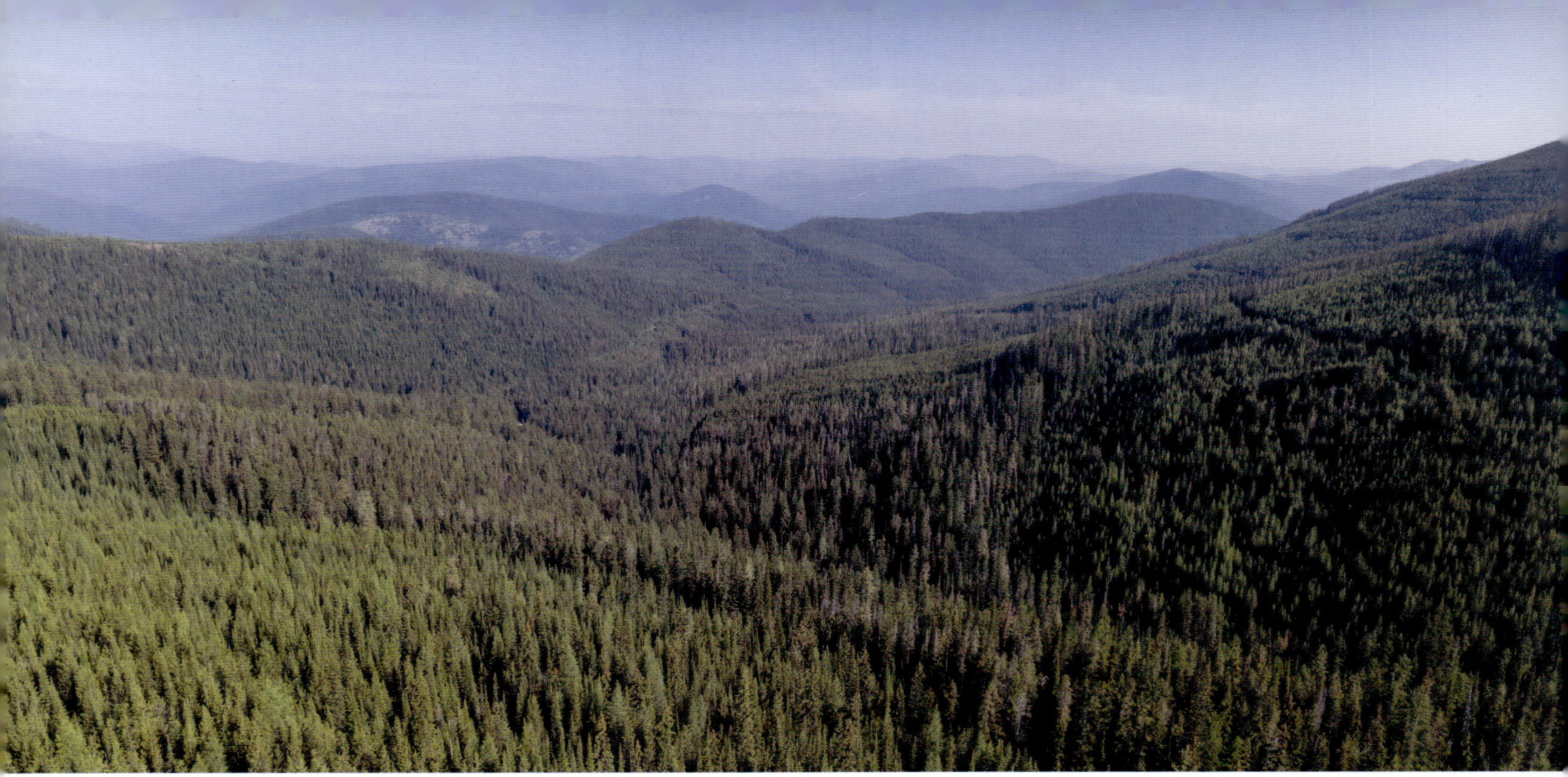

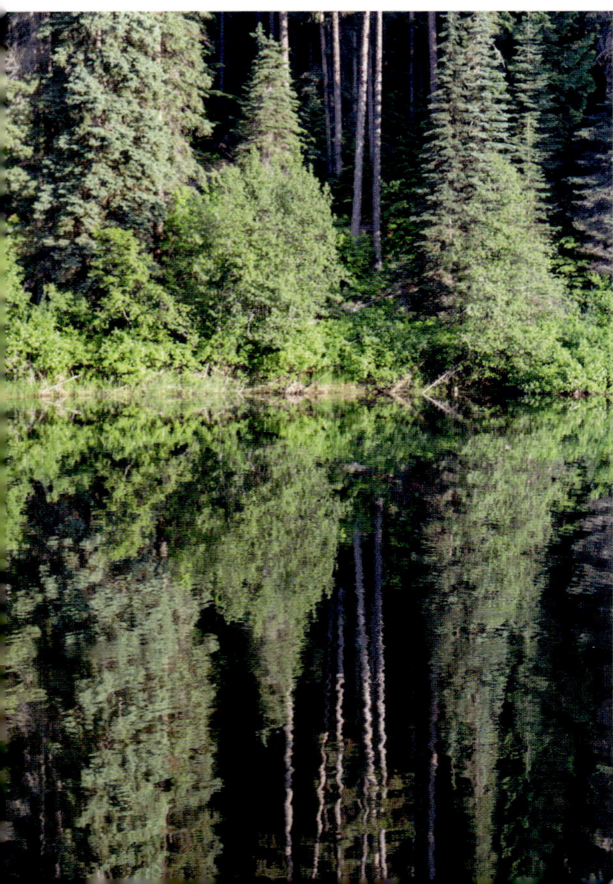
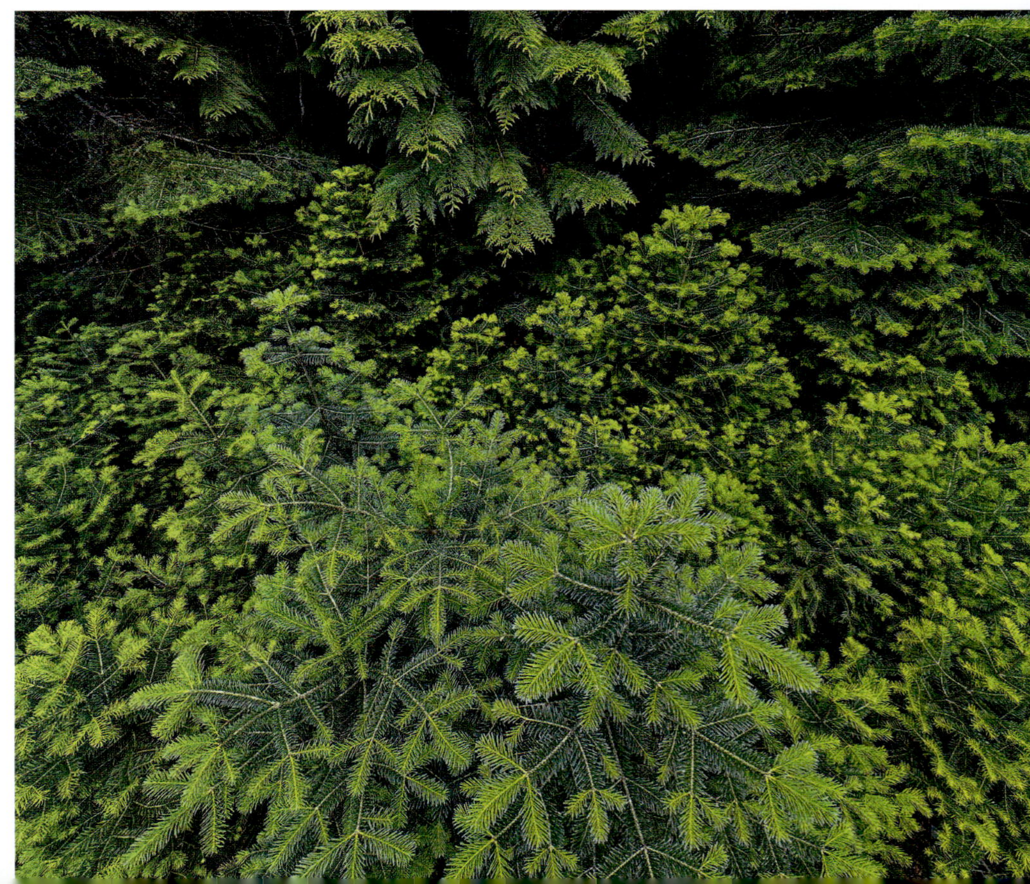

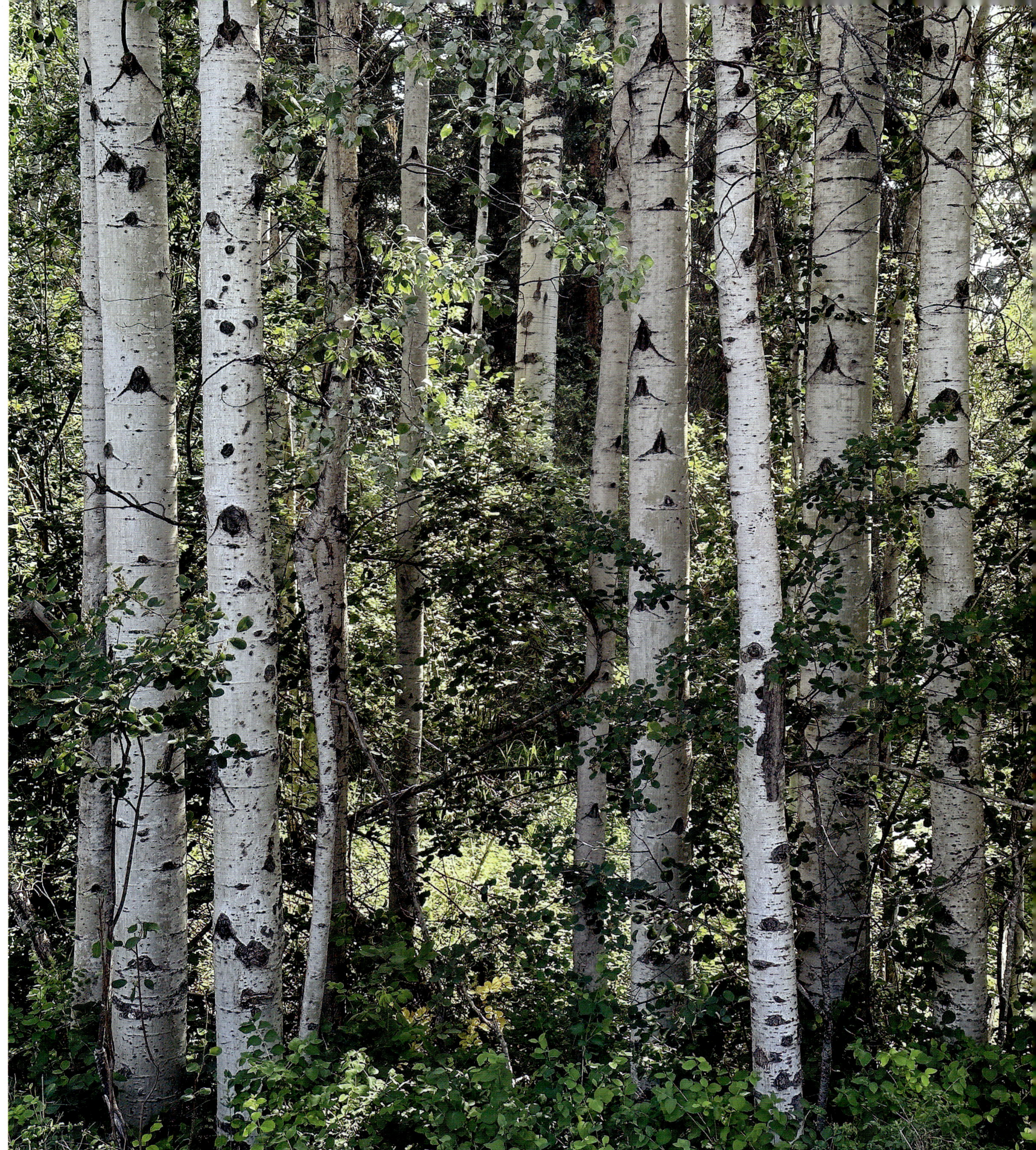

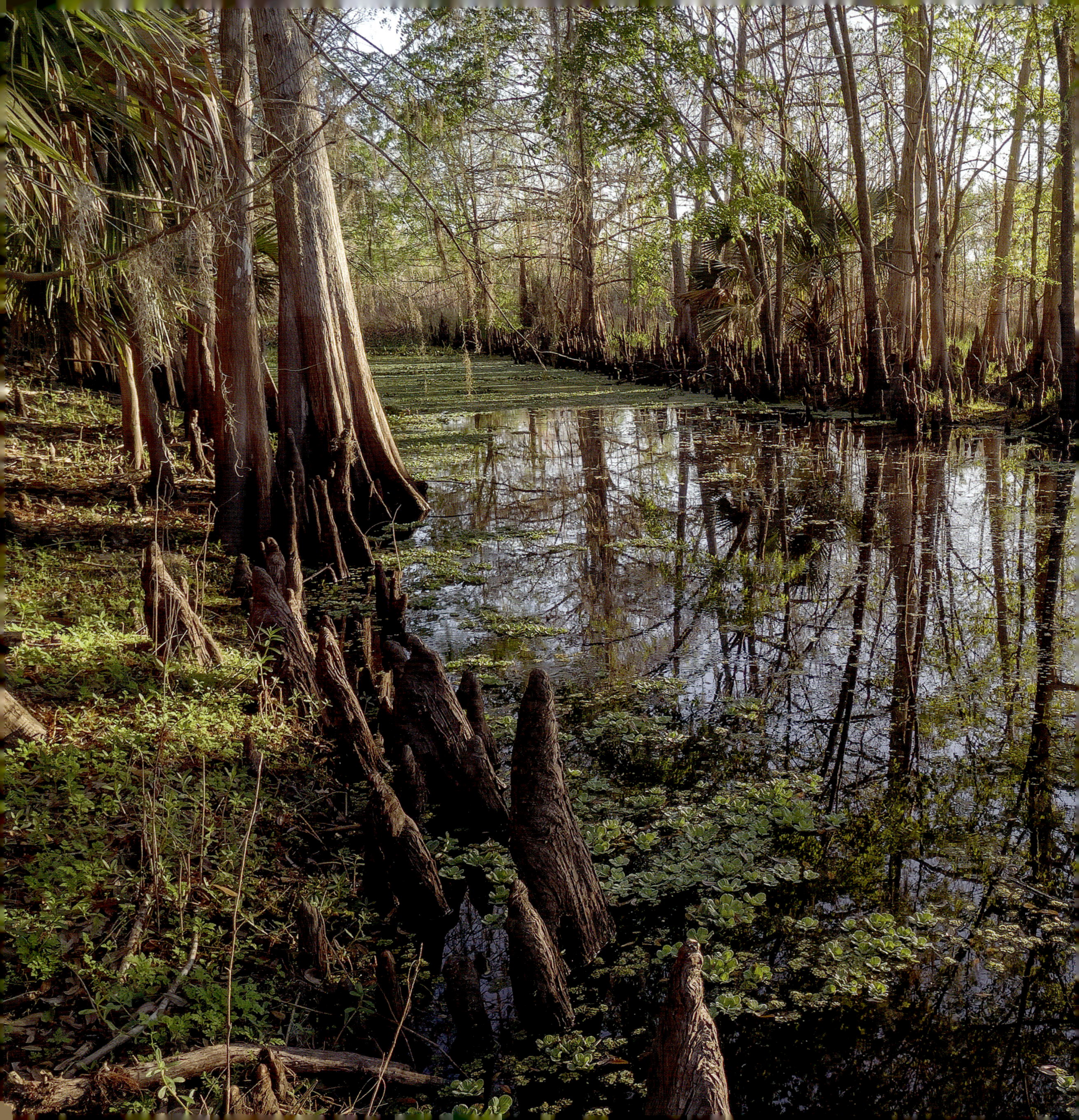

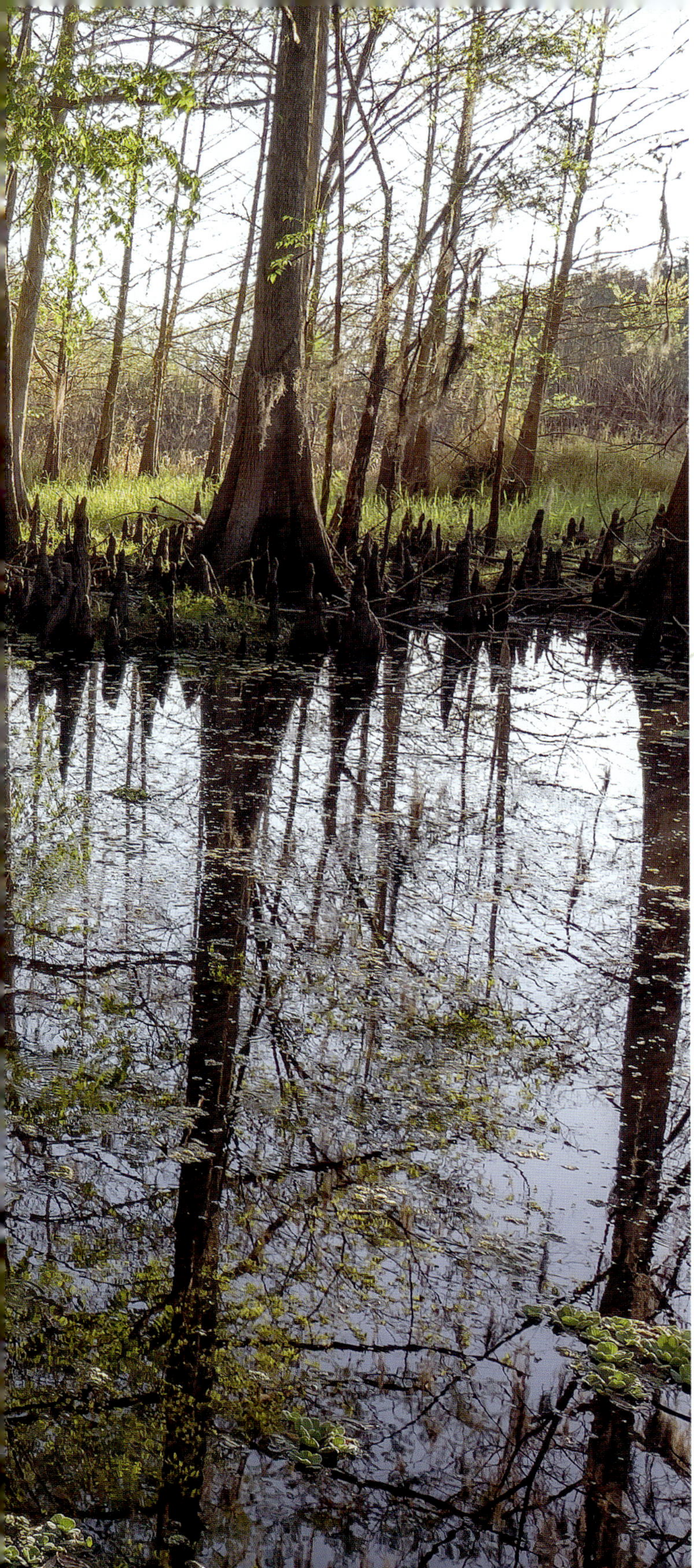

Bill Belleville

FLORIDA

"Wetlands like this that still remain intact become
our time machines, places that can transport
us back to the geological beginnings, and if they
afforded no other benefit, that alone would be
worth the price of admission."

From *Losing It All to Sprawl:
How Progress Ate My Cracker Landscape*

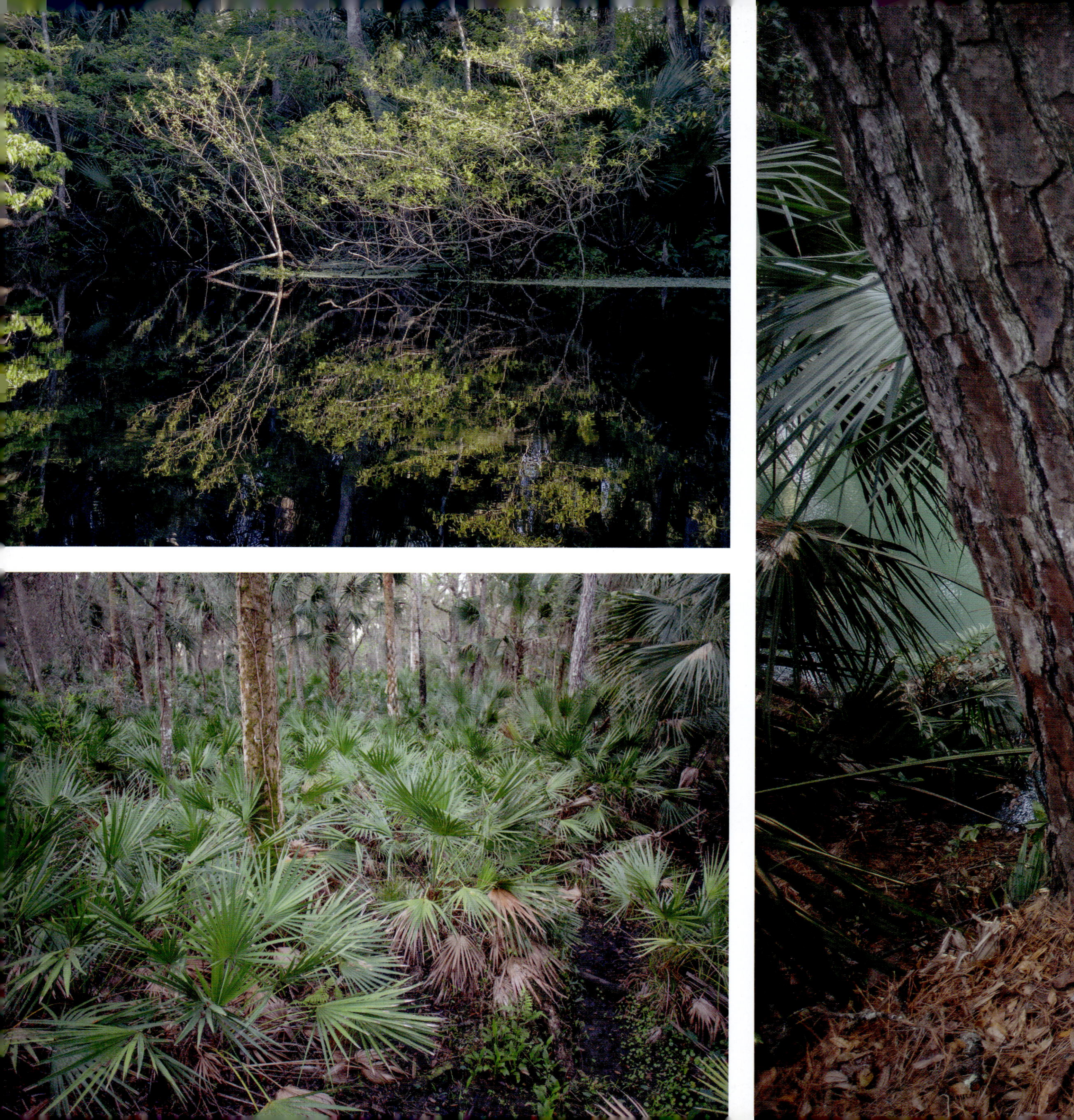

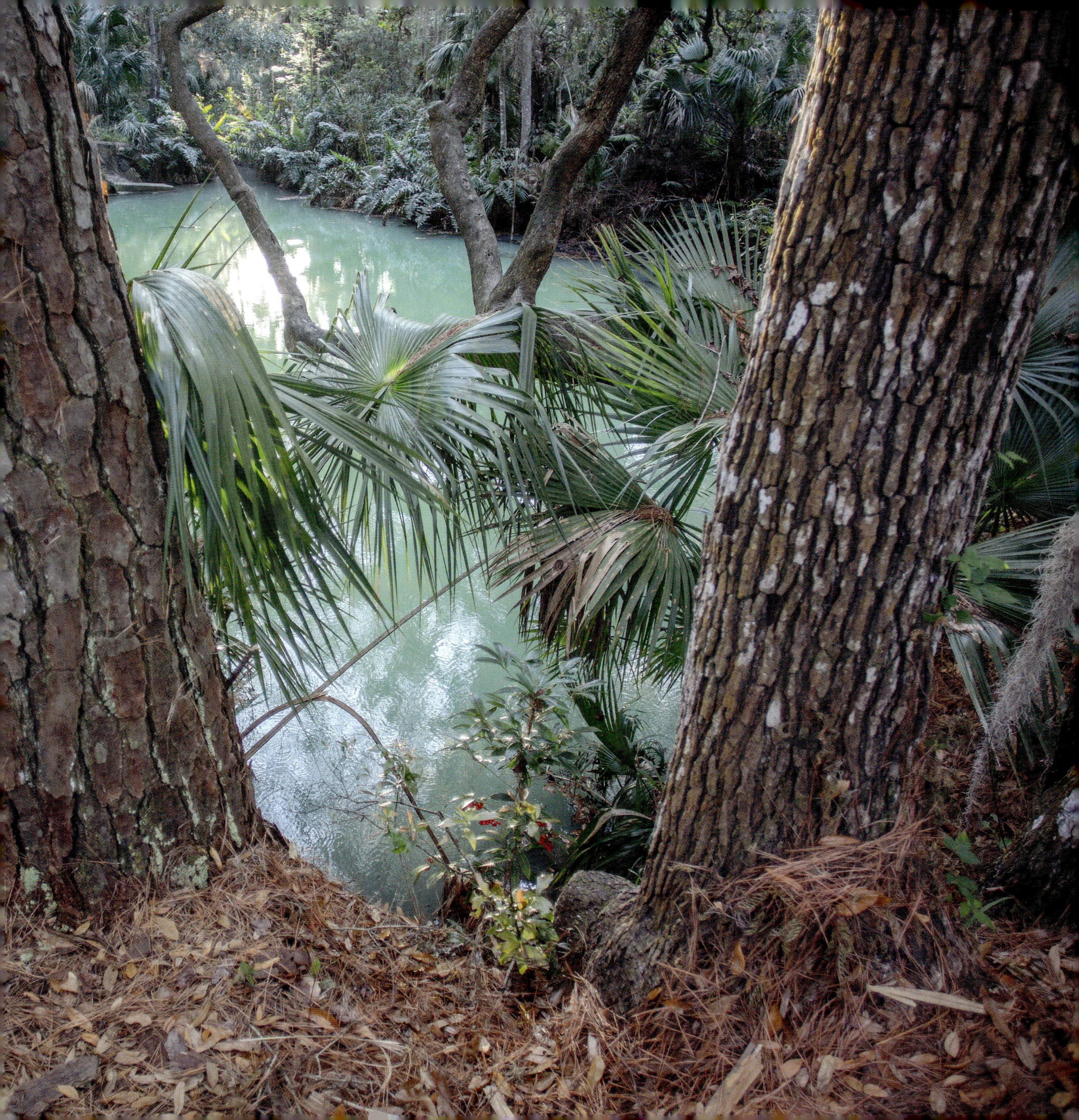

John Burroughs

"The place to observe nature is where you are; the walk to take today is the walk you took yesterday. You will not find just the same things: both the observed and the observer have changed."

From *Signs and Seasons*

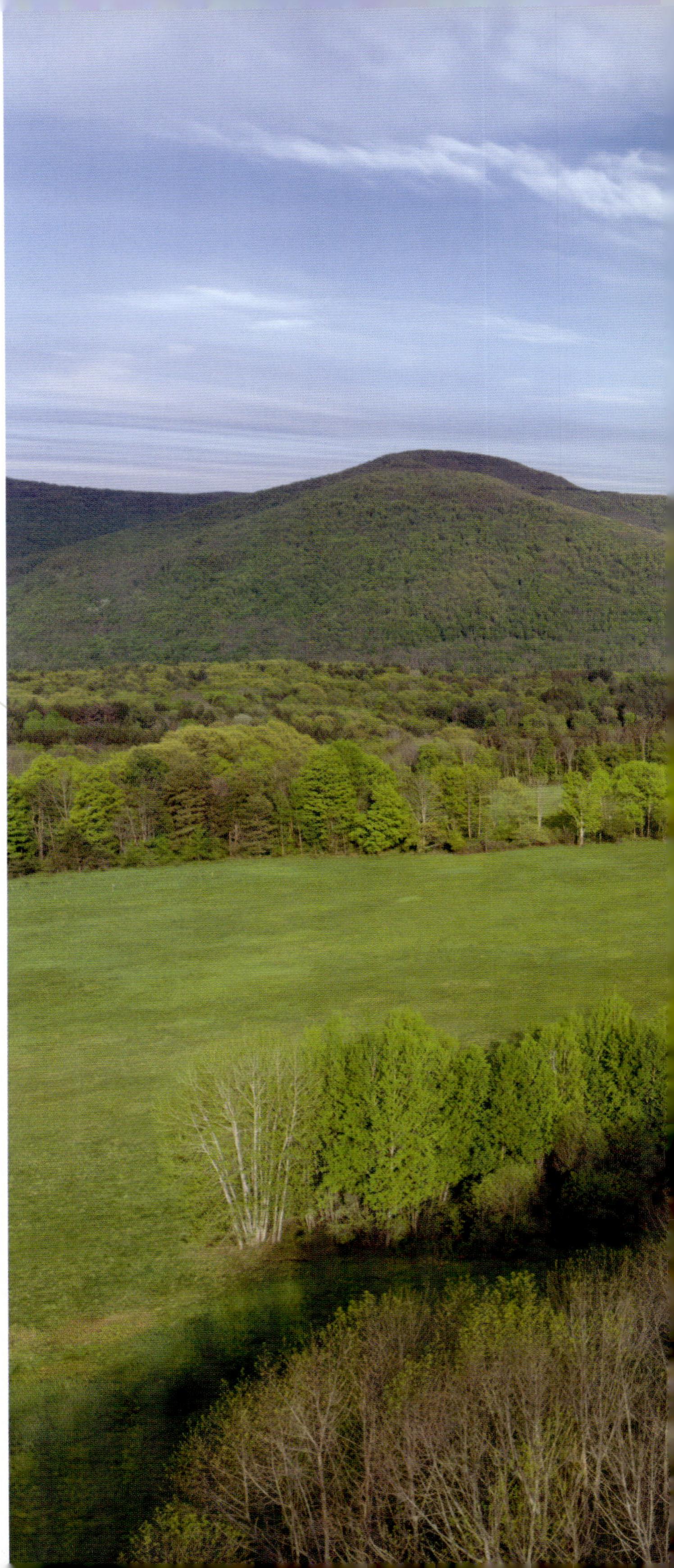

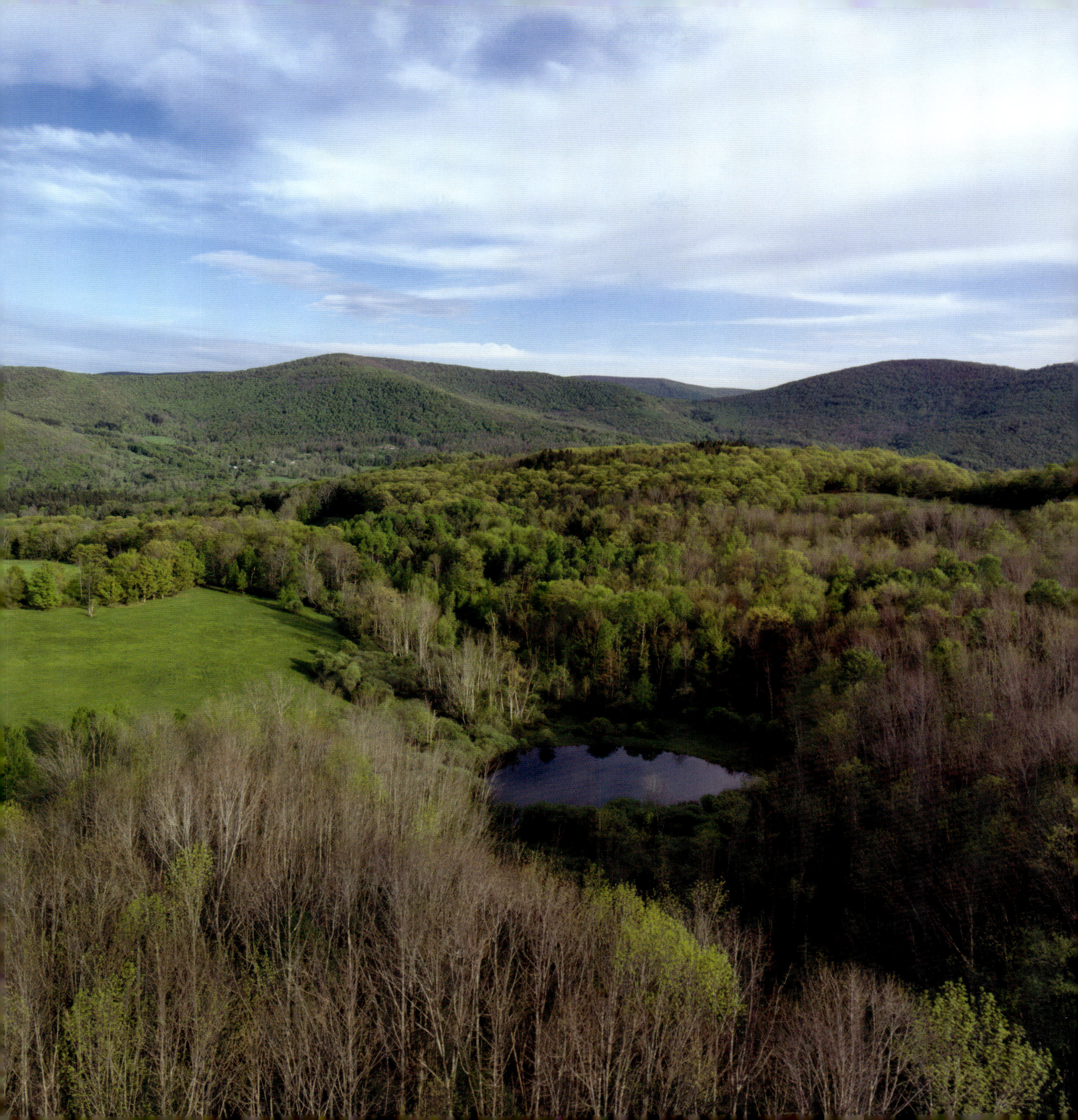

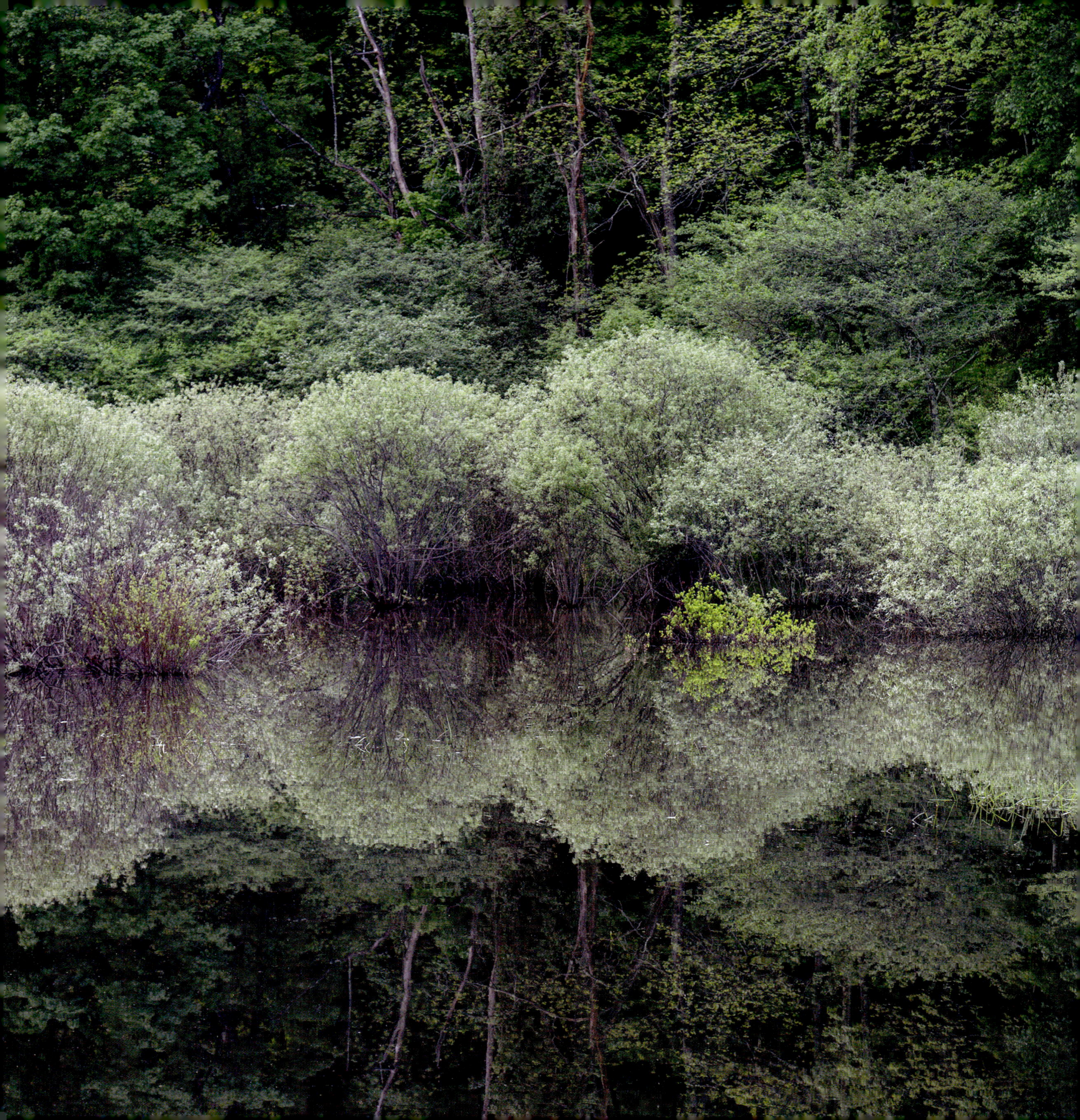

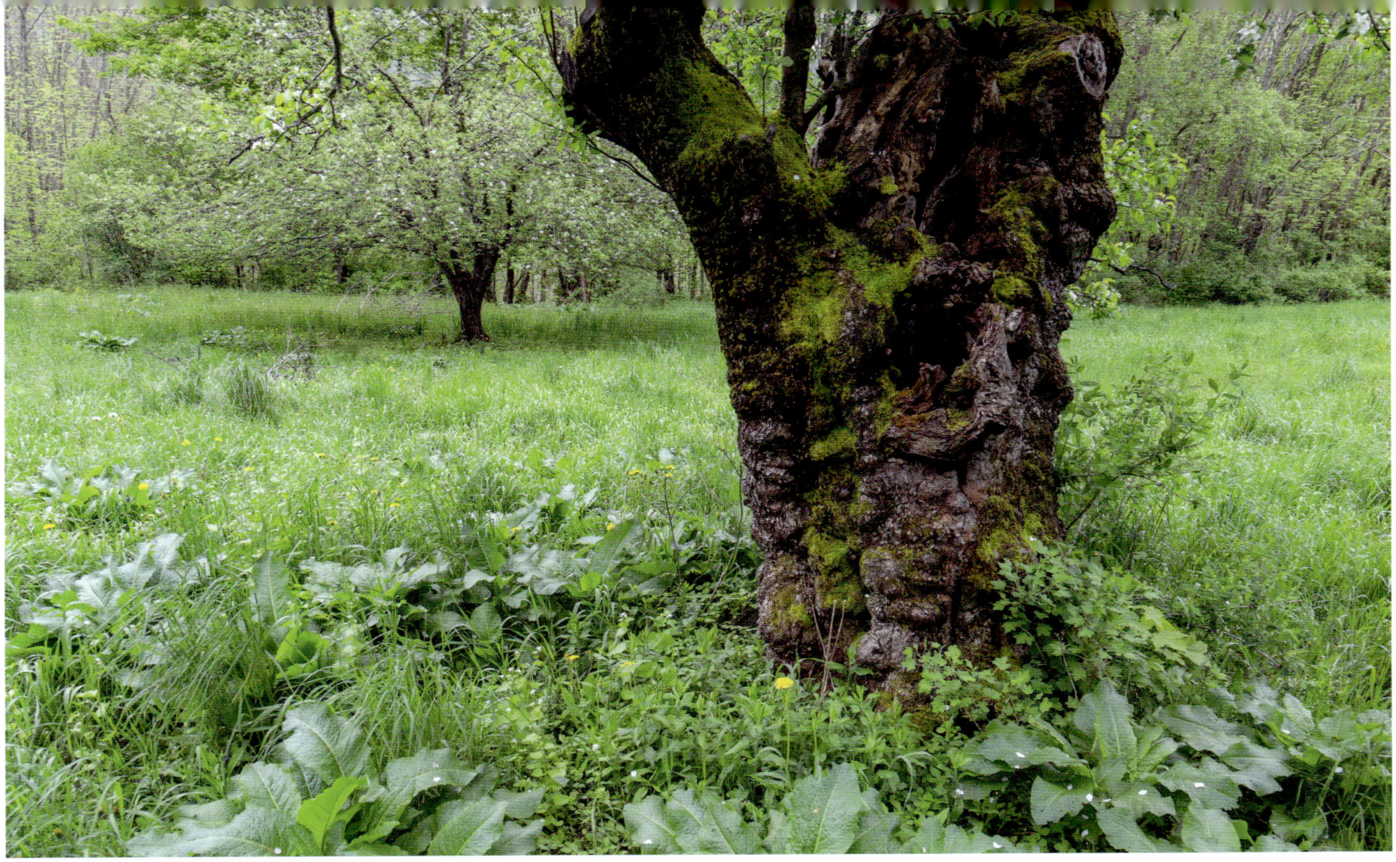

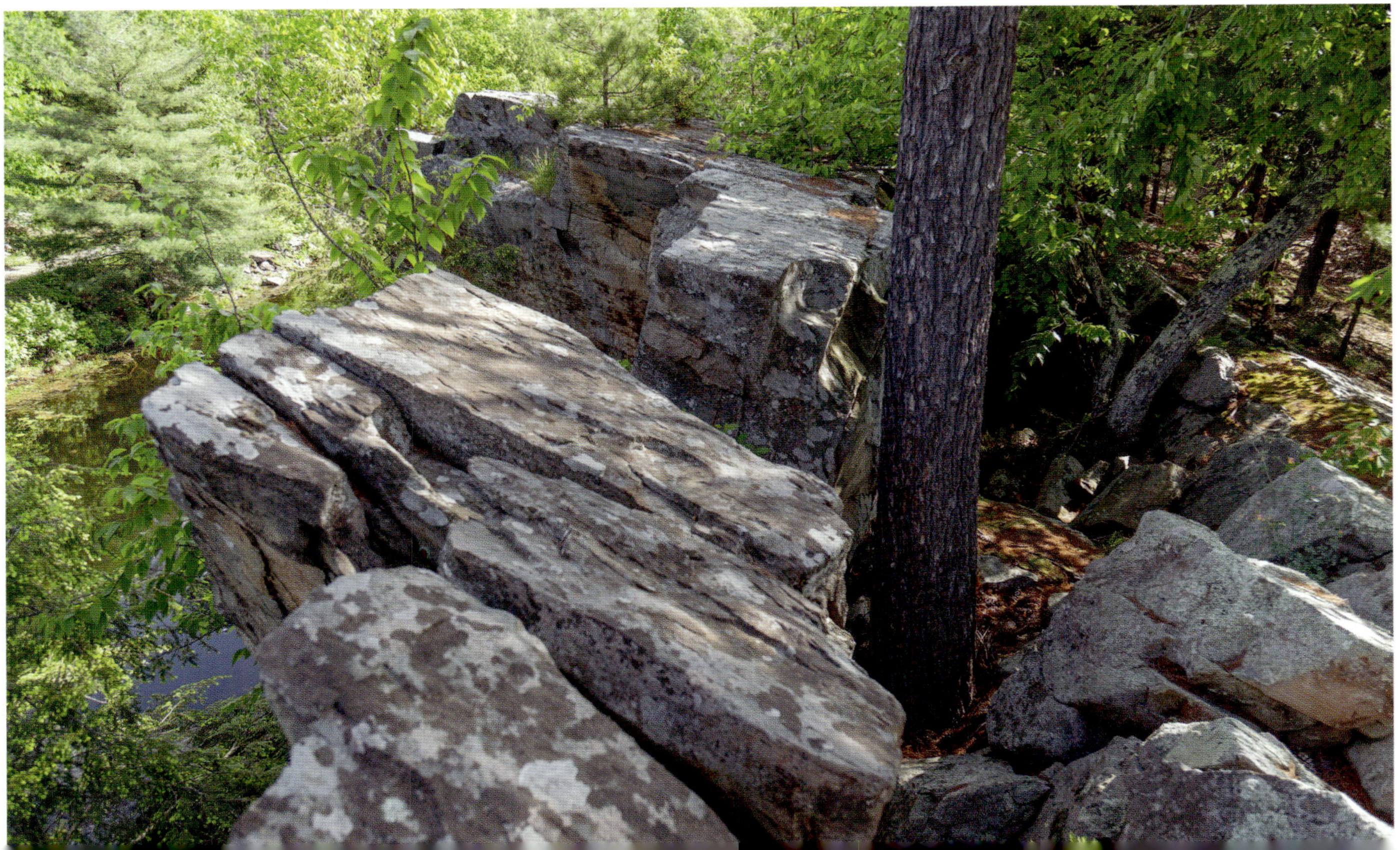

Akiko Busch

NEW YORK

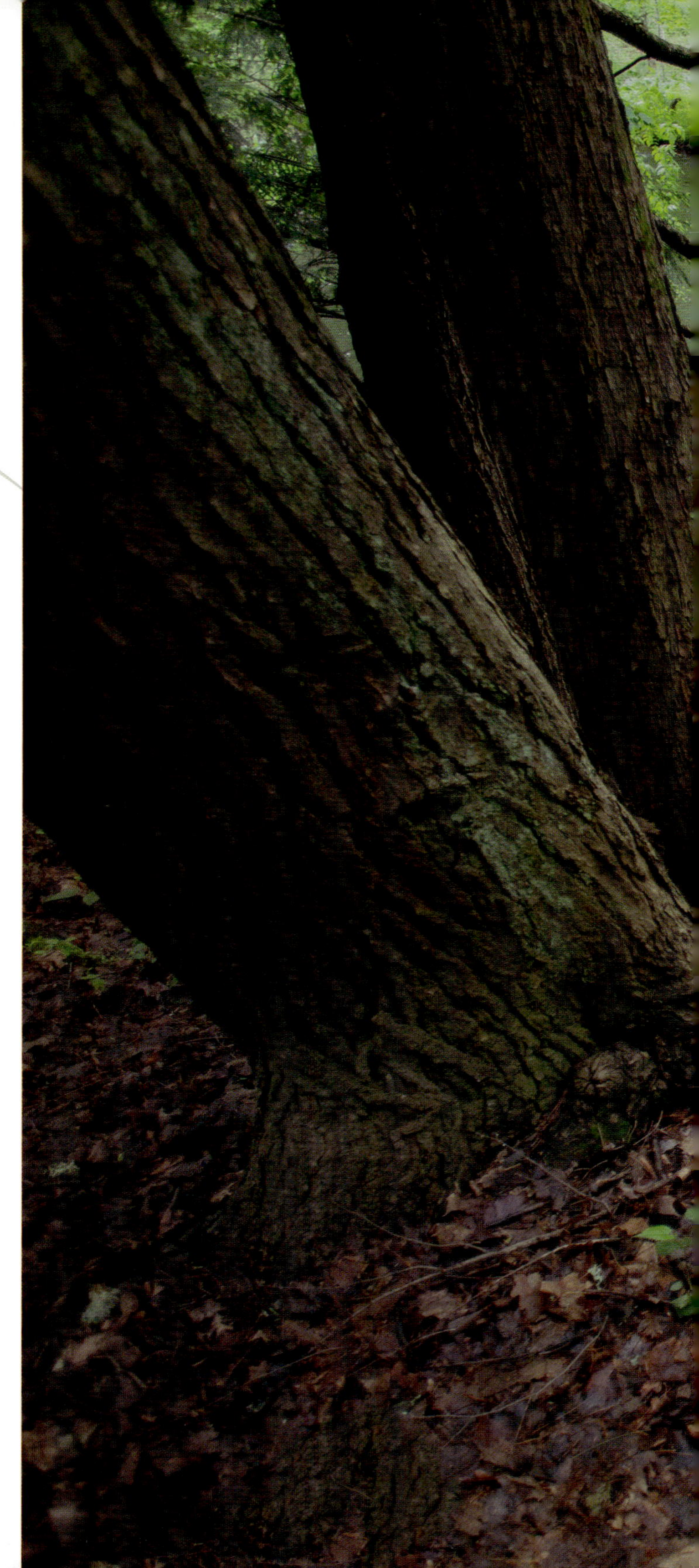

"I have begun to think that those of us who derive comfort from rivers do so because, in one way or another, all rivers are about carving out space. They are about ice and water and the force these gather in trying to find their way. Some do it voraciously and with aggression; others do it with a simpler persistence. It can take seconds or centuries, but all rivers are about making a place for themselves. We are after the same thing, trying as well to find some place on this earth that makes us feel as though we belong there, some crevice or path or course, some sense of give in the earth and rock that will allow us to pass through."

From *Nine Ways to Cross a River: Midstream Reflections
on Swimming and Getting There from Here*

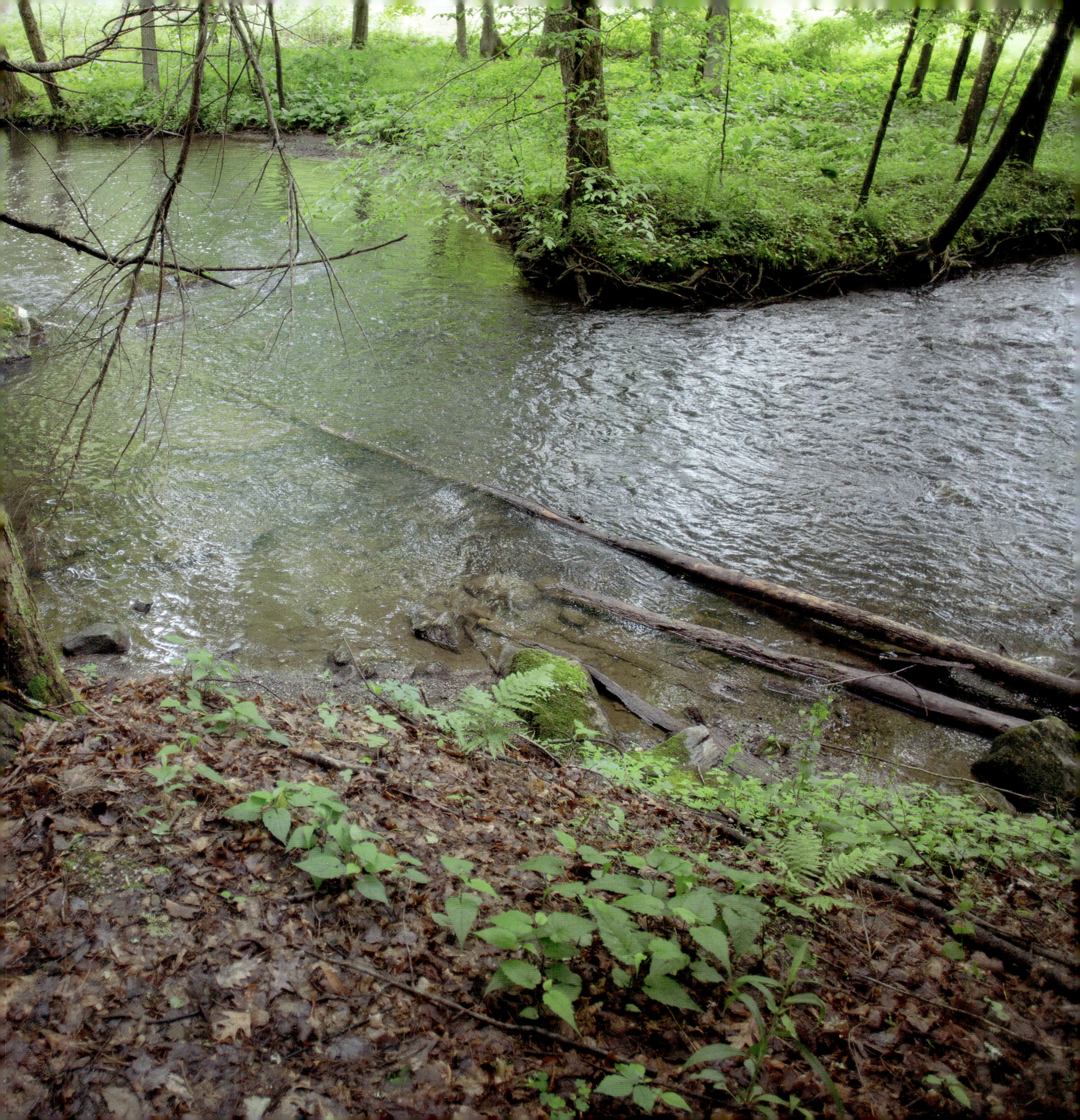

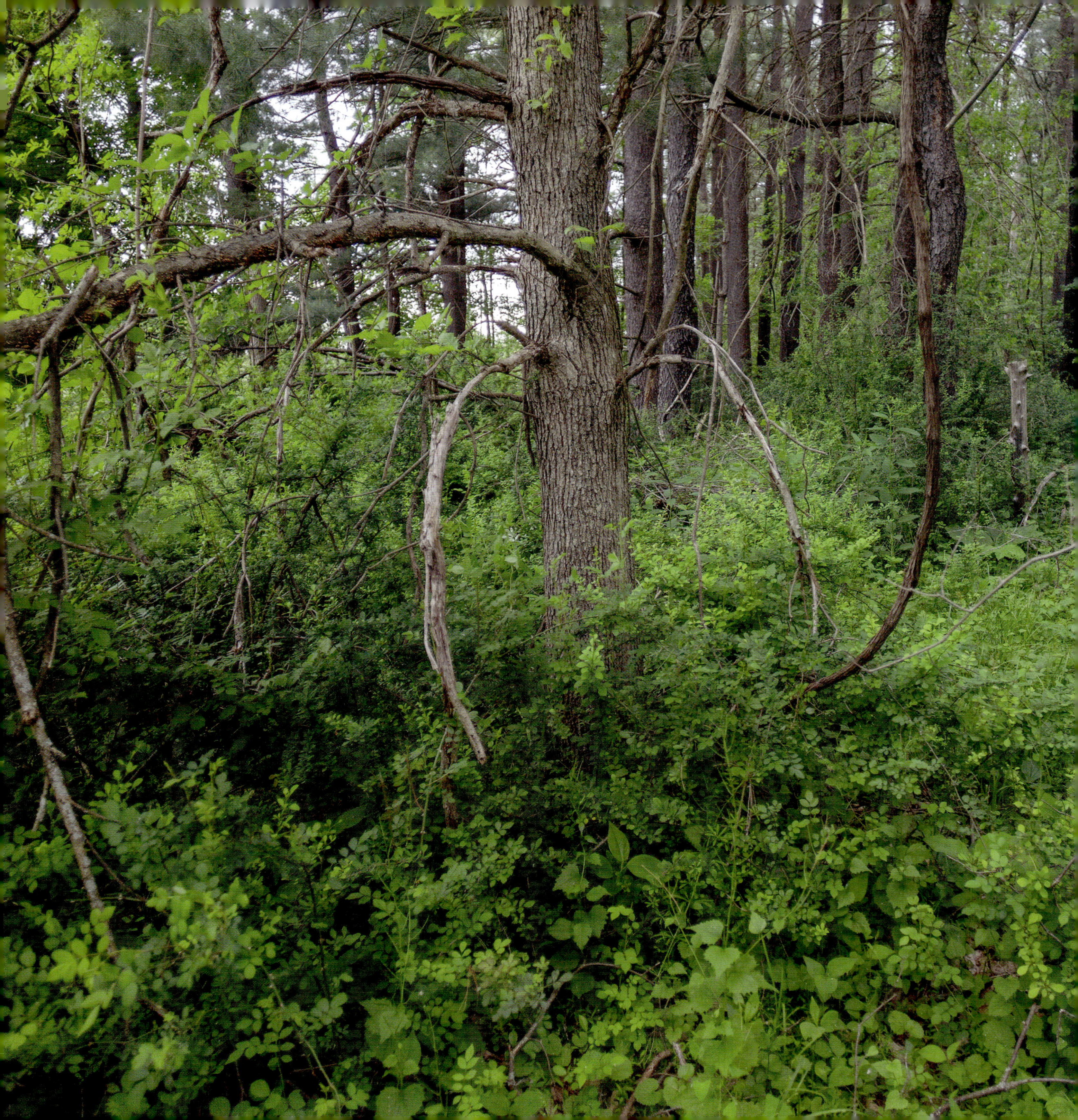

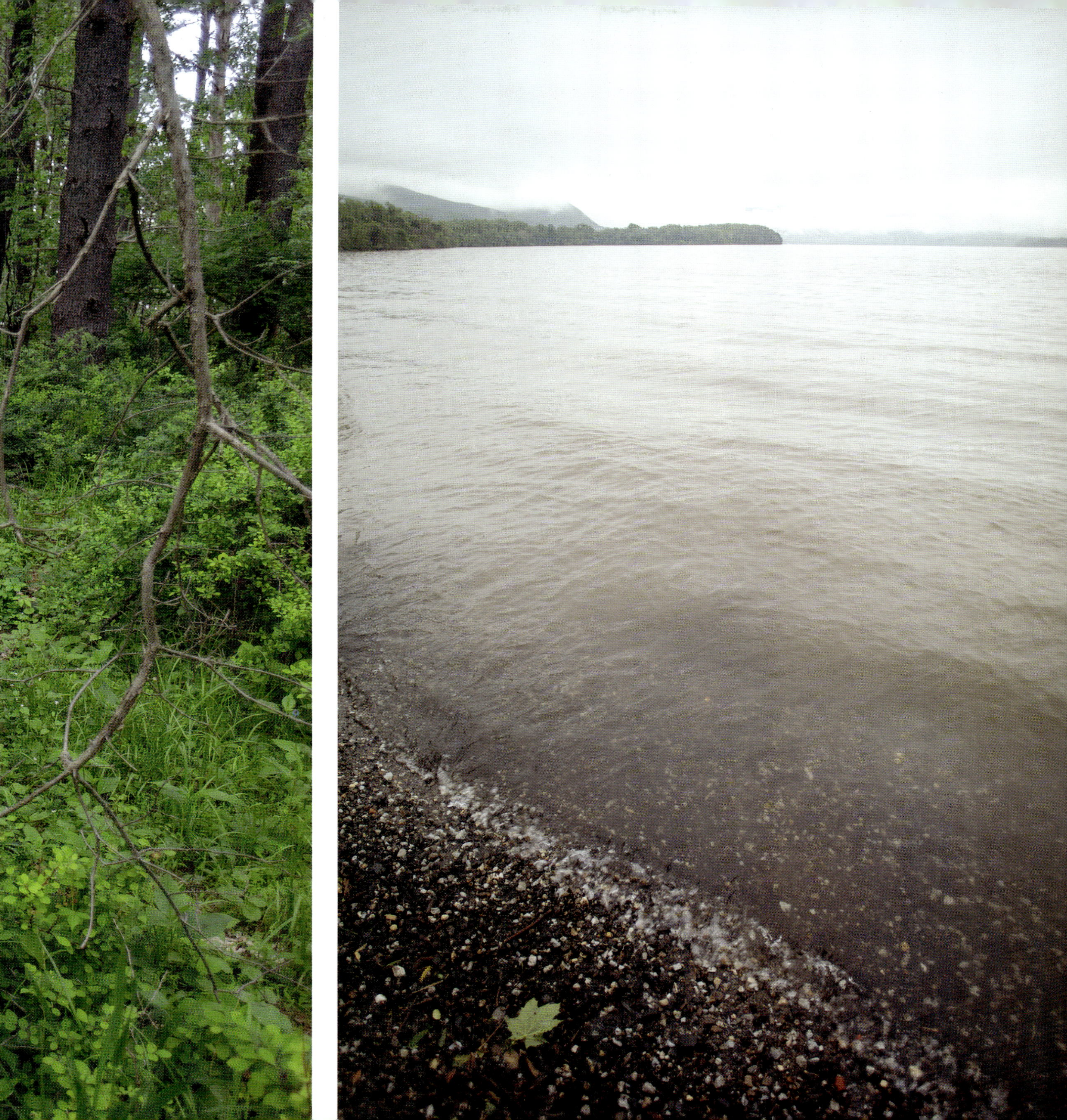

Rachel Carson

"We stand now where two roads diverge. But unlike the roads in Robert Frost's familiar poem, they are not equally fair. The road we have long been traveling is deceptively easy, a smooth superhighway on which we progress with great speed, but at its end lies disaster. The other fork of the road—the one 'less traveled by'—offers our last, our only chance to reach a destination that assures the preservation of our earth."

From *Silent Spring*

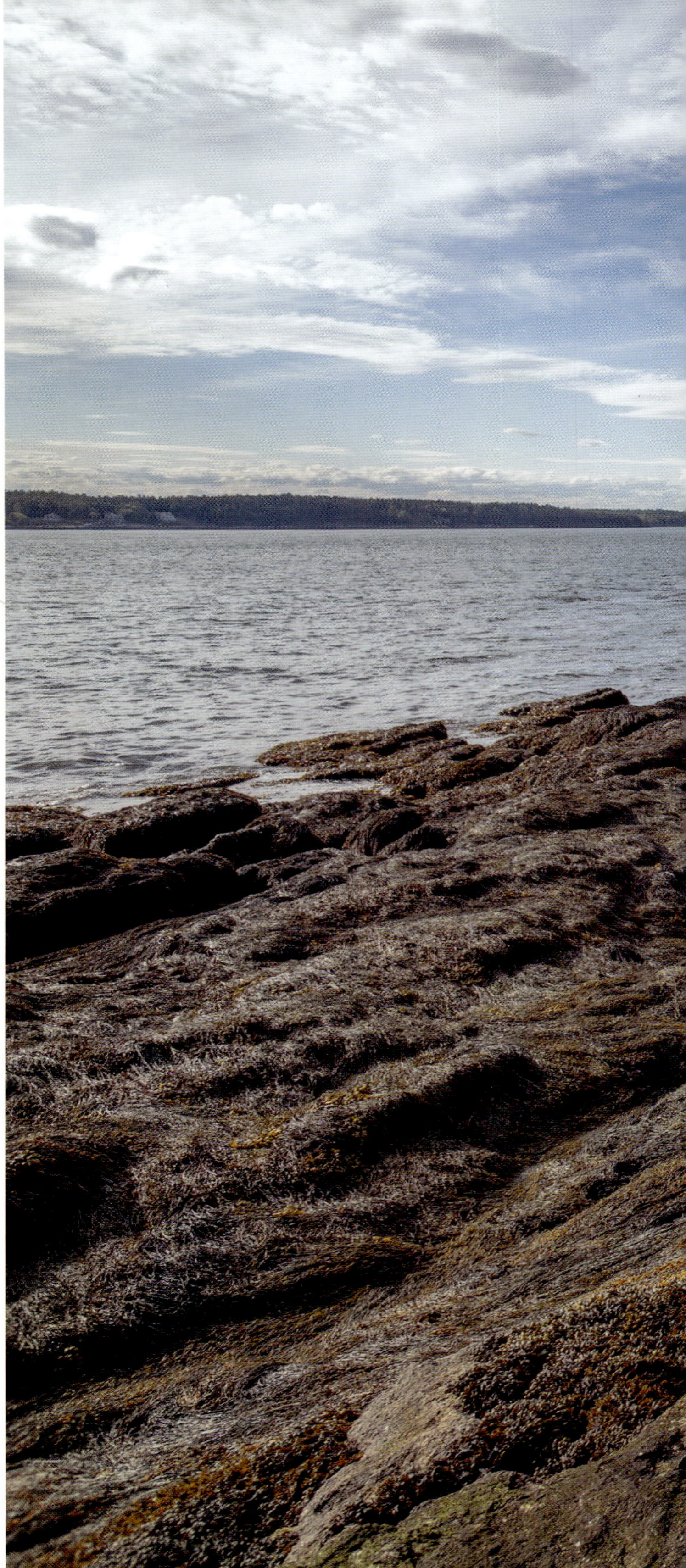

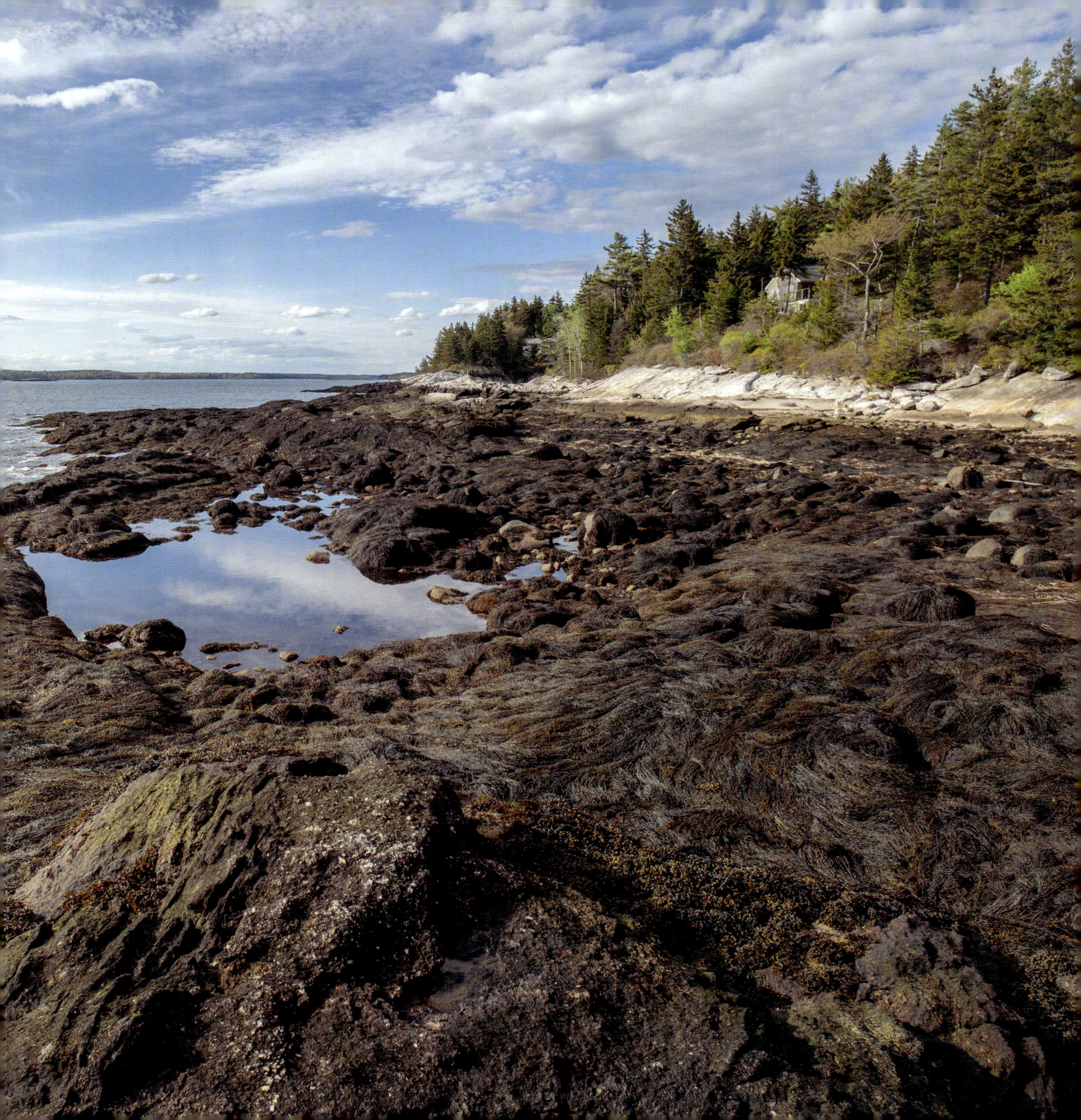

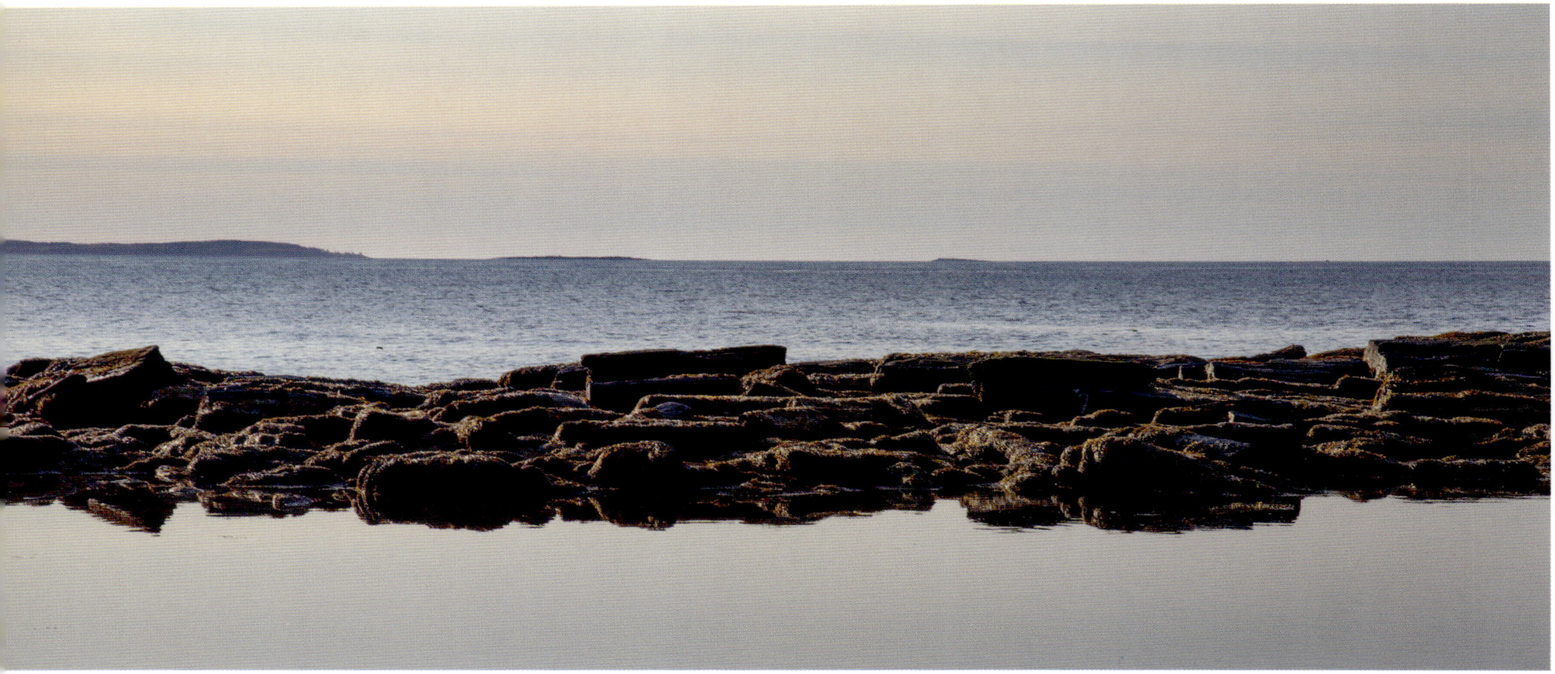

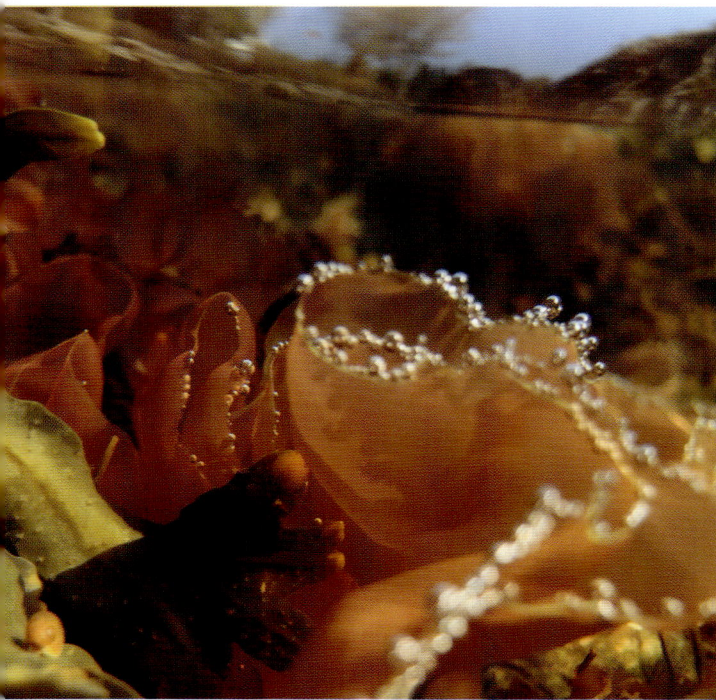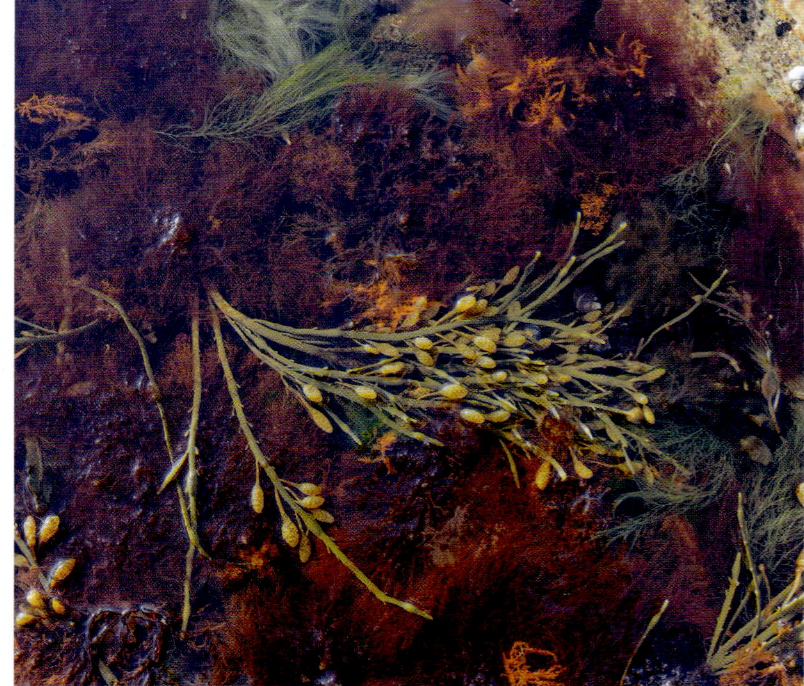

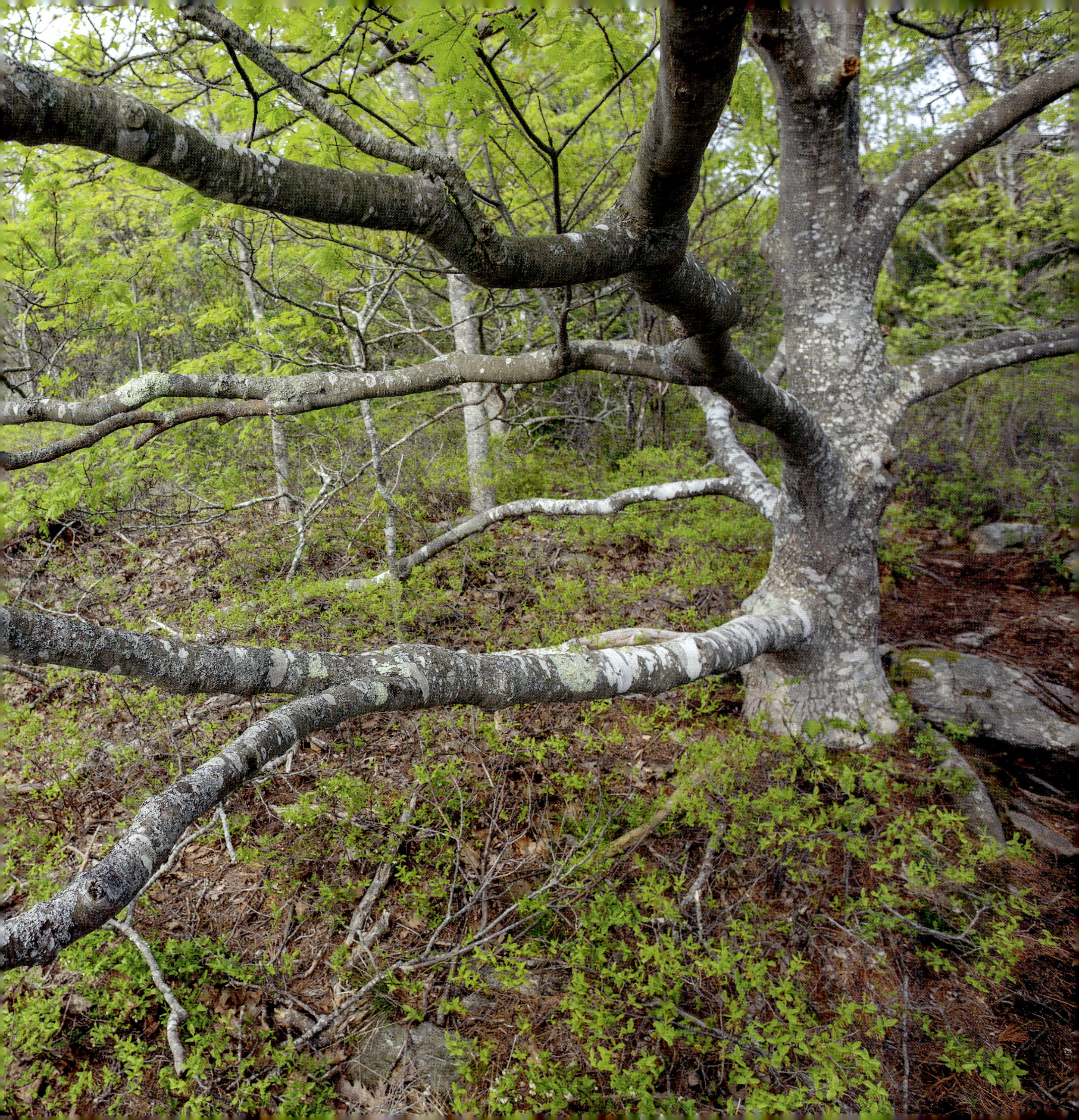

Susan Cerulean

FLORIDA

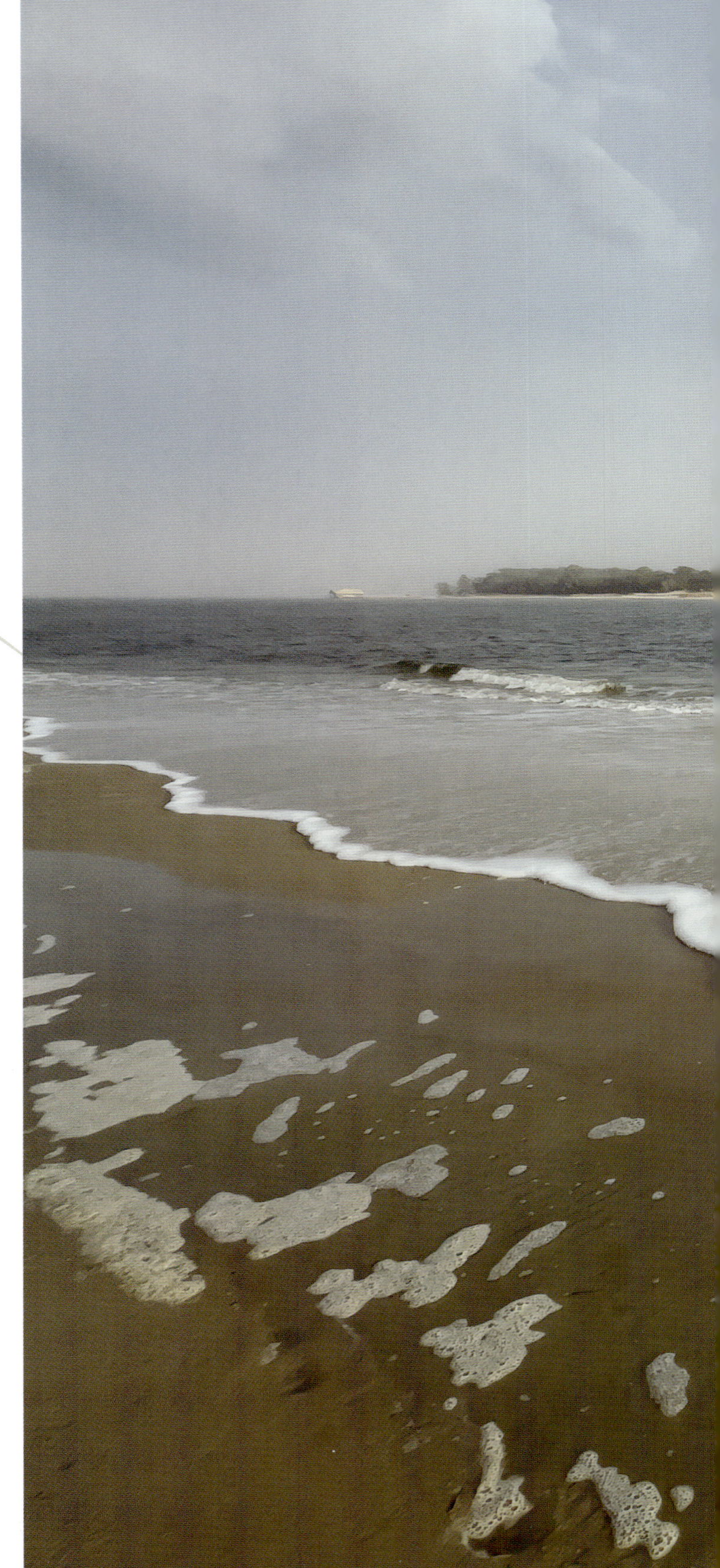

"We love and care for what we have come to know

through immersion, moment by moment by moment,

over long intimate years. Understanding the place

we live in or visit, in this way, leads us to connect

and tend and defend."

From *I Have Been Assigned the
Single Bird: A Daughter's Memoir*

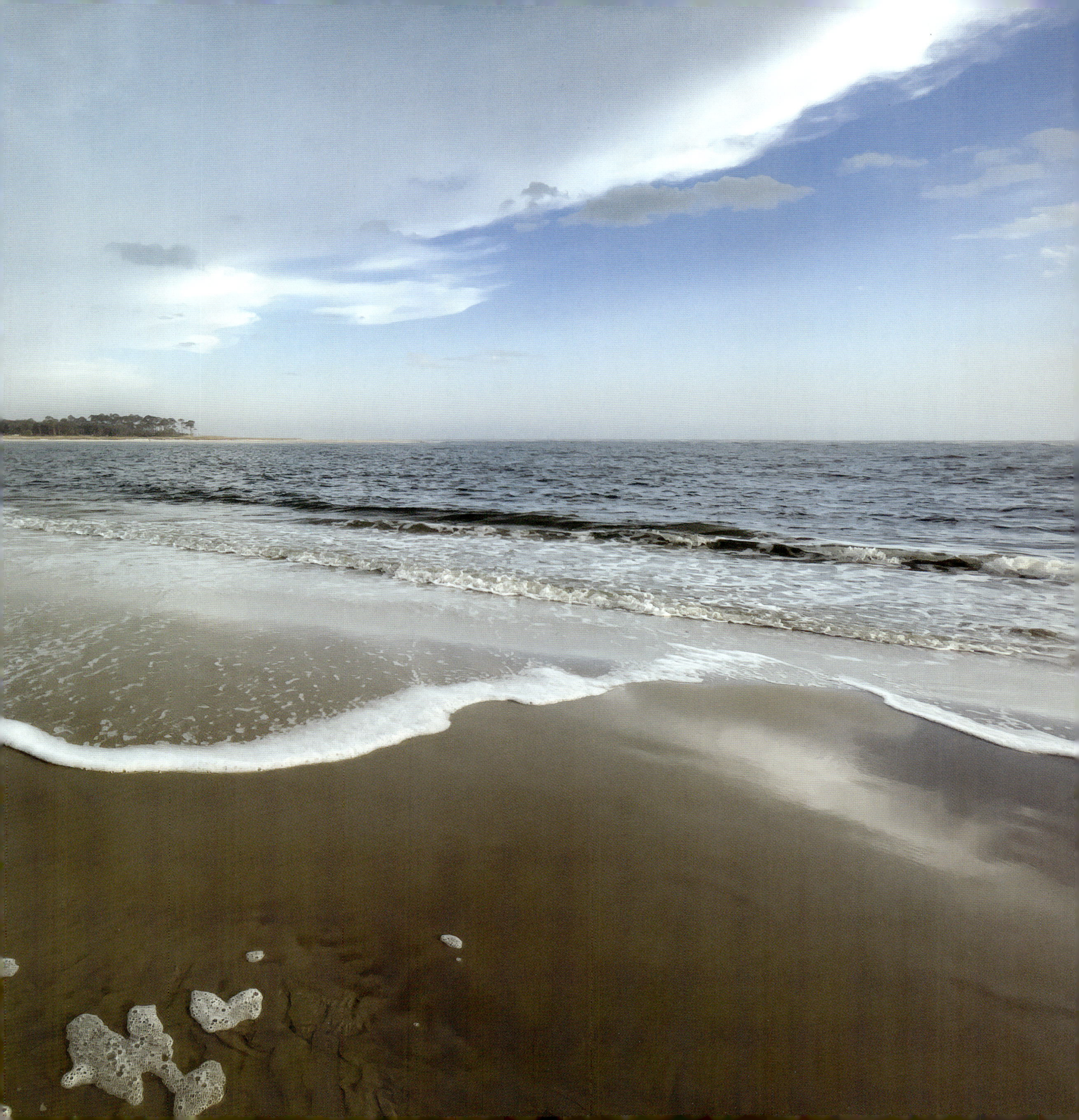

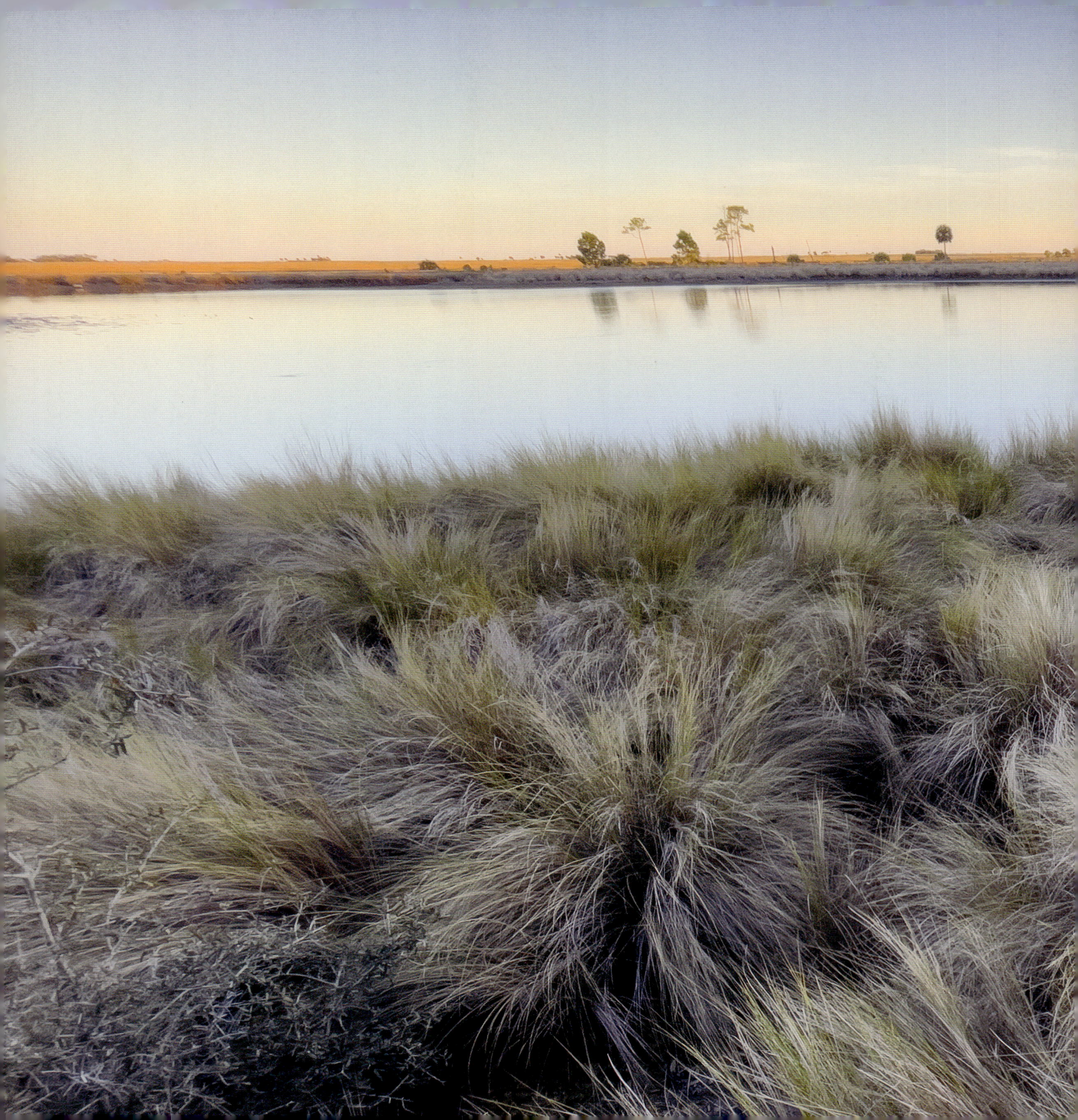

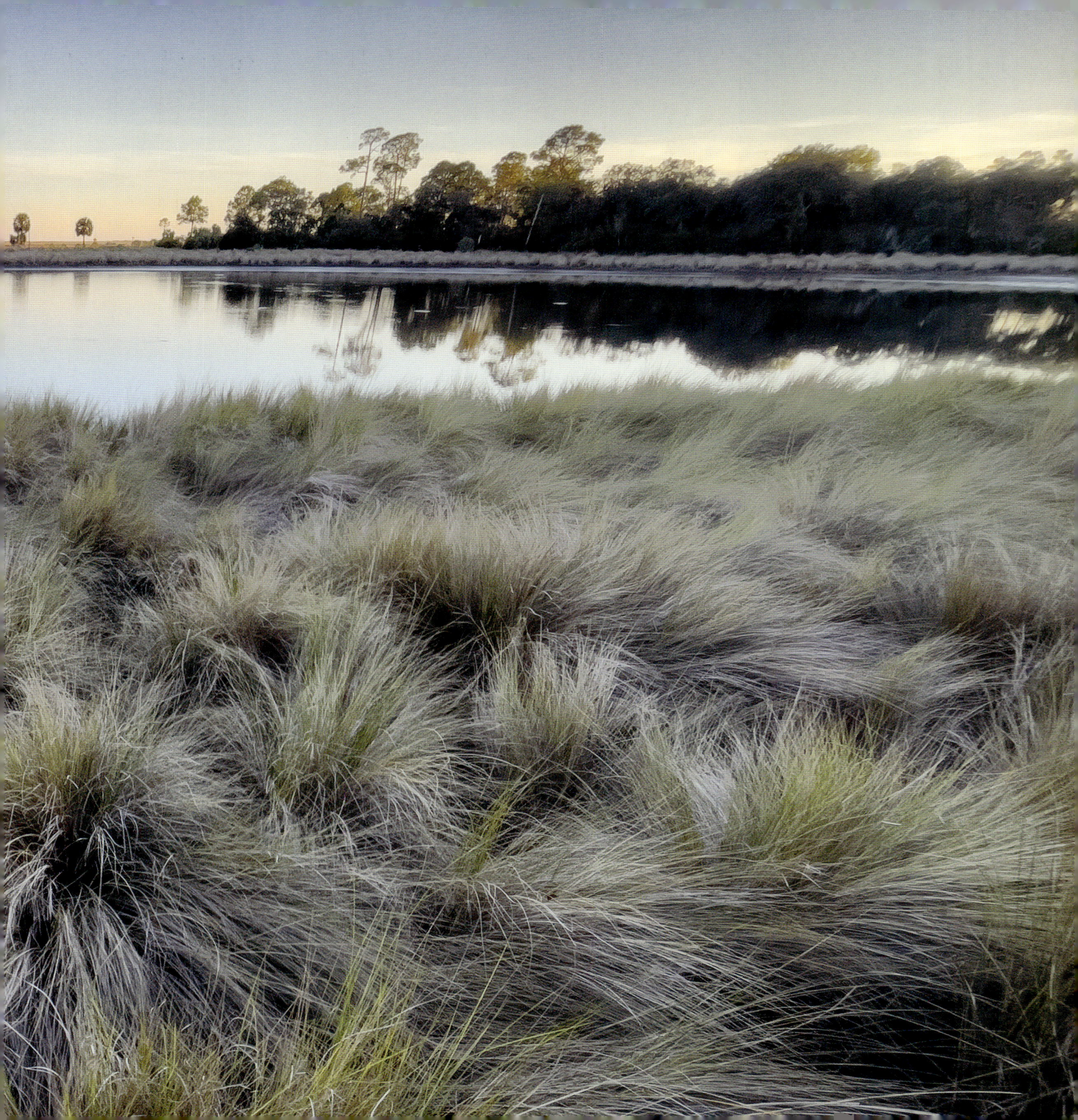

Philip Connors

NEW MEXICO

"I should know by now that nothing lasts and nothing stays the same. My life has been one long lesson in that fact. I want, I suppose, one place I can hold to as immutable, one thing I can count on as fixed. But of course I already have that: the guarantee that I won't be here forever. The knowledge that transformation awaits me too, the transition to nonbeing. I am as ephemeral as the details of any place. More so, given that once I'm gone, the places will remain. So I scribble to mark my passage through those places I have loved most."

From *A Song for the River*

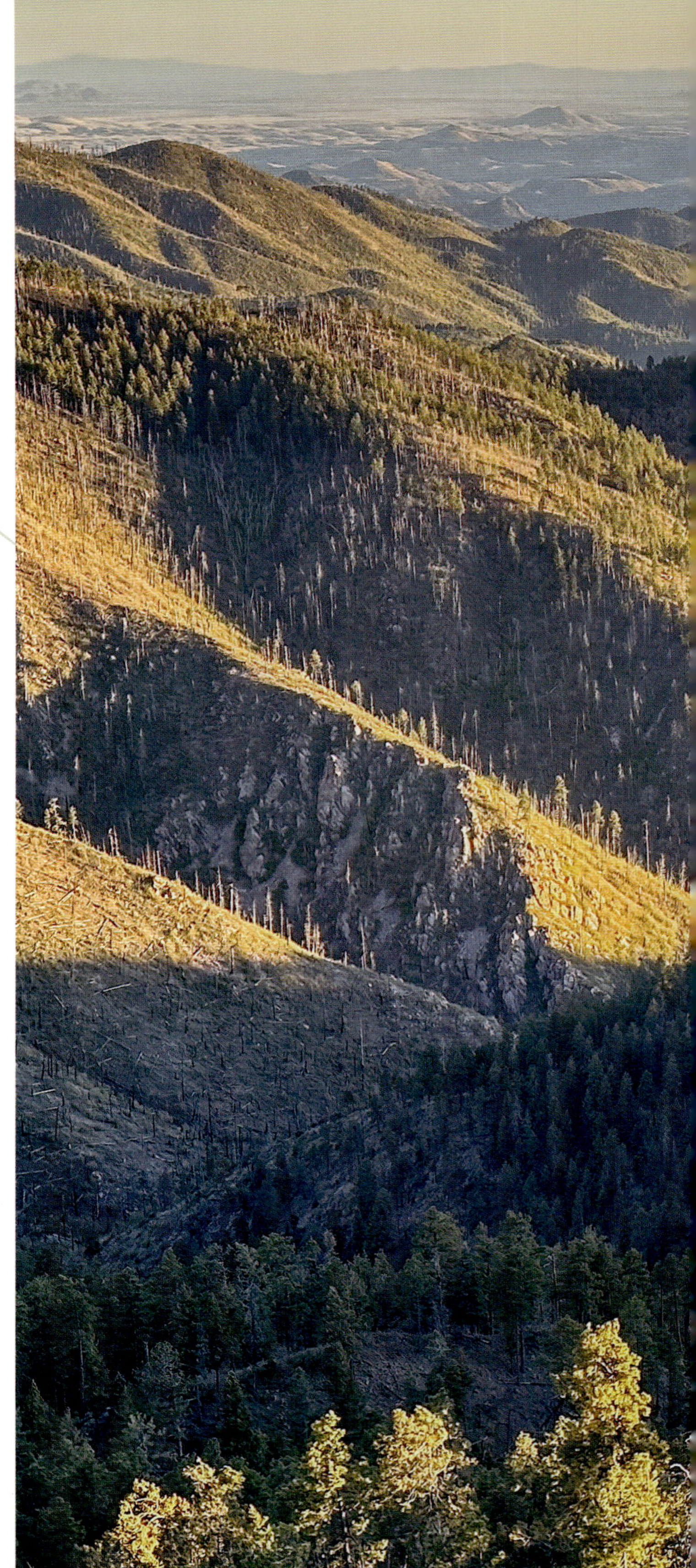

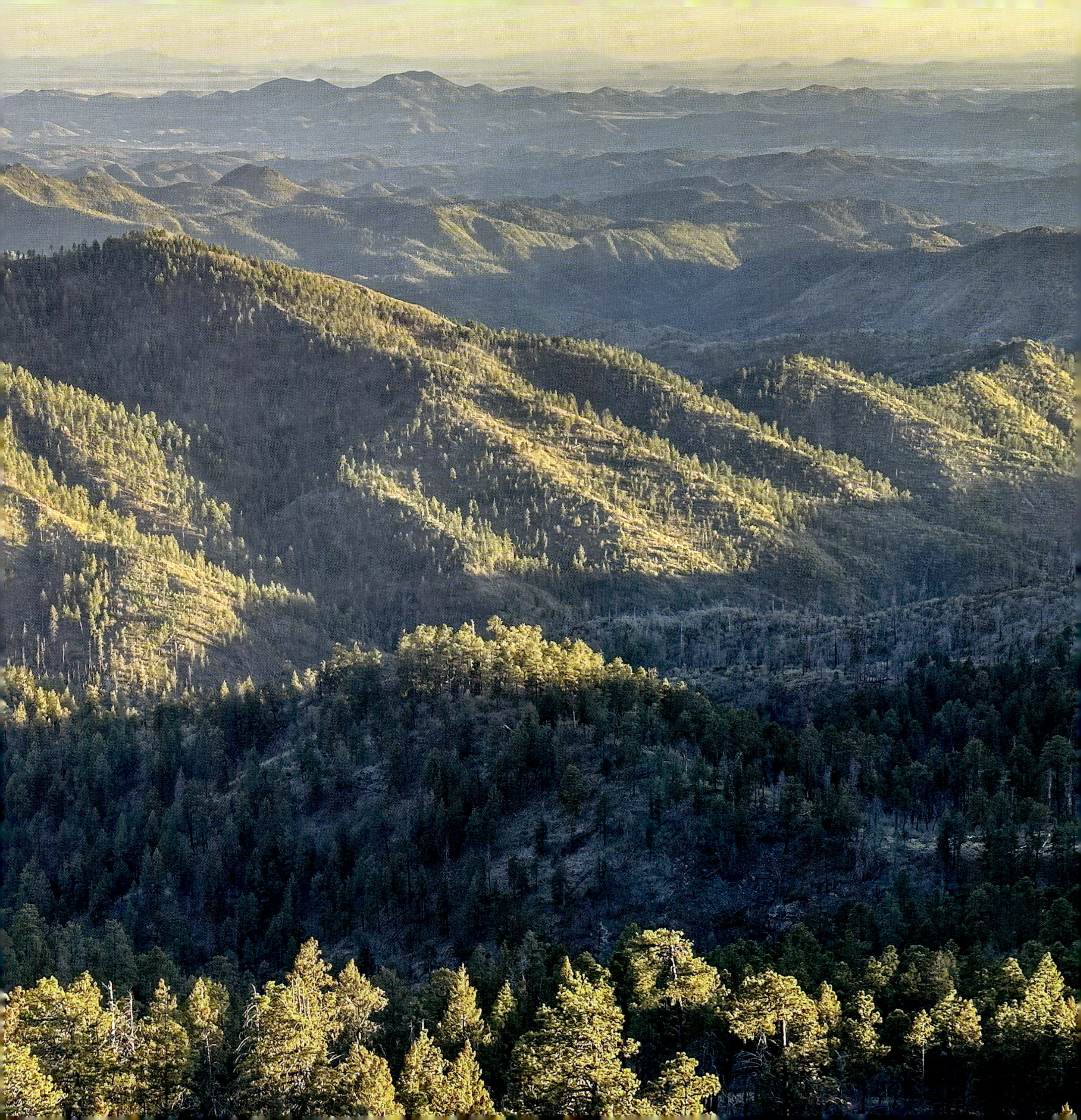

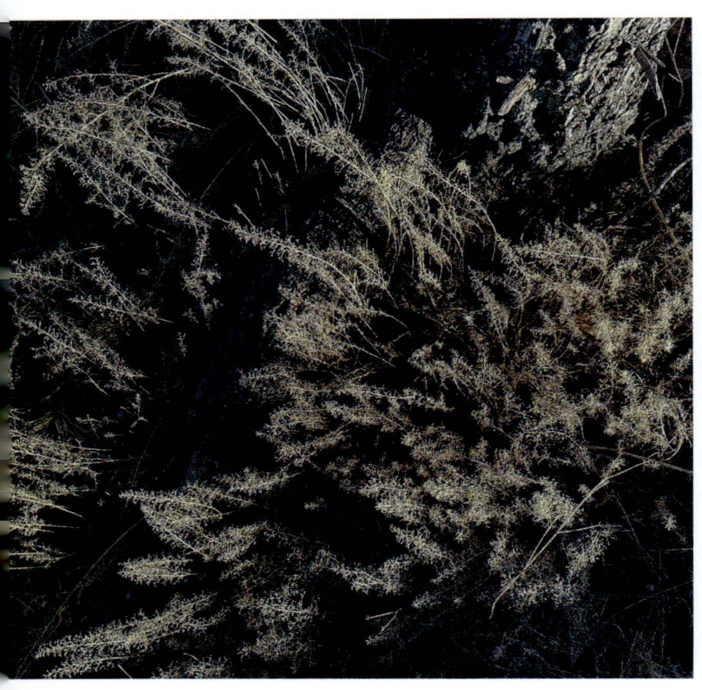
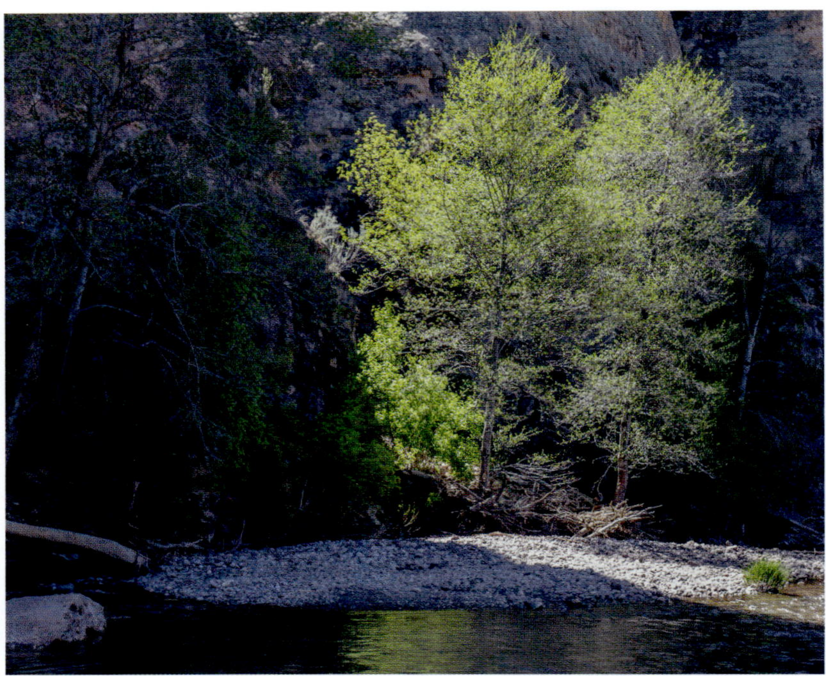

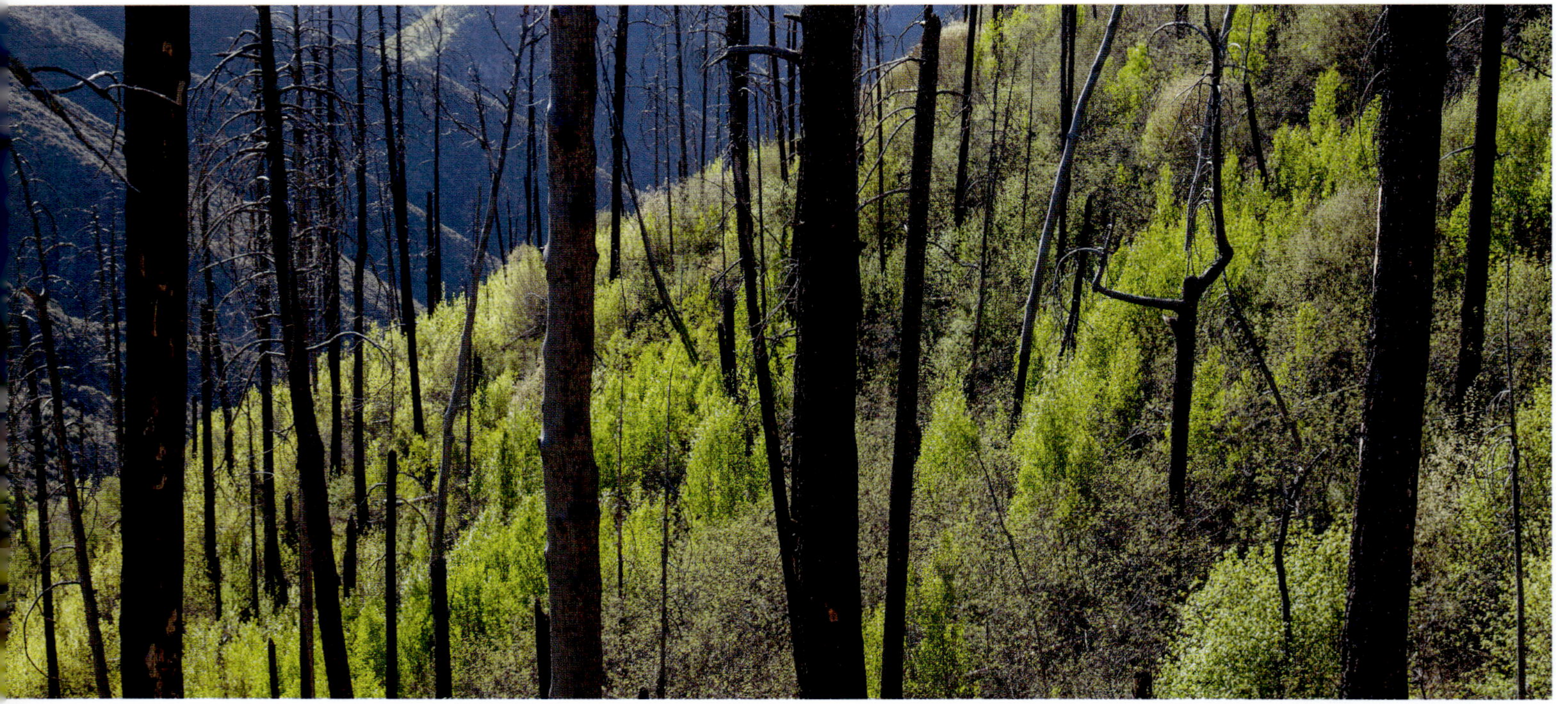

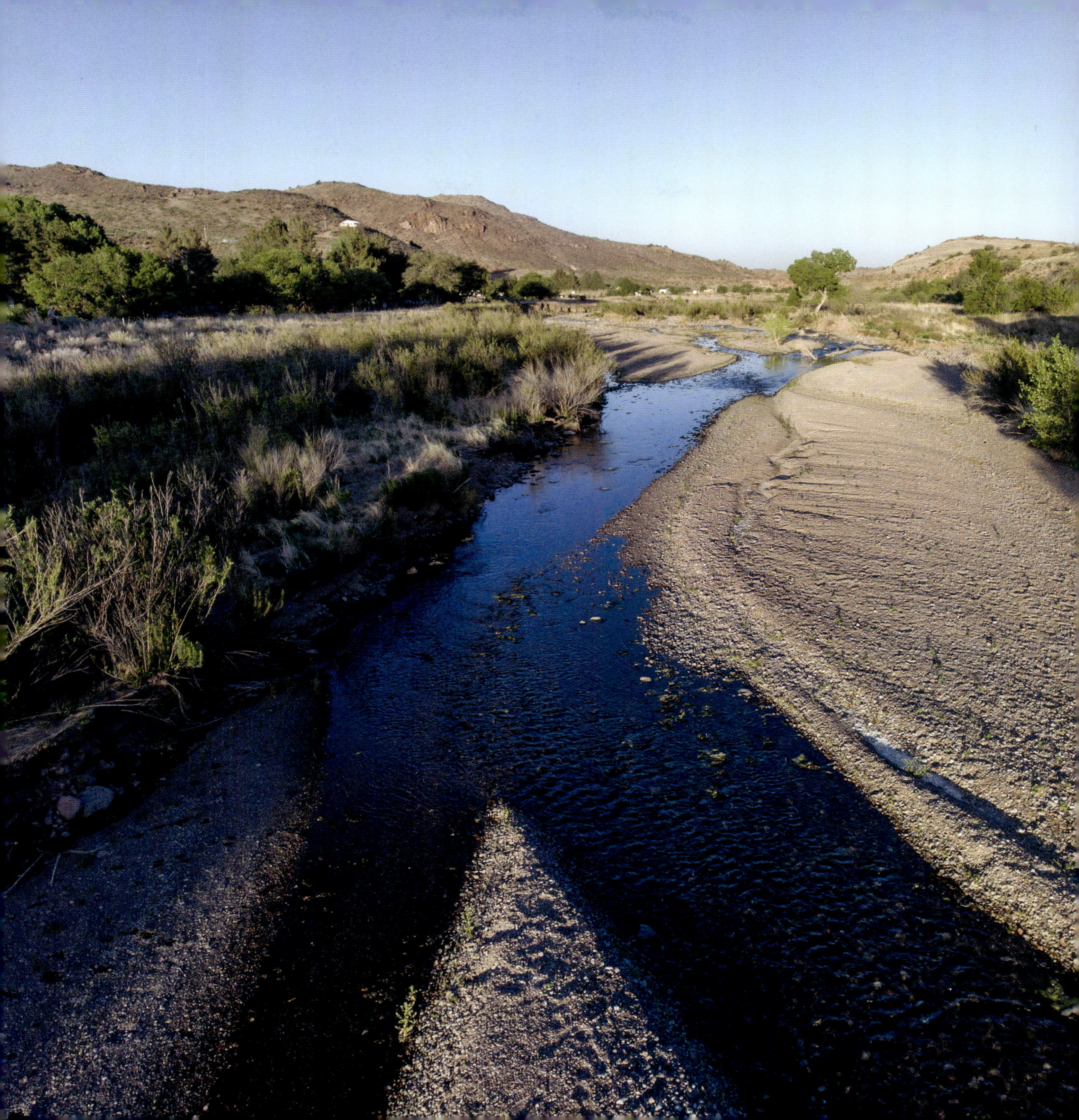

Alison Hawthorne Deming

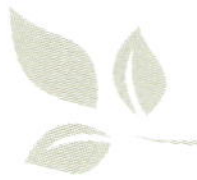

"In my story I may not know how to define the

sacred, but I have felt its presence in nature and

in the coming-into-form that is language and art.

I have felt it in the space inside the body and

in the space between the stars. What holds the

Creation together? Not emptiness."

From *Writing the Sacred into the Real*

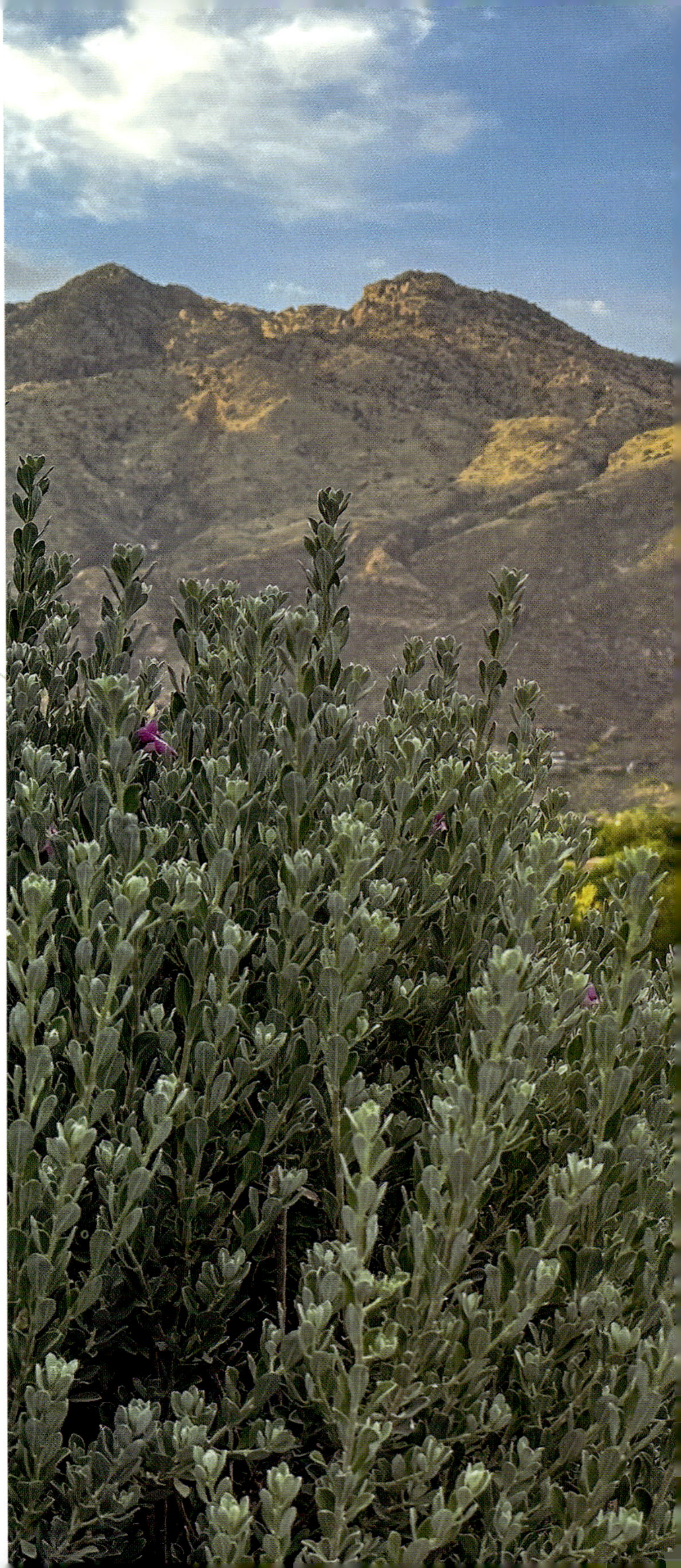

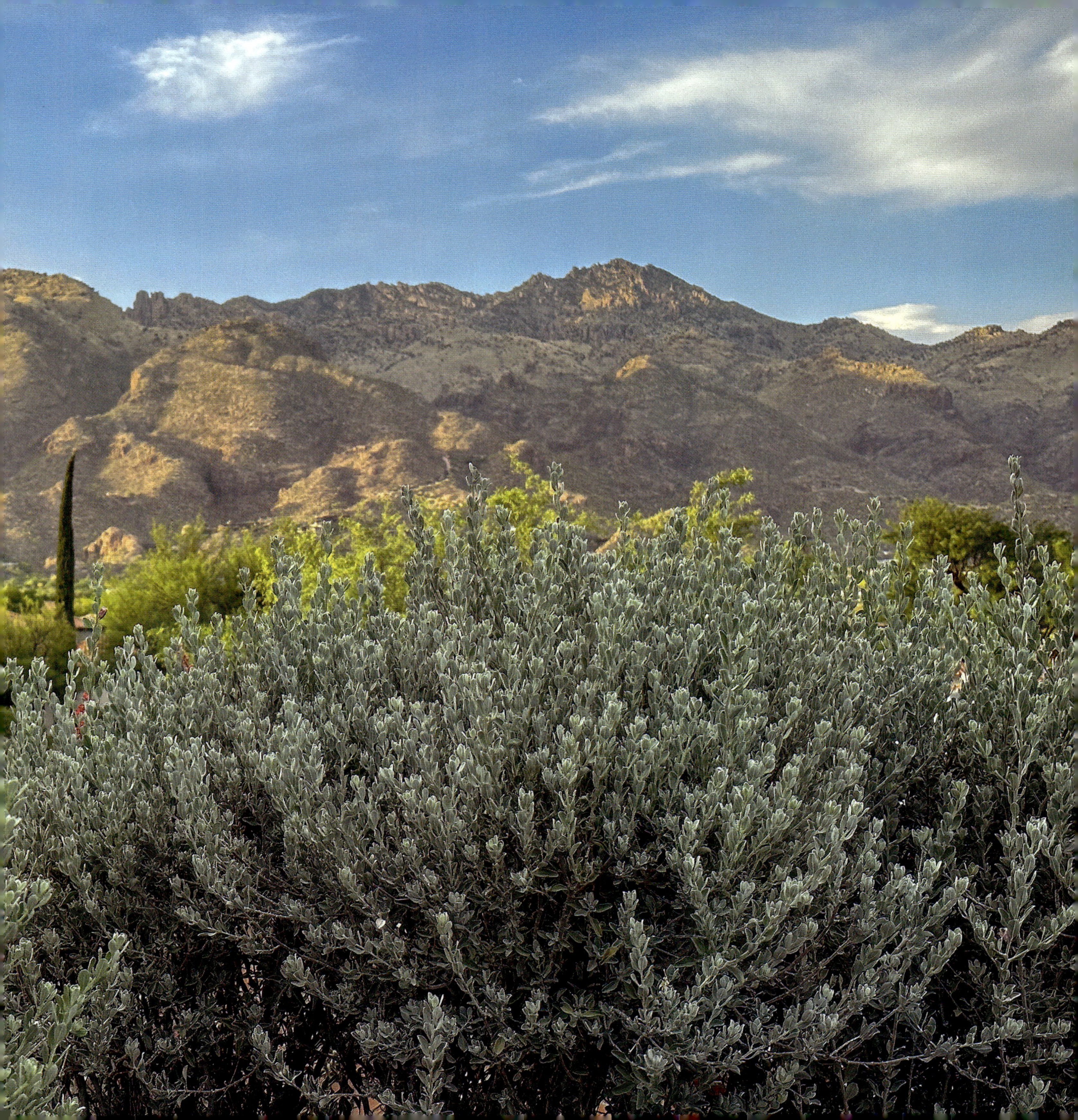

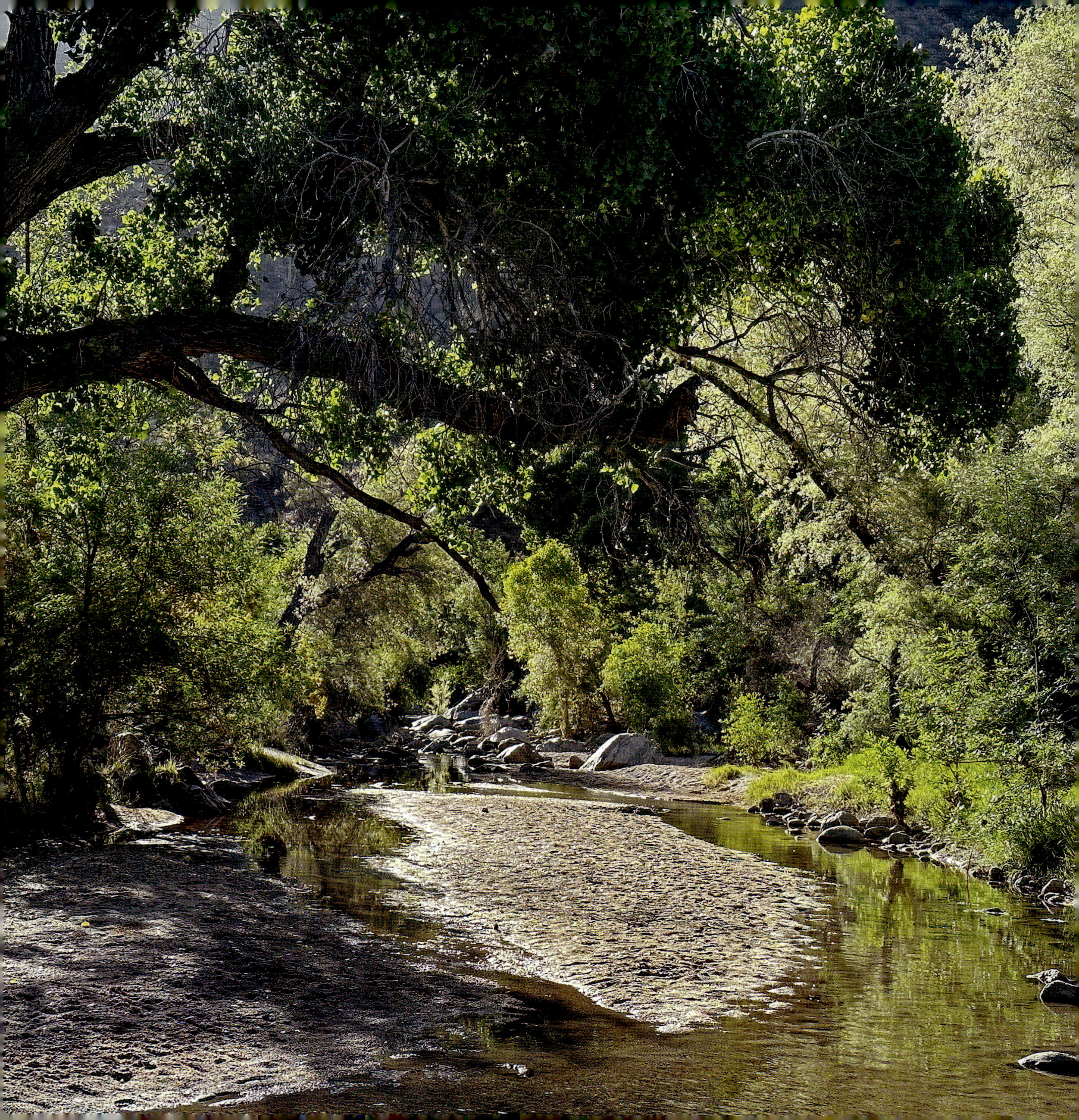

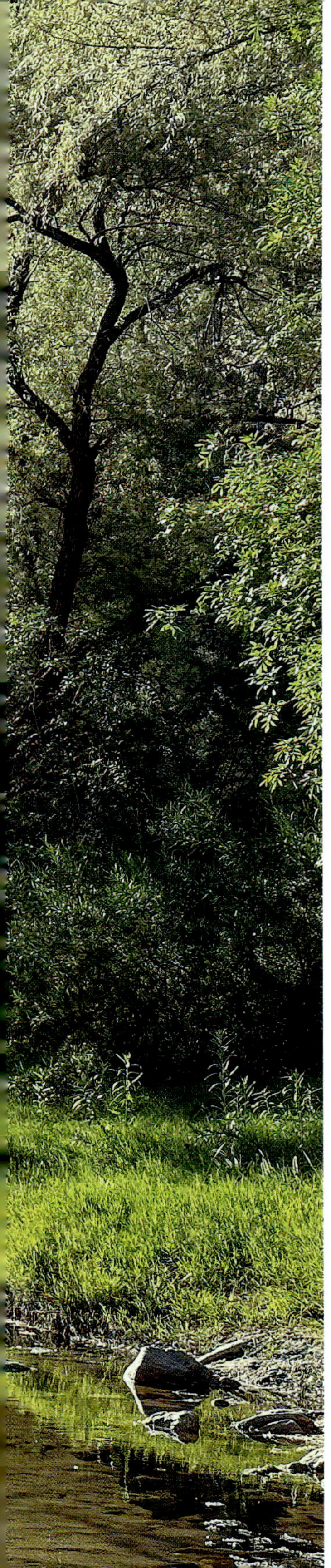

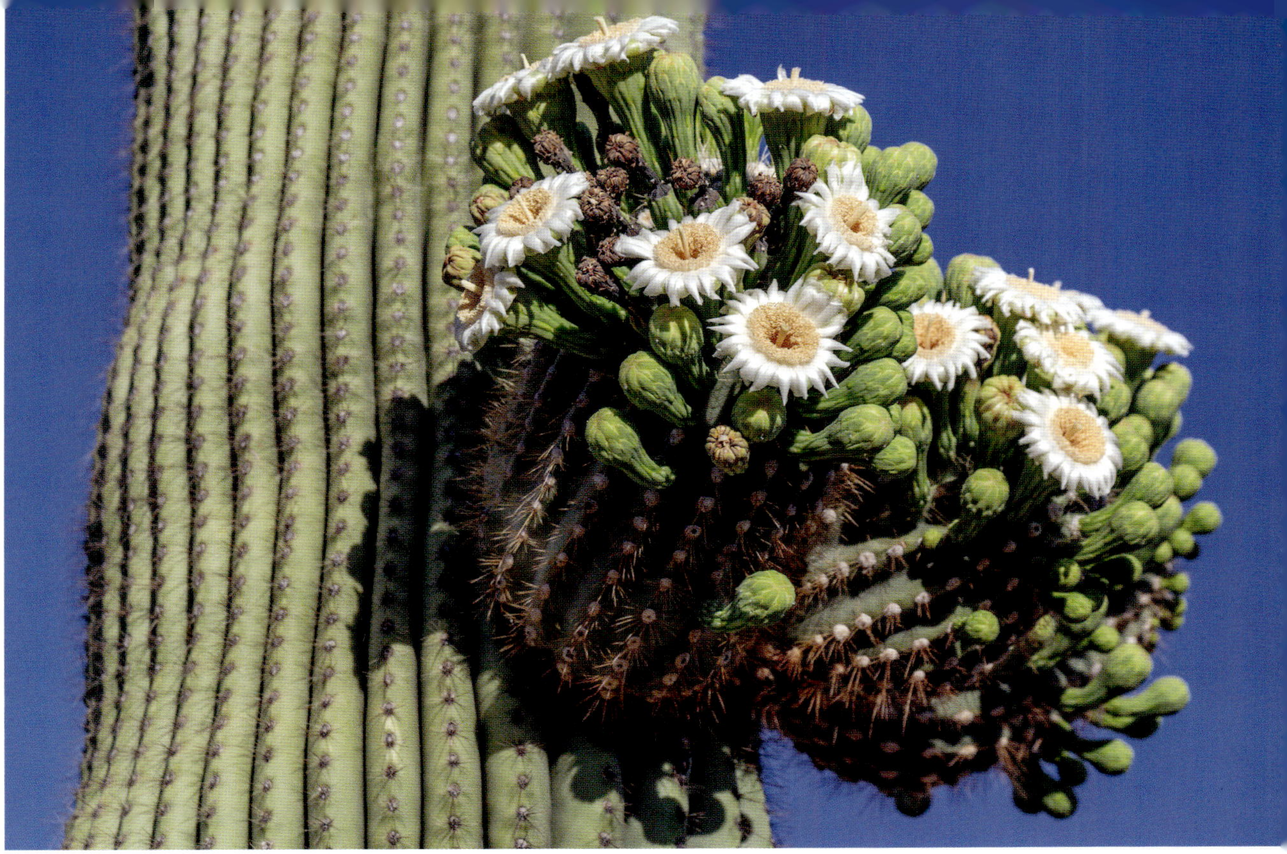

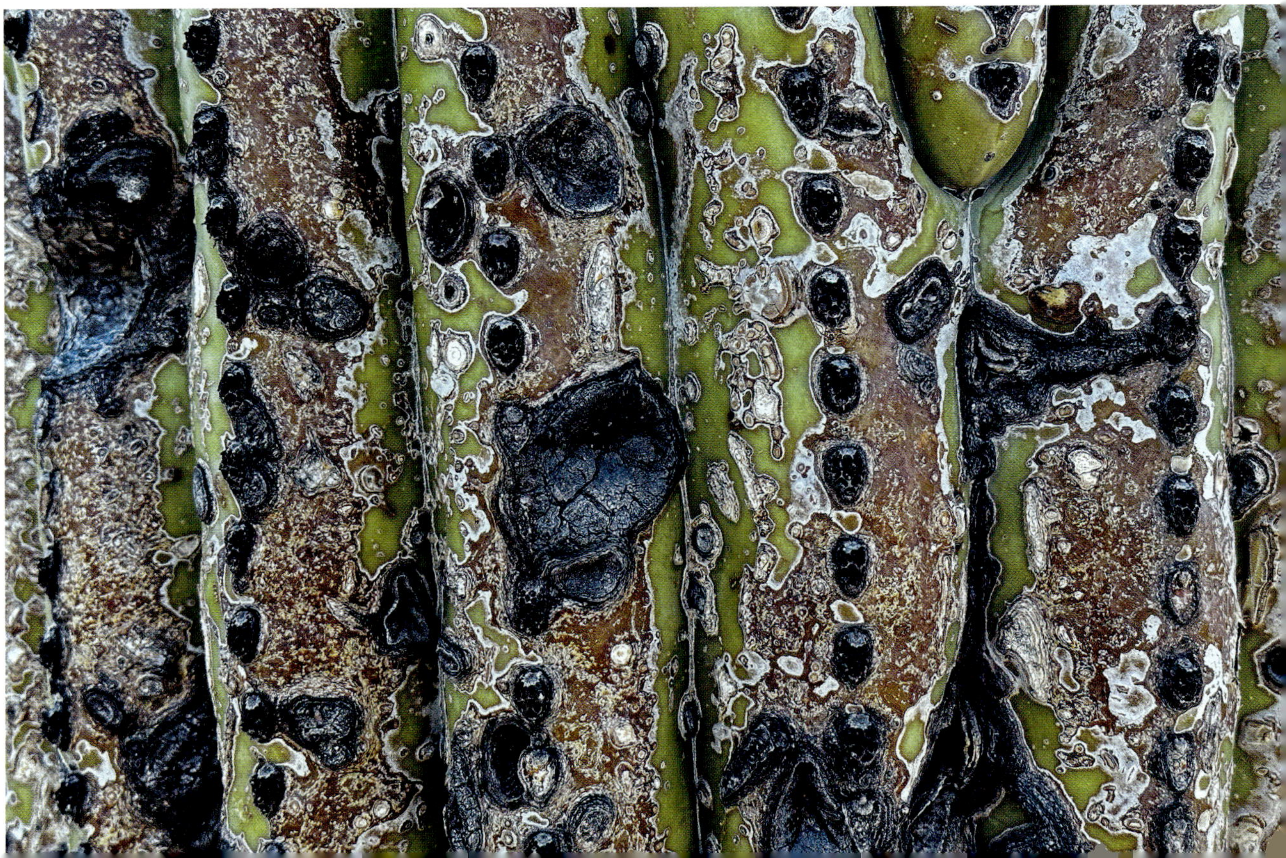

Marjory Stoneman Douglas

"There are no other Everglades in the world. They are, they have always been, one of the unique regions of the earth, remote, never wholly known. Nothing anywhere else is like them: their vast glittering openness, wider than the enormous visible round of the horizon, the racing free saltness and sweetness of their massive winds, under the dazzling blue heights of space. They are unique also in the simplicity, the diversity, the related harmony of the forms of life they enclose. The miracle of the light pours over the green and brown expanse of saw grass and of water, shining and slow-moving below, the grass and water that is the meaning and the central fact of the Everglades of Florida. It is a river of grass."

From *The Everglades: River of Grass*

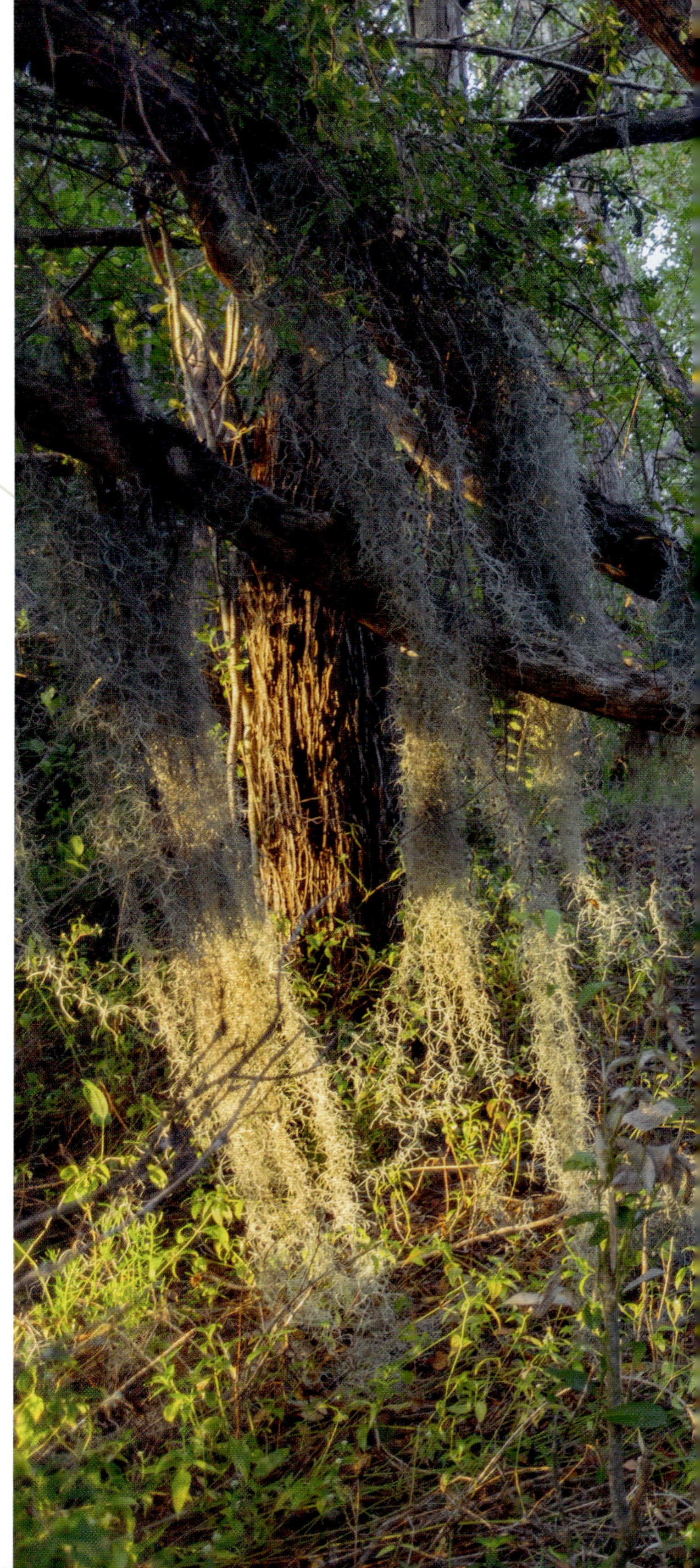

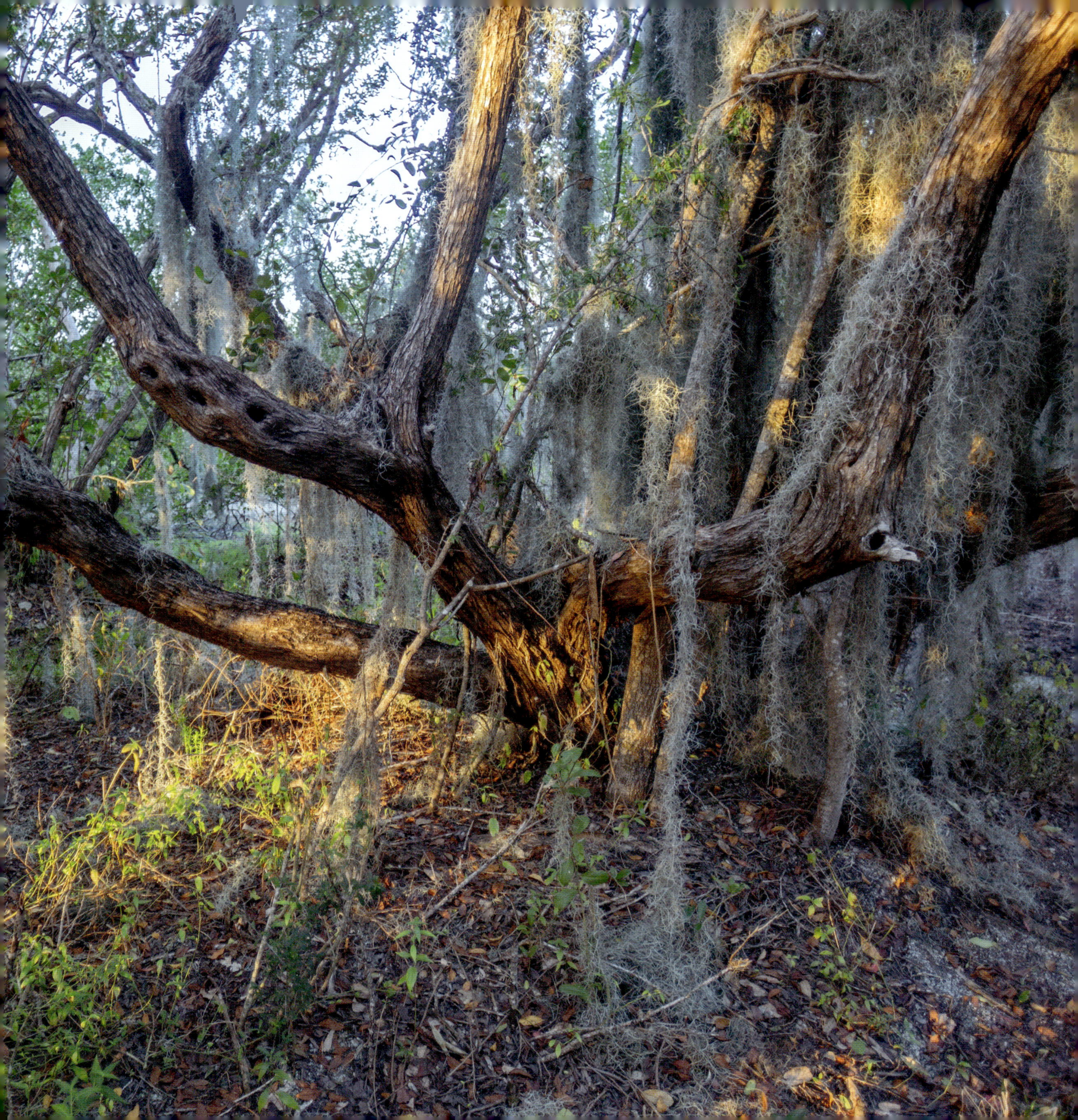

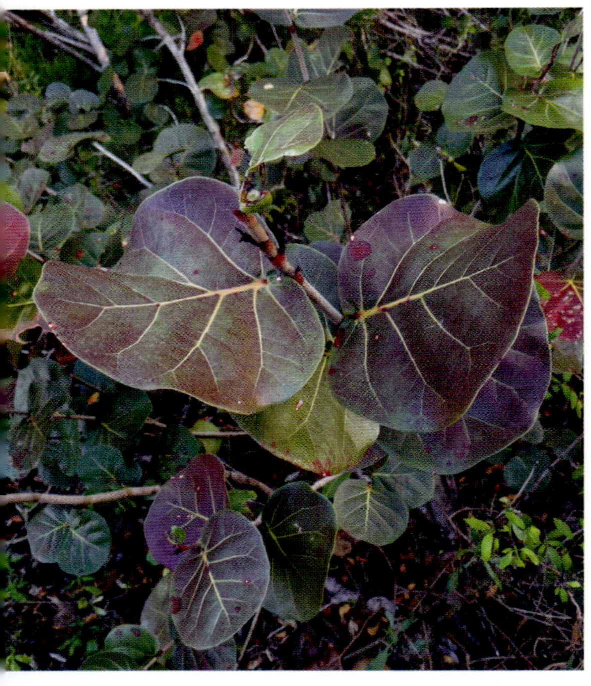
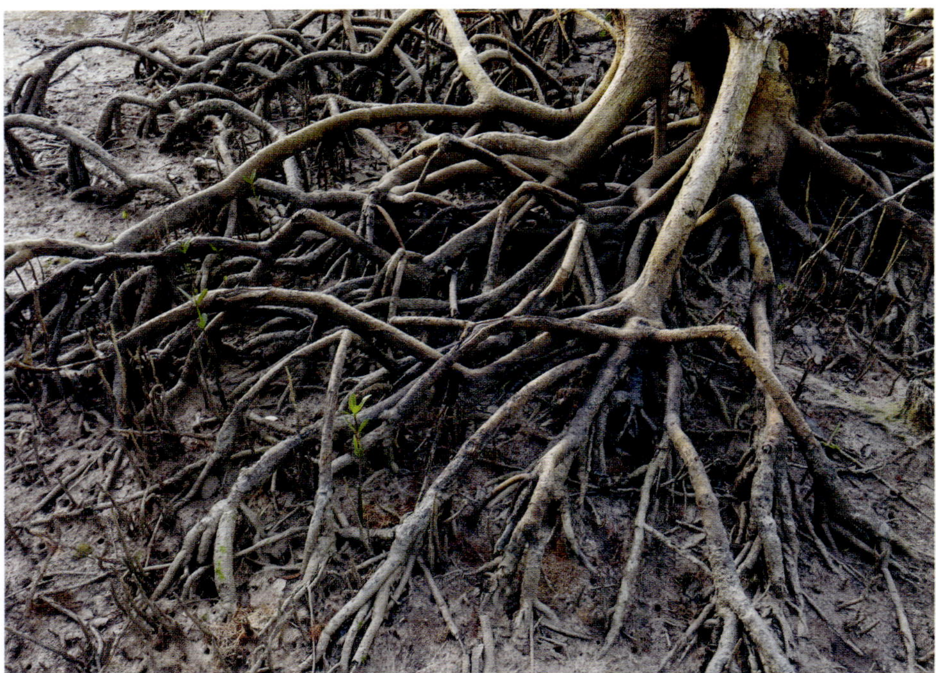

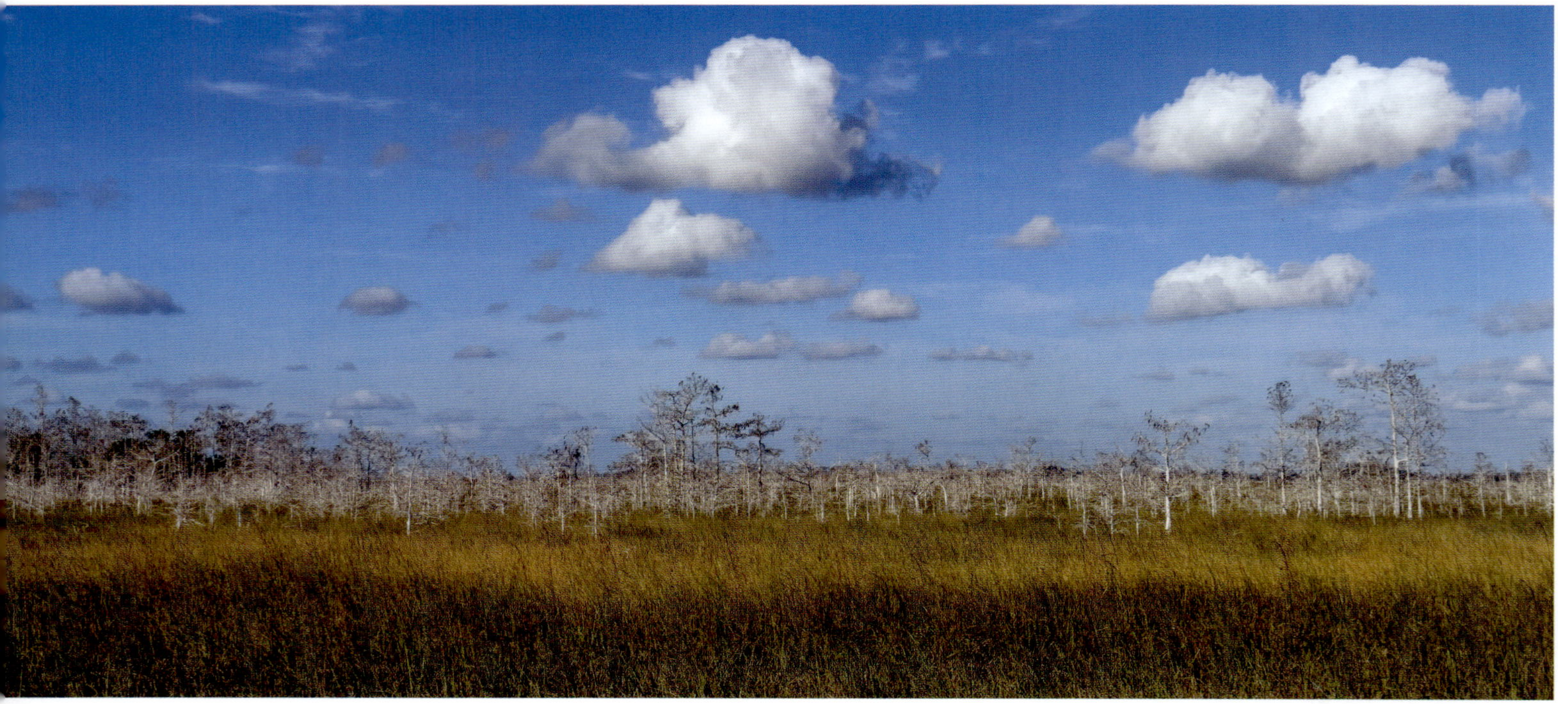

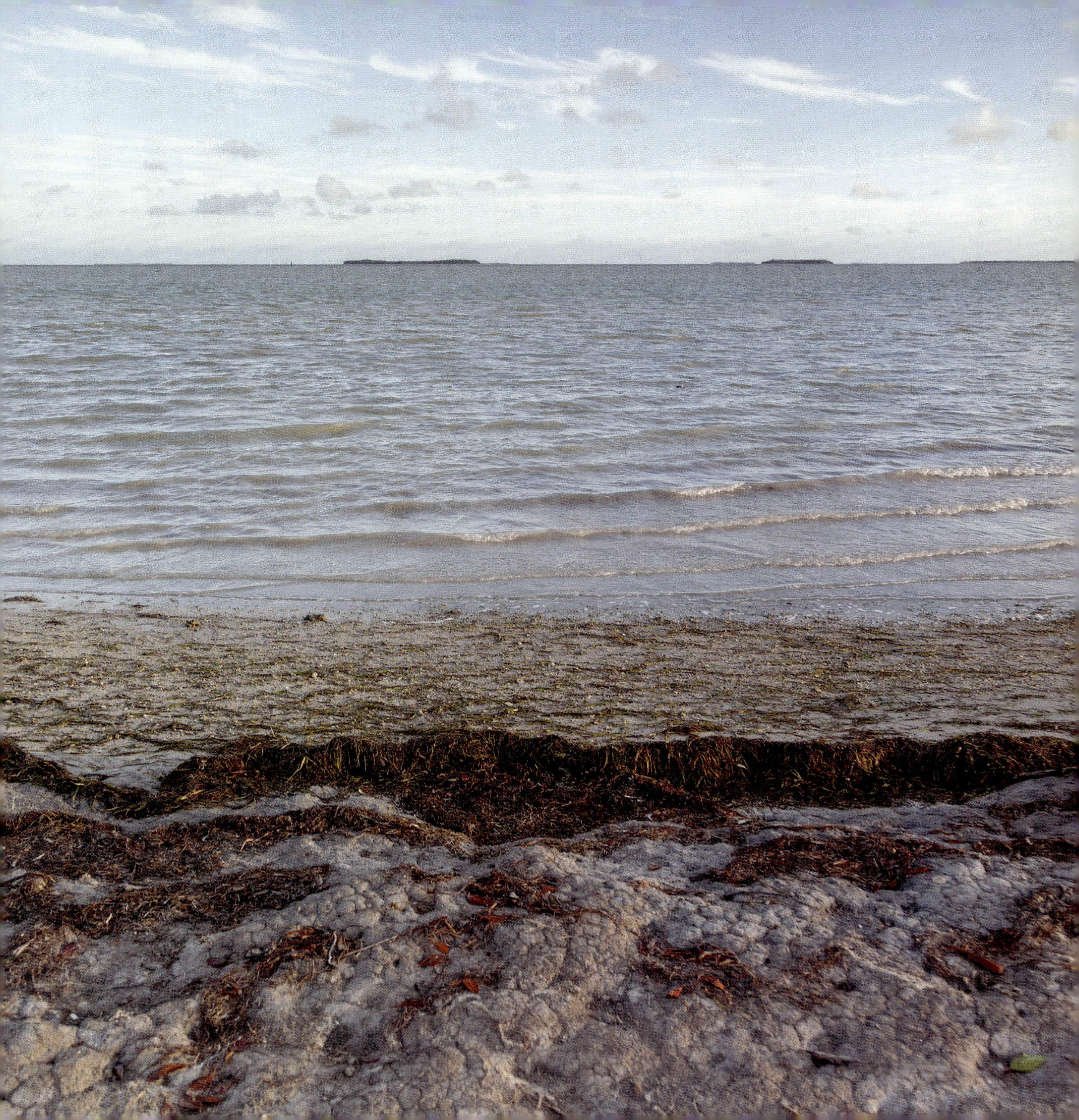

Camille T. Dungy

COLORADO

"Whether a plot in a yard or pots in a window, every politically engaged person should have a garden. By politically engaged, I mean everyone with a vested interest in the direction the people on this planet take in relationship to others. We should all take some time to plant life in the soil. Even when such planting isn't easy."

From *Soil: The Story of a Black Mother's Garden*

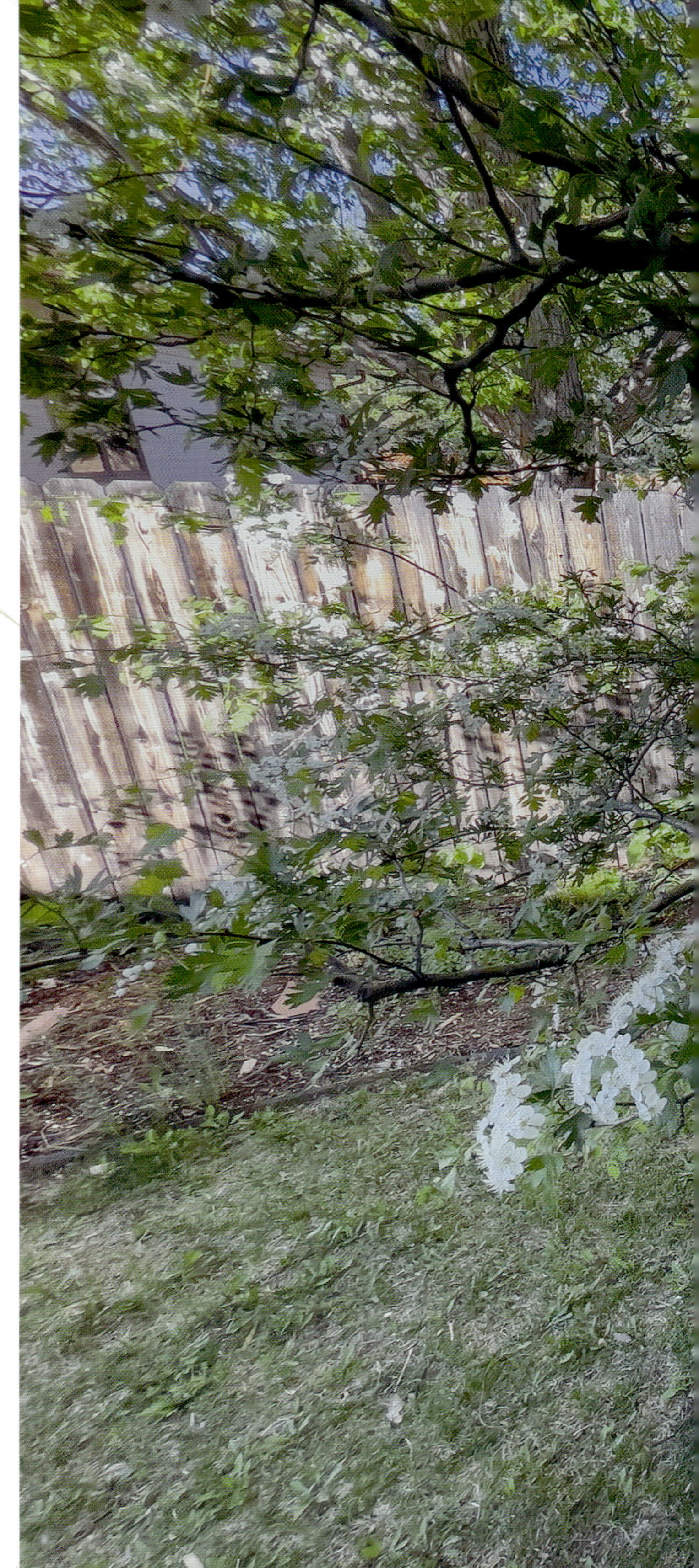

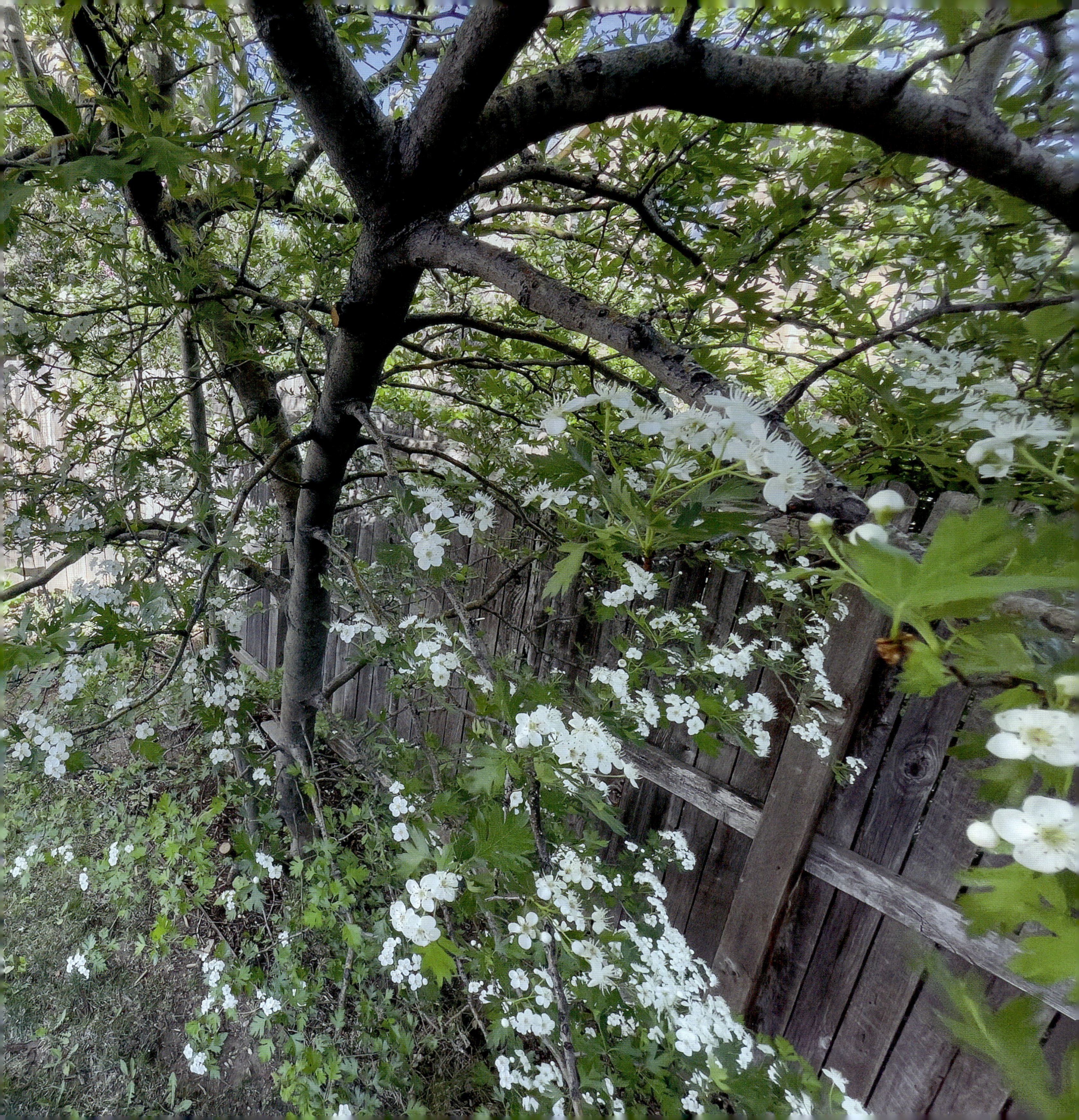

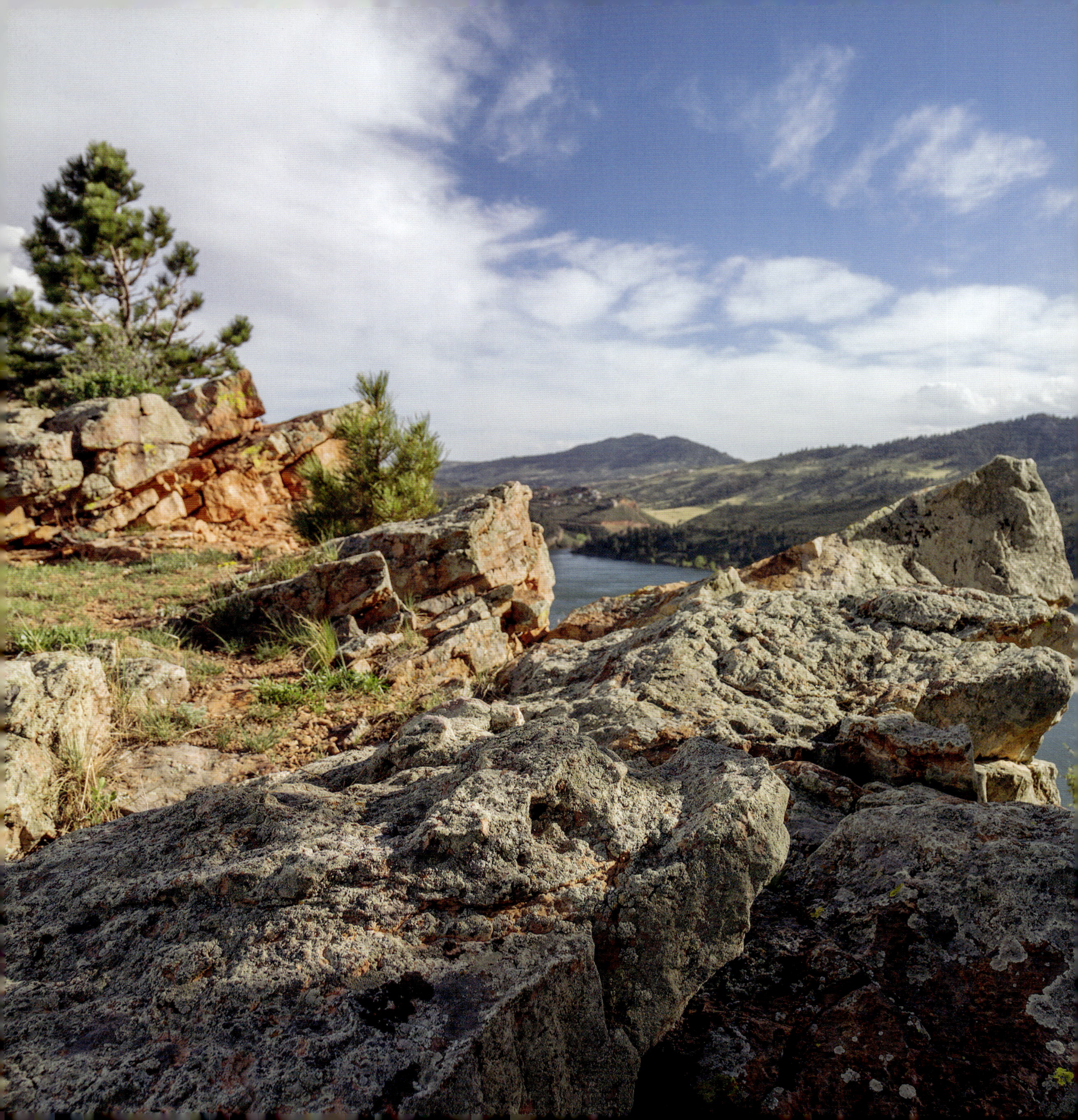

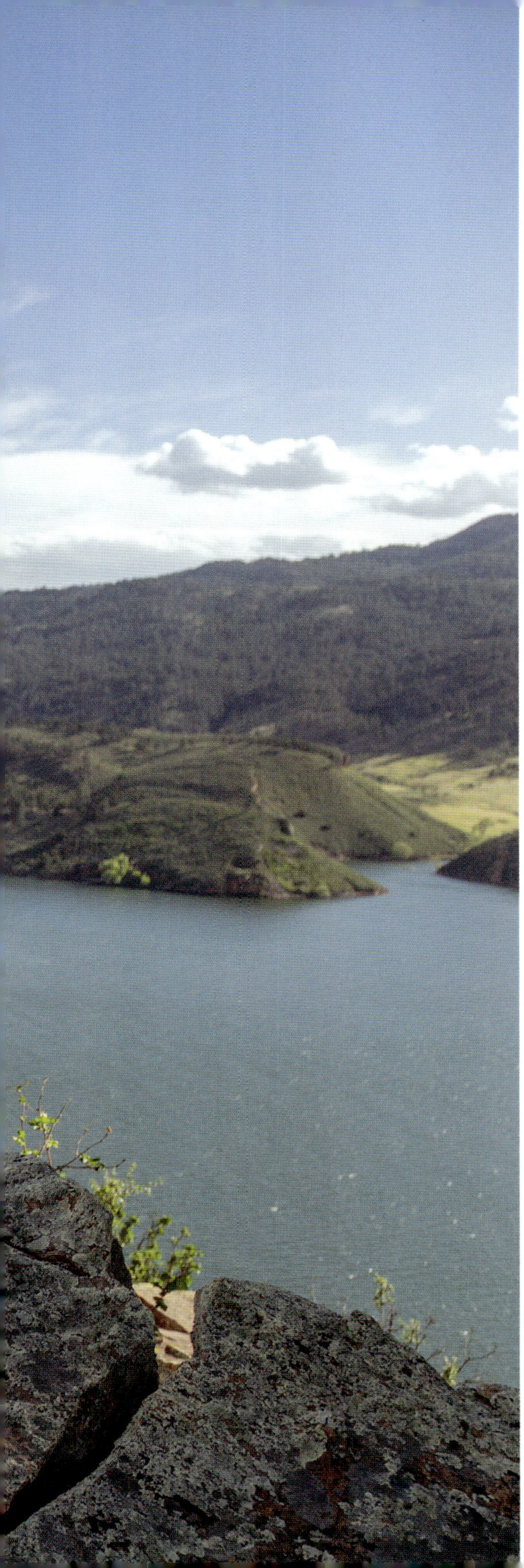

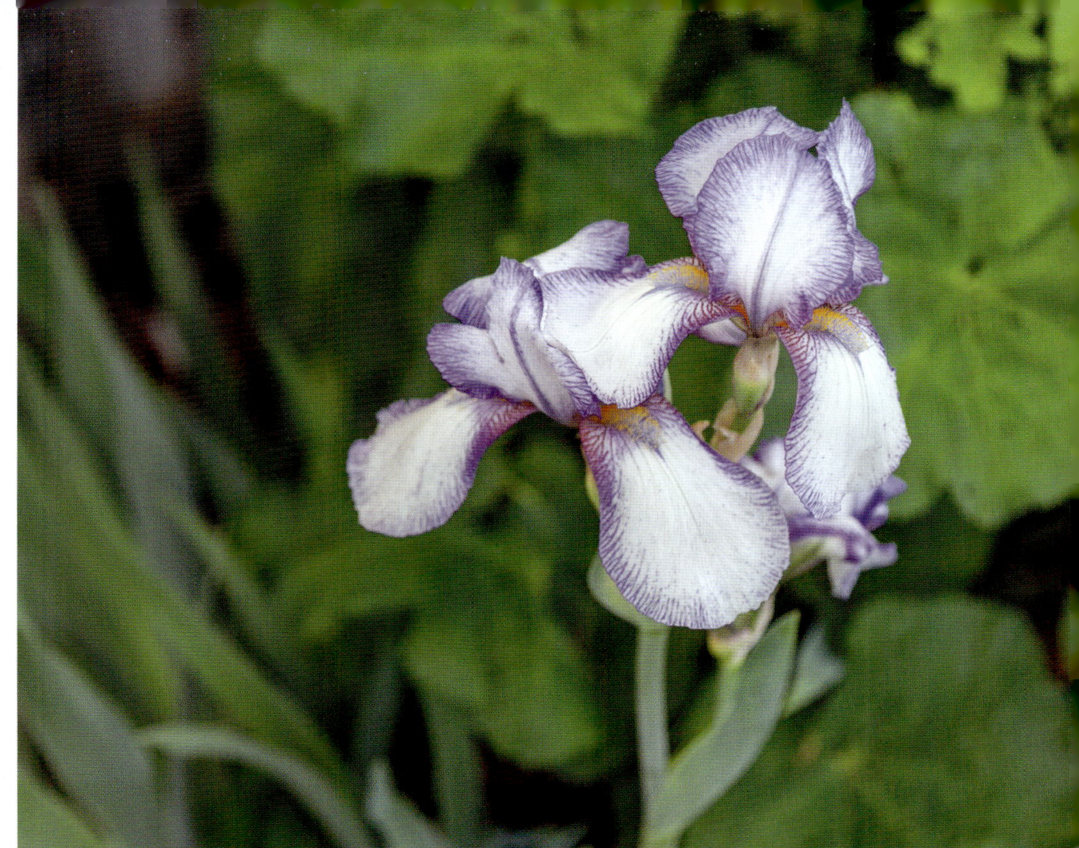

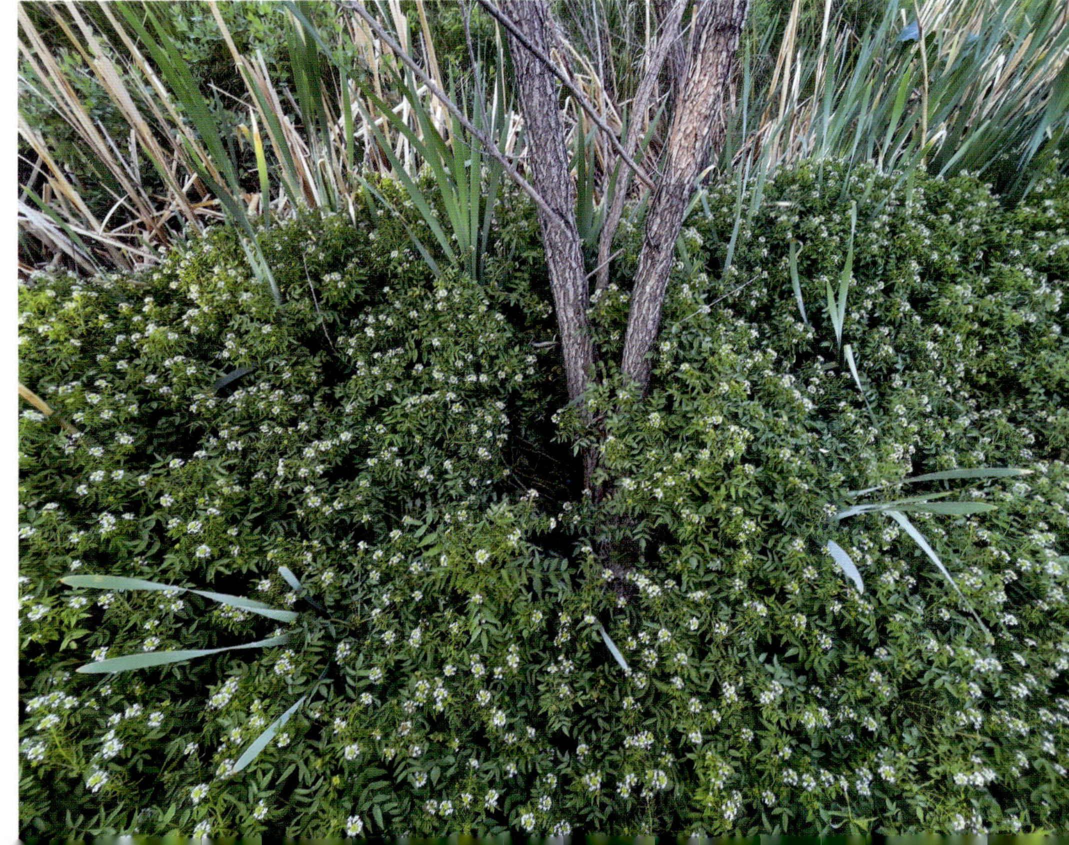

Gretel Ehrlich

M O N T A N A   &   W Y O M I N G

"Becoming 'native to a place' doesn't have to be about
secured boundaries of blood and territory but can
allude to a deep, growing knowledge of that place.
The way one feasts on it and becomes nourished and
gives thanks. And hands it over to be shared."

From *Unsolaced: Along the Way to All That Is*

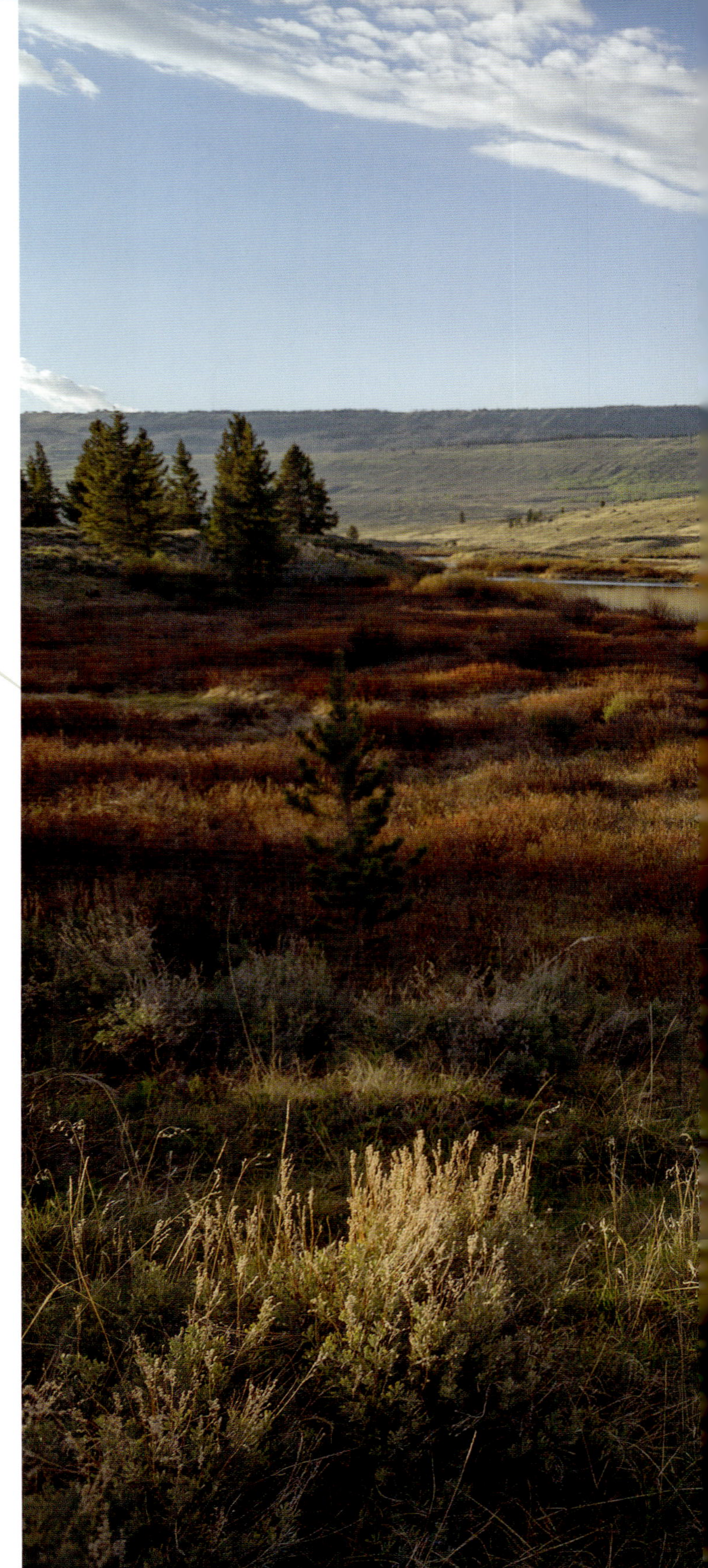

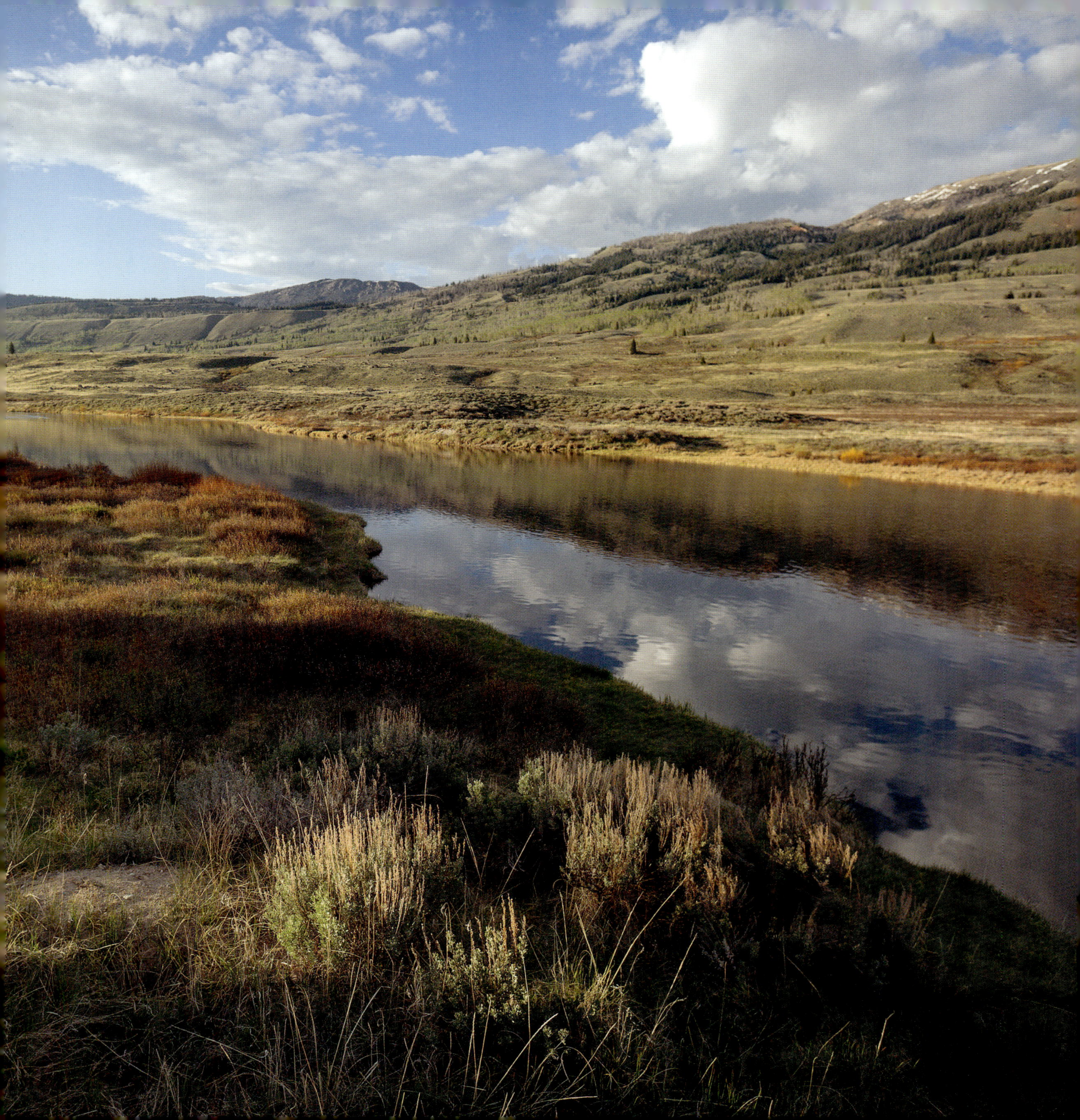

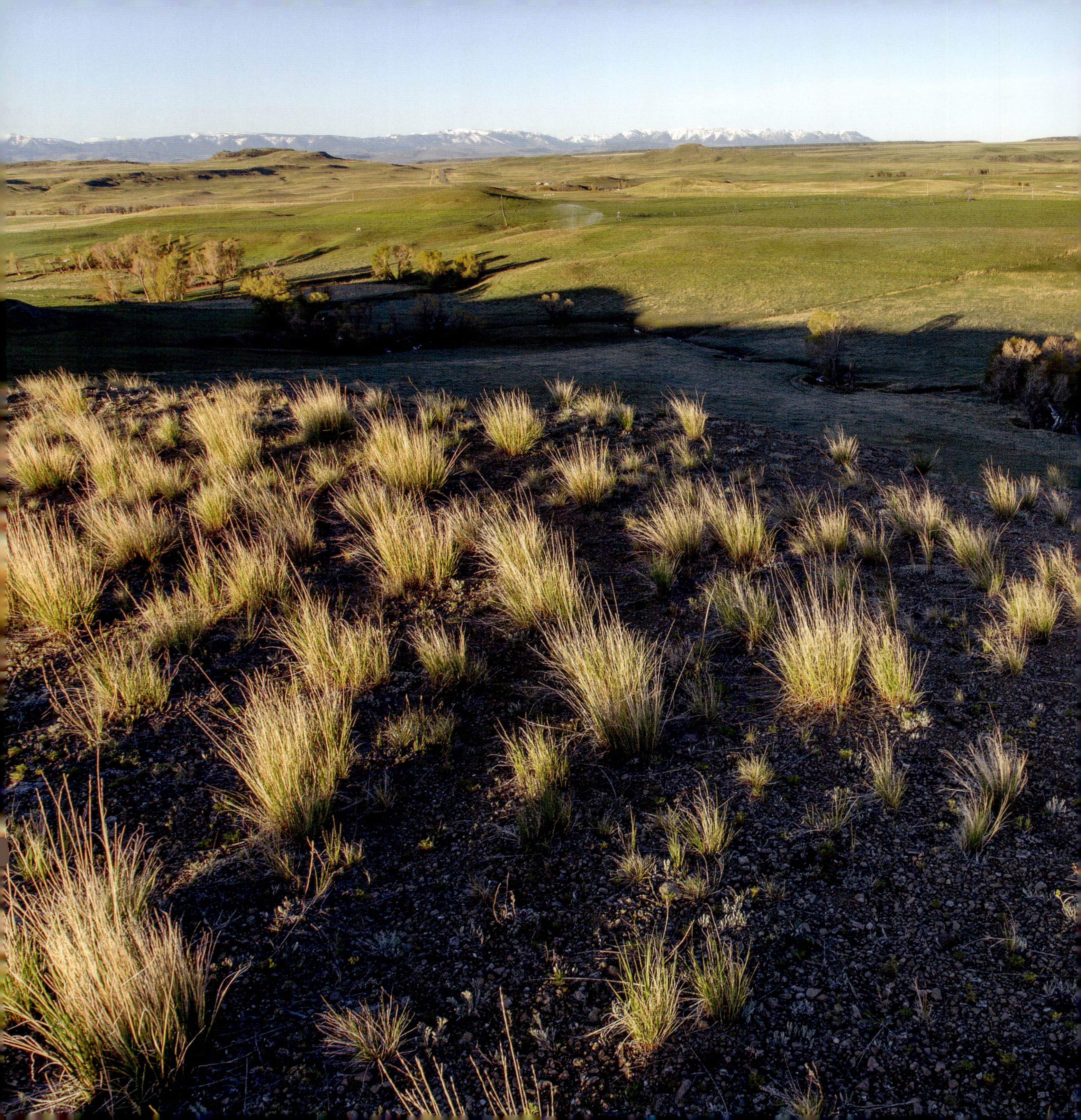

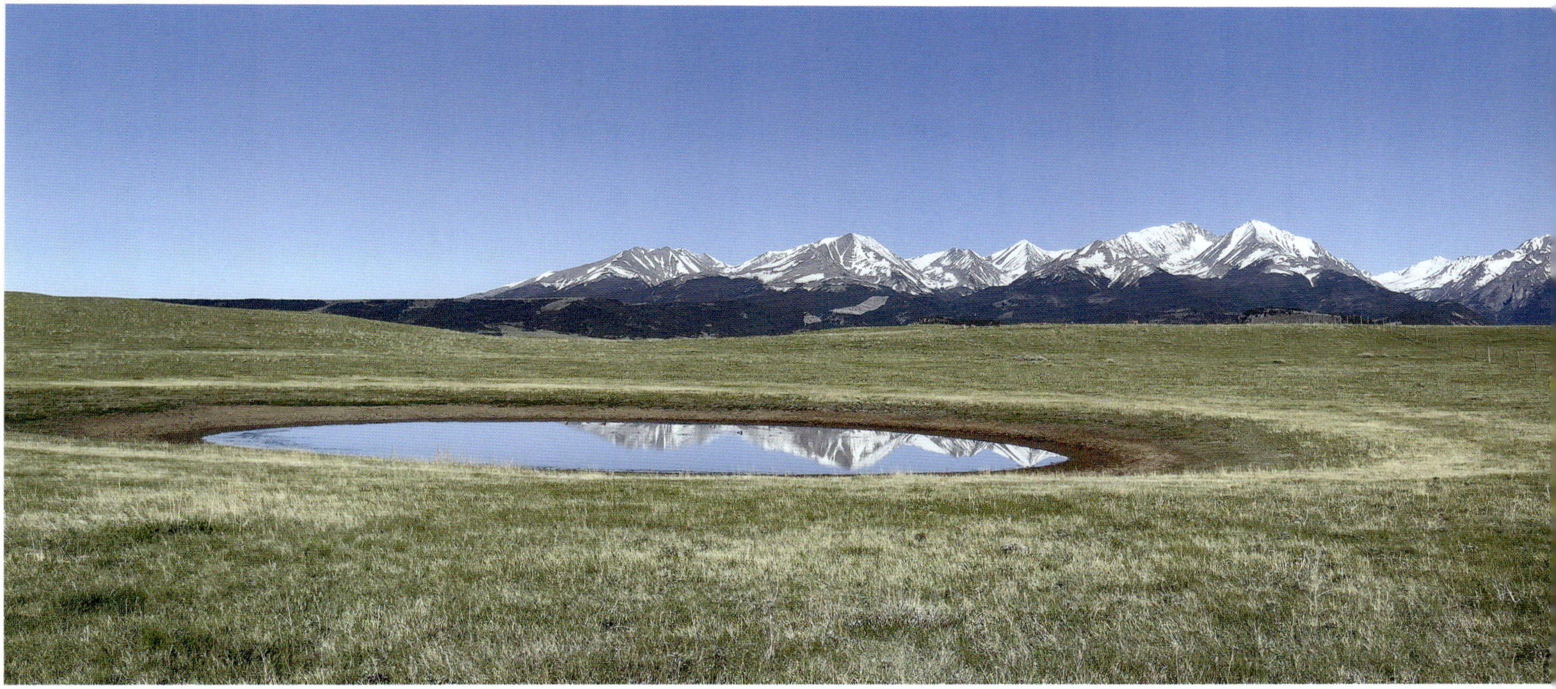

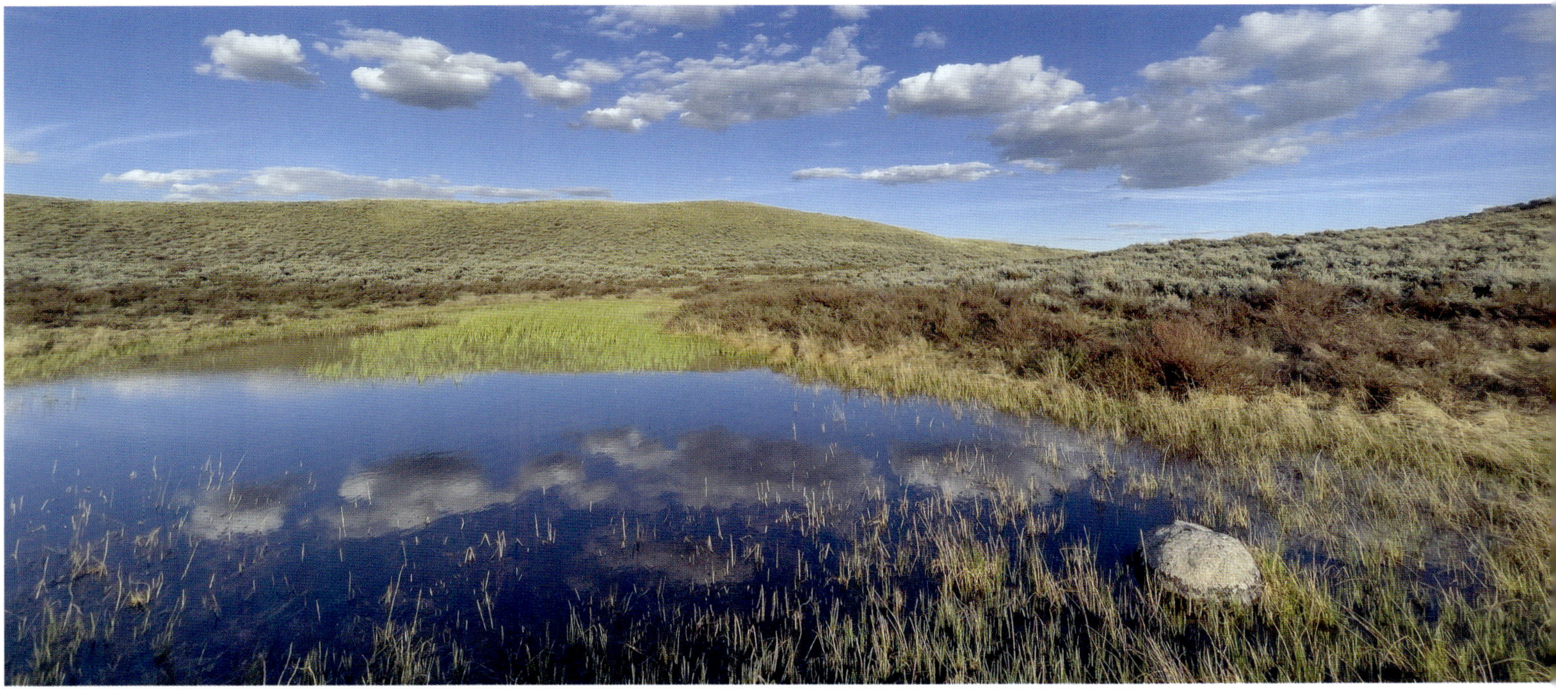

Robert Finch

"This would be a perfect time and place to meditate,
if I practiced meditation. But I don't want to empty
my mind. Rather, I want to *fill* it more deeply with
what is there. I don't wish to detach myself from this
solid, perishable world, but to feel it even closer,
to pay it the attention it deserves."

From *The Outer Beach: A Thousand-Mile
Walk on Cape Cod's Atlantic Shore*

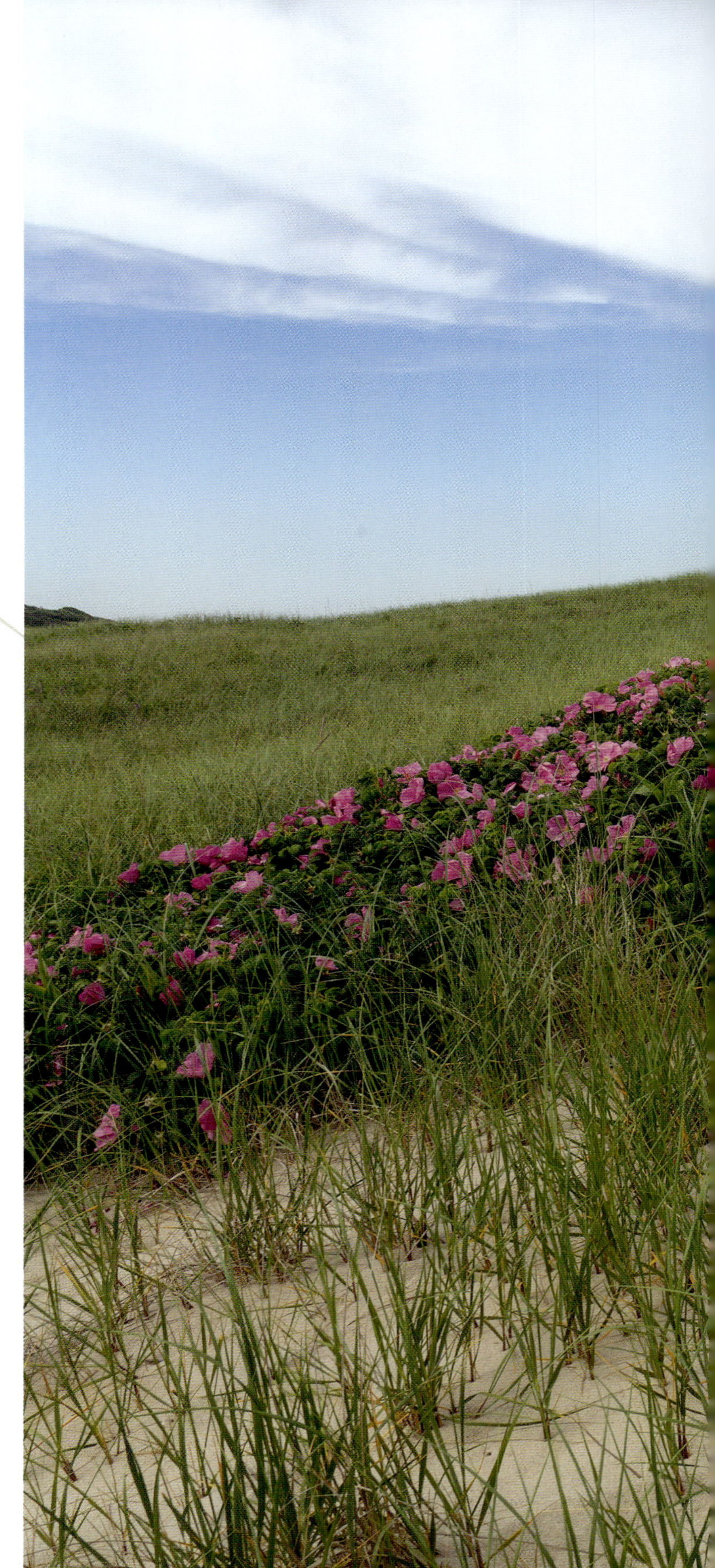

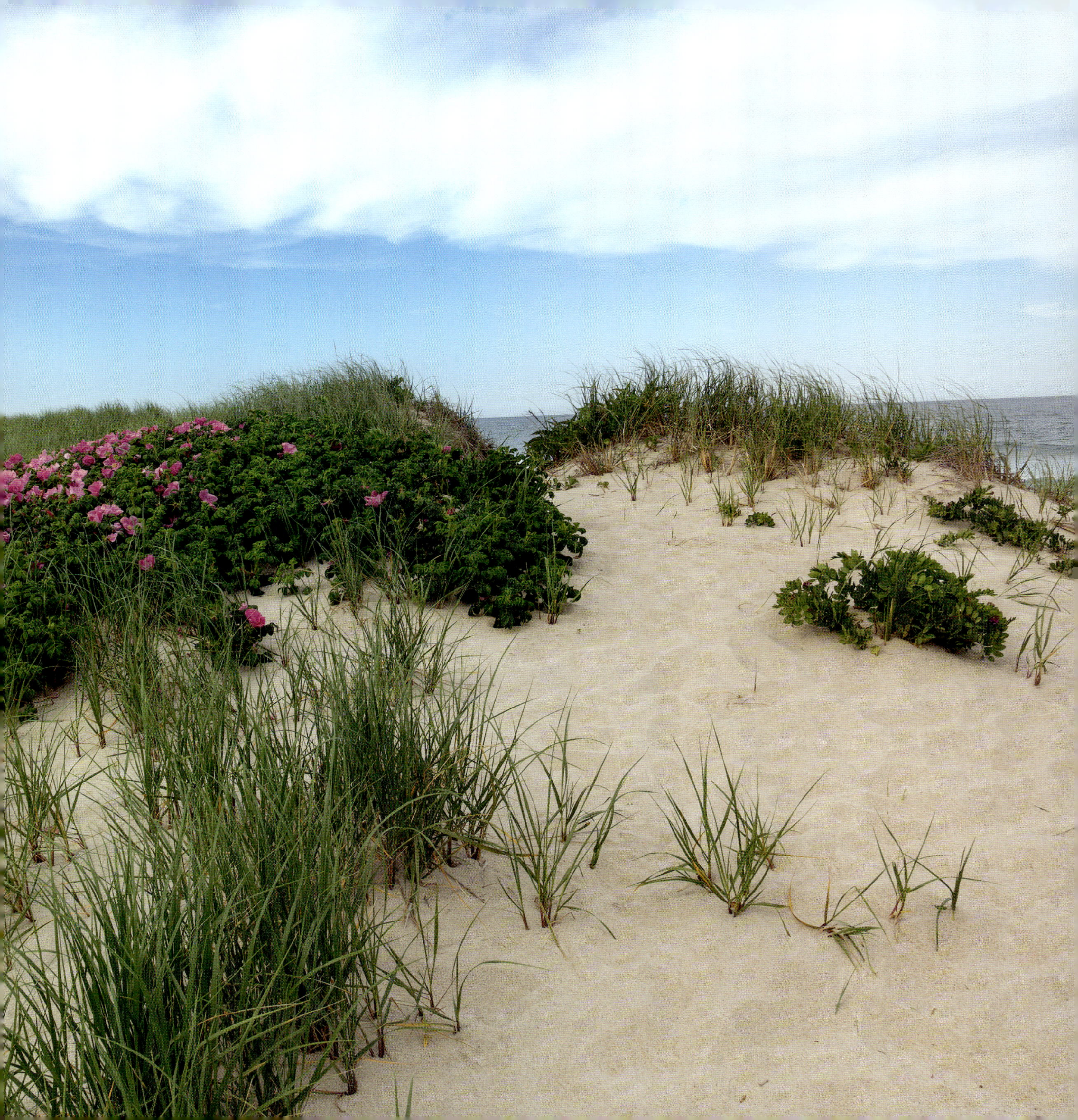

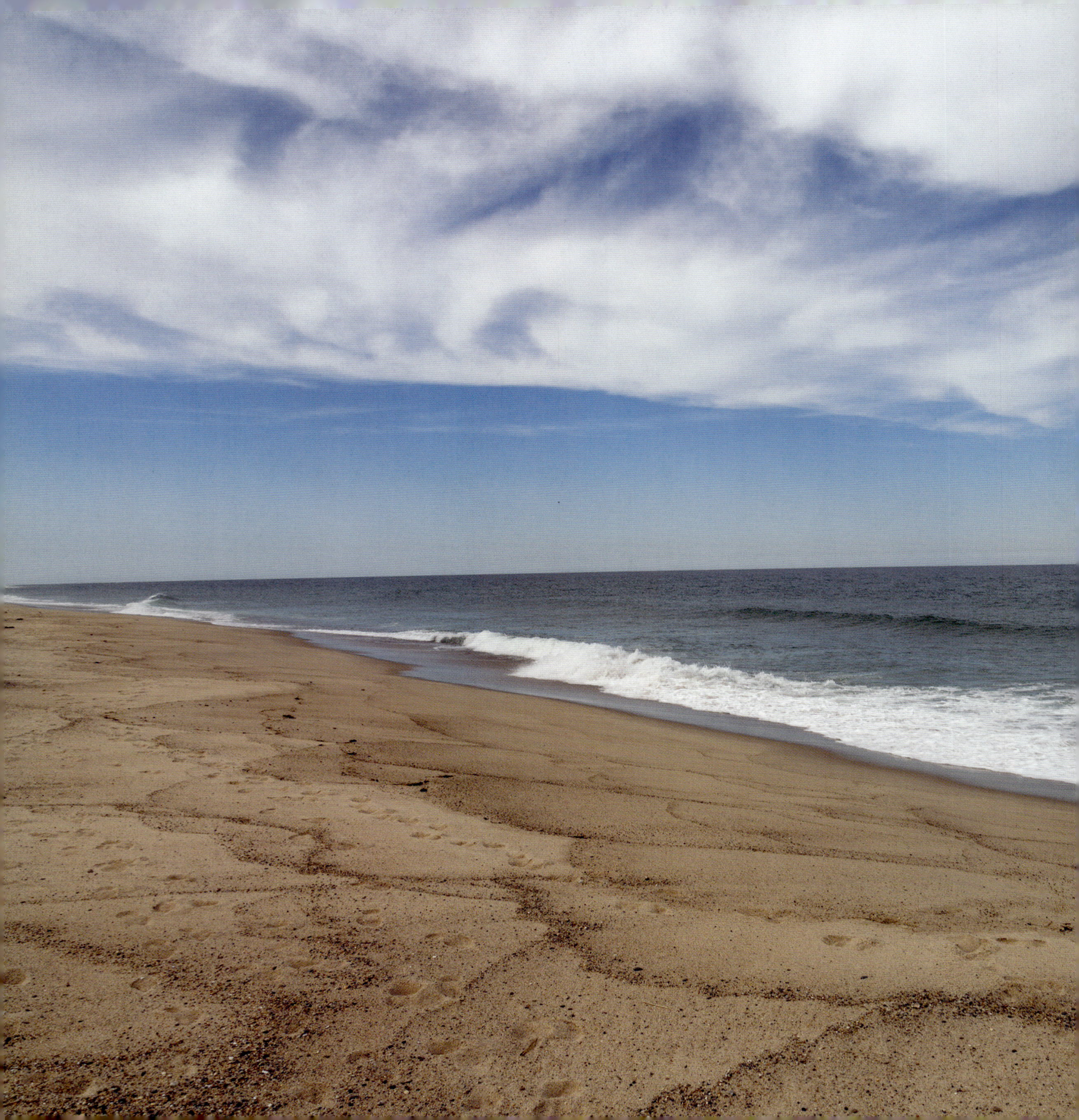

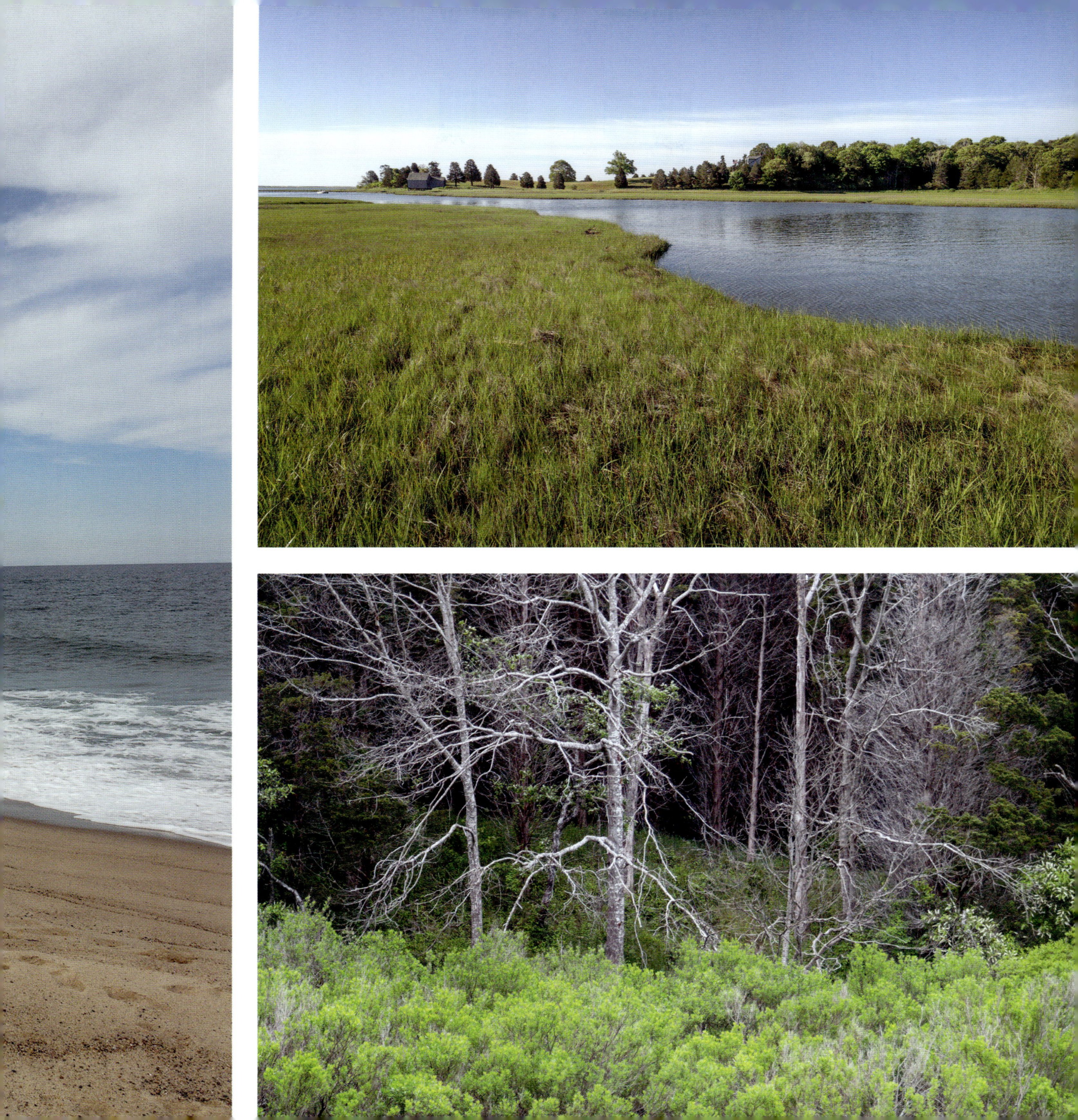

Scott Freeman

WASHINGTON

"Ecology tells us we are part of a community;
evolution tells us we are part of a family. Earth is the
only place in the universe where life exists, as far as
we know, and all of that life is unified: through our
interactions in a common environment and through
sharing a common history. We are not separate or
isolated—we are part of a whole."

From *Saving Tarboo Creek:*
One Family's Quest to Heal the Land

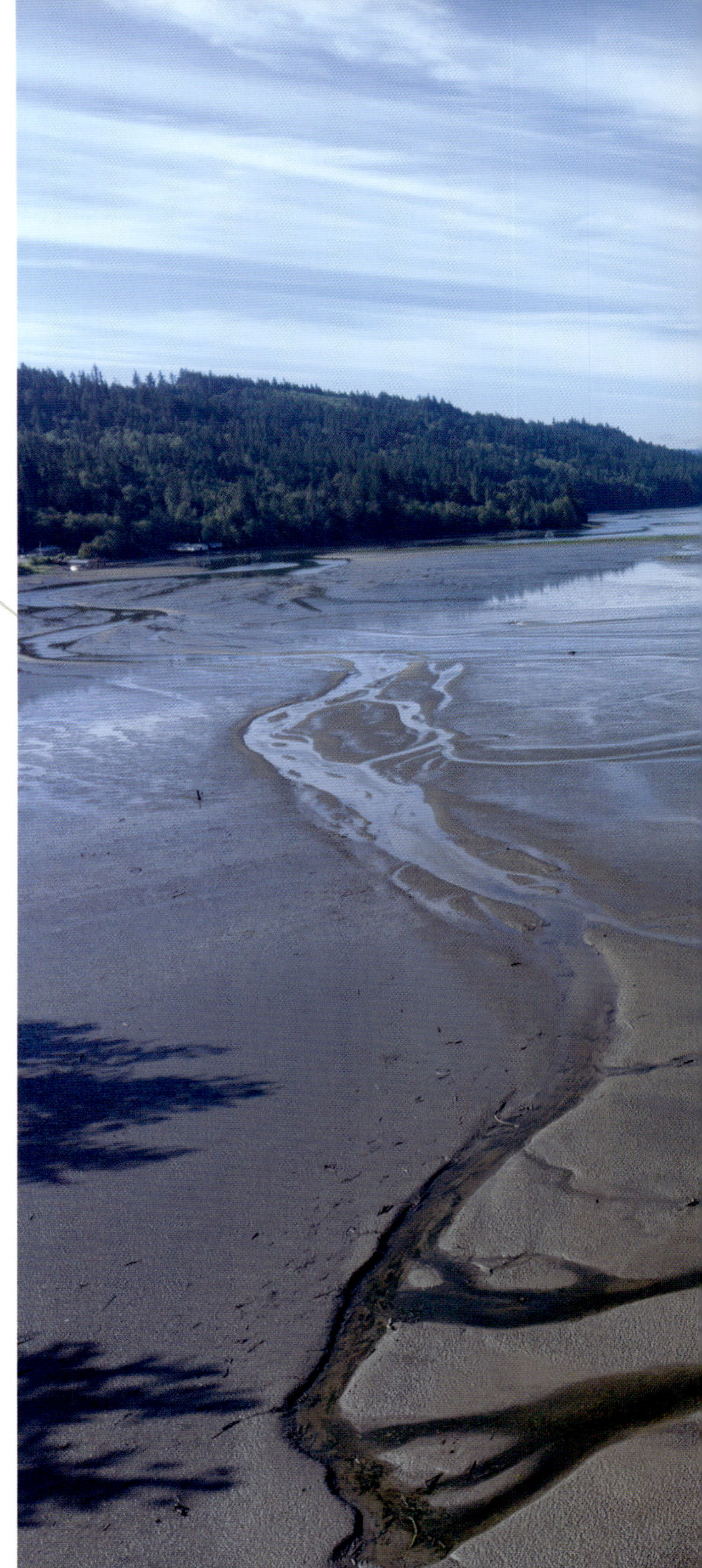

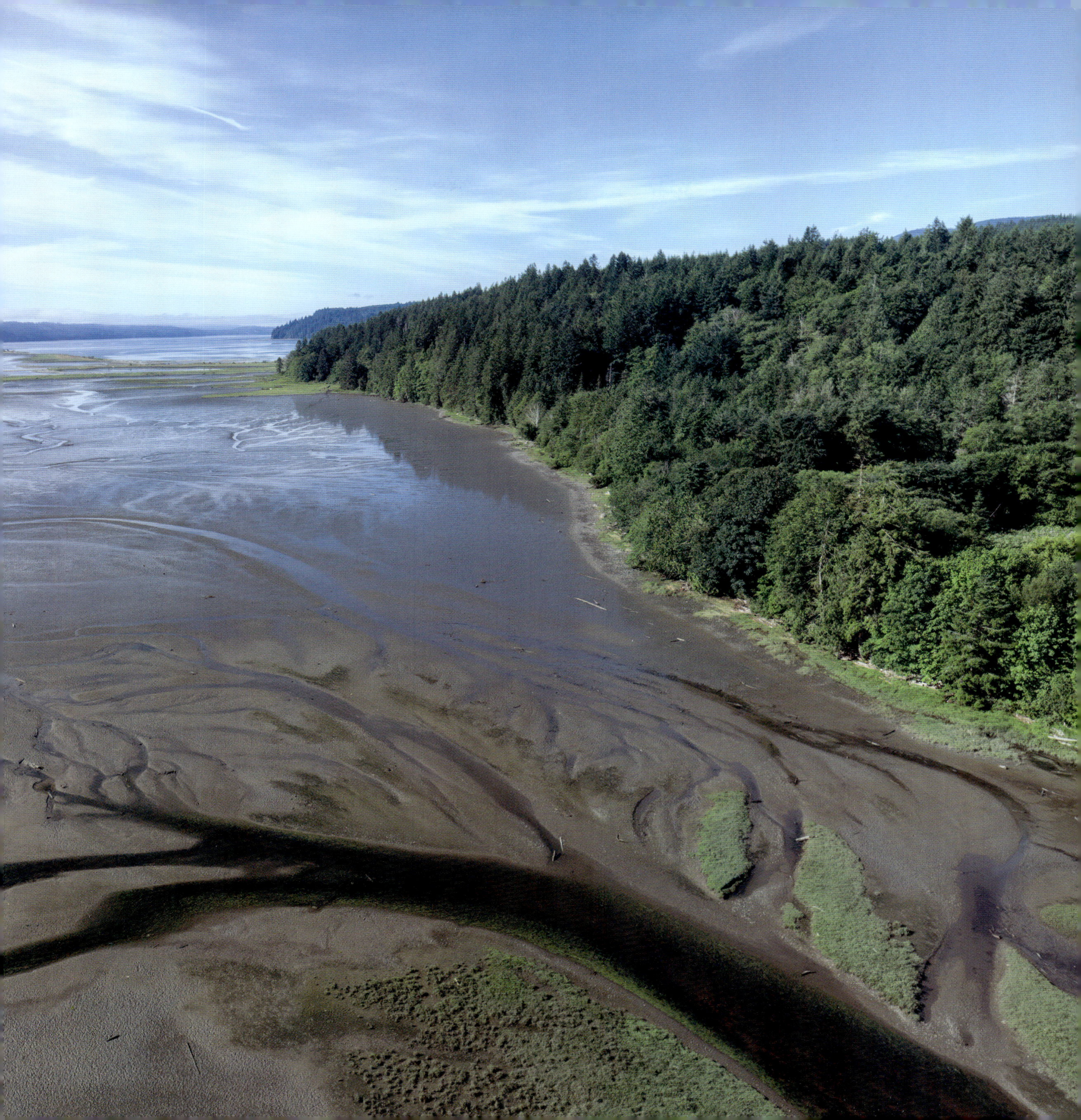

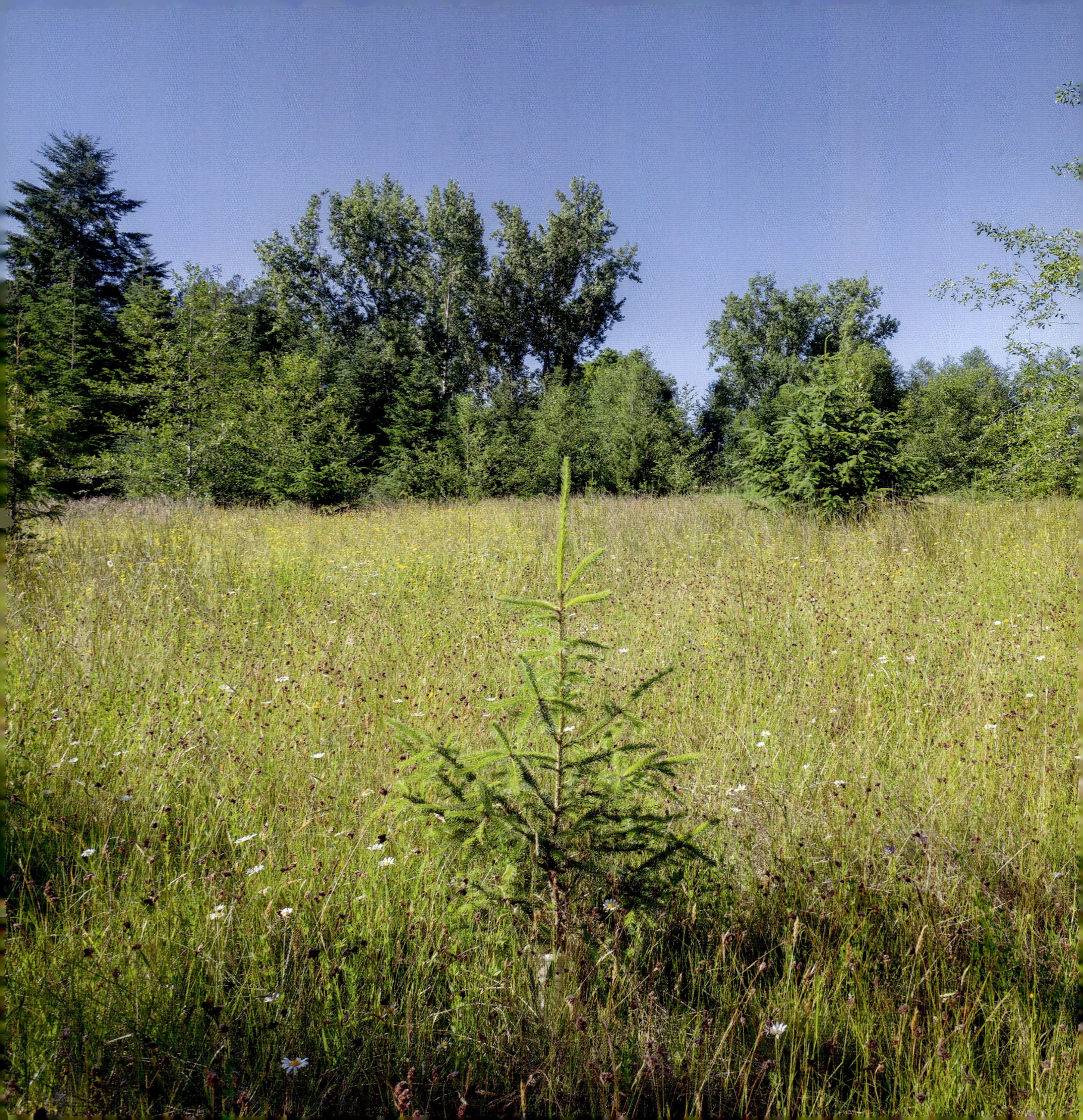

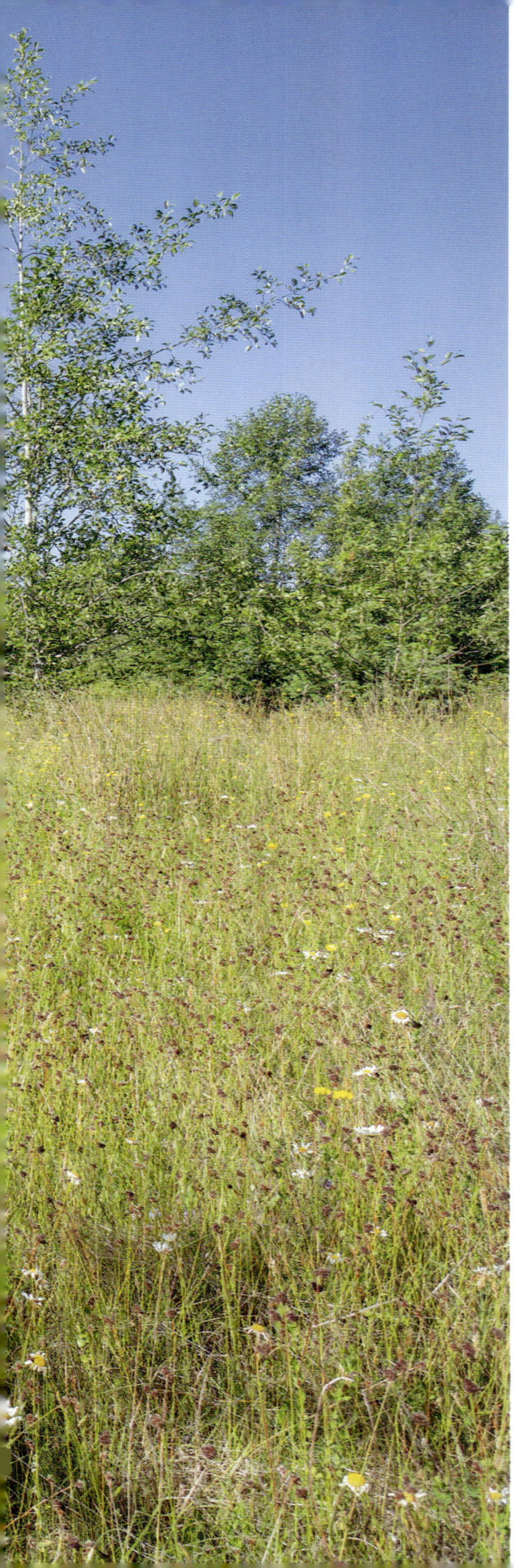

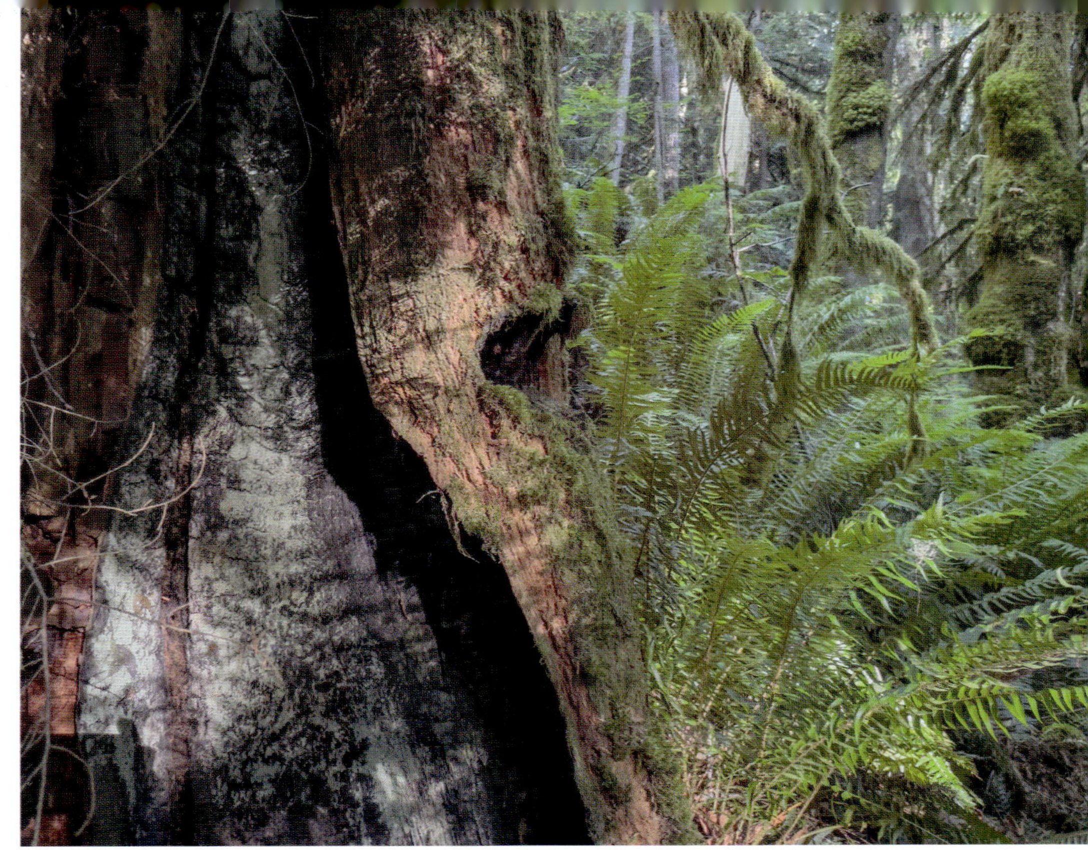
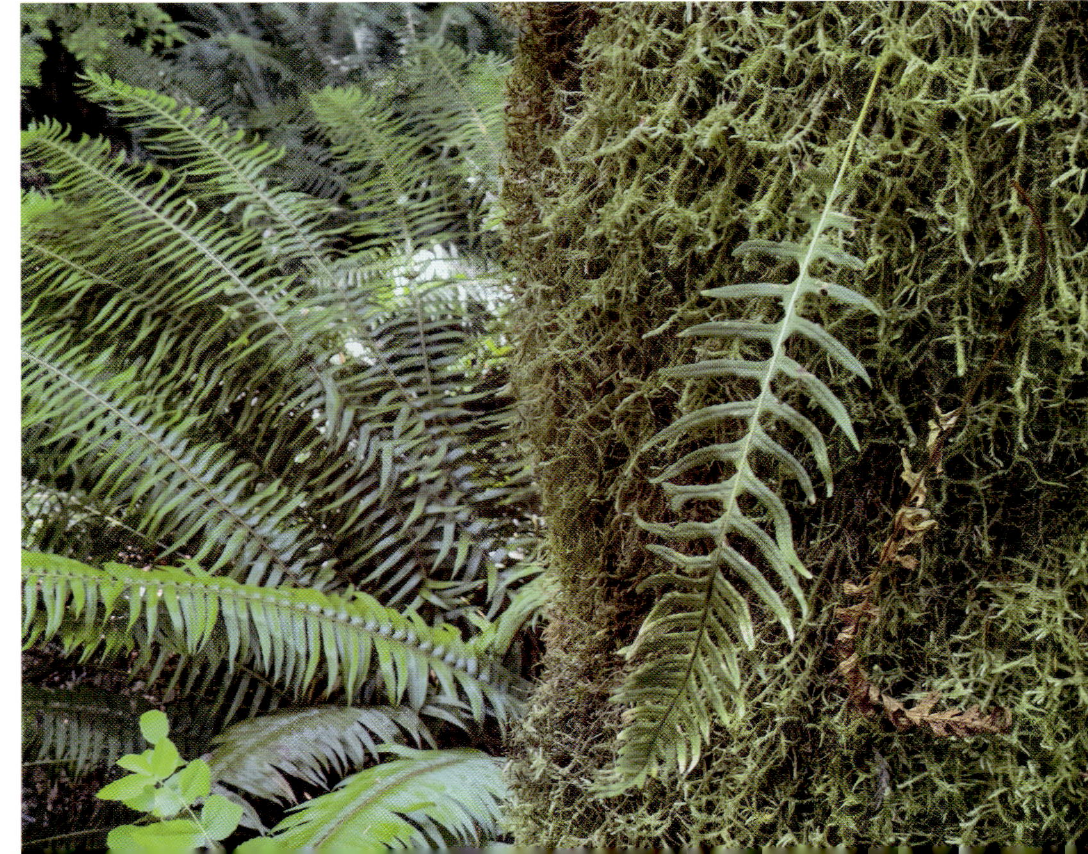

David Gessner

NORTH CAROLINA

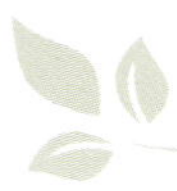

"We used to think the world was so big. So indestructible. So *fun*. We still can't completely believe that it is as small and serious, as threatened and vulnerable, as we have made it."

From *All the Wild That Remains: Edward Abbey,
Wallace Stegner, and the American West*

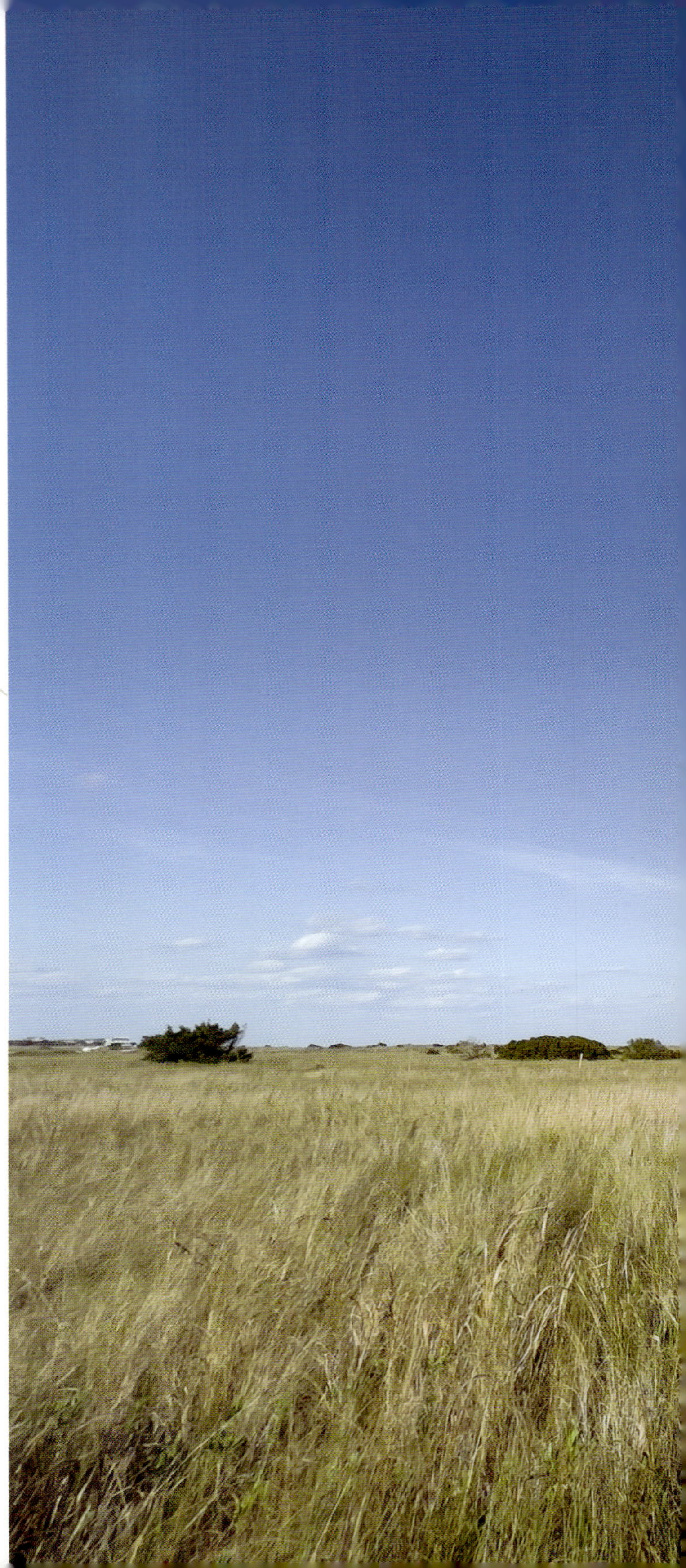

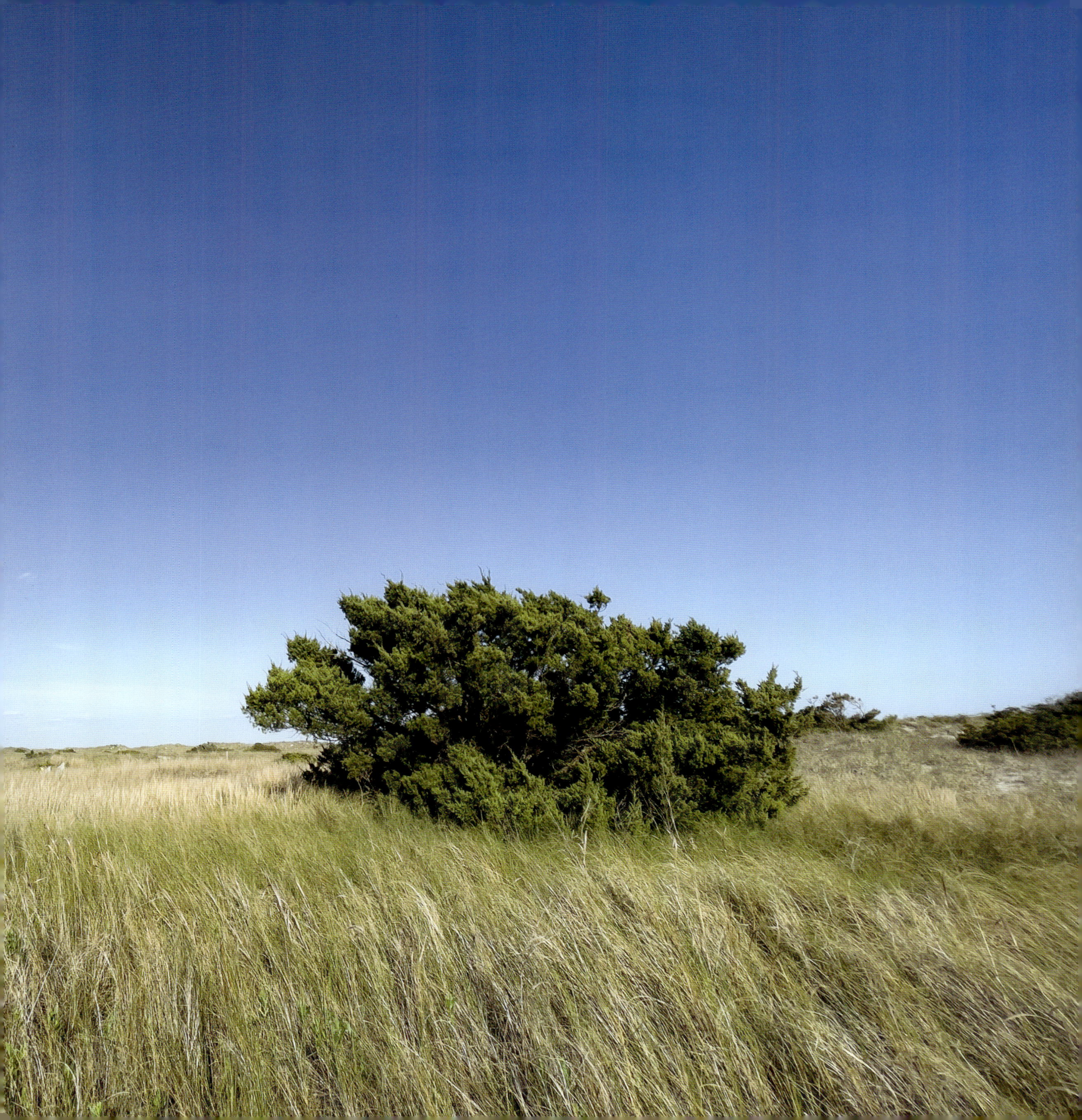

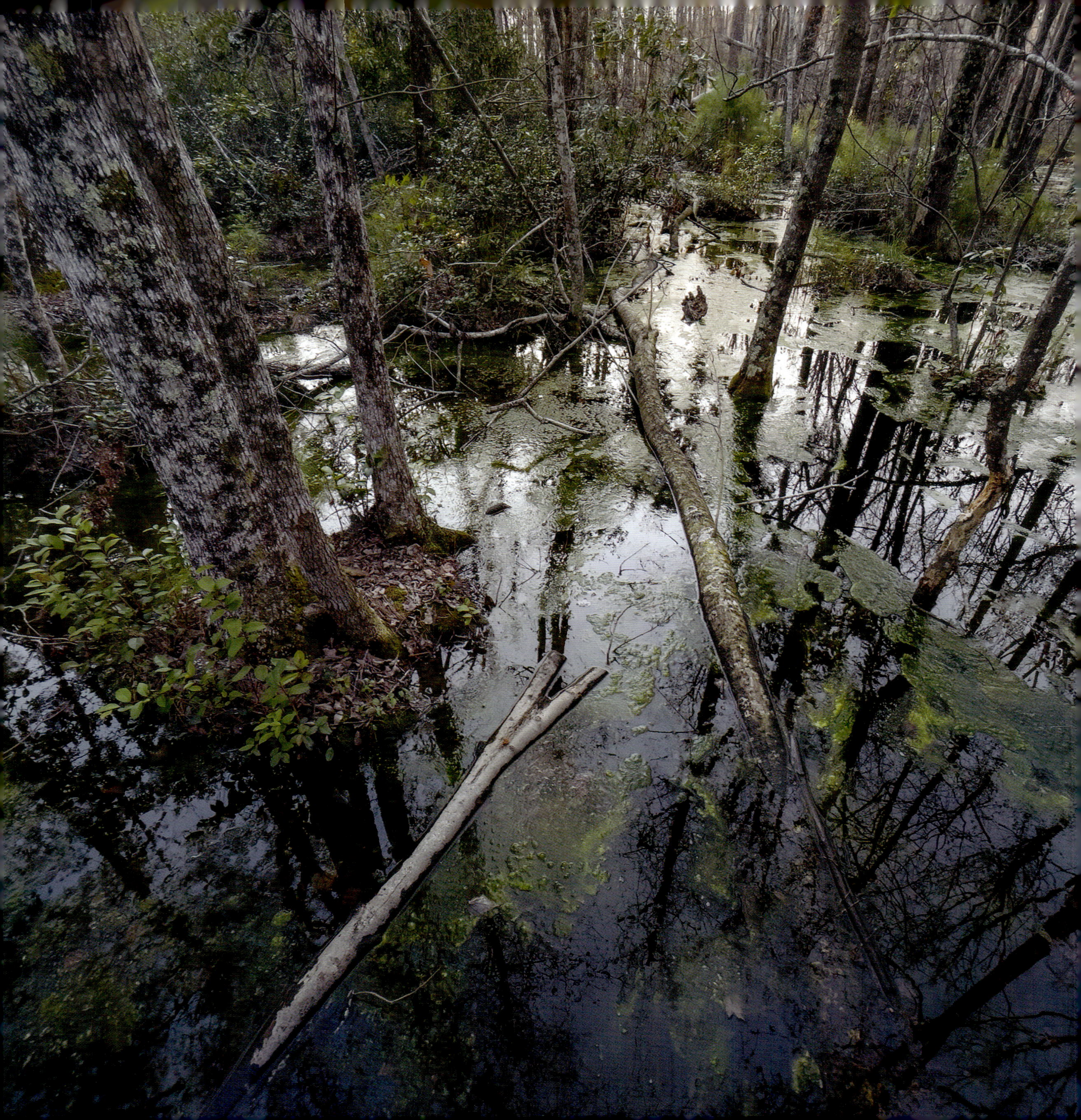

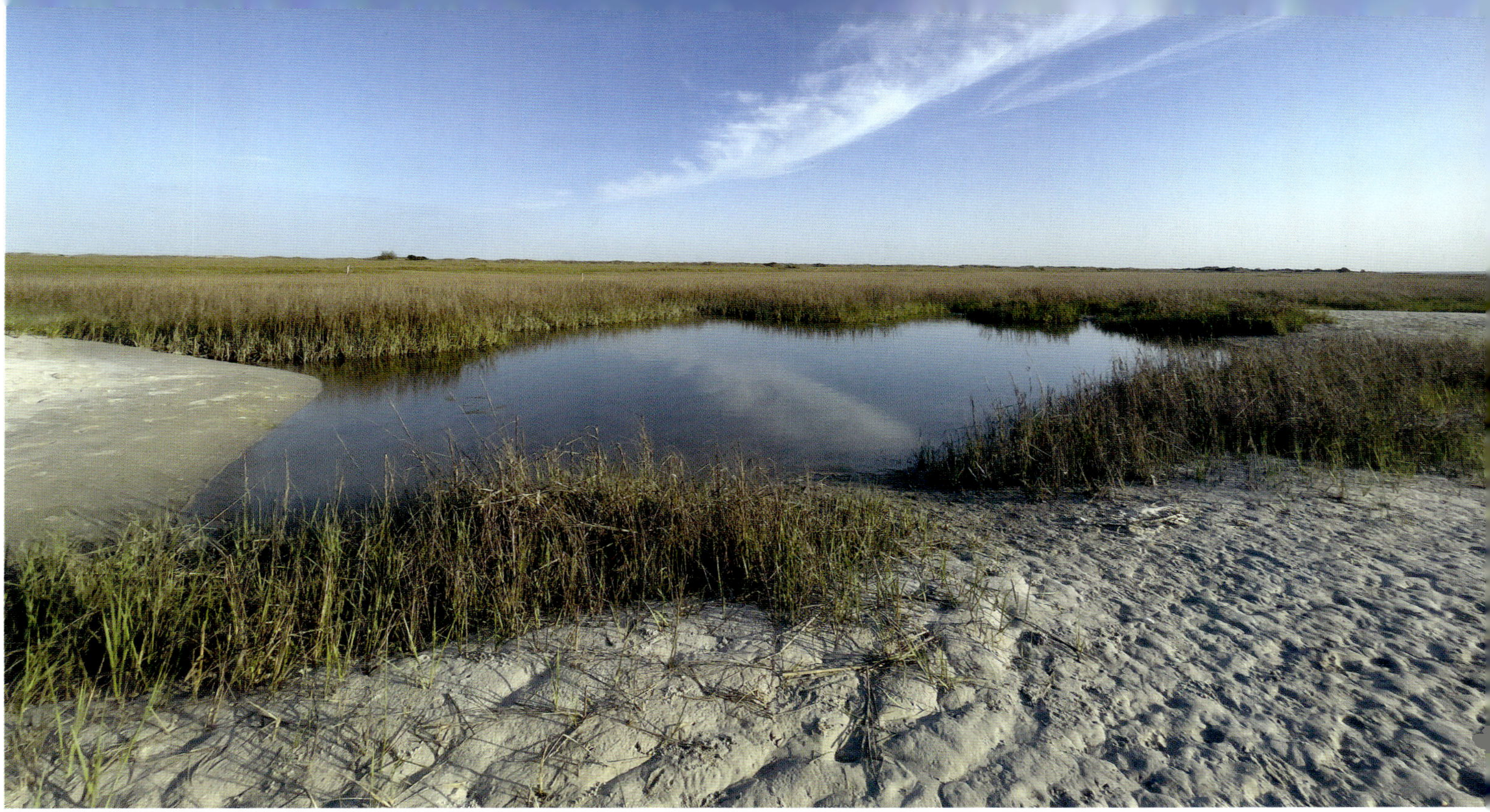

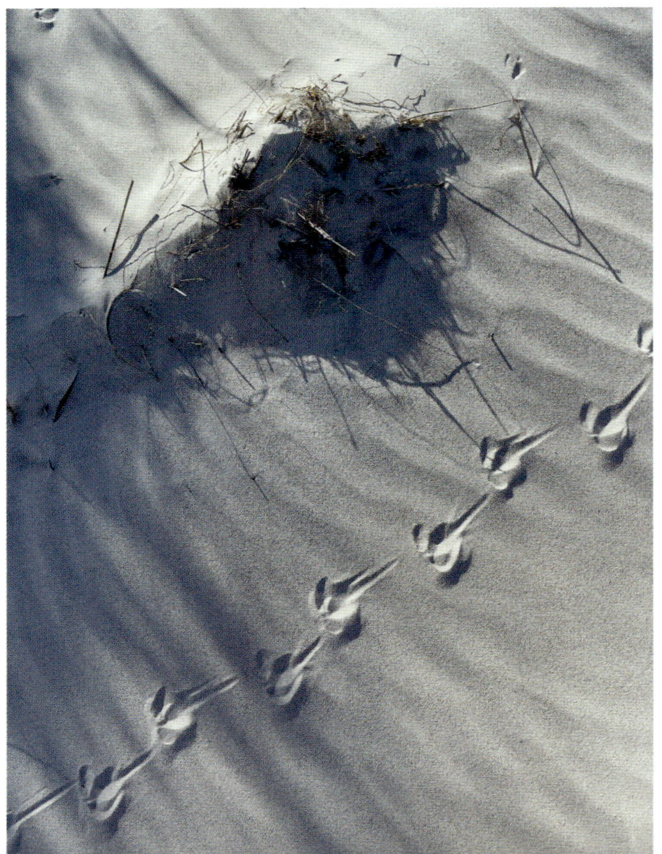

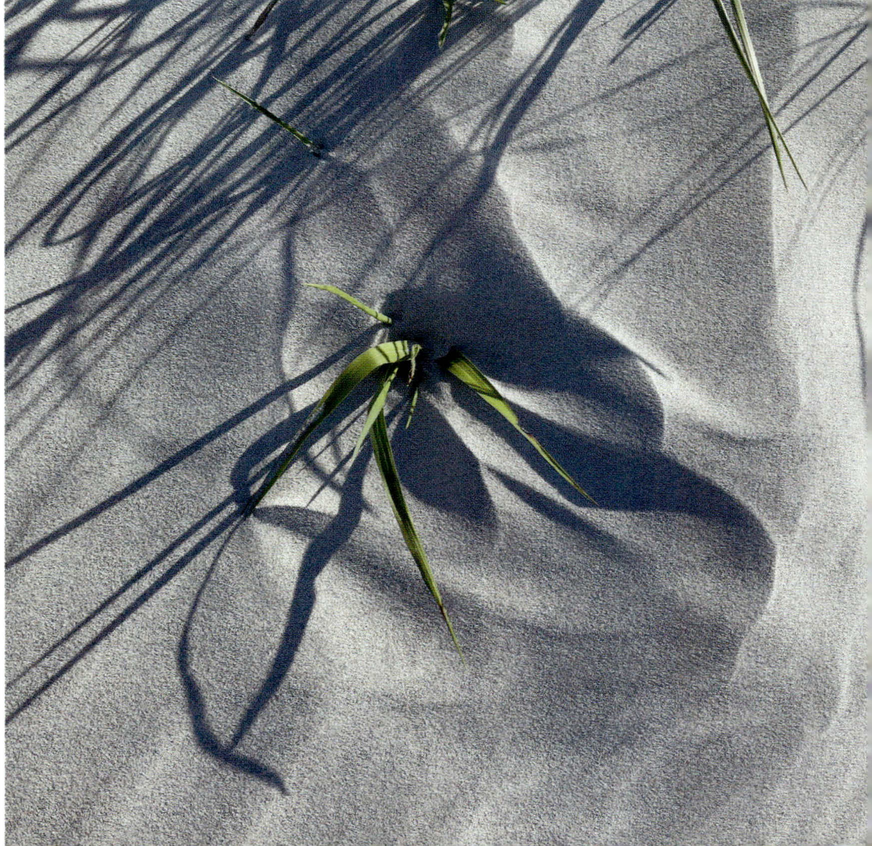

John Graves

"We don't know much about solitude these days, nor do we want to. A crowded world thinks that aloneness is always loneliness, and that to seek it is perversion. Maybe so."

From *Goodbye to a River: A Narrative*

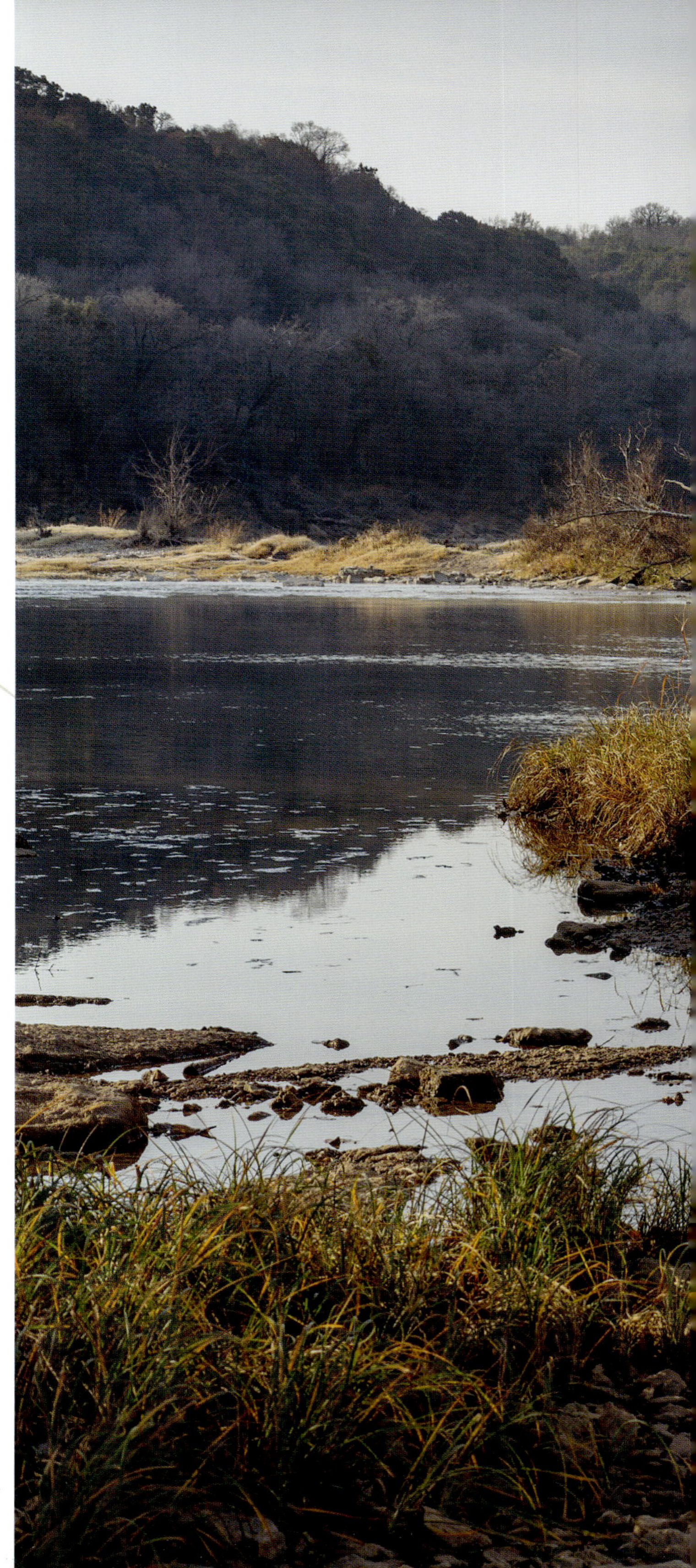

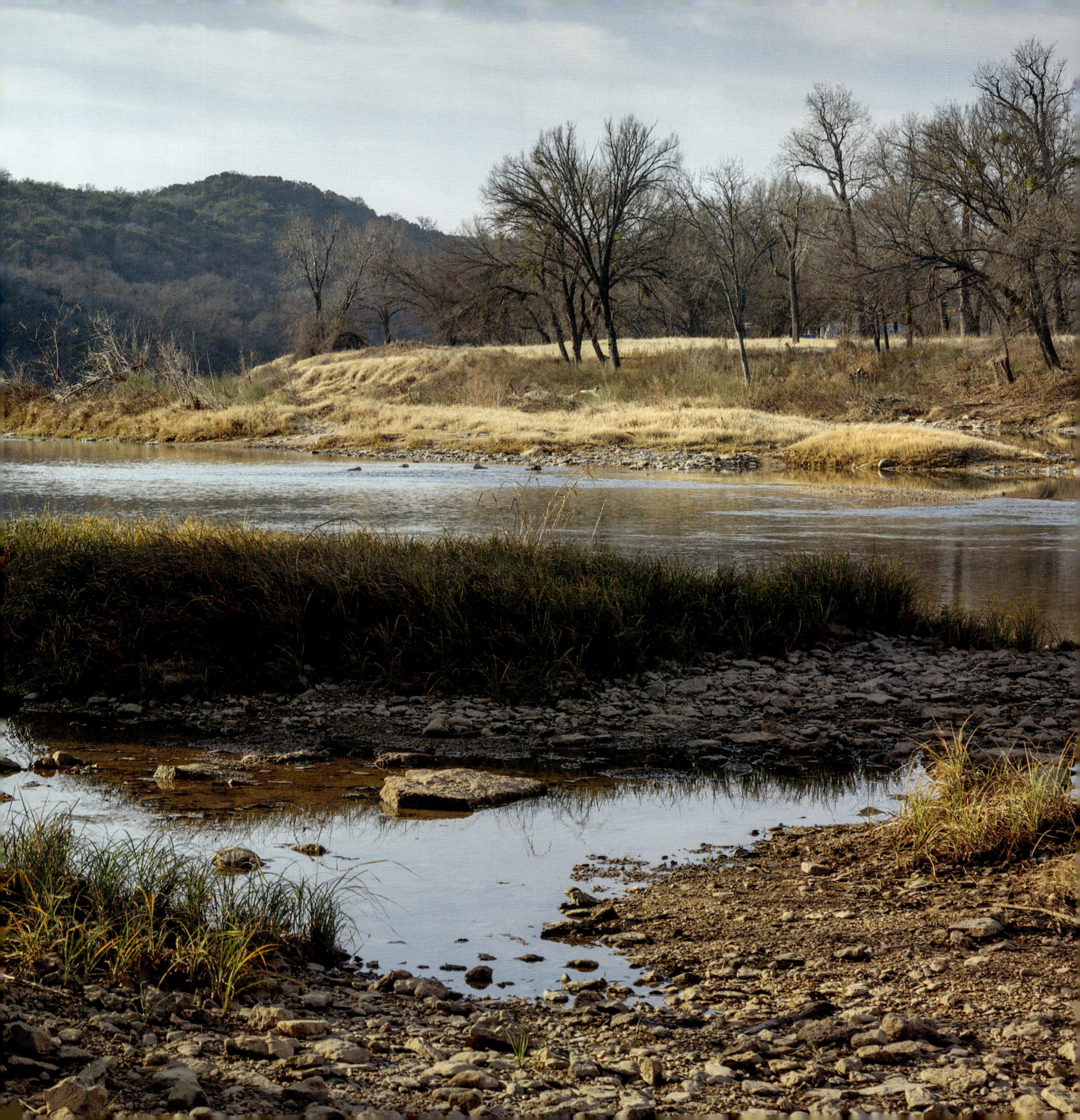

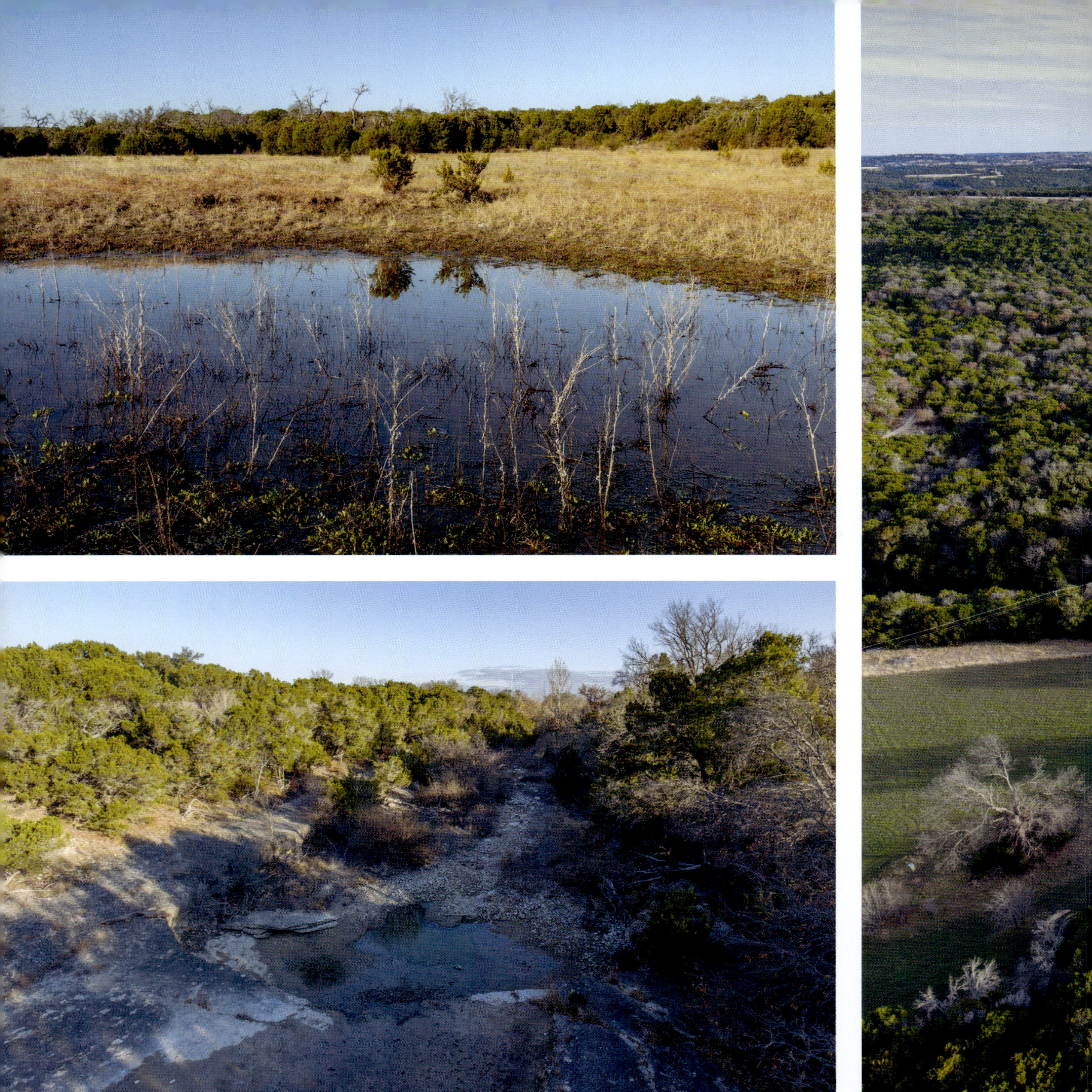

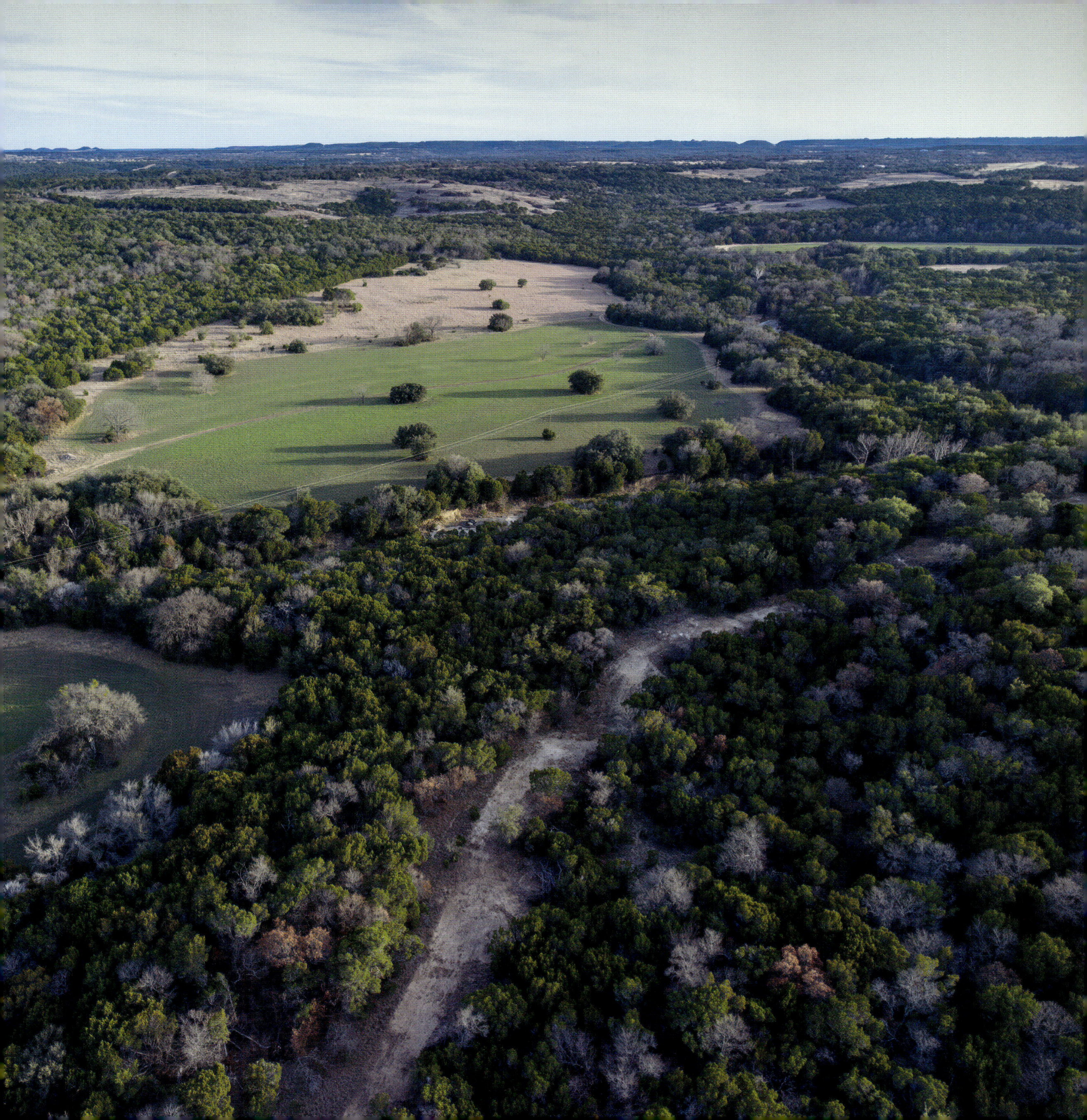

Paul Gruchow

MINNESOTA

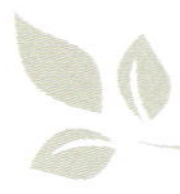

"To live on the prairie is to daydream. It is the only

conceivable response to such immensity. It is when

we are smallest that our daydreams come quickest."

From *Journal of a Prairie Year*

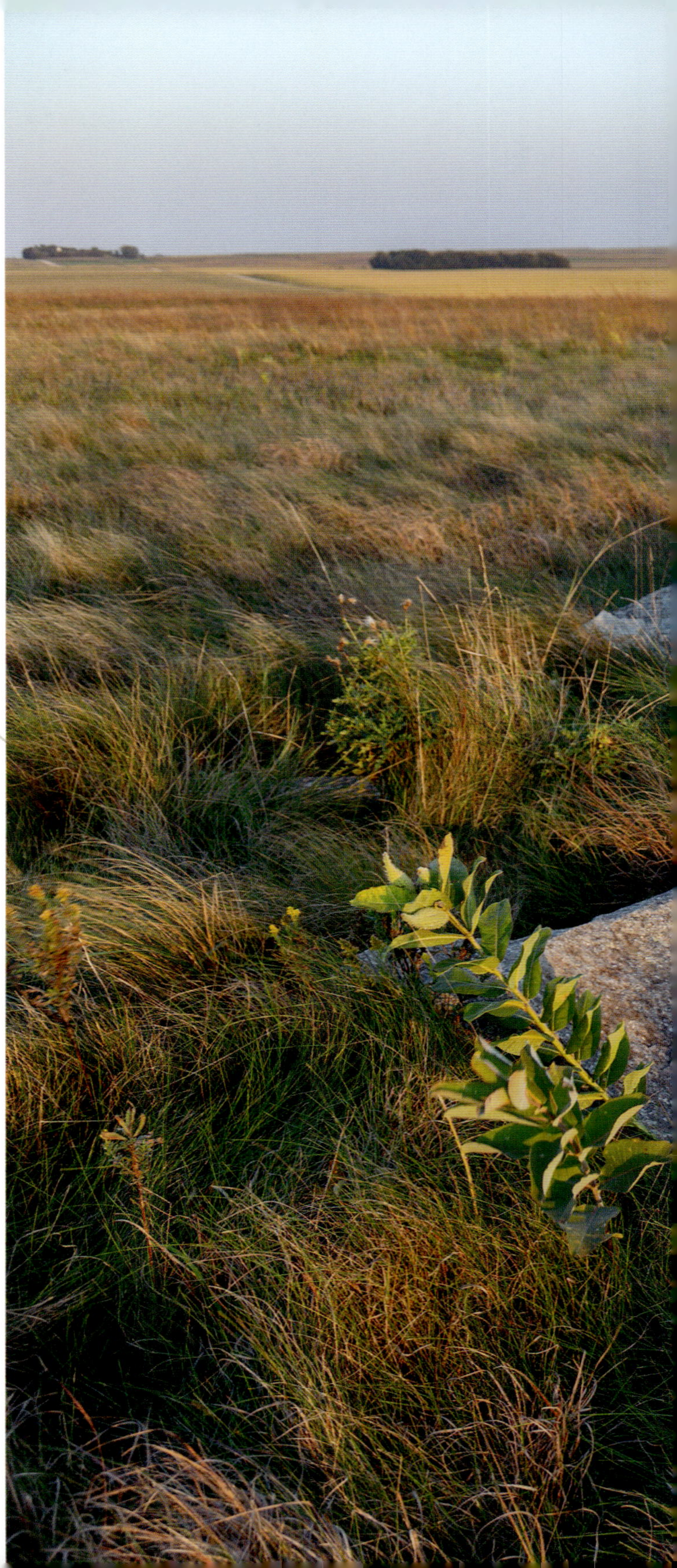

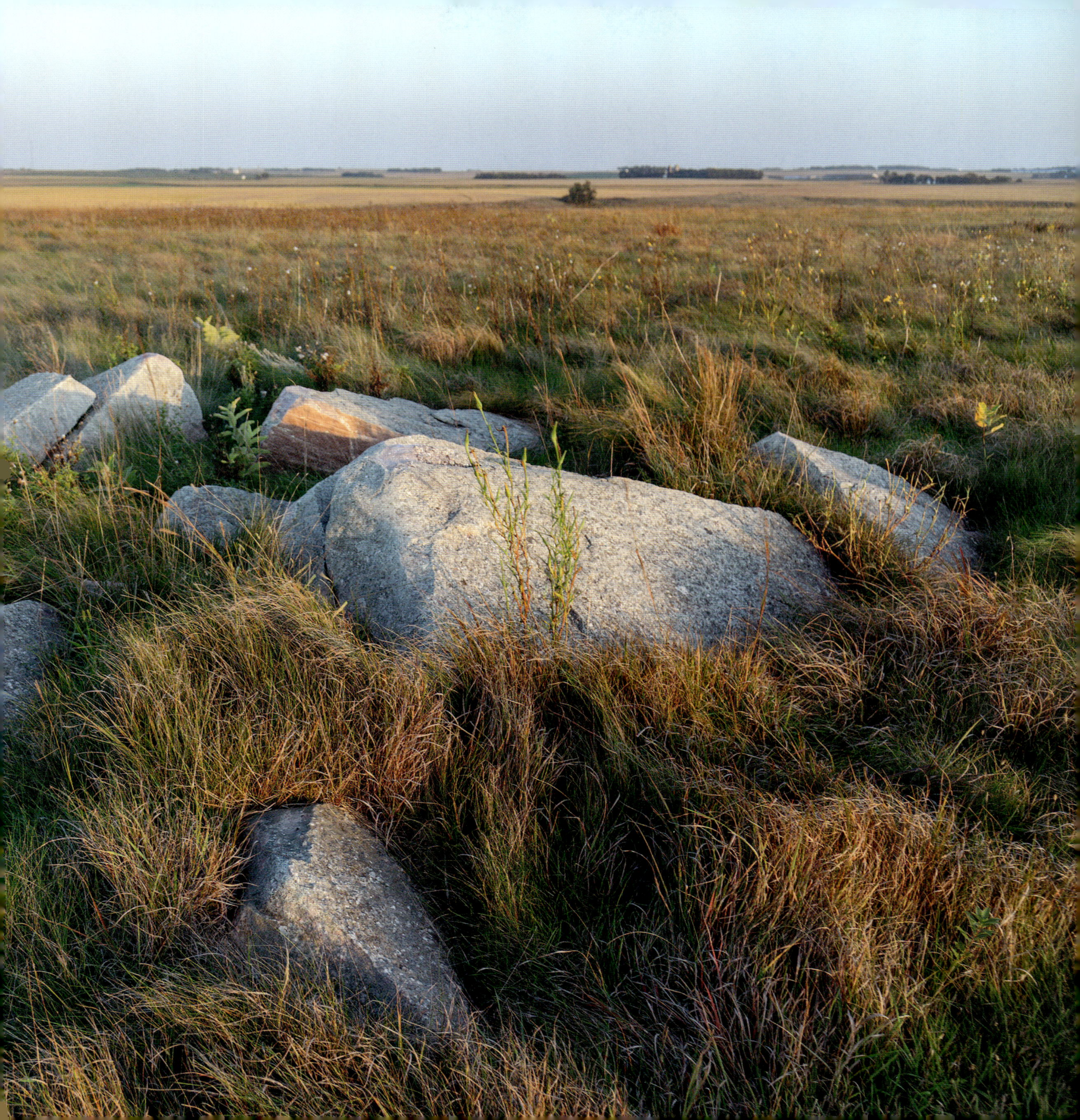

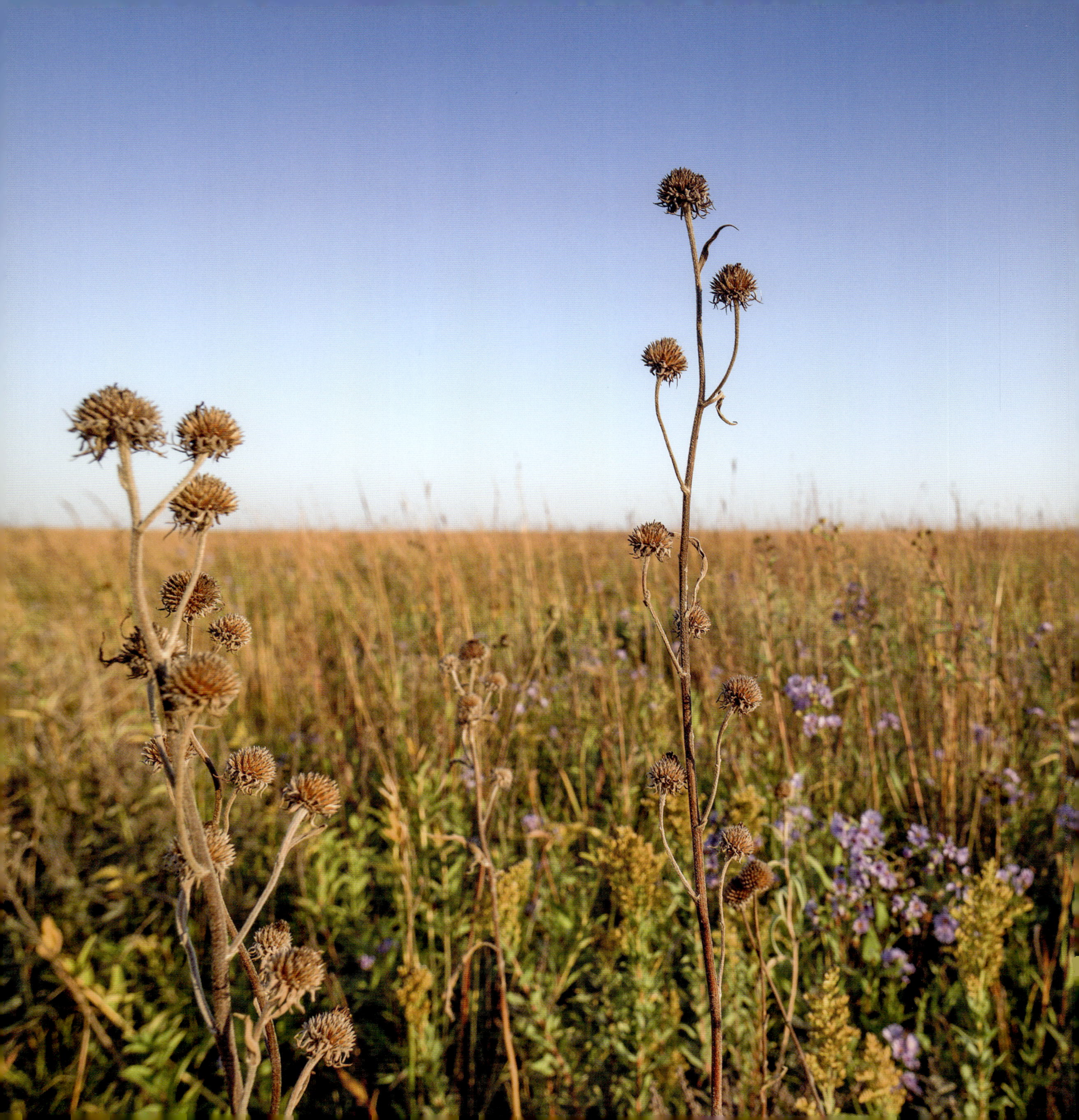

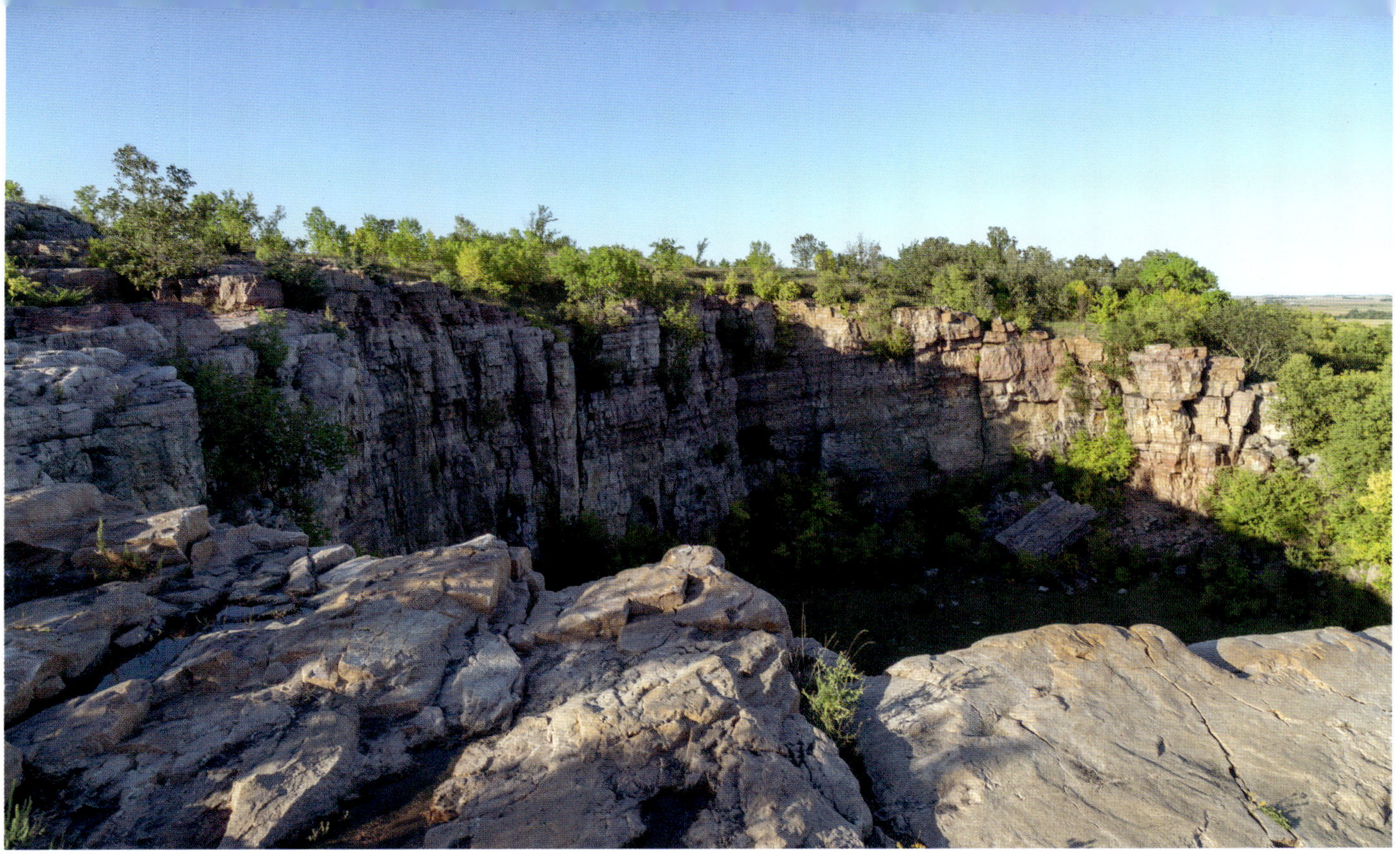

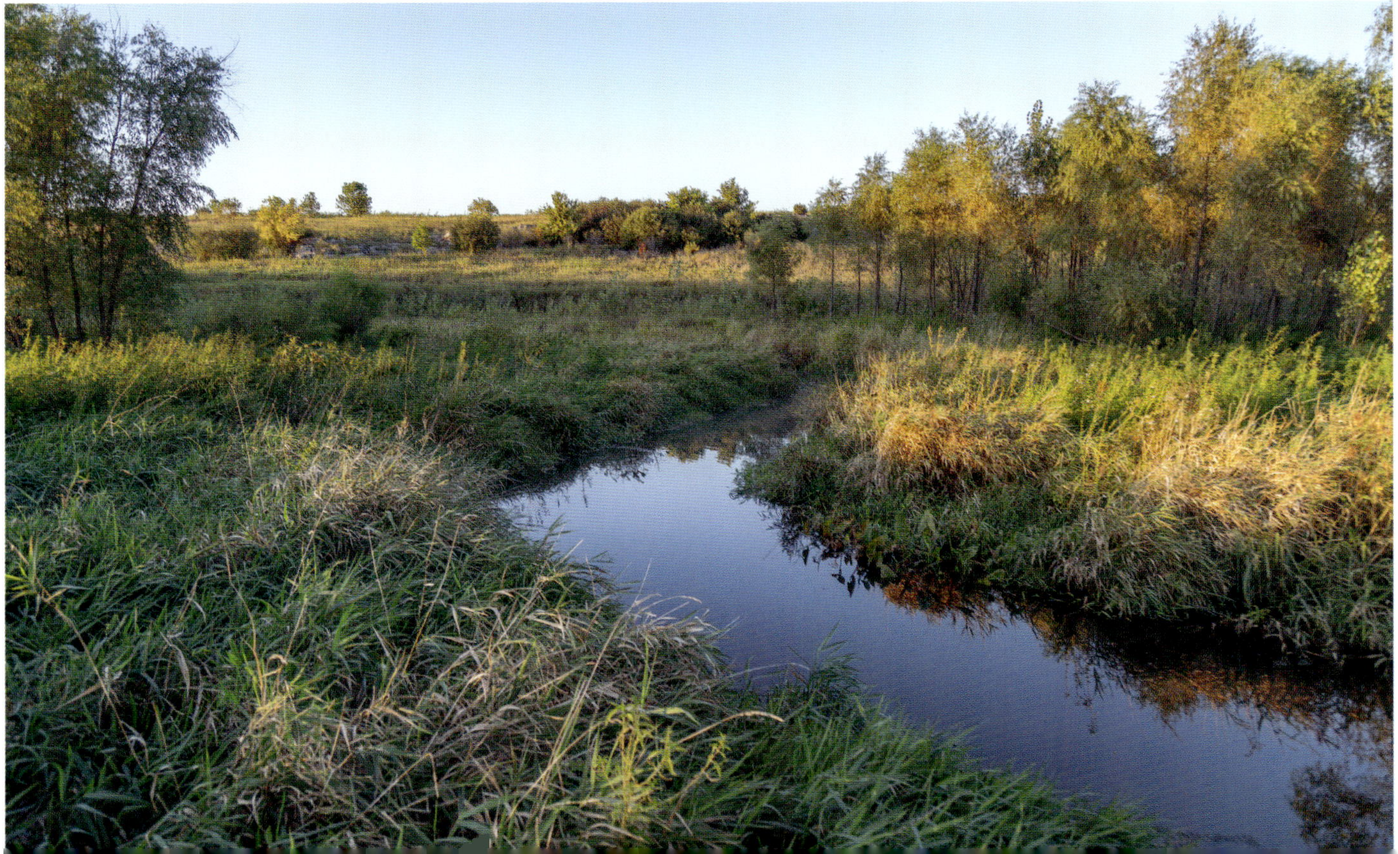

David George Haskell

TENNESSEE

"But, to love nature and to hate humanity is illogical.
Humanity is part of the whole. To truly love the
world is also to love human ingenuity and playfulness.
Nature does not need to be cleansed of human
artifacts to be beautiful or coherent. Yes, we should
be less greedy, untidy, wasteful, and shortsighted.
But let us not turn responsibility into self-hatred.
Our biggest failing is, after all, lack of compassion
for the world. Including ourselves."

From *The Forest Unseen:*
A Year's Watch in Nature

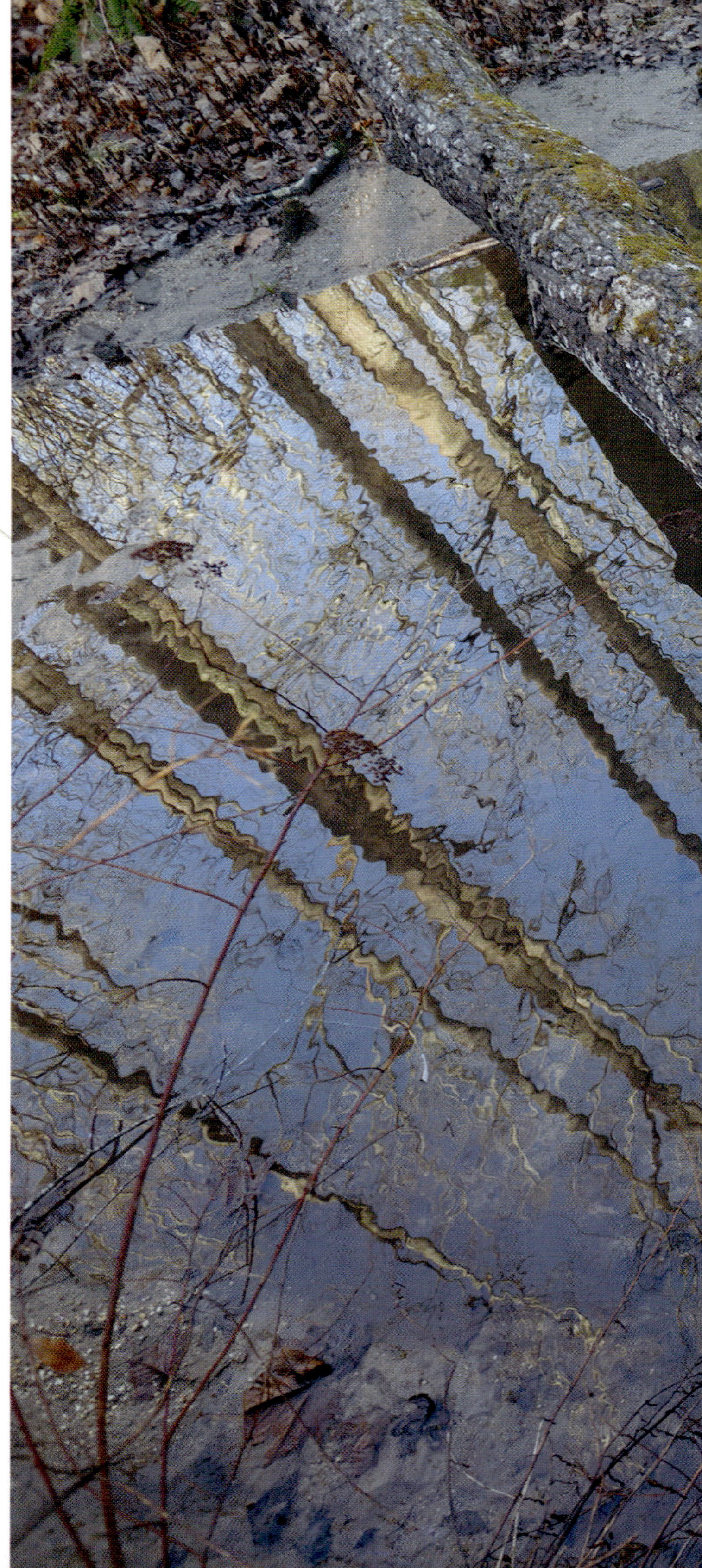

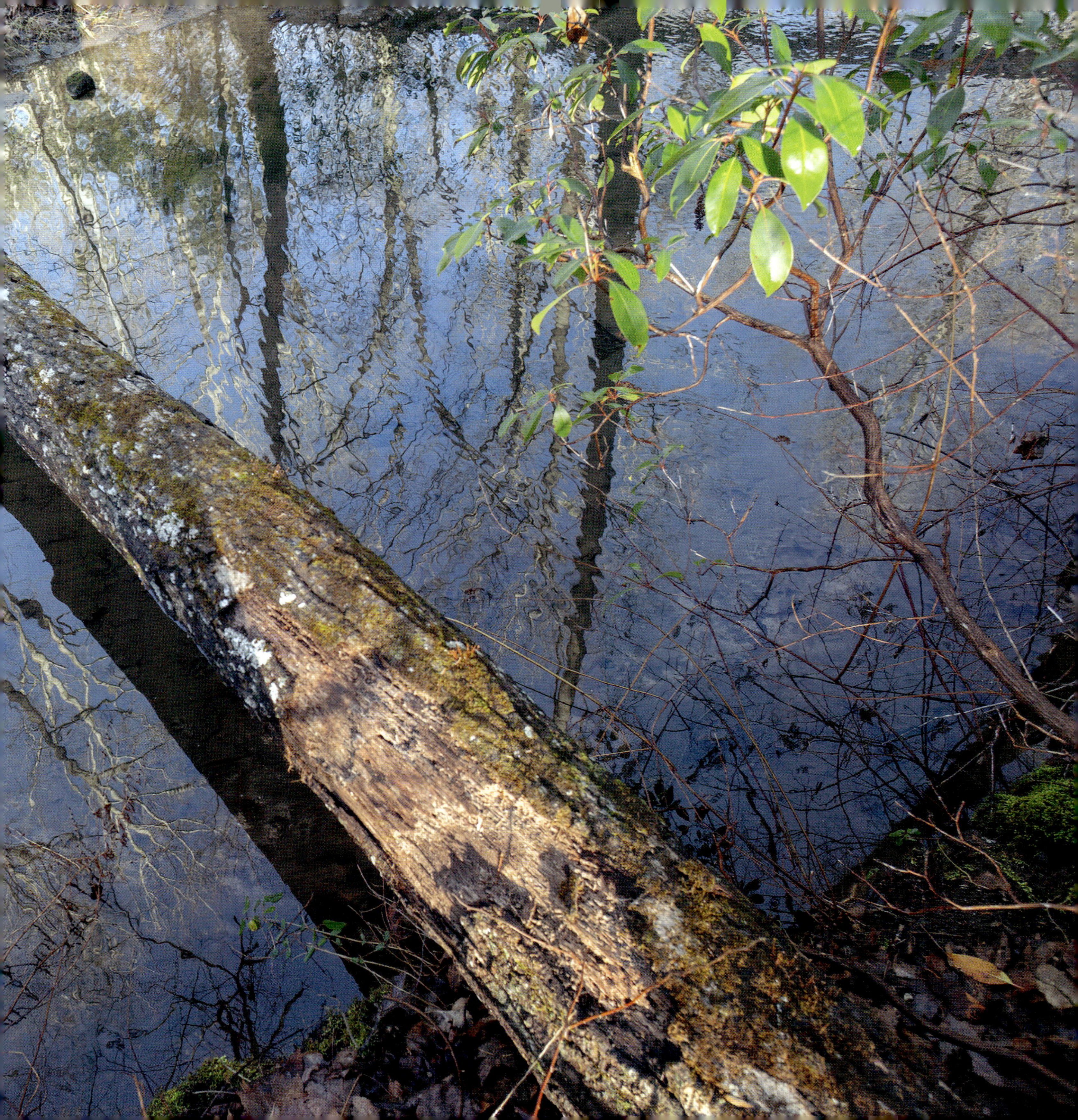

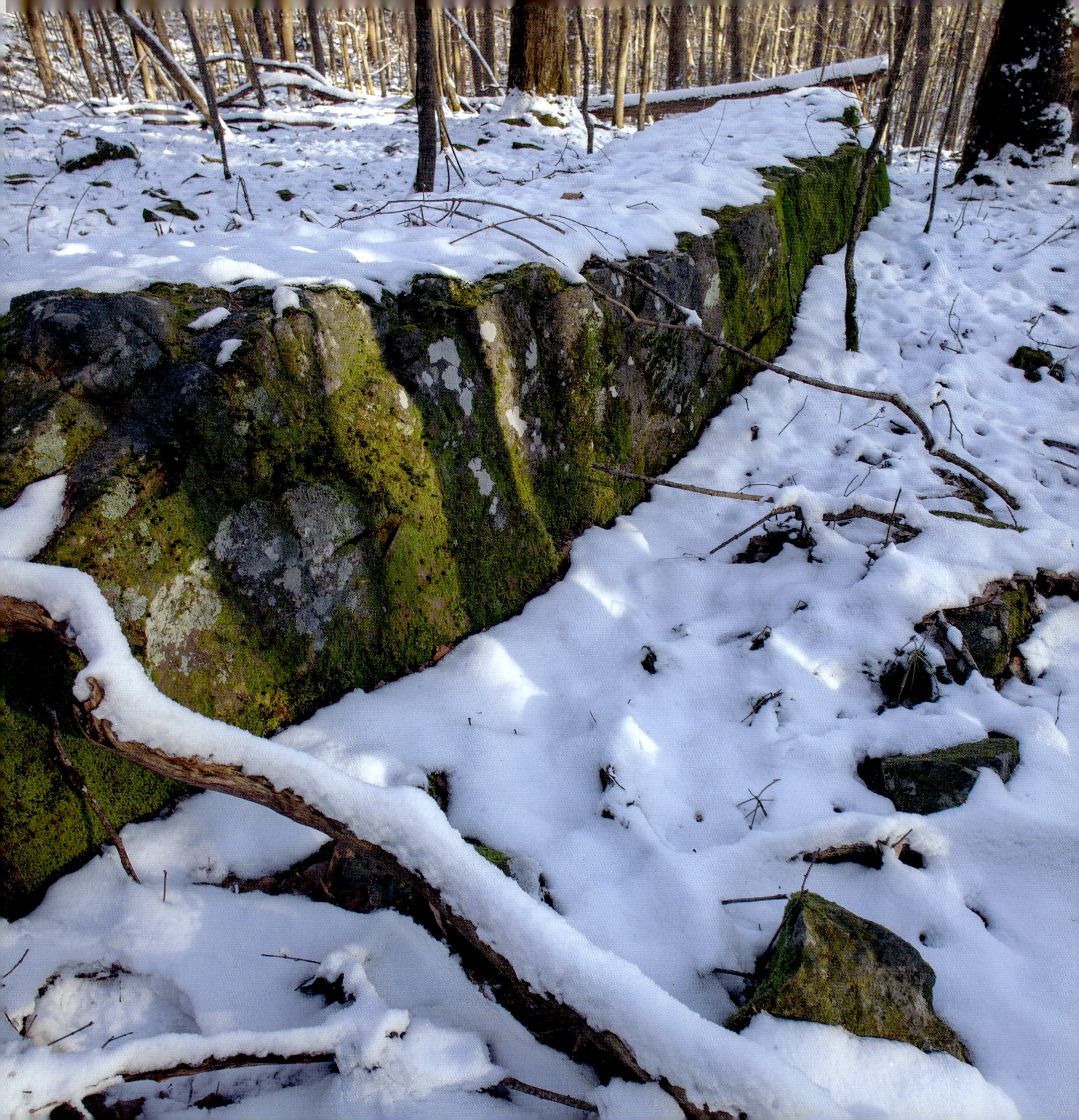

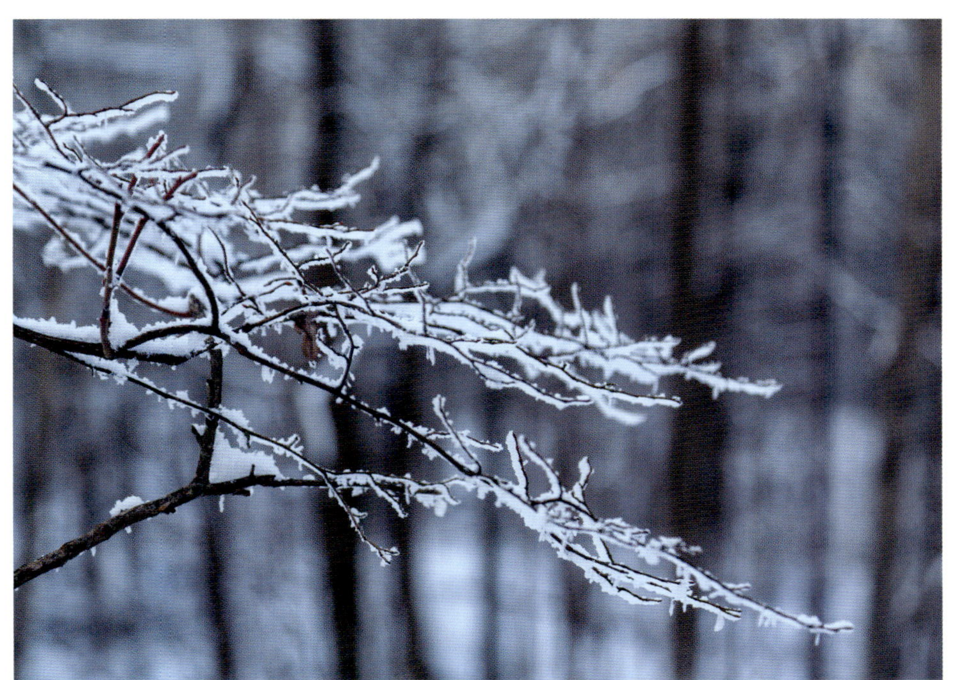
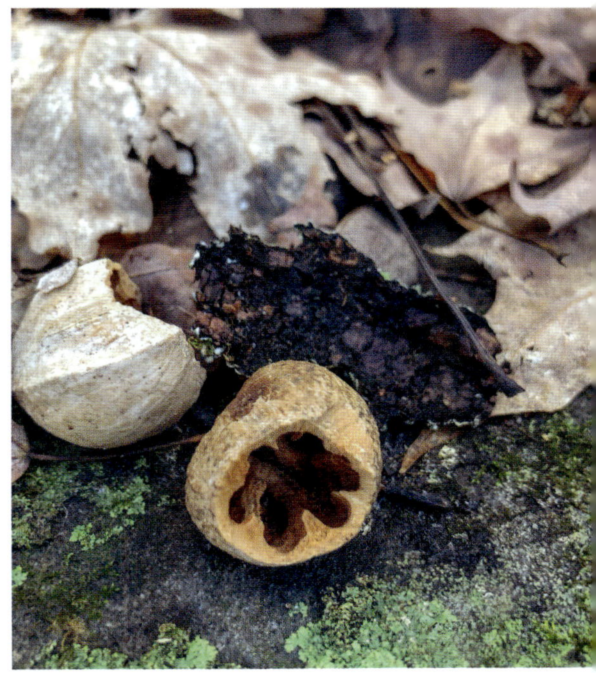

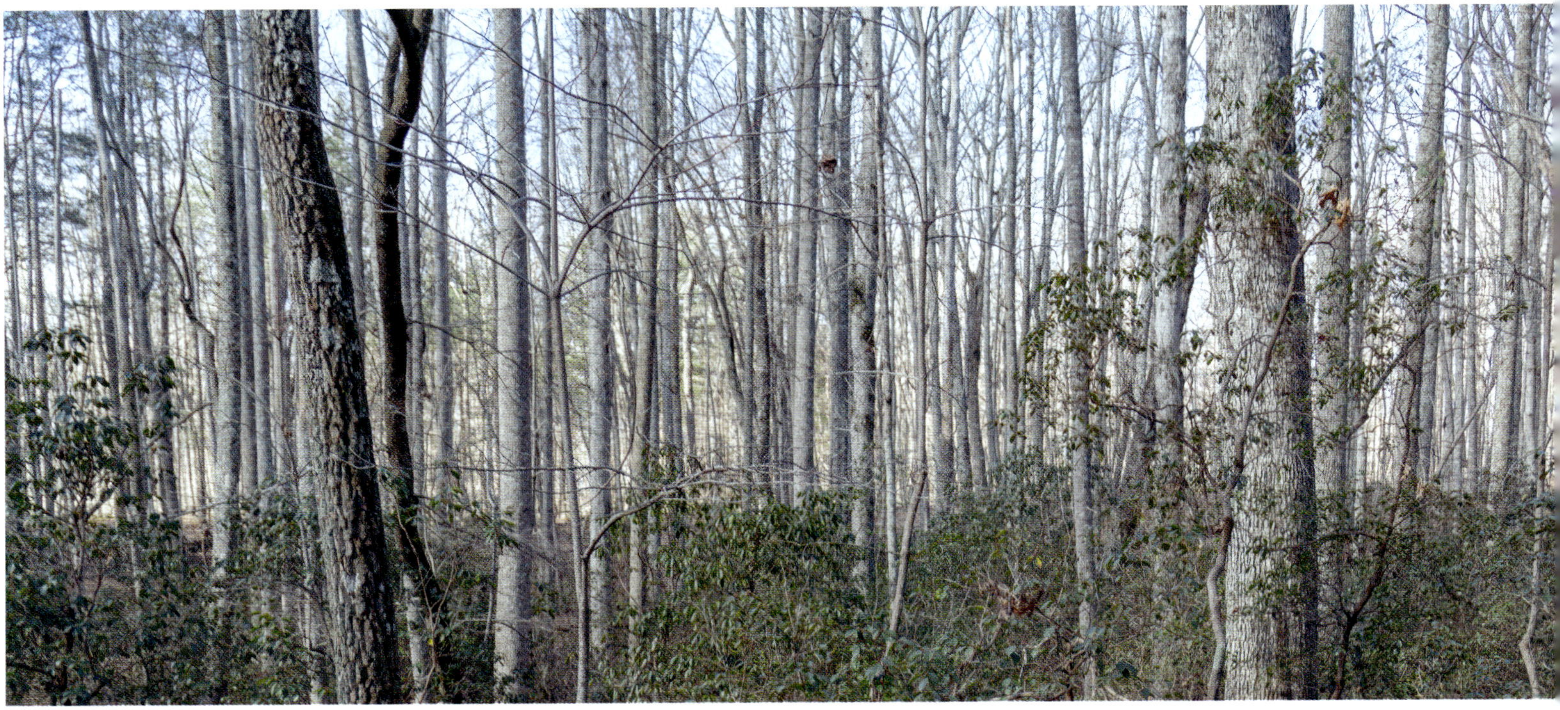

Linda M. Hasselstrom

SOUTH DAKOTA

"Read this book, and others about nature. But
remember to go outside, to experience and study
the place nearest your home where you are
closest to the earth, whether it's a patch of weeds
amid concrete, or an estate. Visit the wilderness
if you can, but attend to your home first."

From *Between Grass and Sky:*
Where I Live and Work

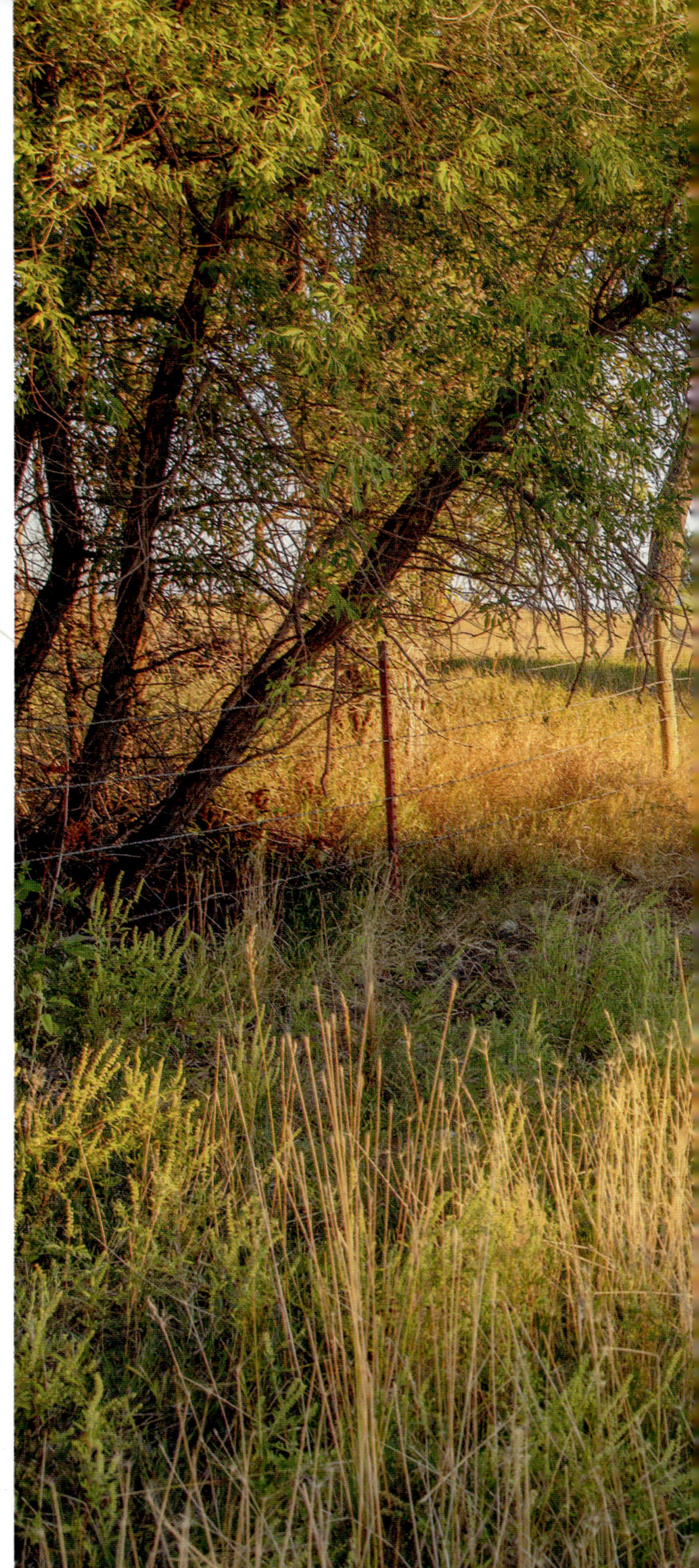

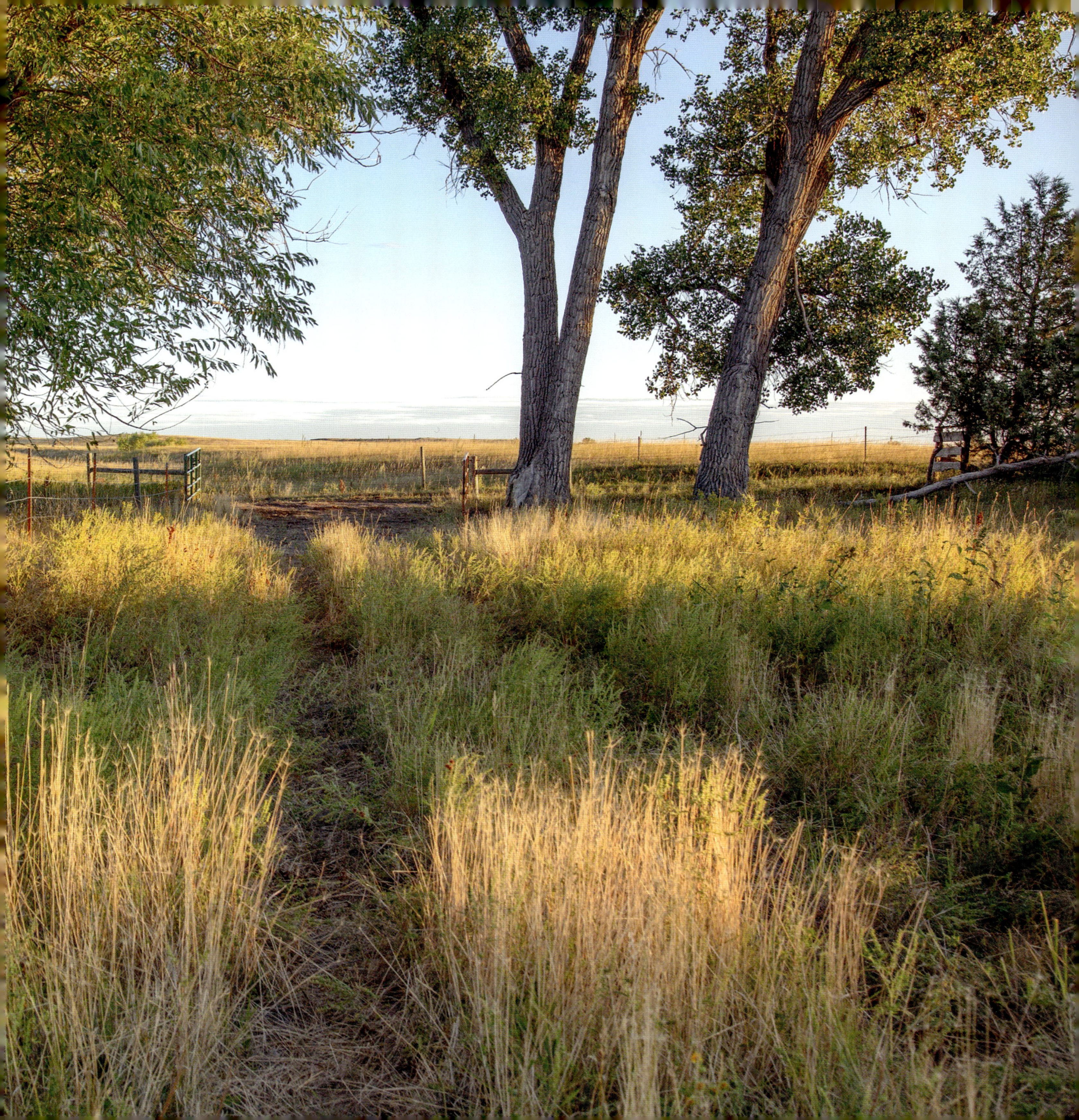

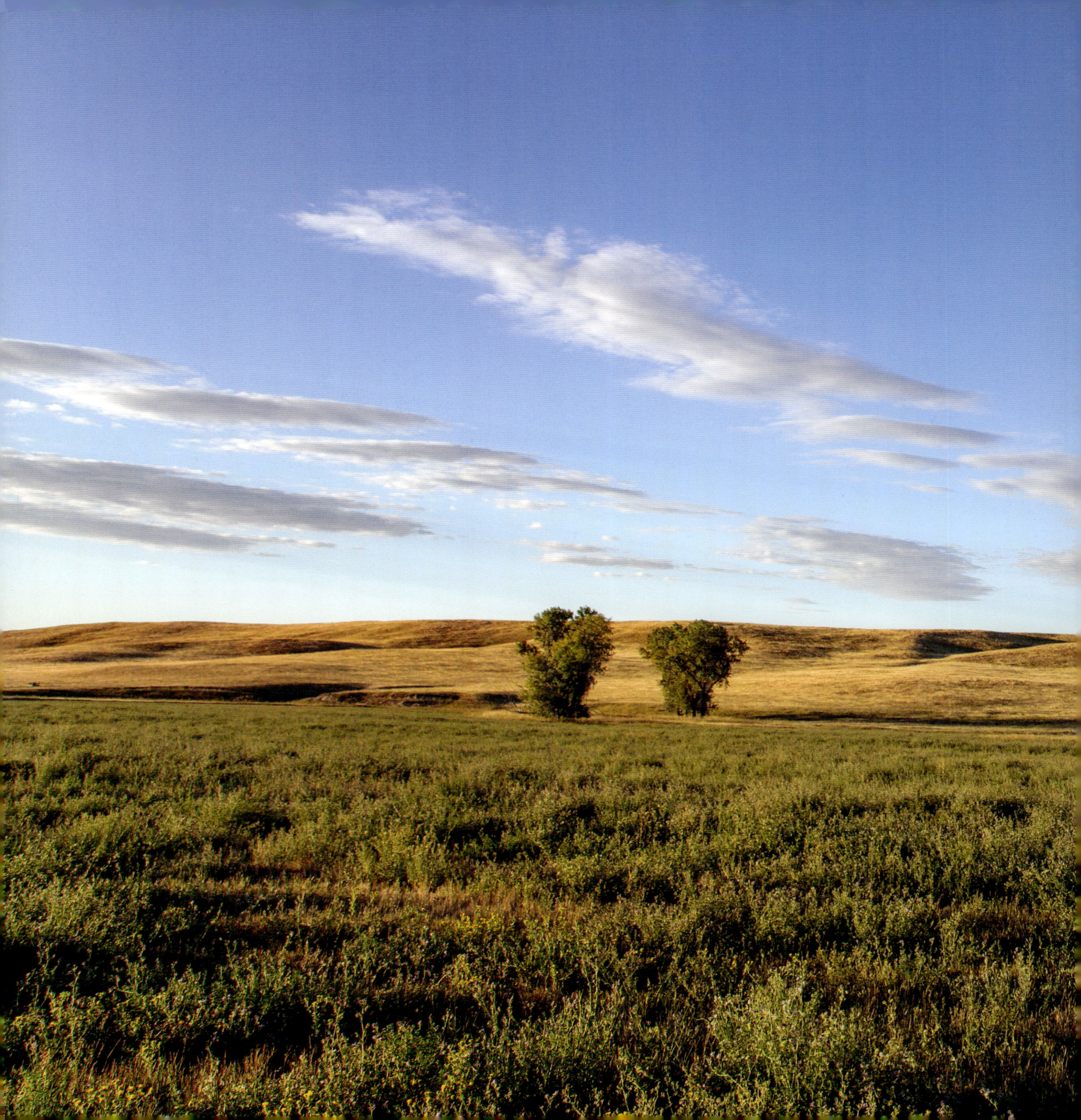

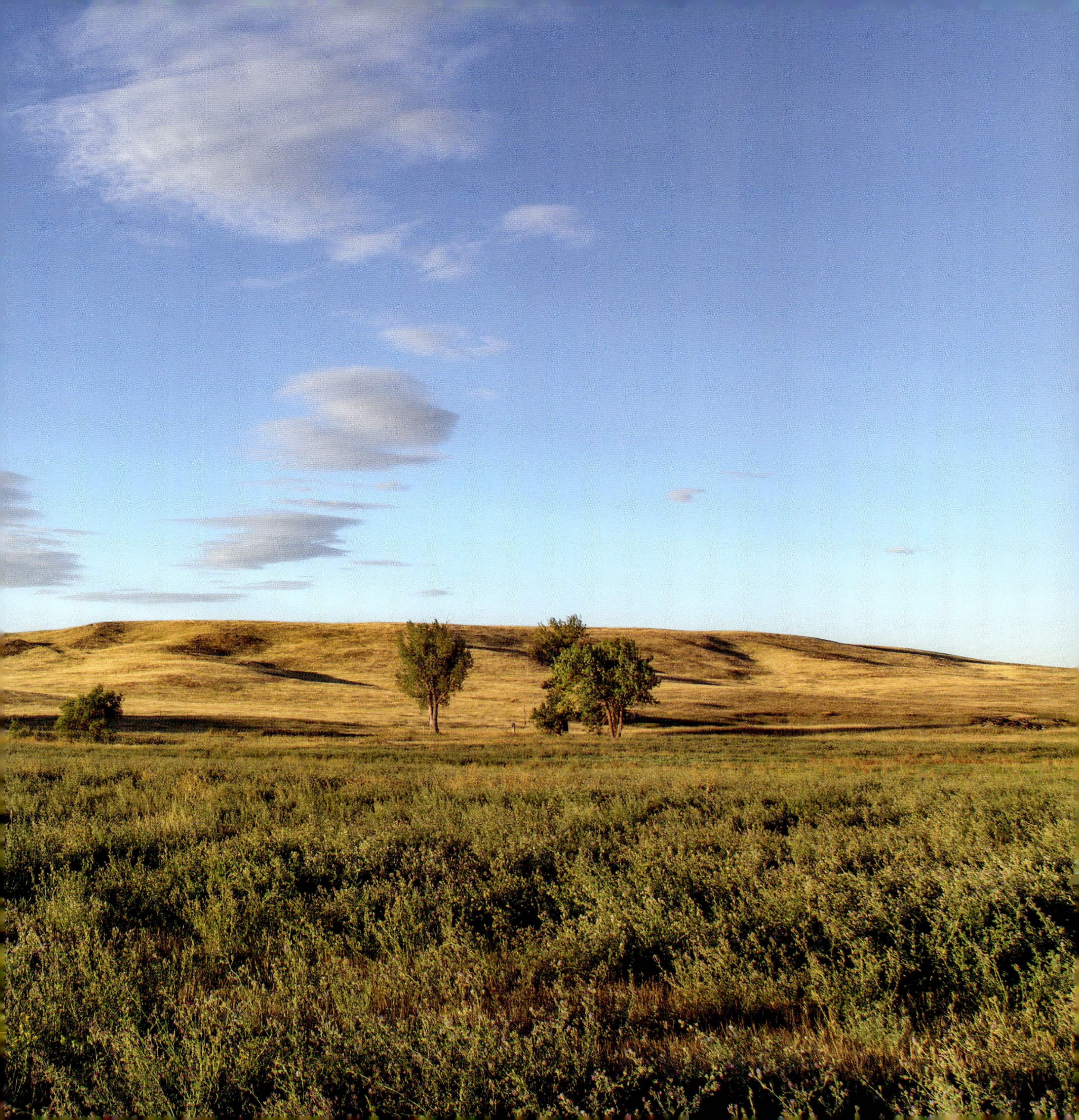

Lyanda Lynn Haupt

WASHINGTON

"This is one of the blessings of the urban nature project: without the overtly magnificent to stop us in our tracks, we must seek out the more subversively magnificent. Our sense of what constitutes *wildness* is expanded, and our sense of wonder along with it."

From *Crow Planet: Essential Wisdom from the Urban Wilderness*

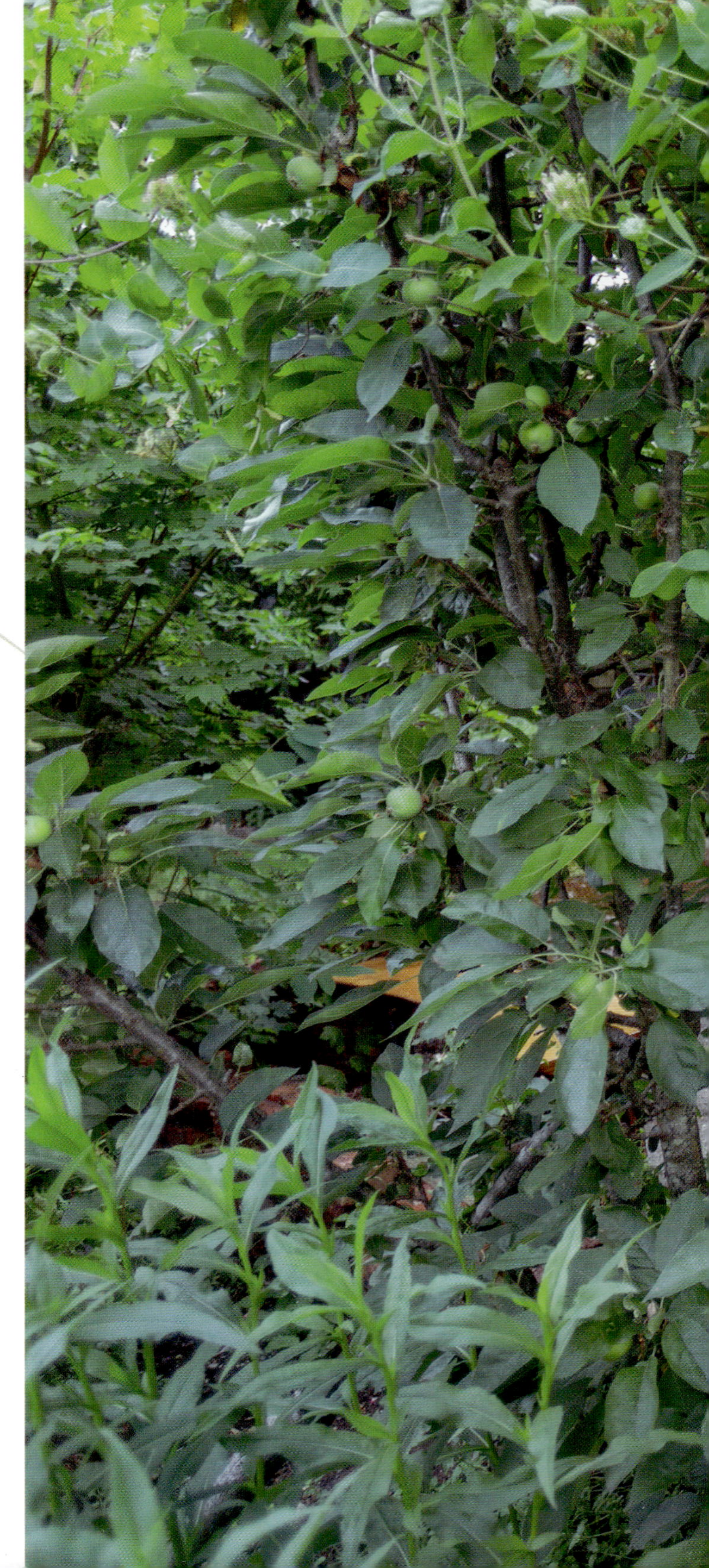

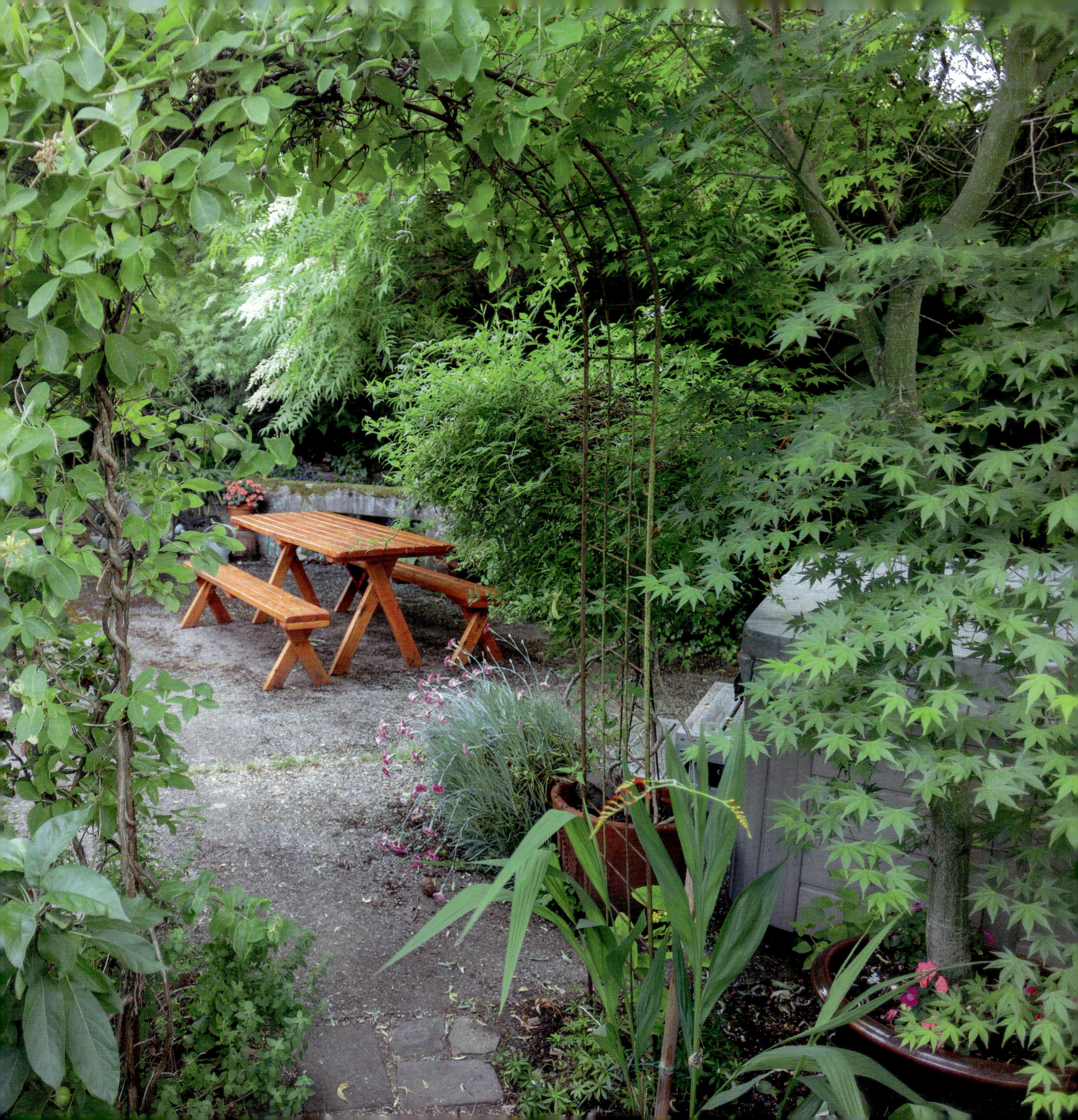

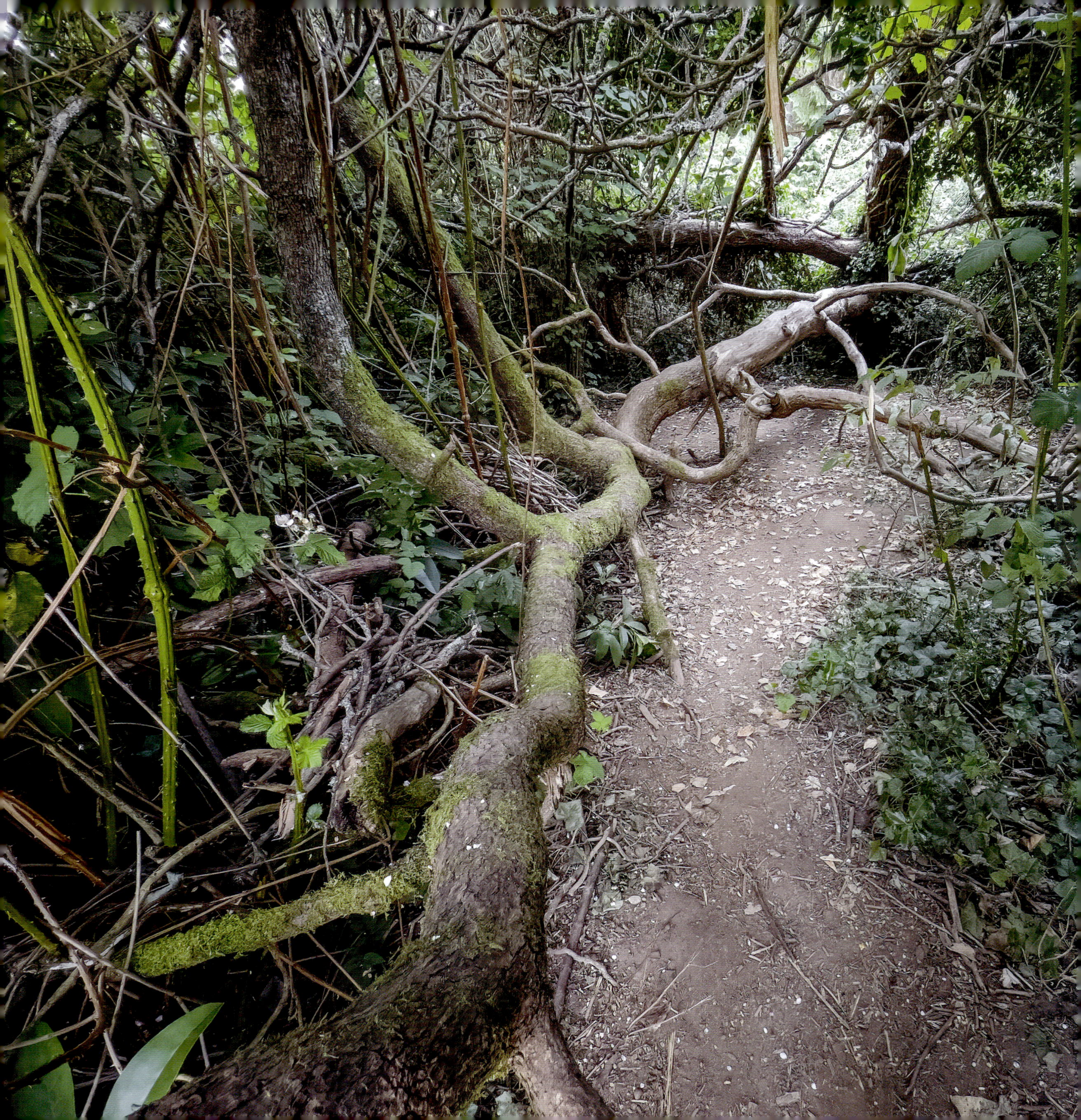

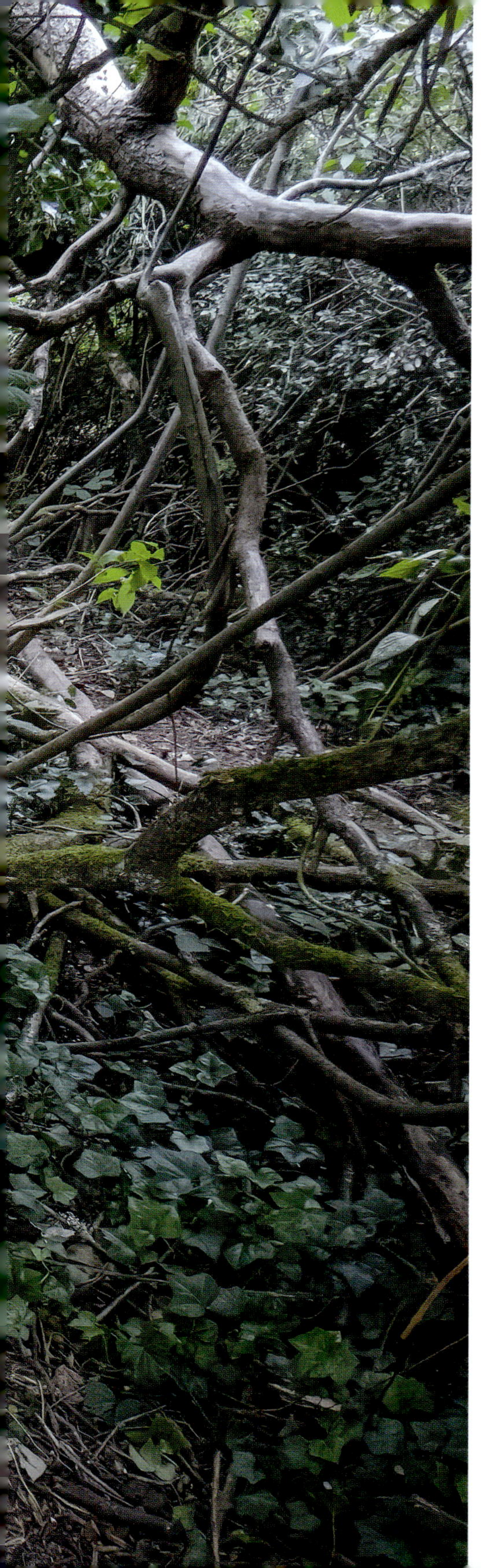
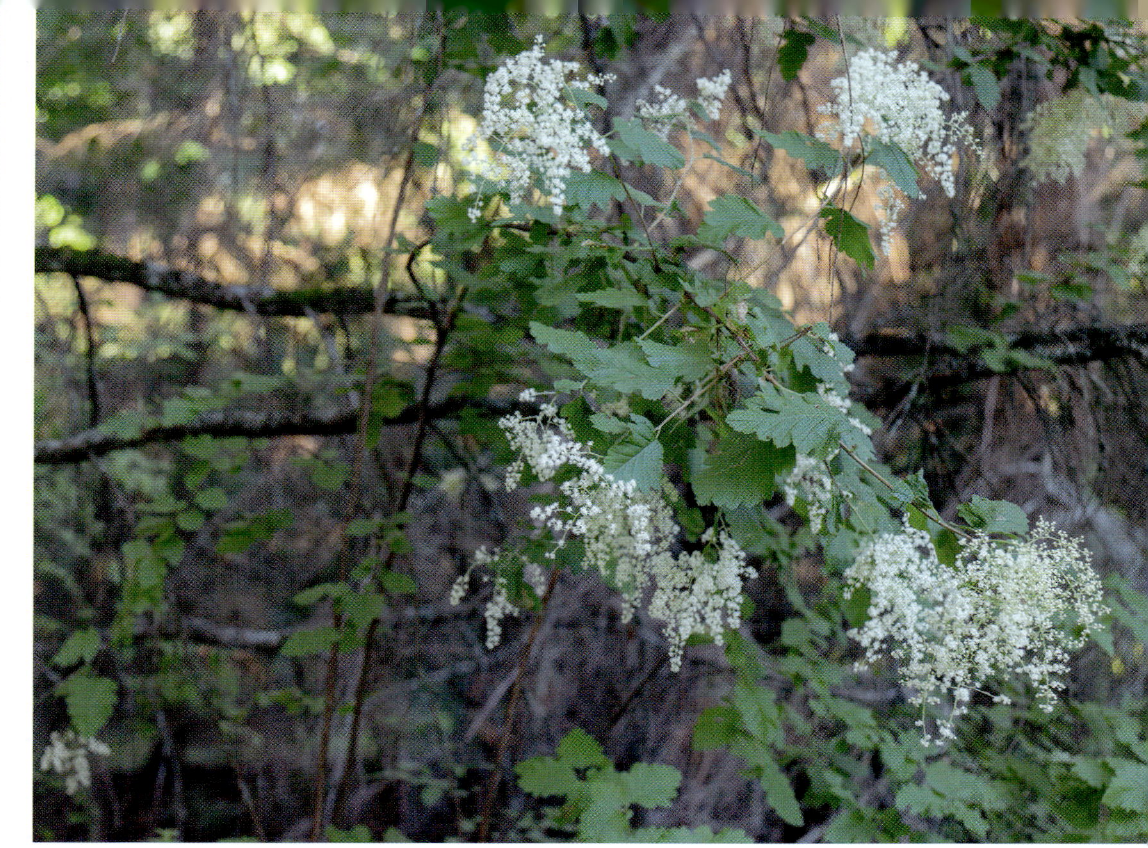
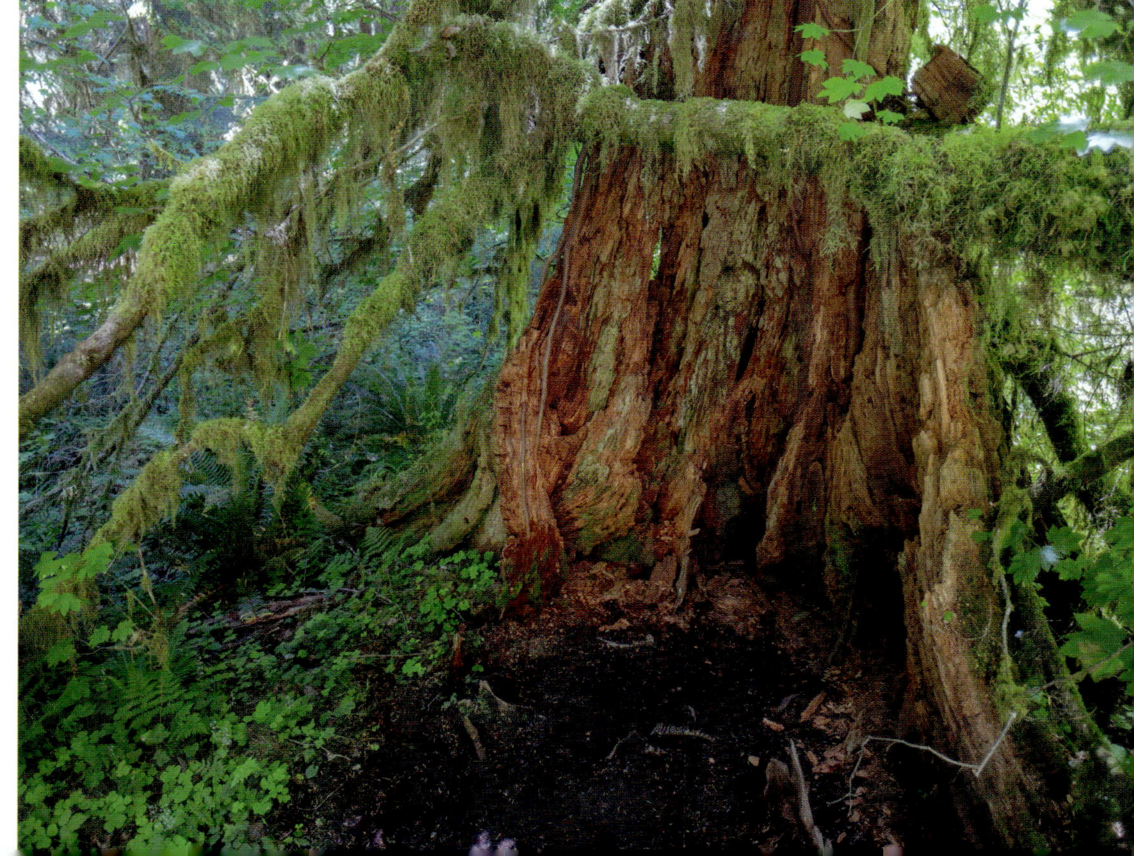

Edward Hoagland

"The question of whether it's God's green earth is not center stage, except in the sense that if so, one is reminded with some regularity that He may be dying."

From the essay "Revolution II: The Sequel,"
from *Balancing Acts: Essays*

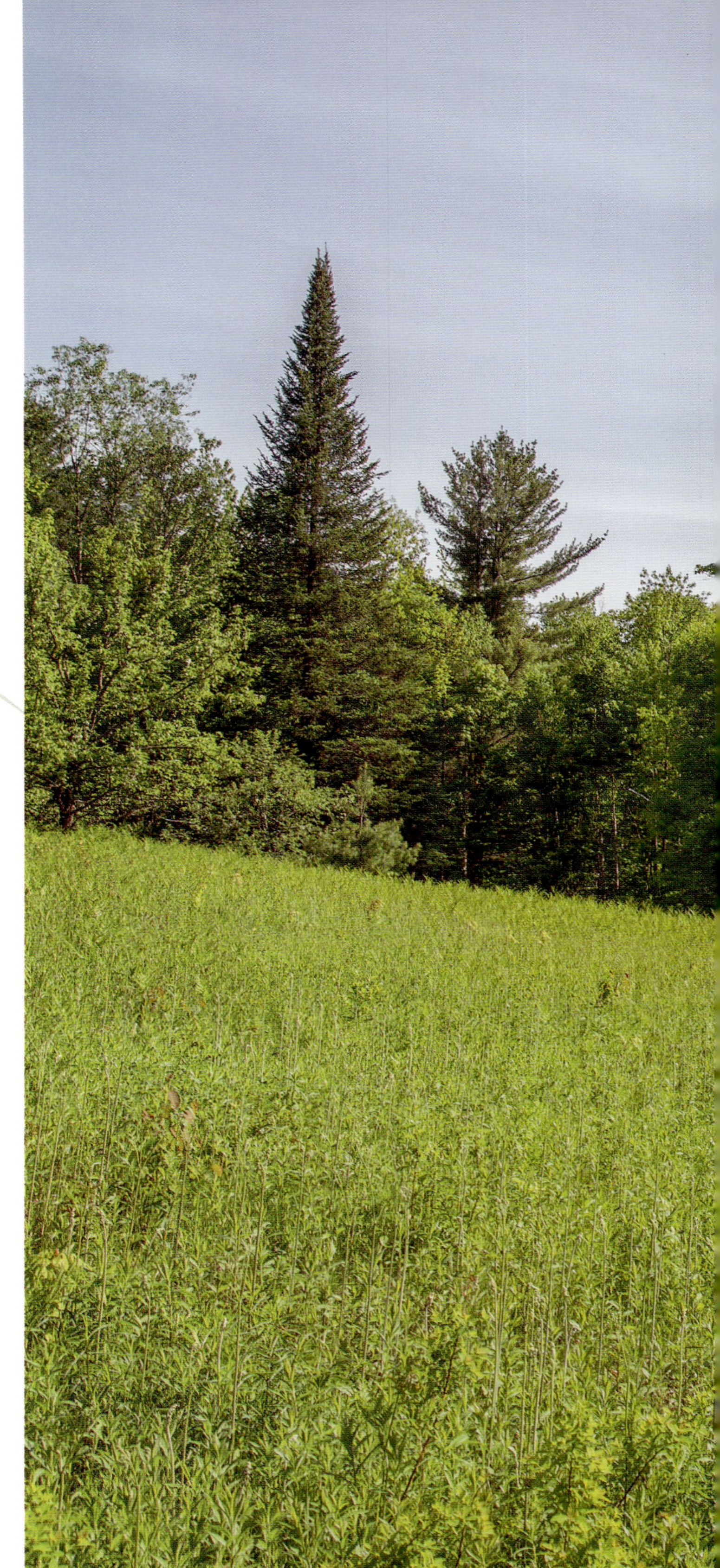

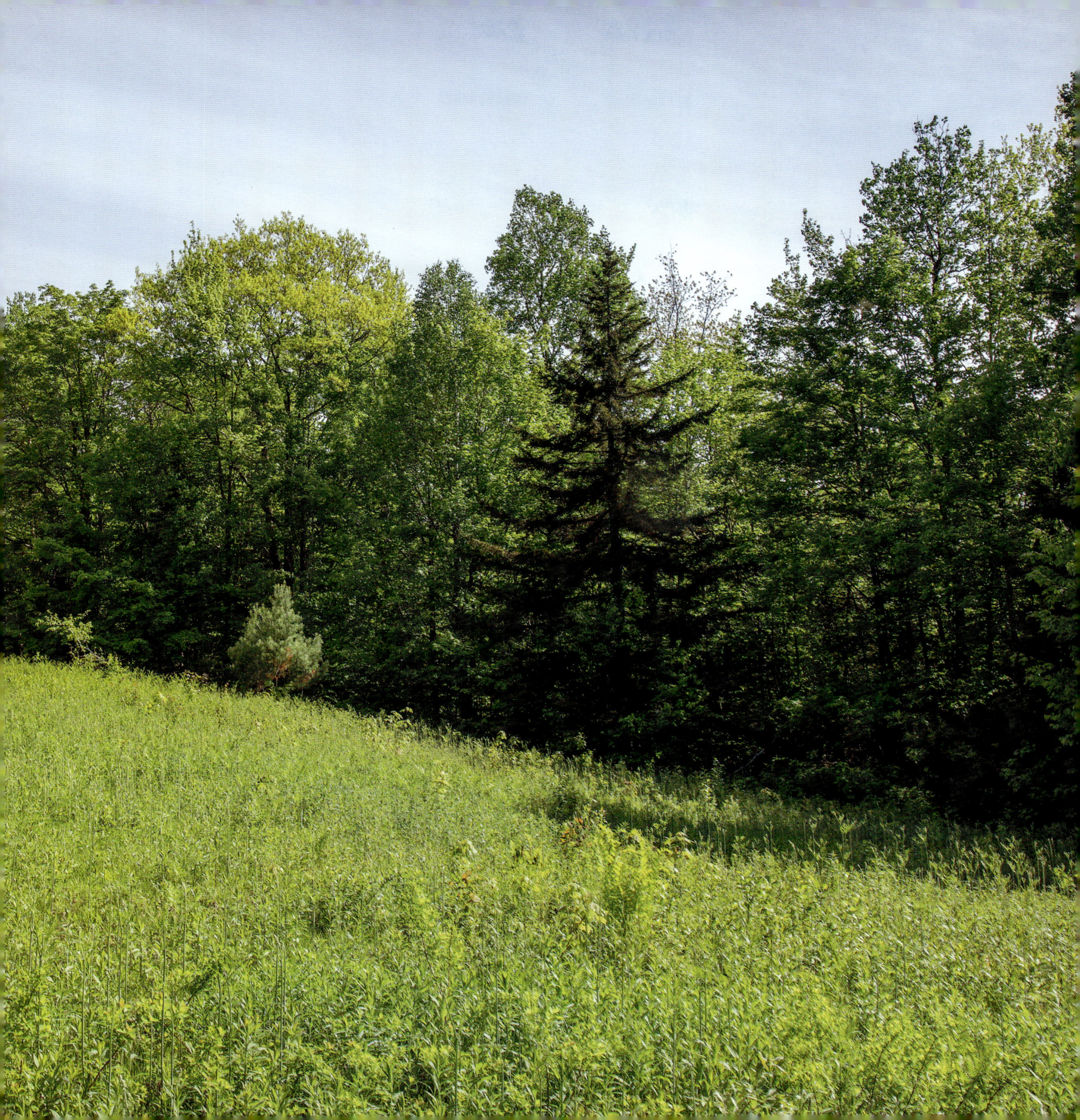

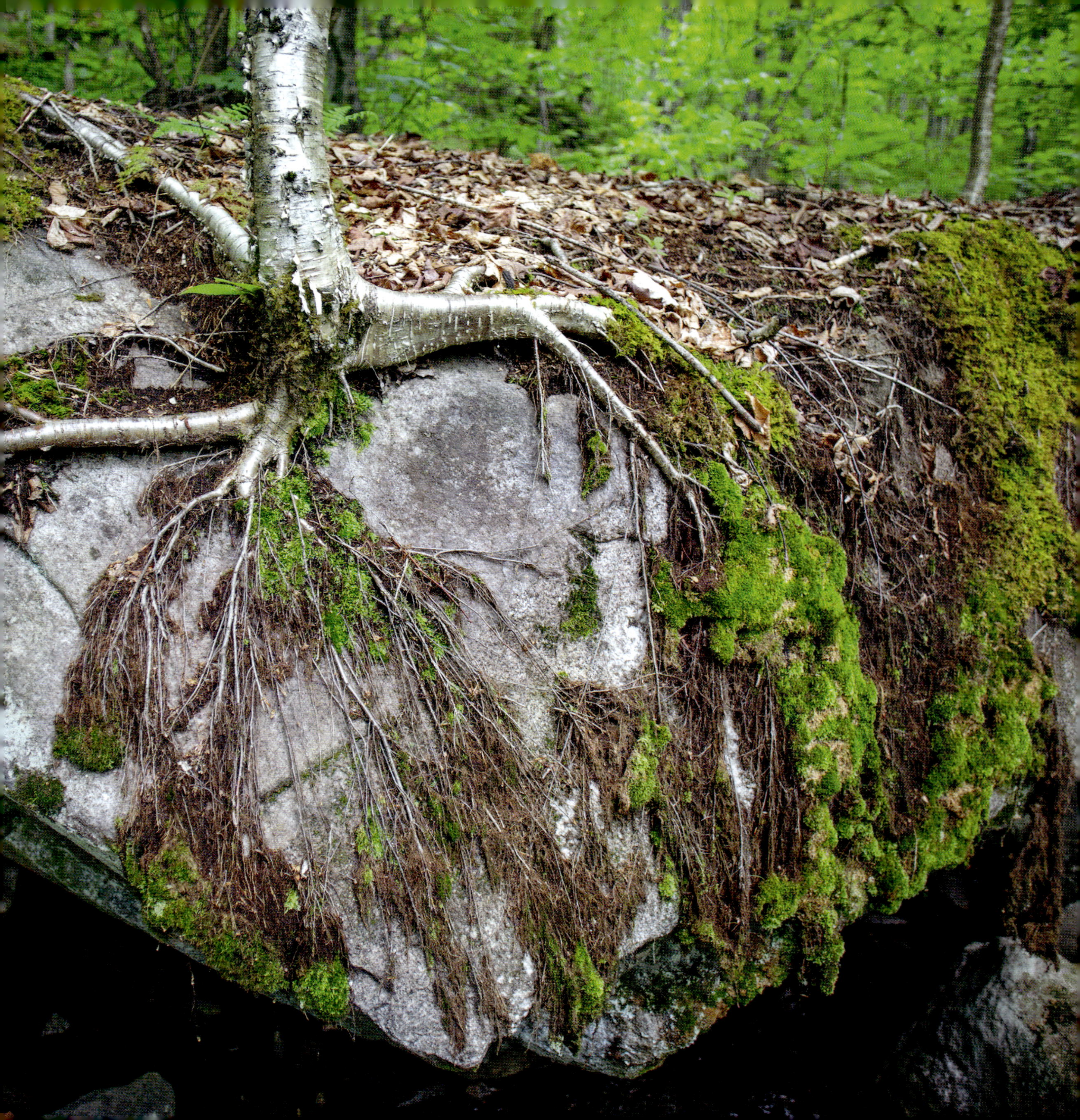

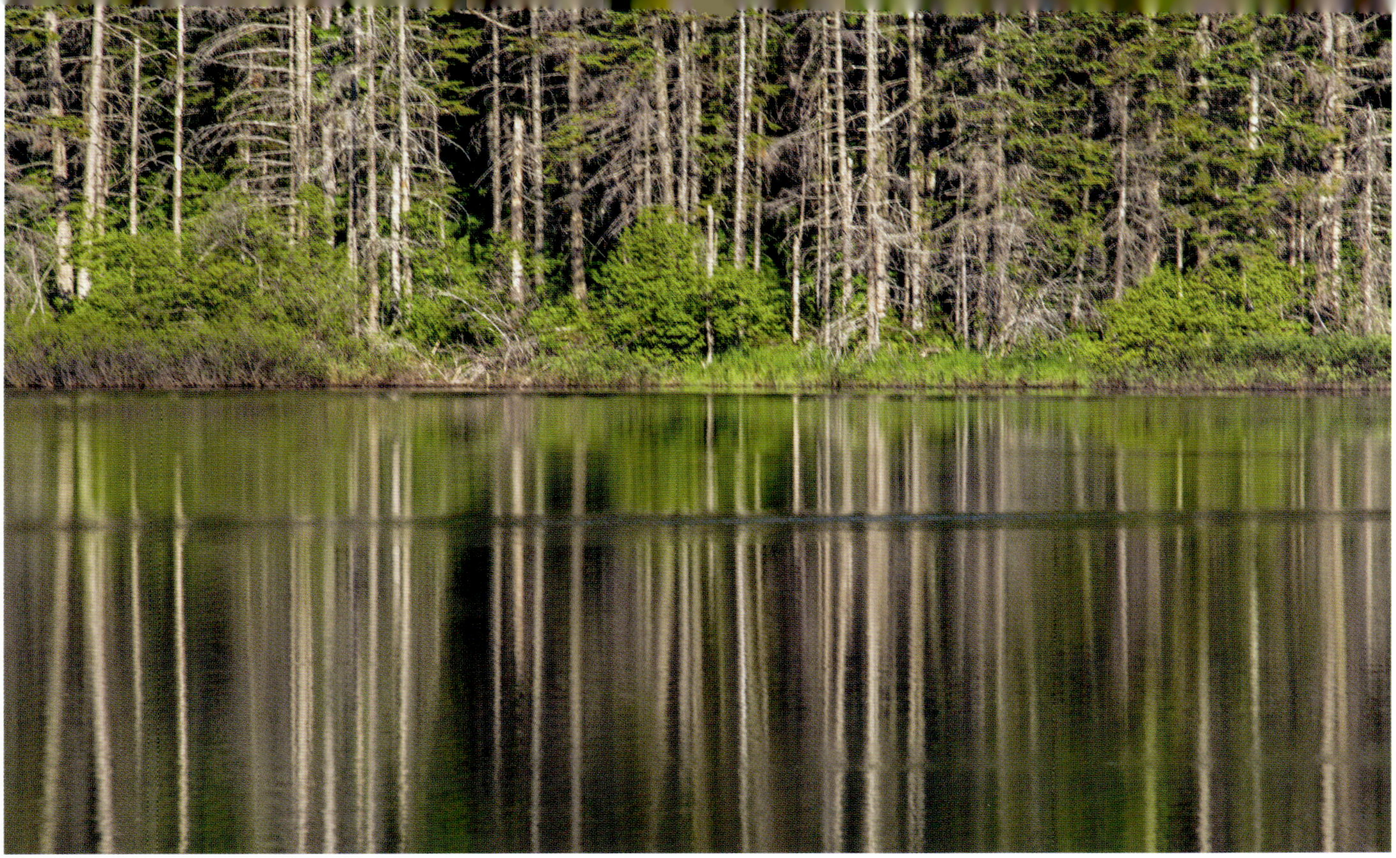

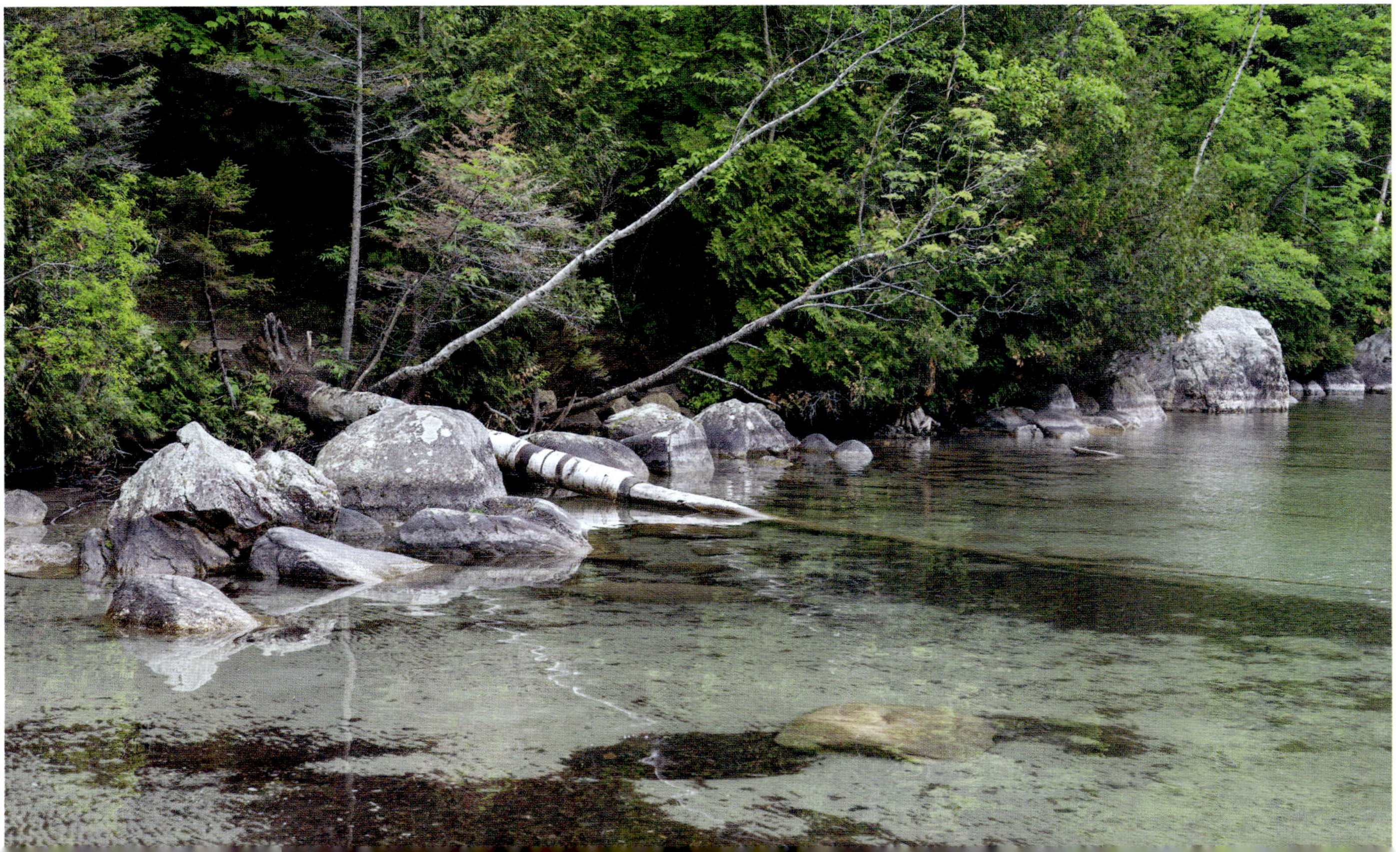

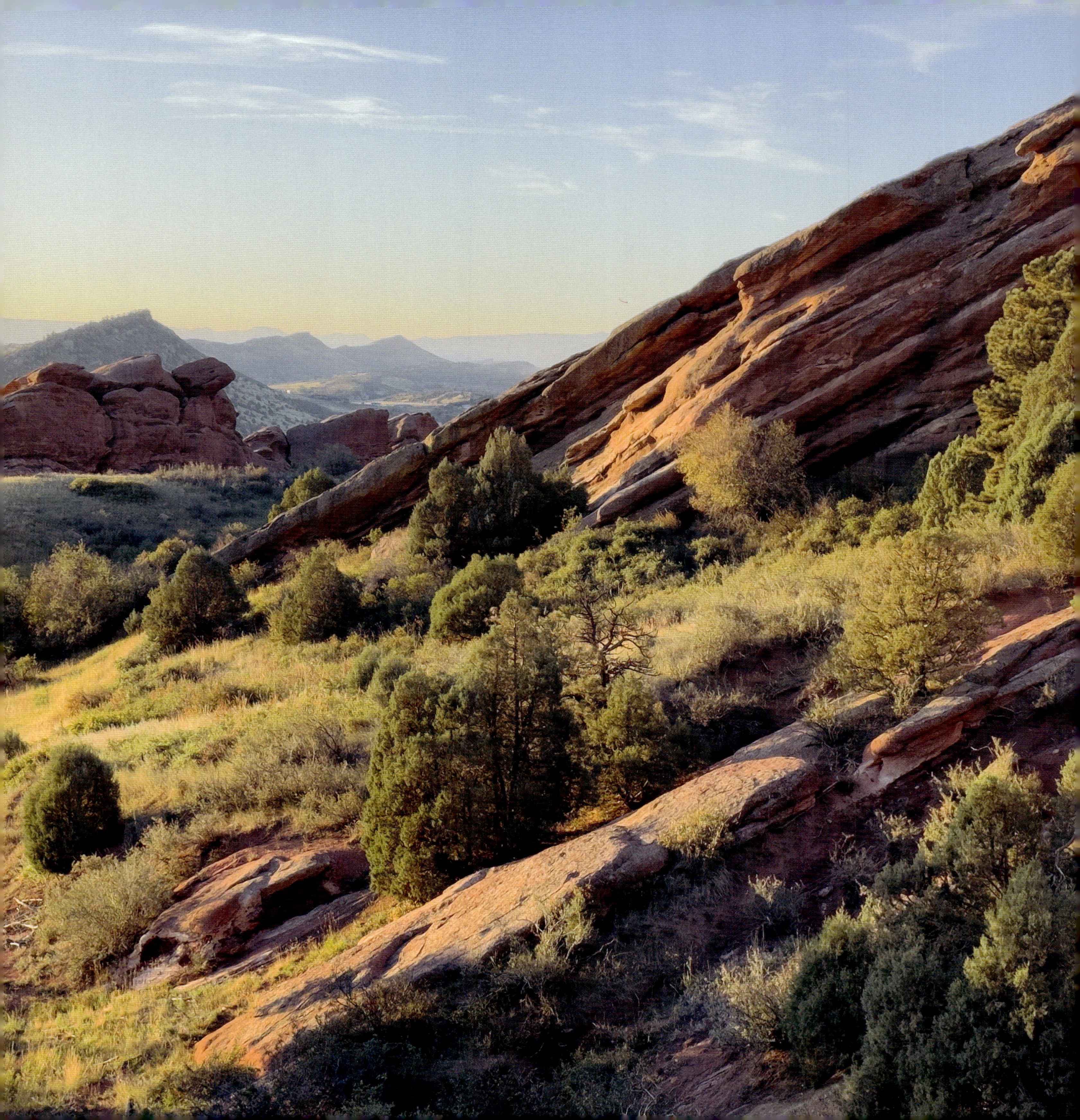

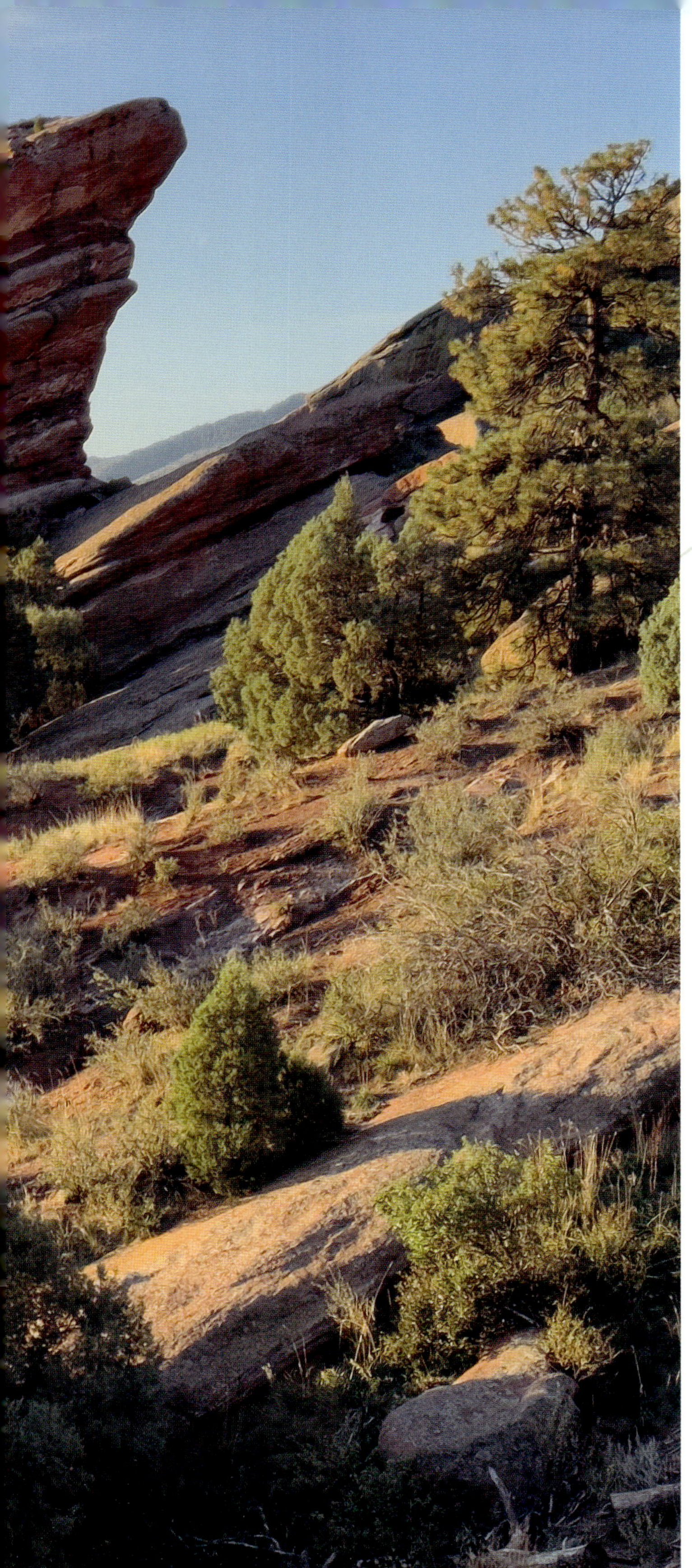

Linda Hogan

COLORADO & OKLAHOMA

"A change is required of us, a healing of the betrayed trust between humans and earth. Caretaking is the utmost spiritual and physical responsibility of our time, and perhaps that stewardship is finally our place in the web of life, our work, the solution to the mystery of what we are. There are already so many holes in the universe that will never again be filled, and each of them forces us to question why we permitted such loss, such tearing away at the fabric of life, and how we will live with our planet in the future."

From *Dwellings: A Spiritual History of the Living World*

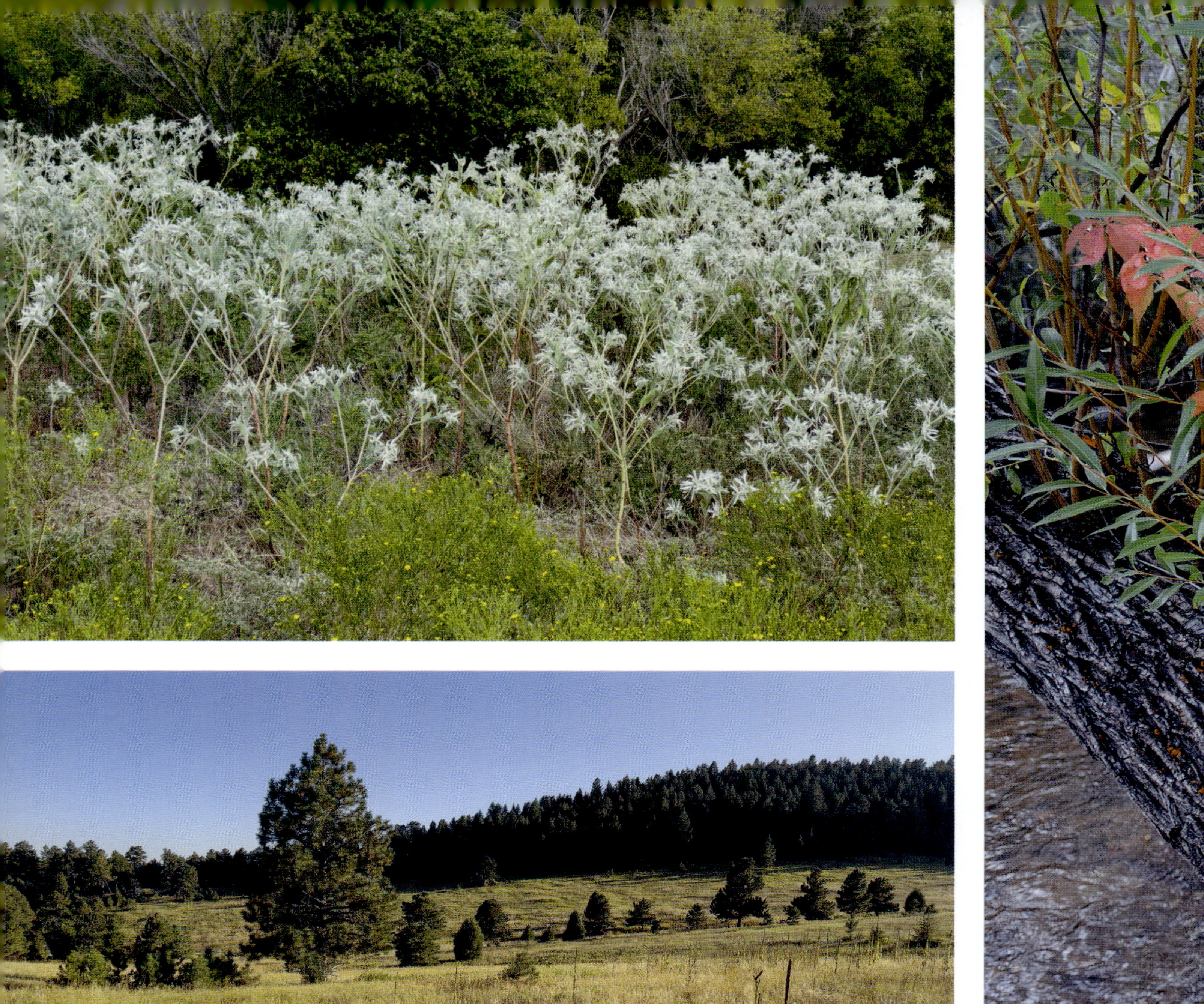

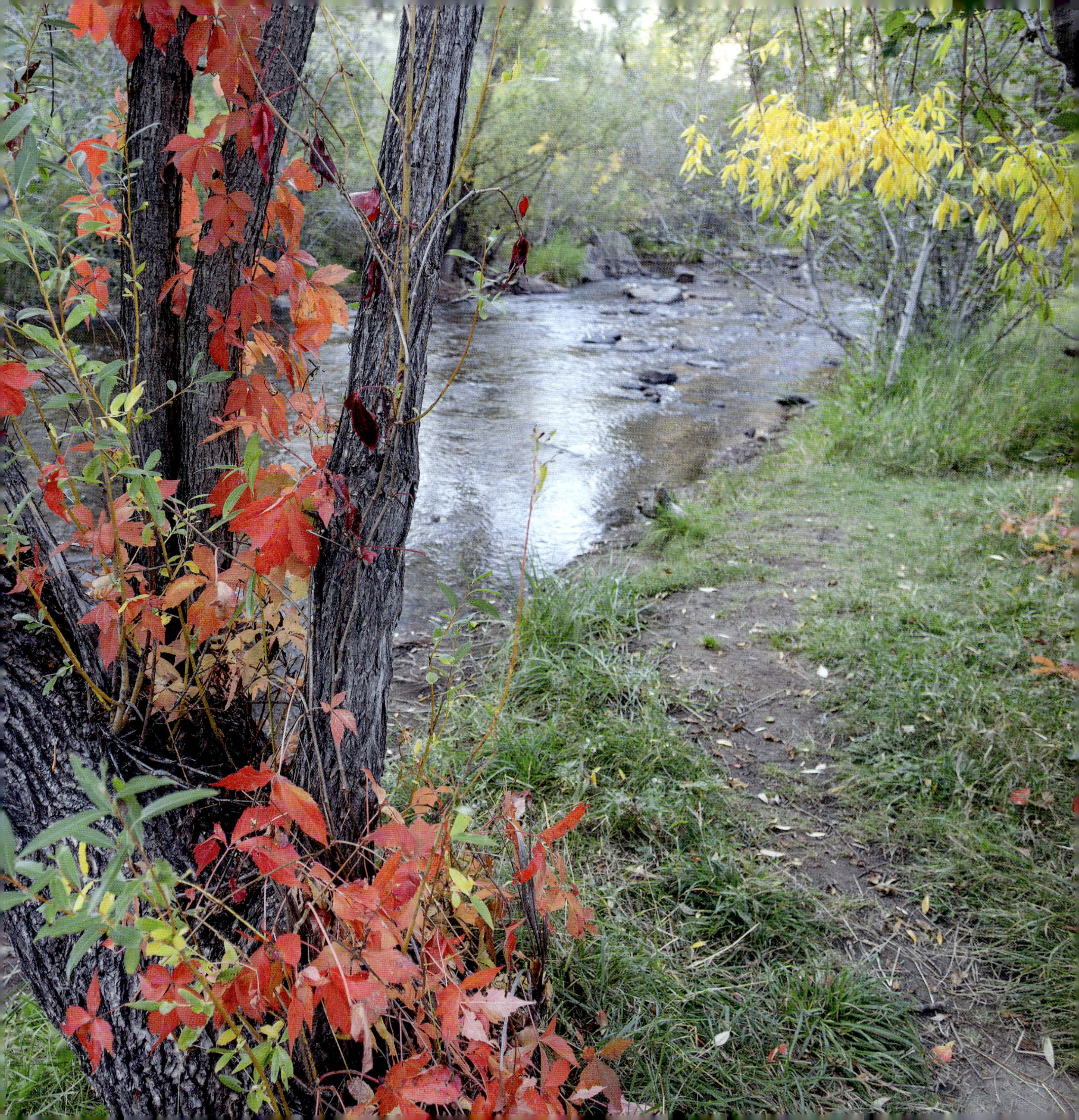

Pam Houston

COLORADO

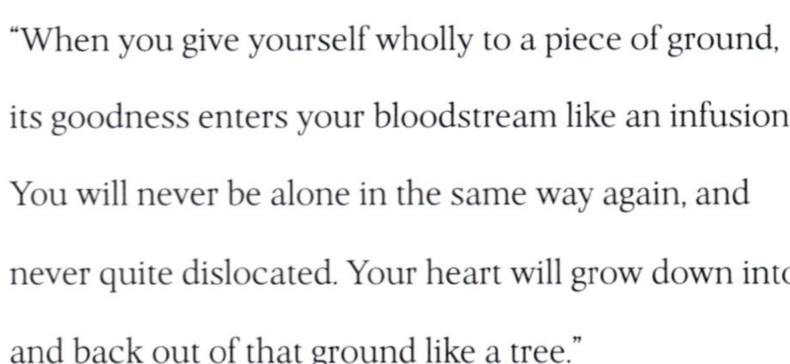

"When you give yourself wholly to a piece of ground,
its goodness enters your bloodstream like an infusion.
You will never be alone in the same way again, and
never quite dislocated. Your heart will grow down into
and back out of that ground like a tree."

From *Deep Creek: Finding Hope in the High Country*

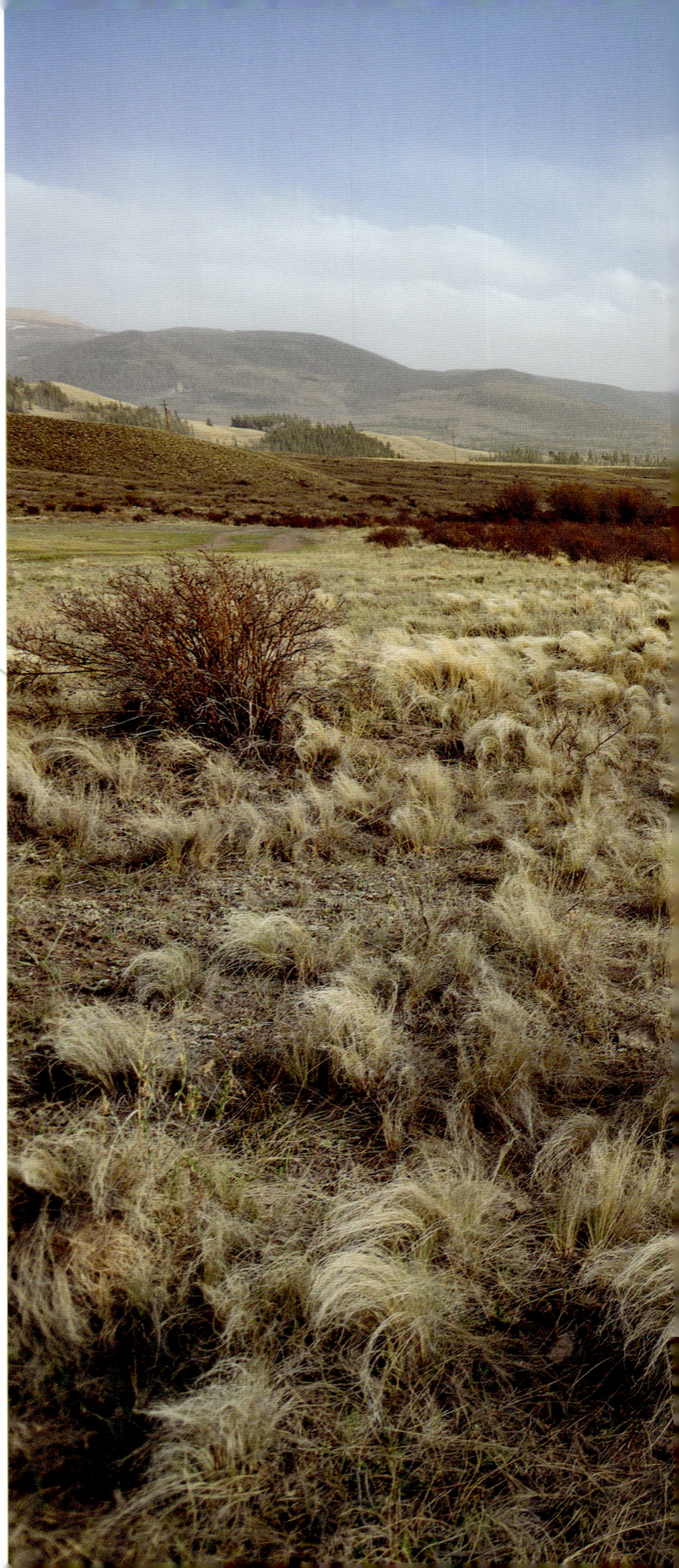

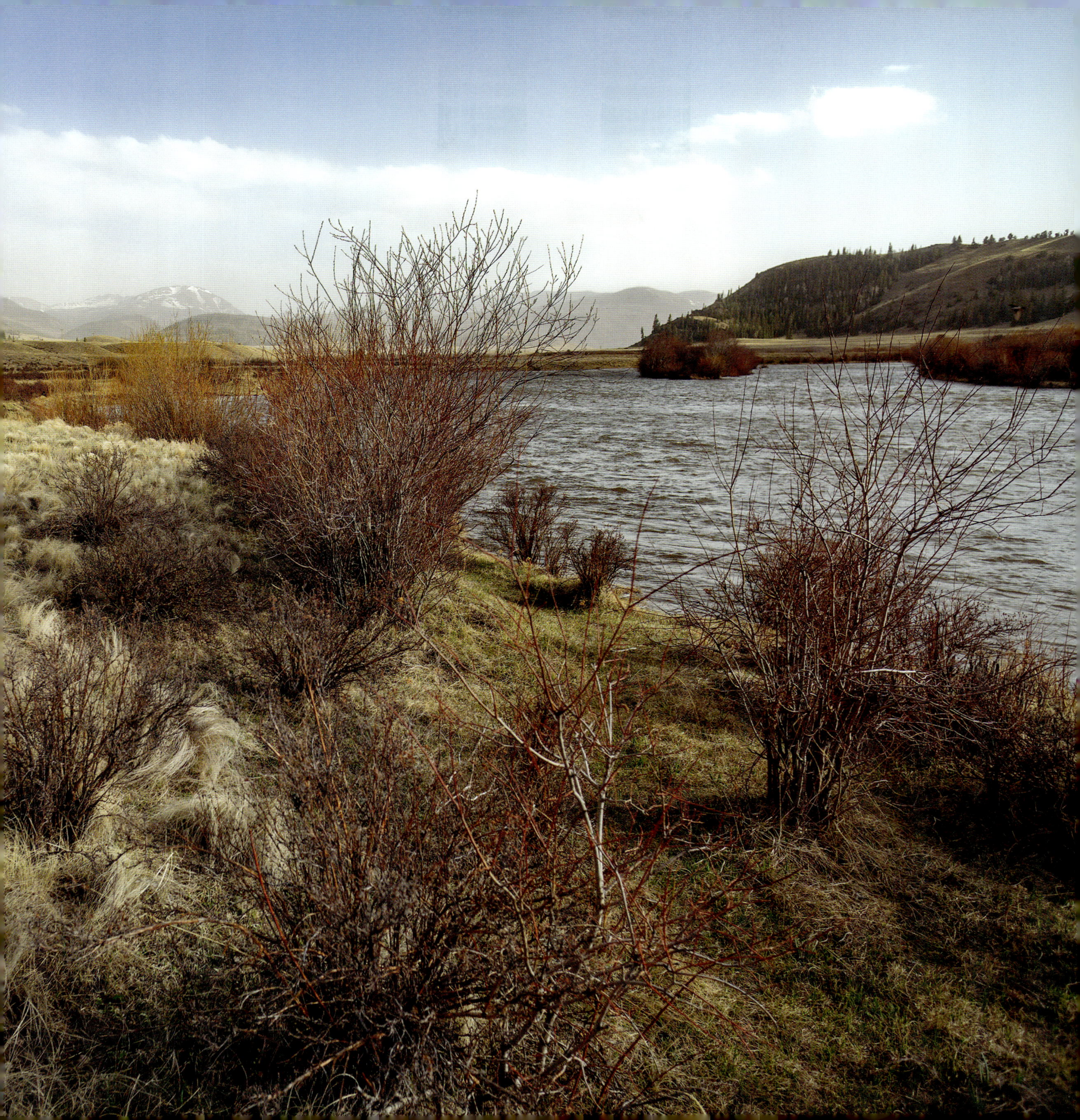

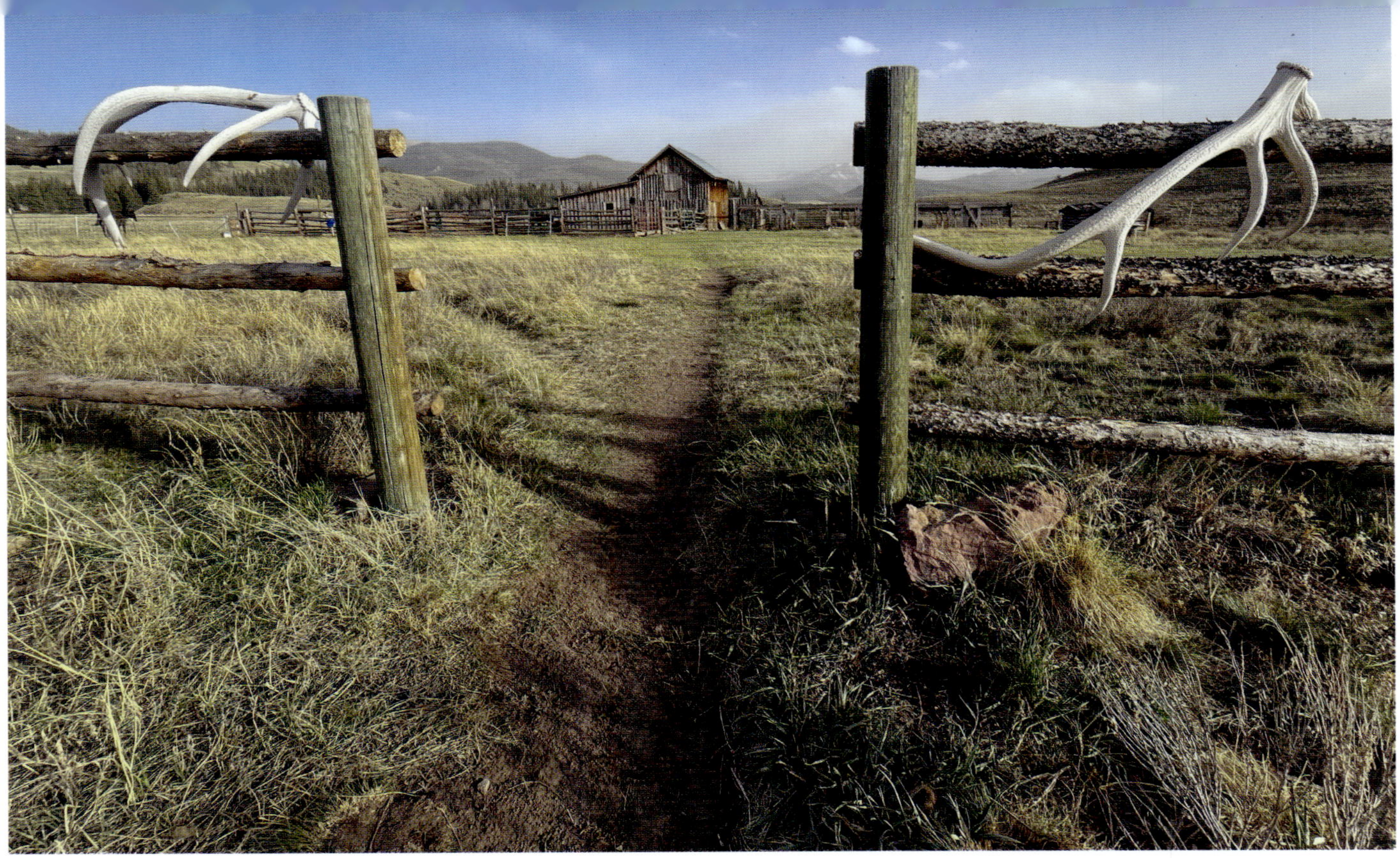

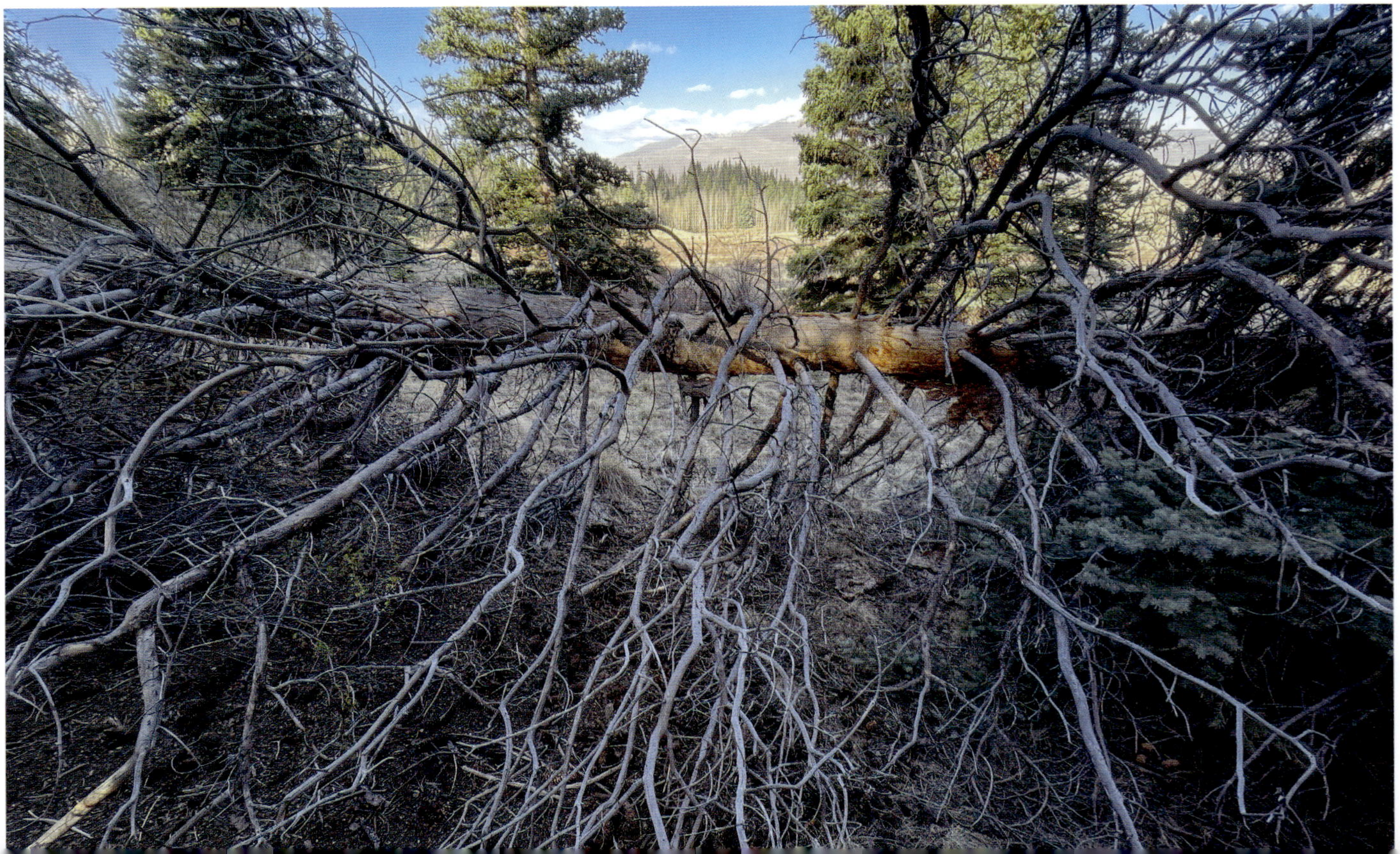

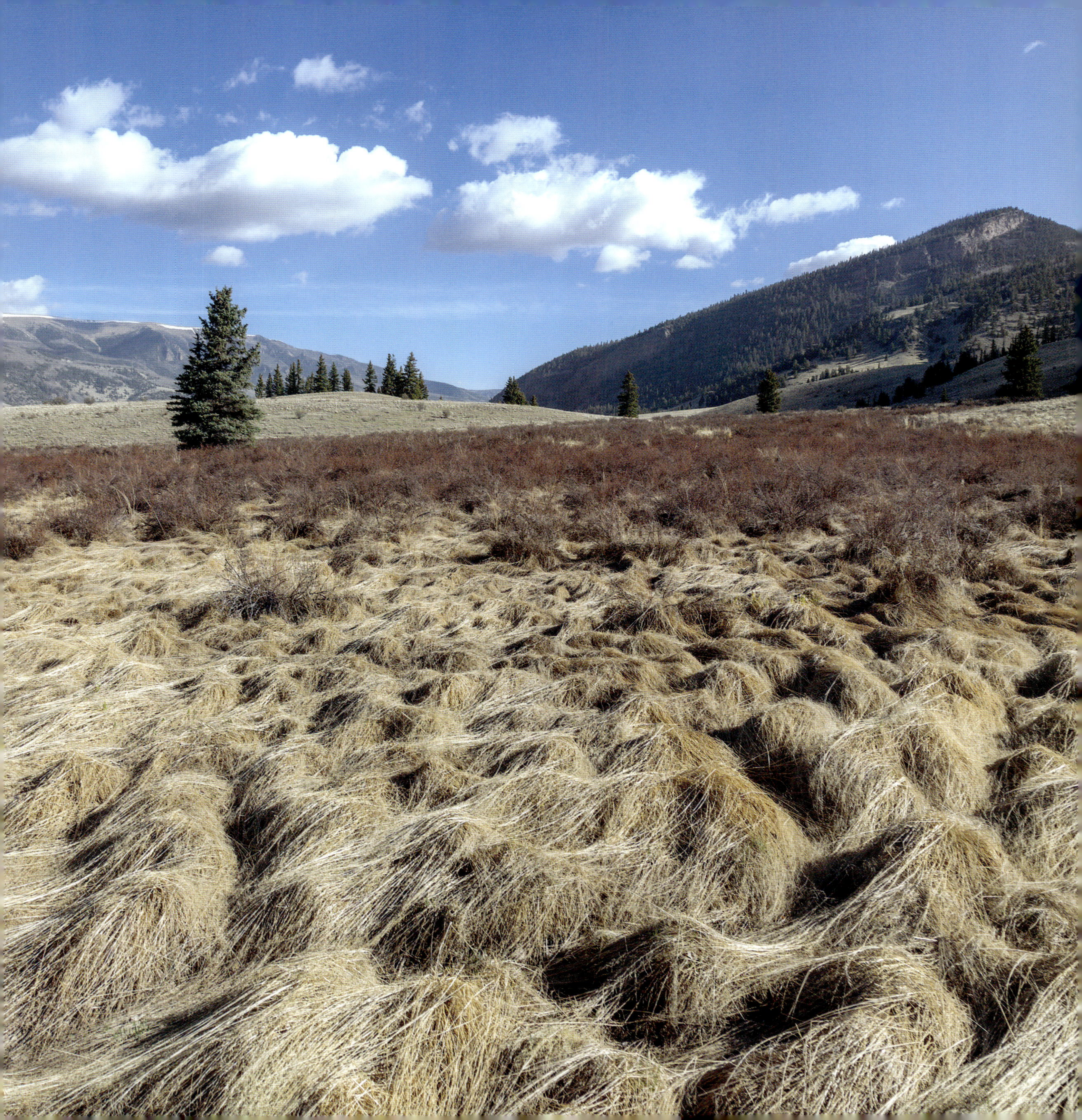

Robinson Jeffers

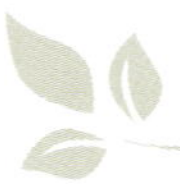

"A little too abstract, a little too wise

It is time for us to kiss the earth again,

It is time to let the leaves rain from the skies,

Let the rich life run to the roots again."

From the poem "Return," from *The Wild God
of the World: An Anthology of Robinson Jeffers*

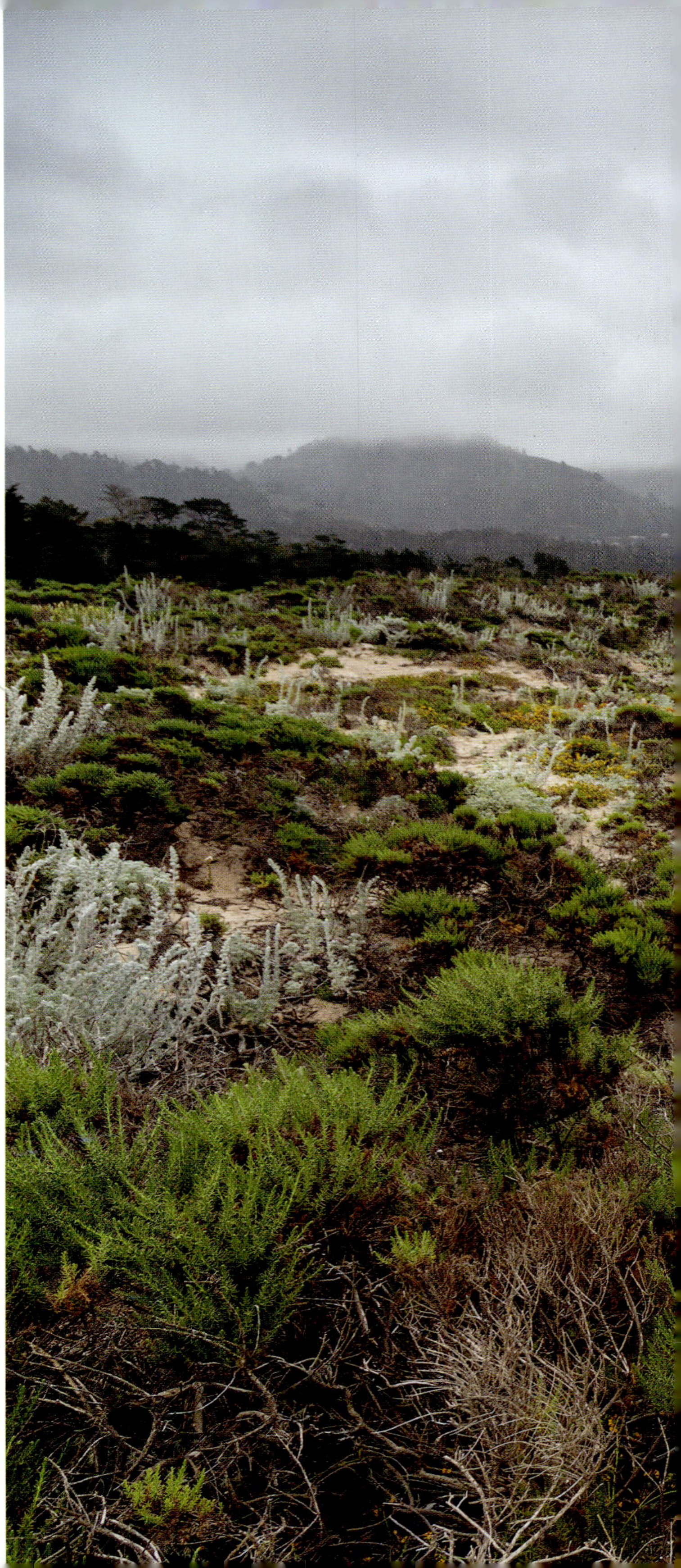

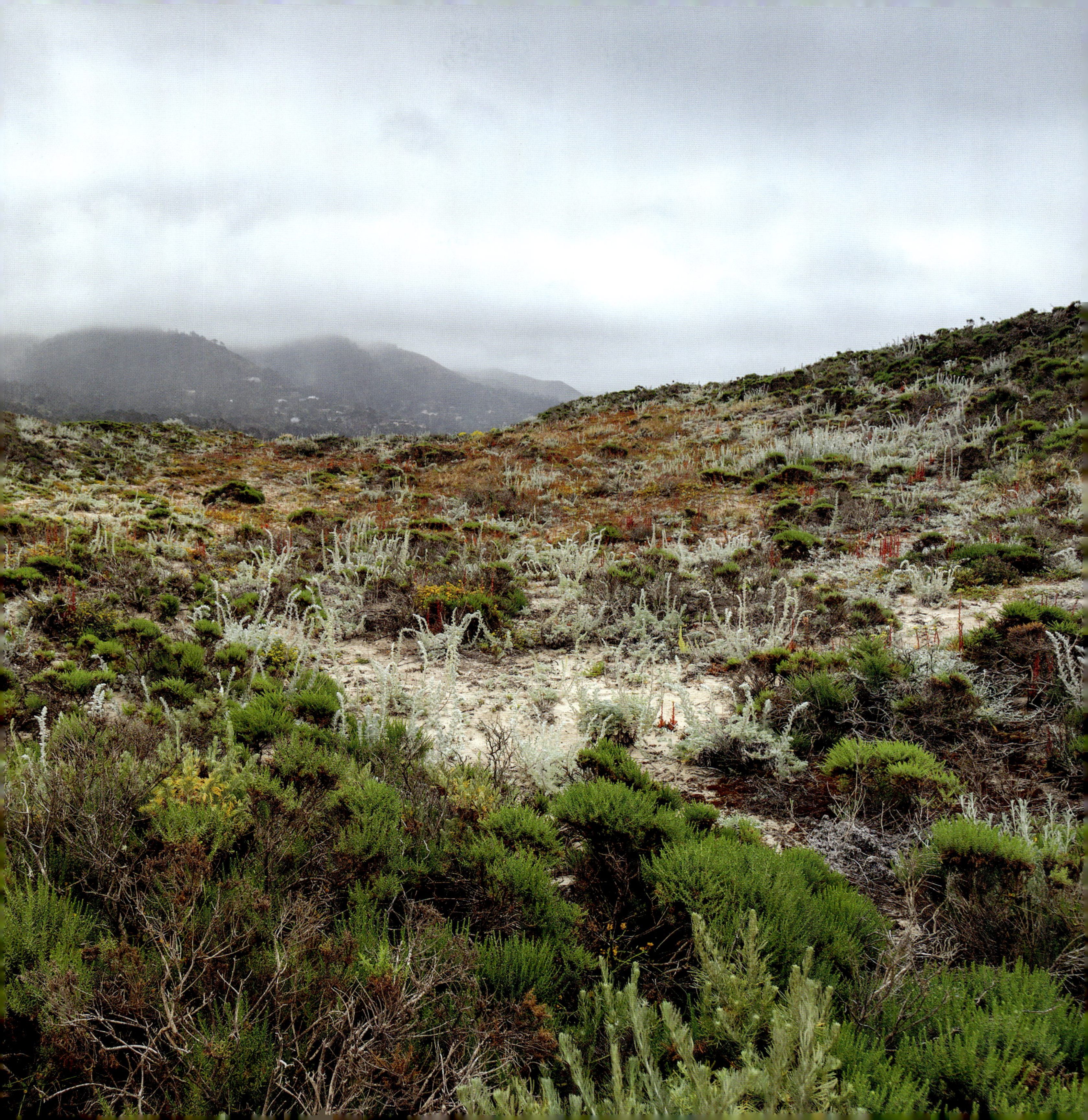

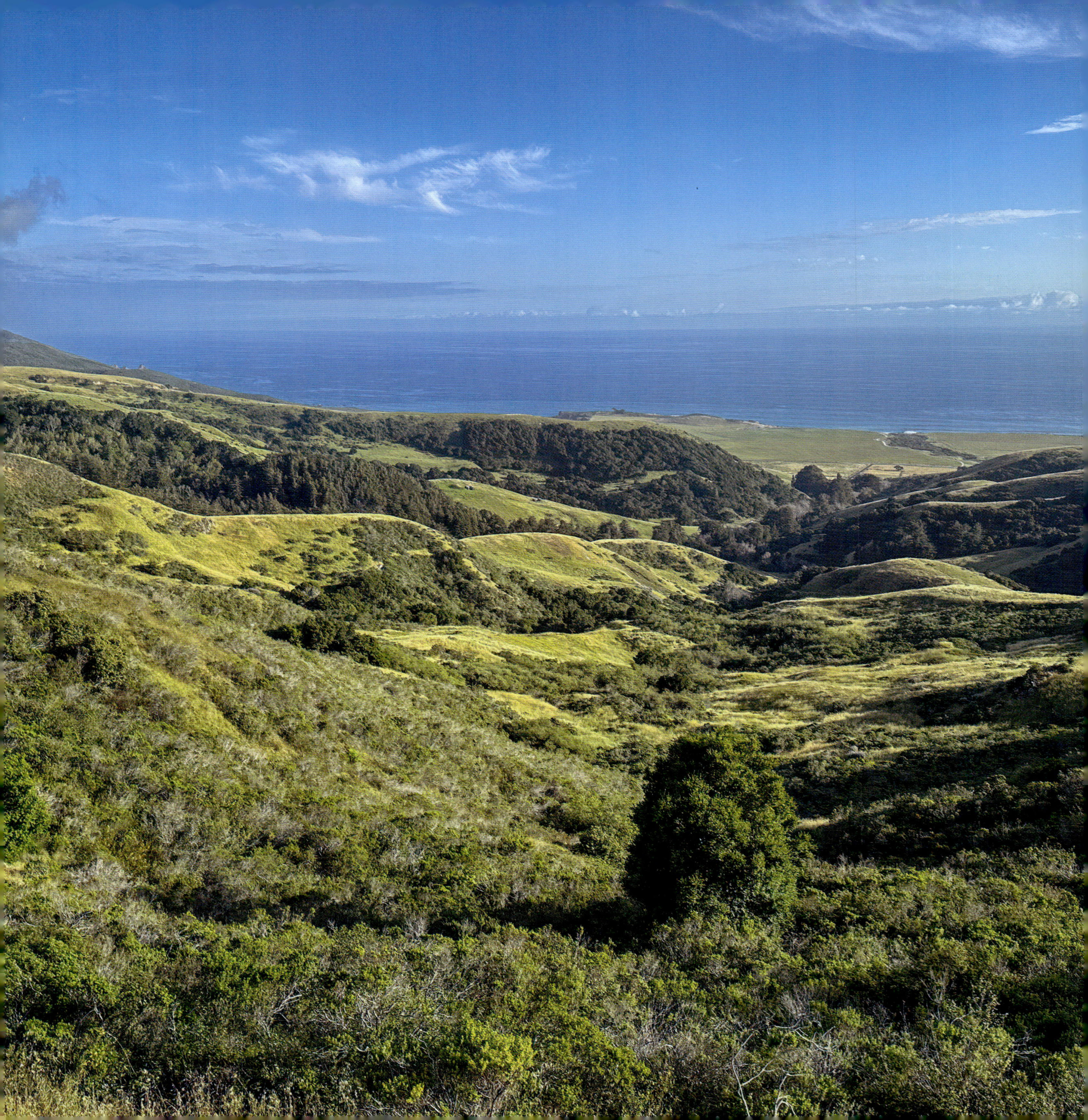

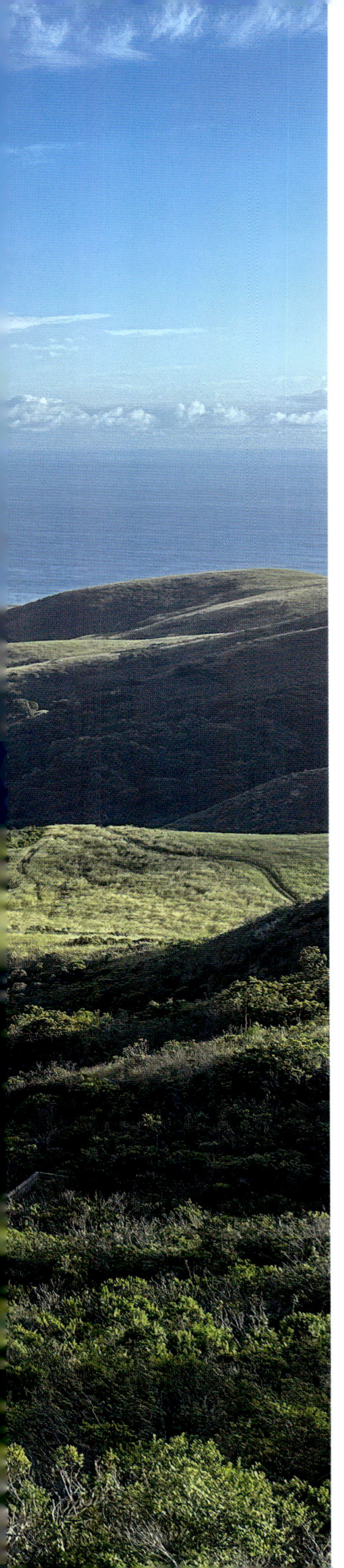

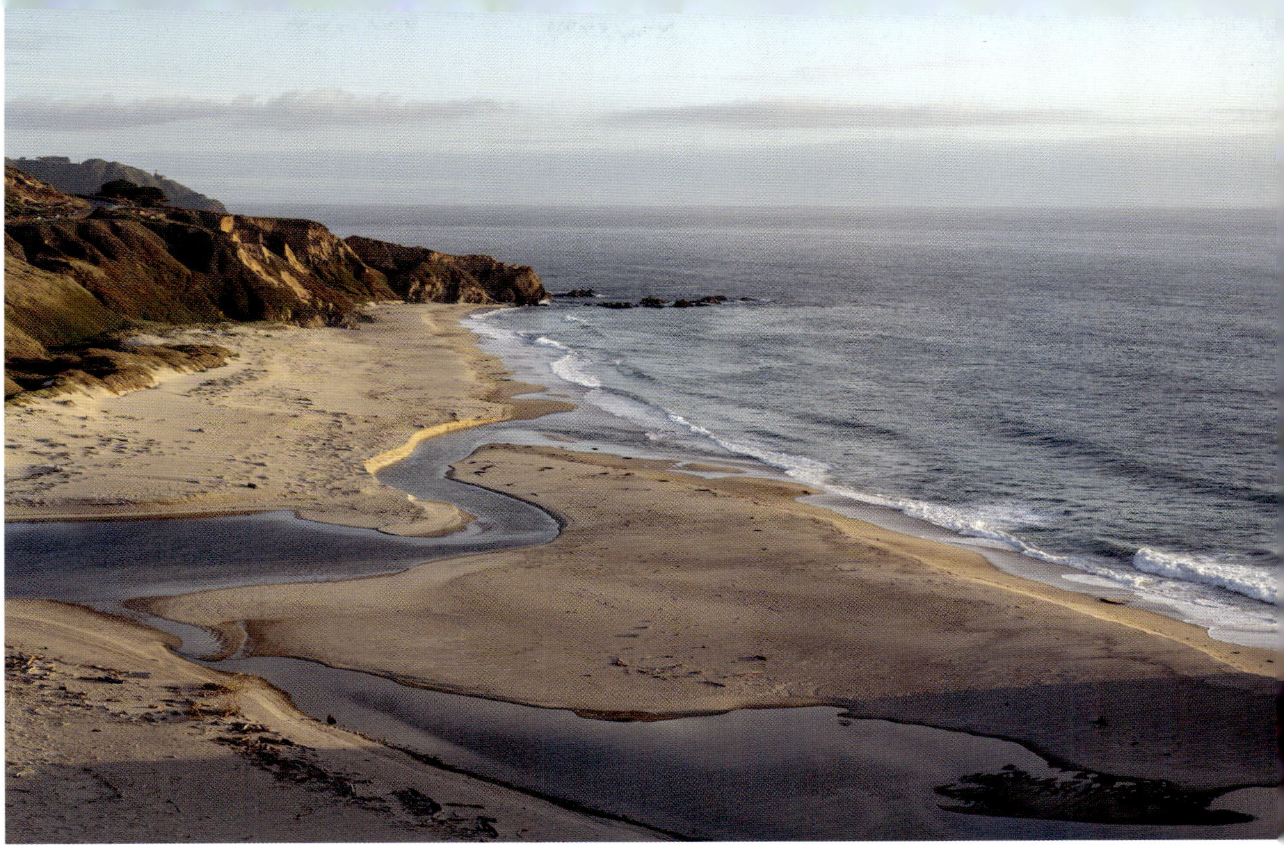

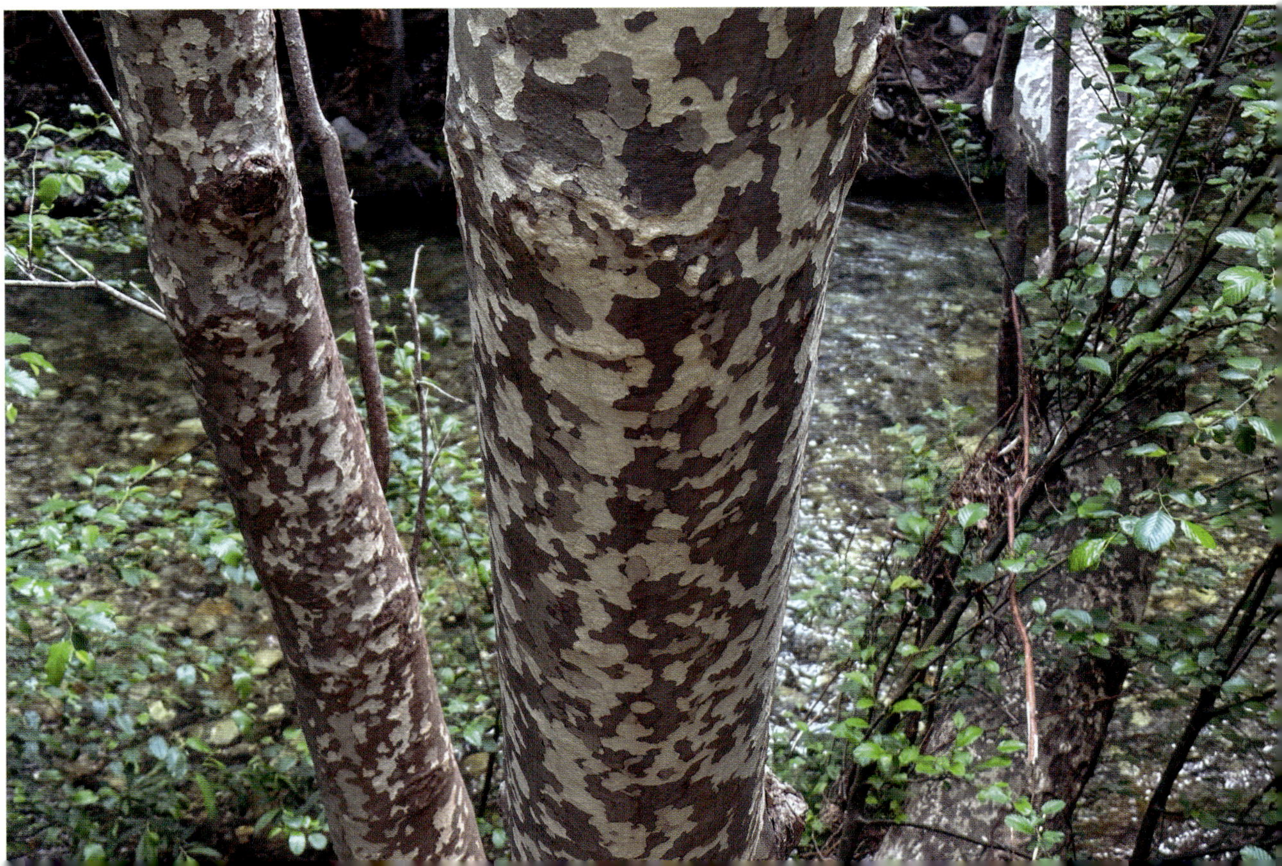

Barbara Kingsolver

"What we lose in our great human exodus from the land is a rooted sense, as deep and intangible as religious faith, of why we need to hold on to the wild and beautiful places that once surrounded us."

From the essay "Knowing Our Place,"
from *Small Wonder: Essays*

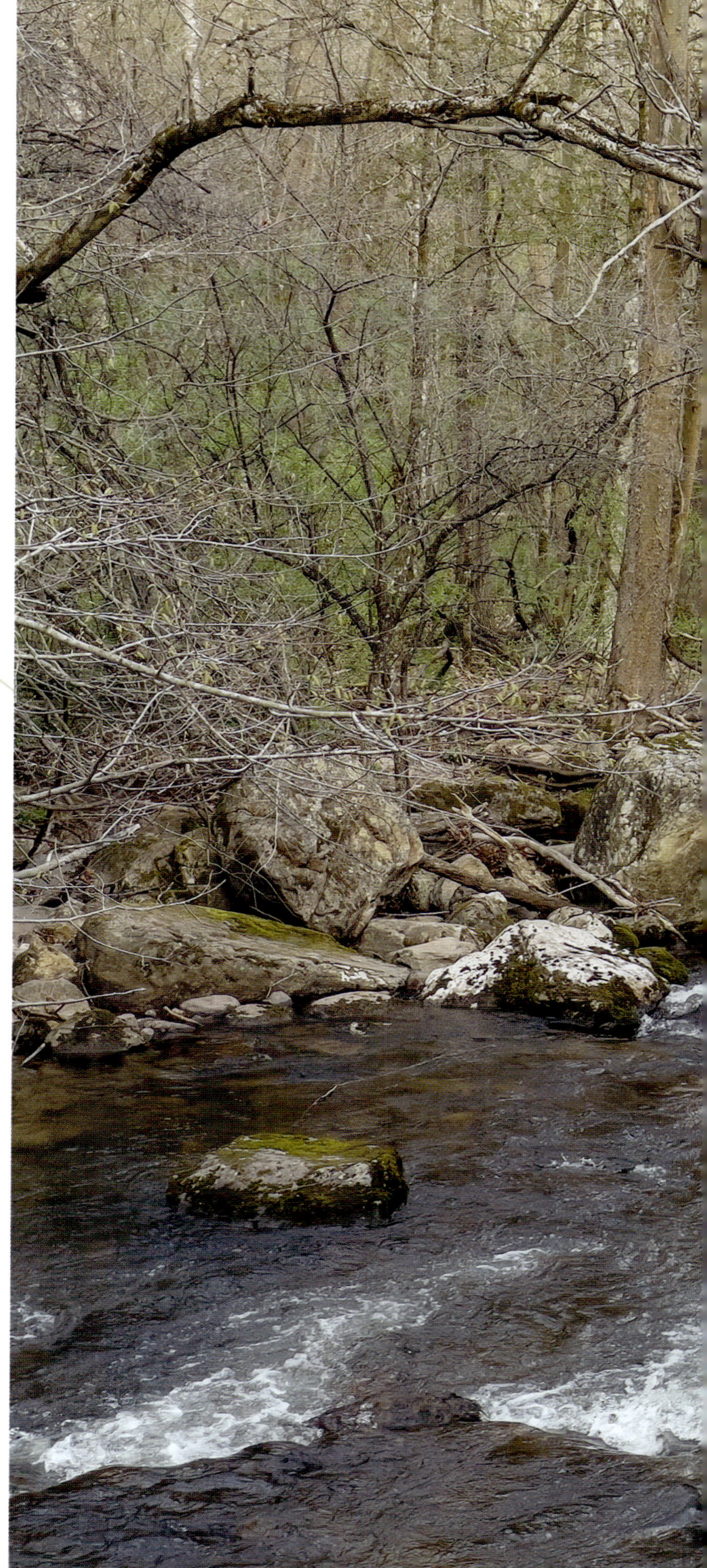

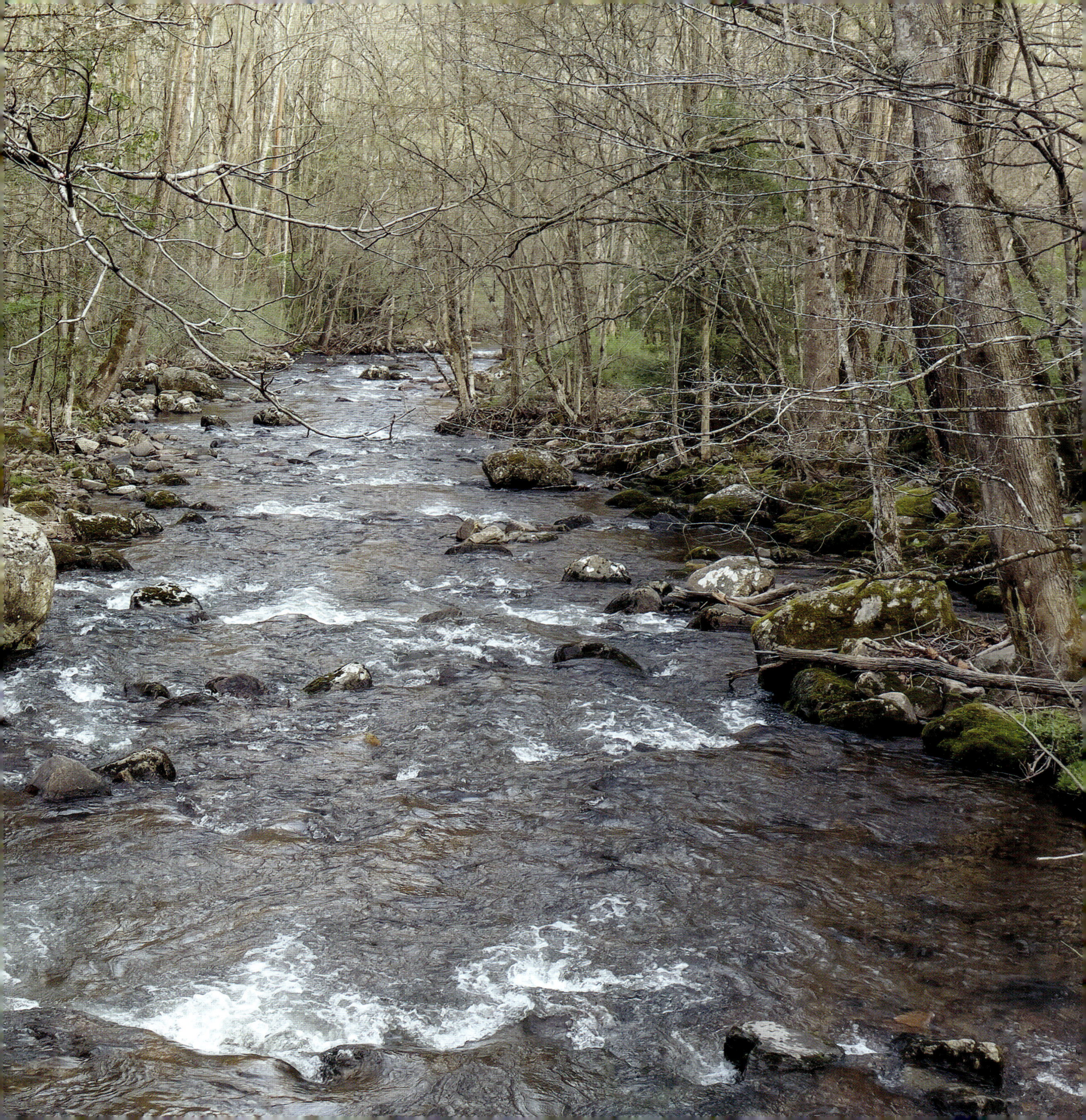

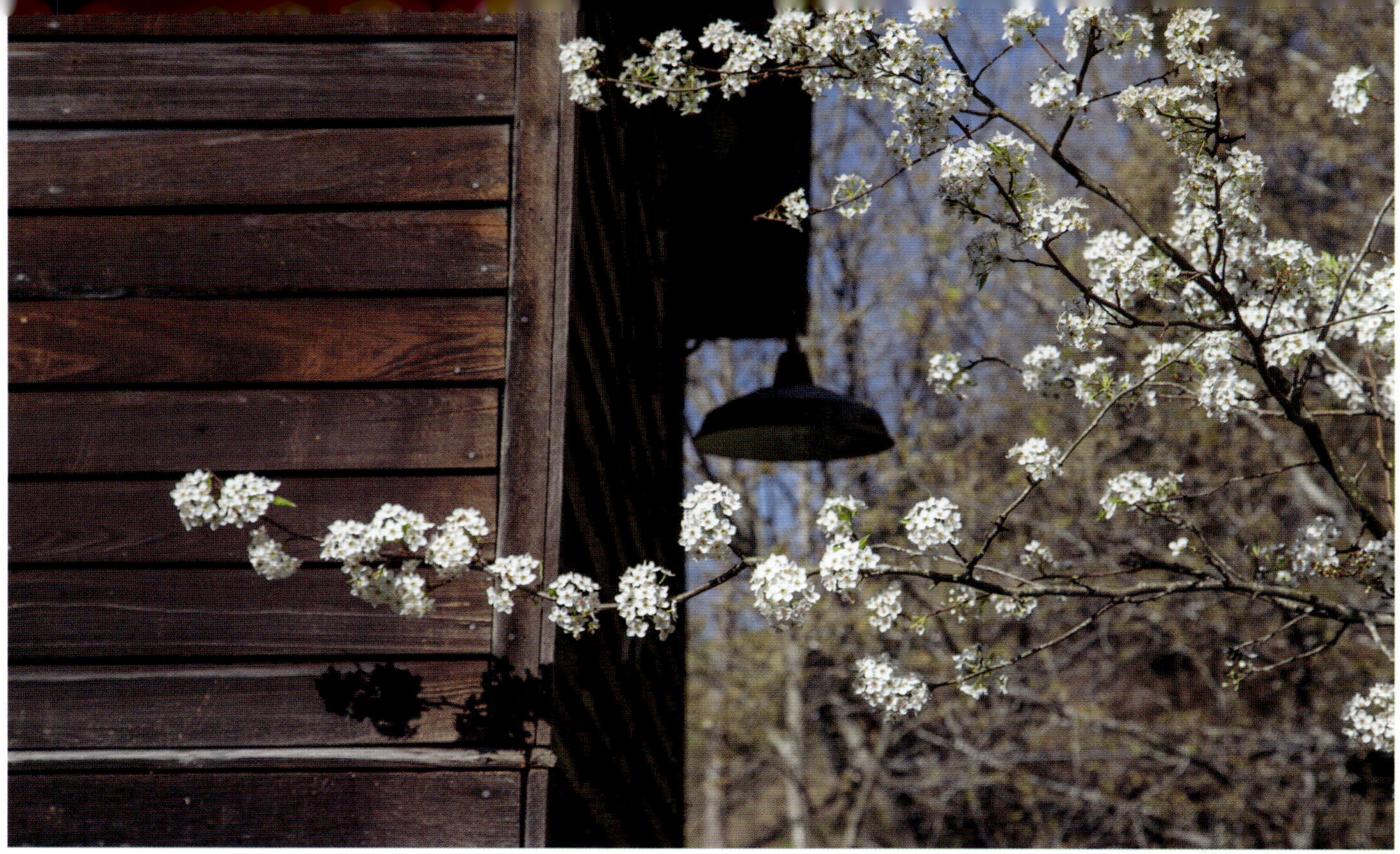

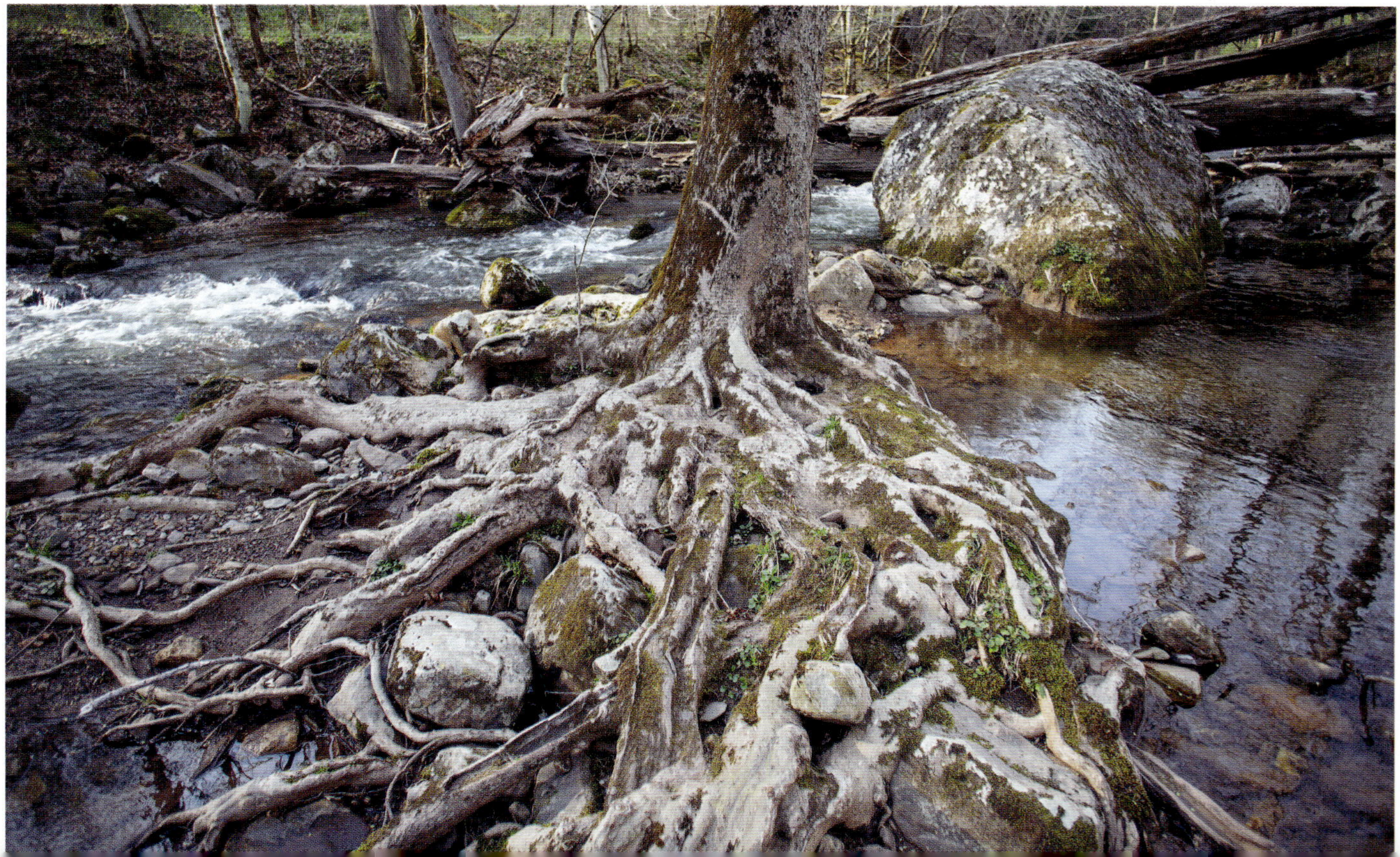

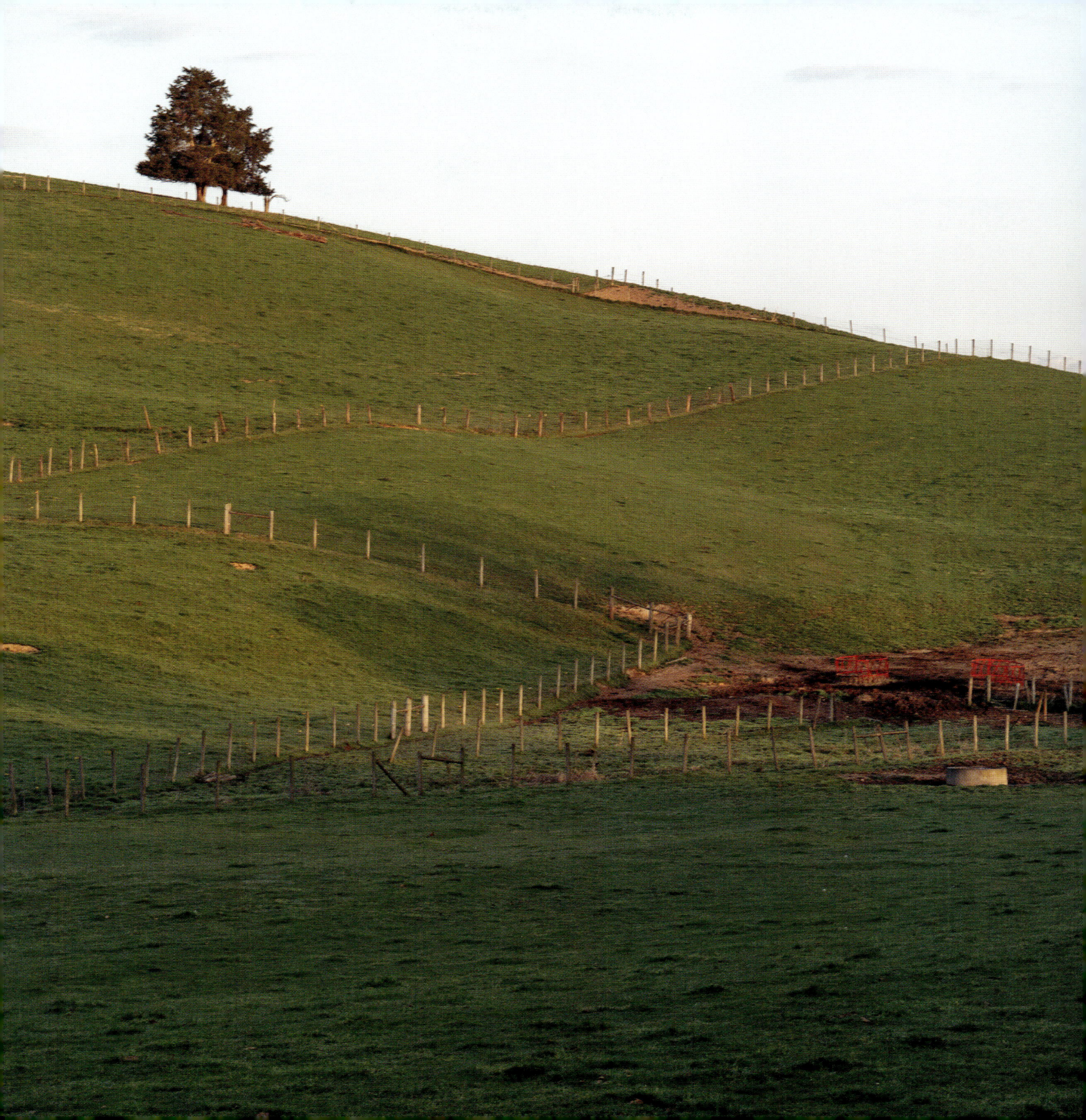

J. Drew Lanham

SOUTH CAROLINA

"Our responsibility is to pass something on to those coming after. As young people of color reconnect with what so many of their ancestors knew—that our connections to the land run deep, like the taproots of mighty oaks; that the land renews and sustains us— maybe things will begin to change."

From *The Home Place: Memoirs of a Colored Man's Love Affair with Nature*

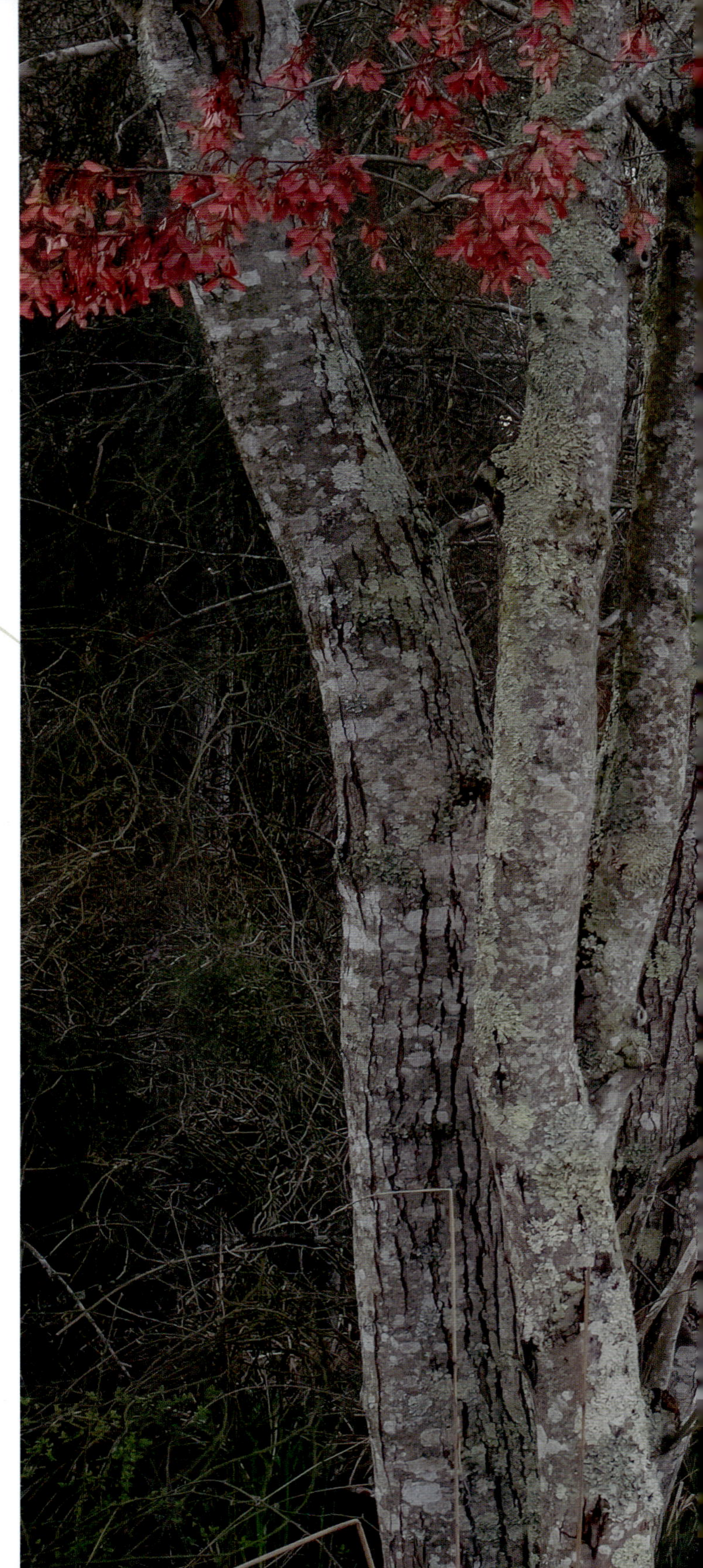

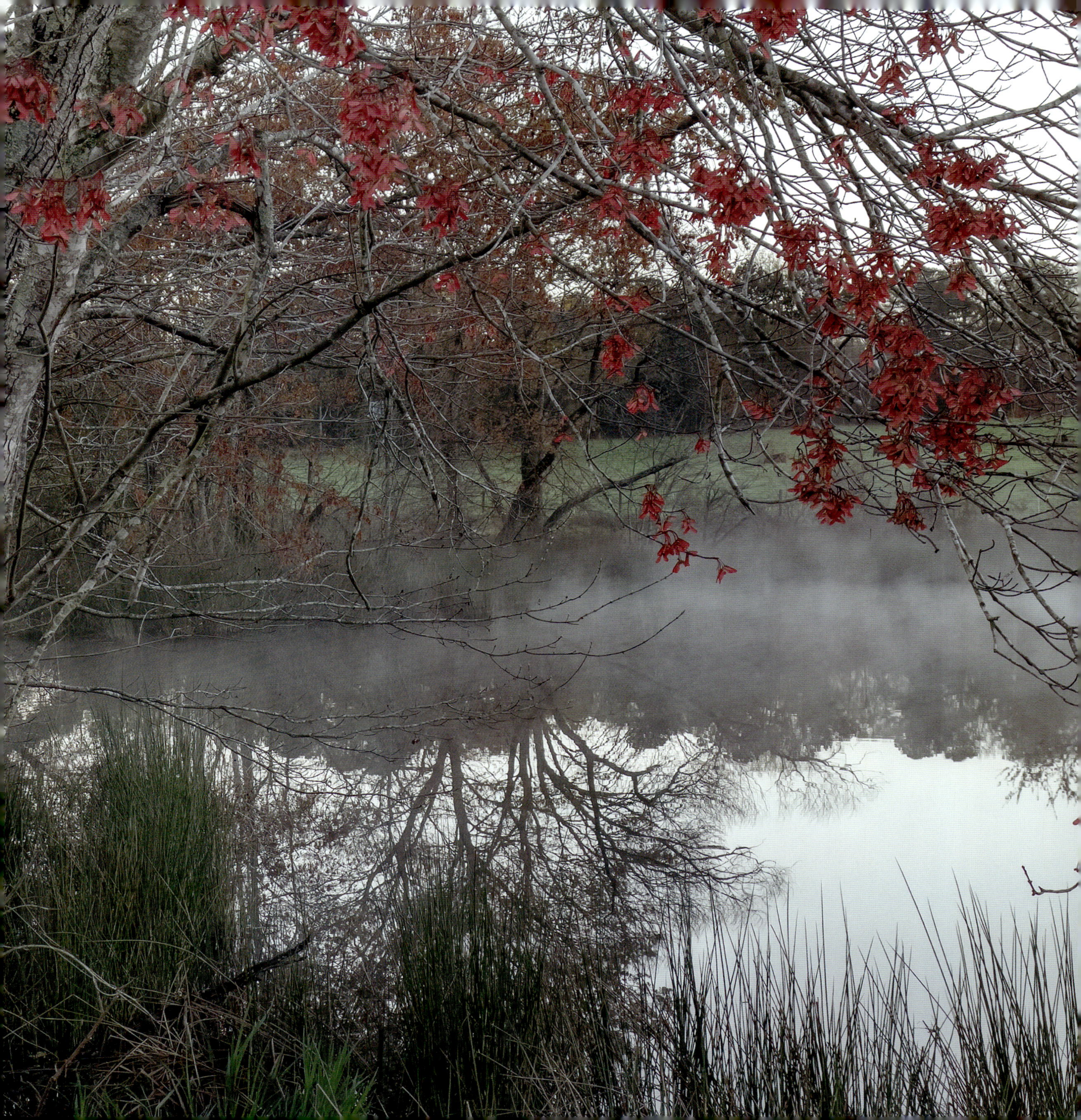

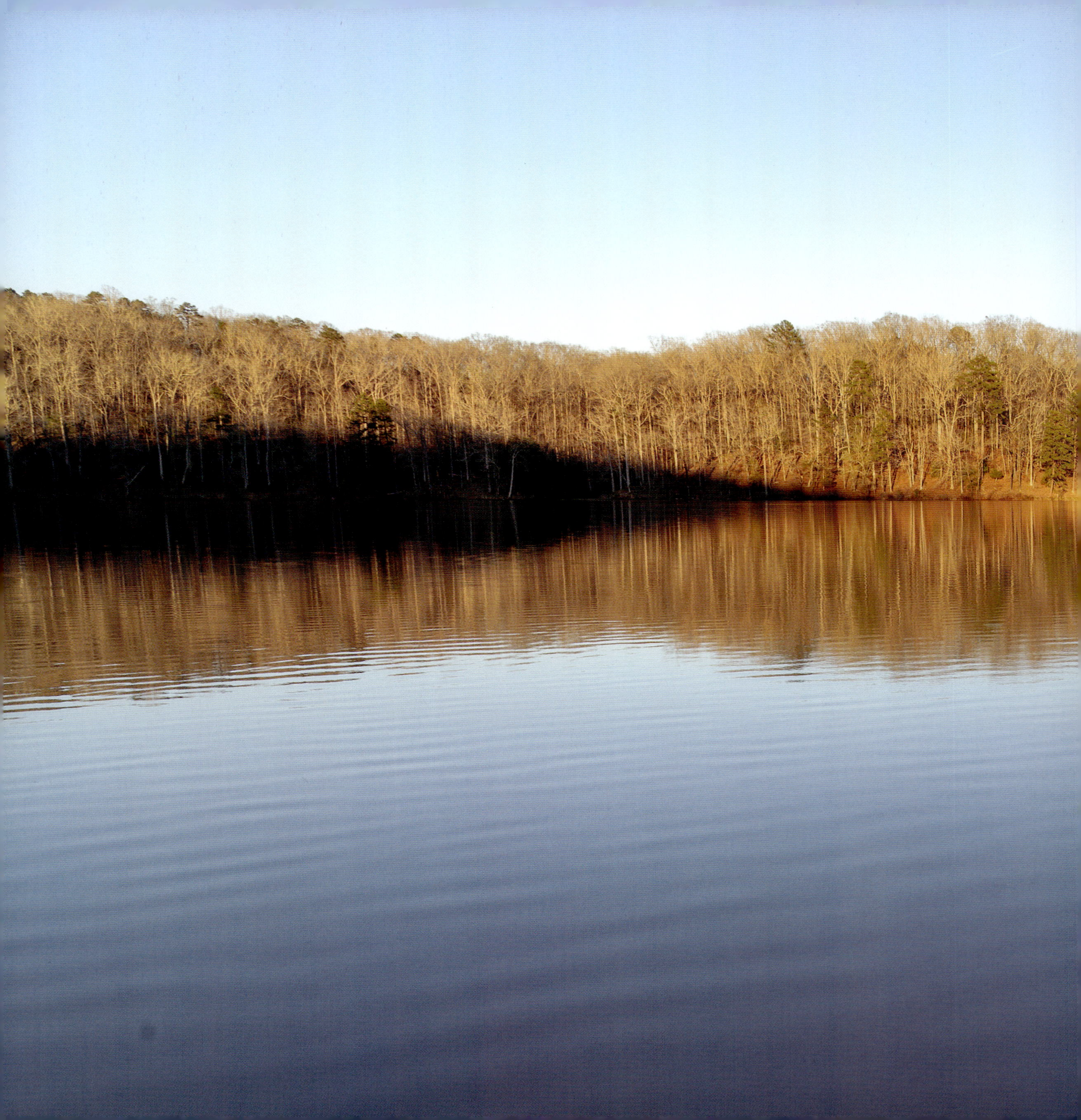

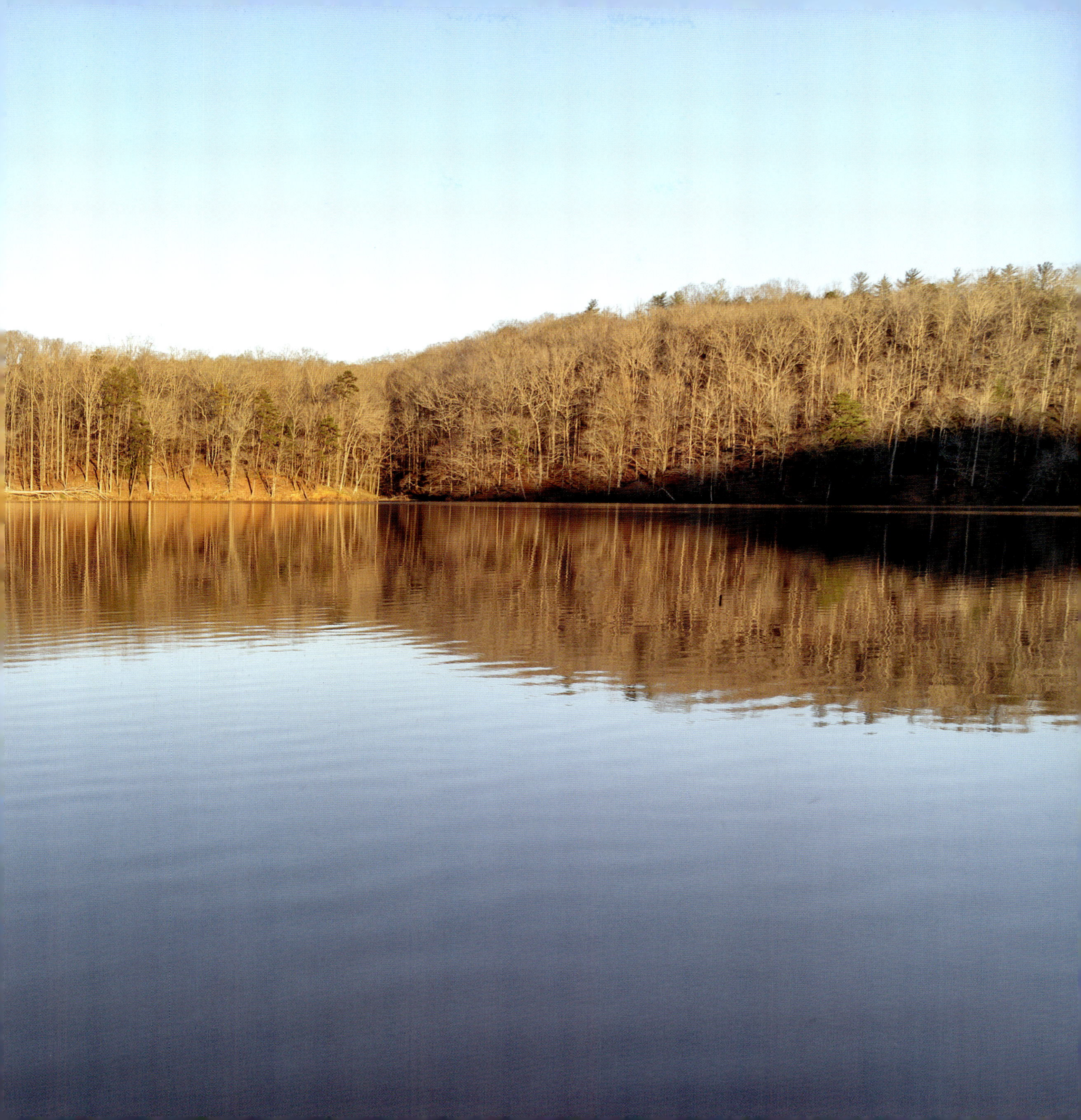

Aldo Leopold

"Acts of creation are ordinarily reserved for gods
and poets, but humbler folk may circumvent this
restriction if they know how. To plant a pine, for
example, one need be neither god nor poet; one
need only own a shovel. By virtue of this curious
loophole in the rules, any clodhopper may say:
Let there be a tree—and there will be one."

From *A Sand County Almanac:
And Sketches Here and There*

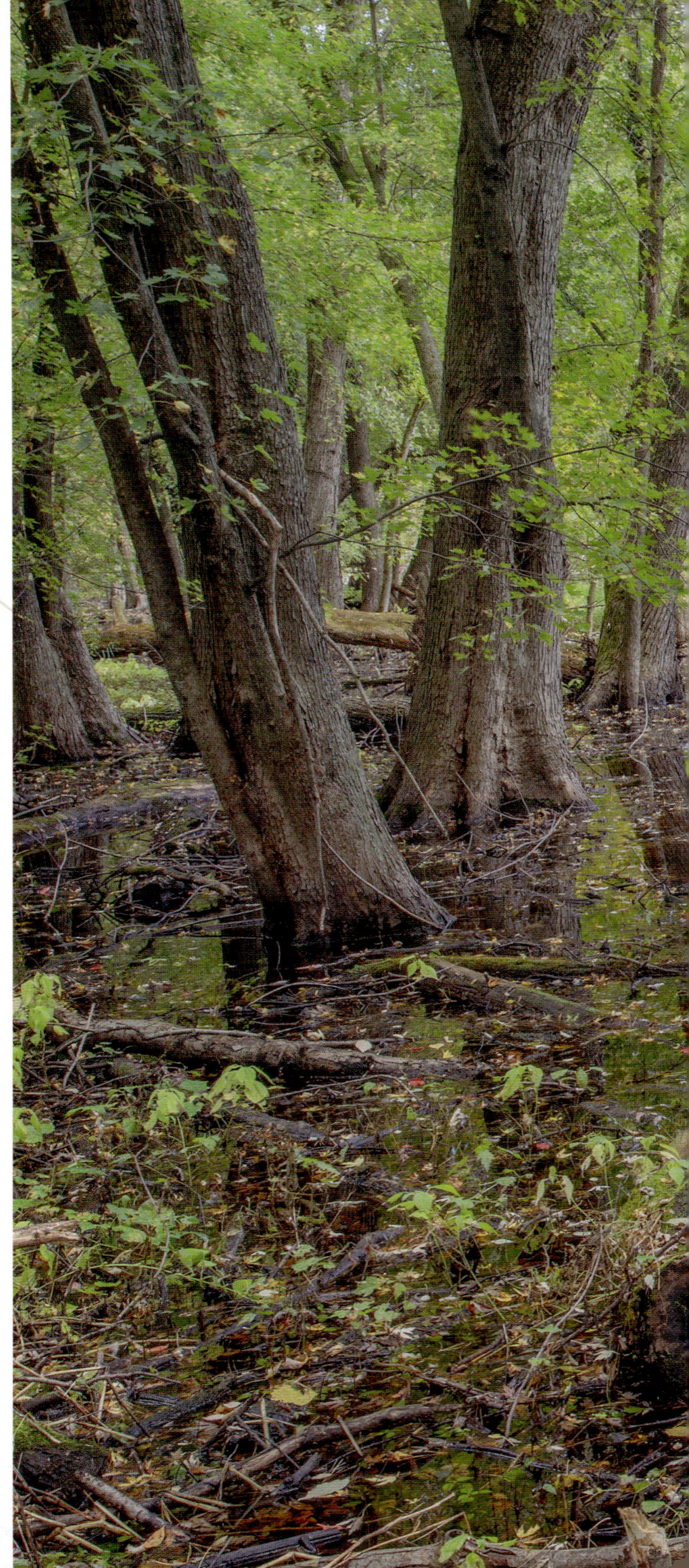

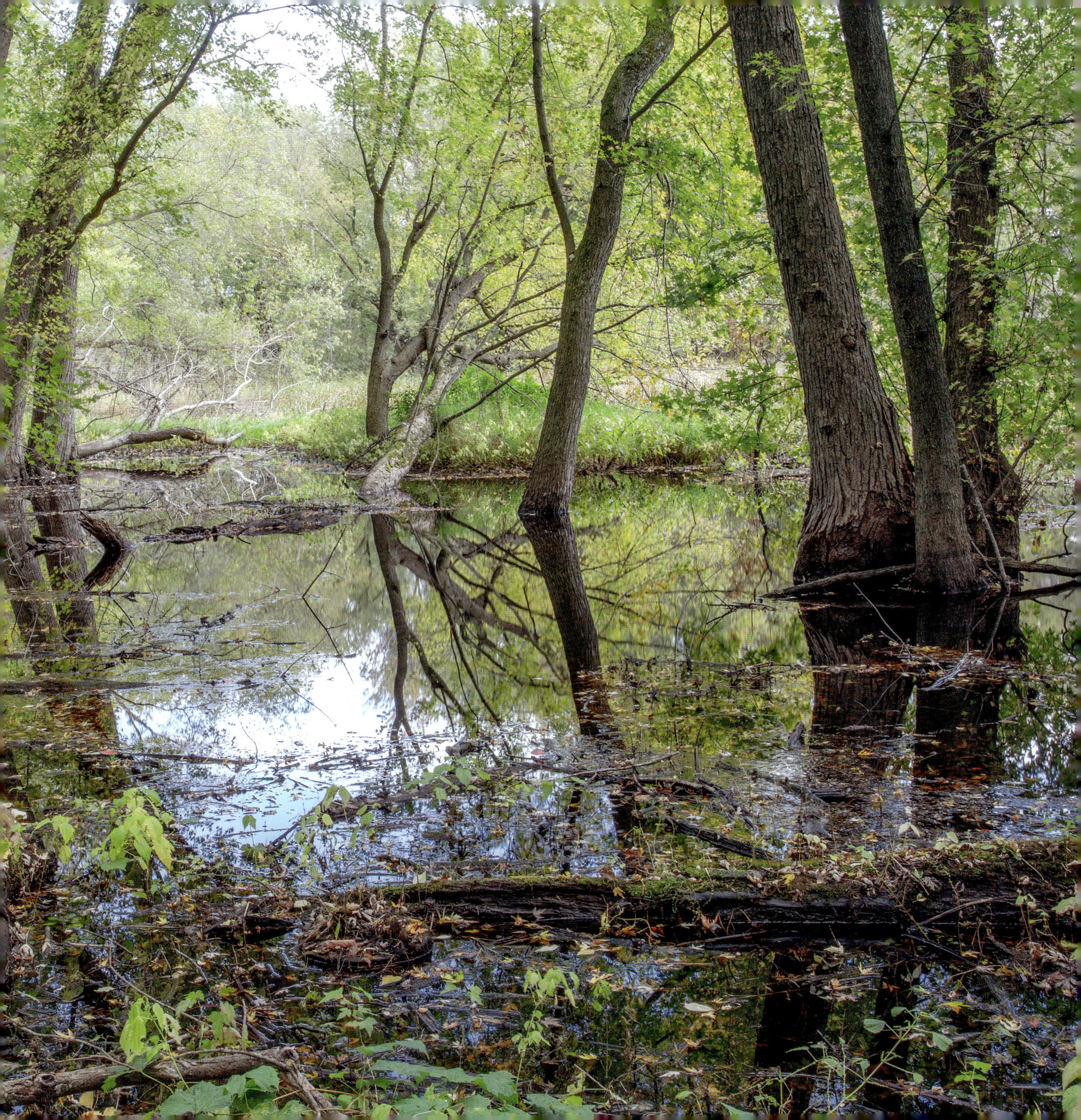

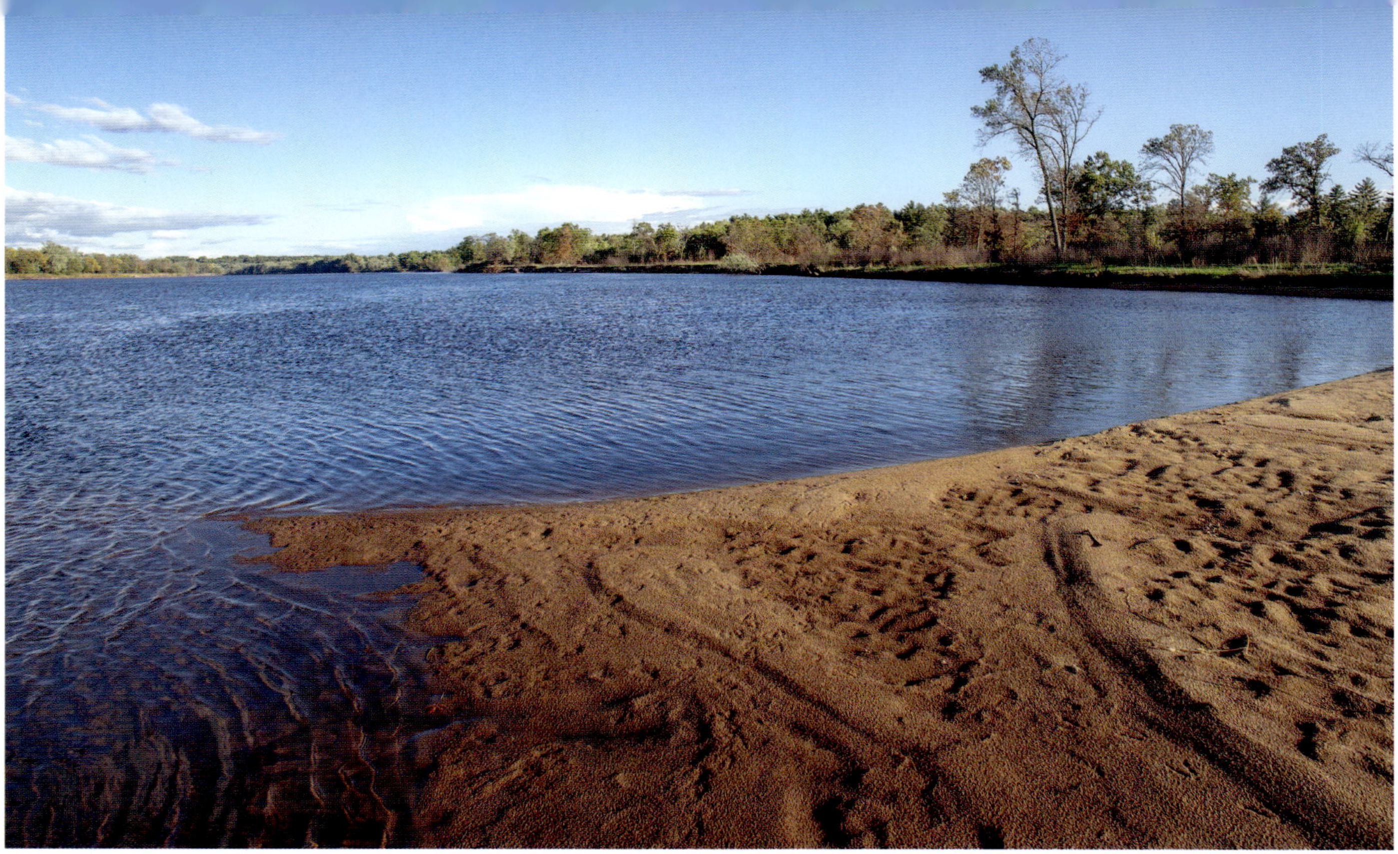

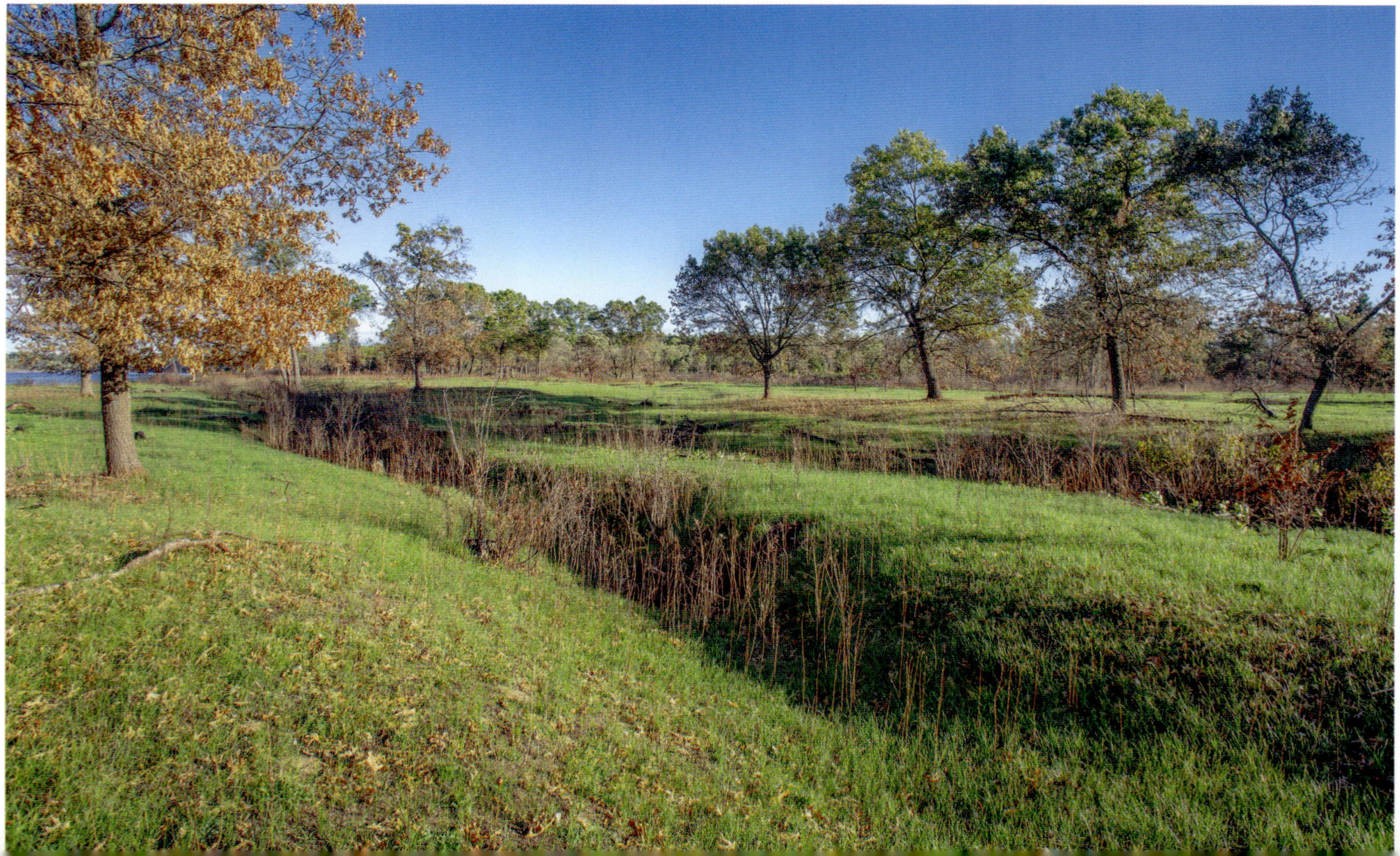

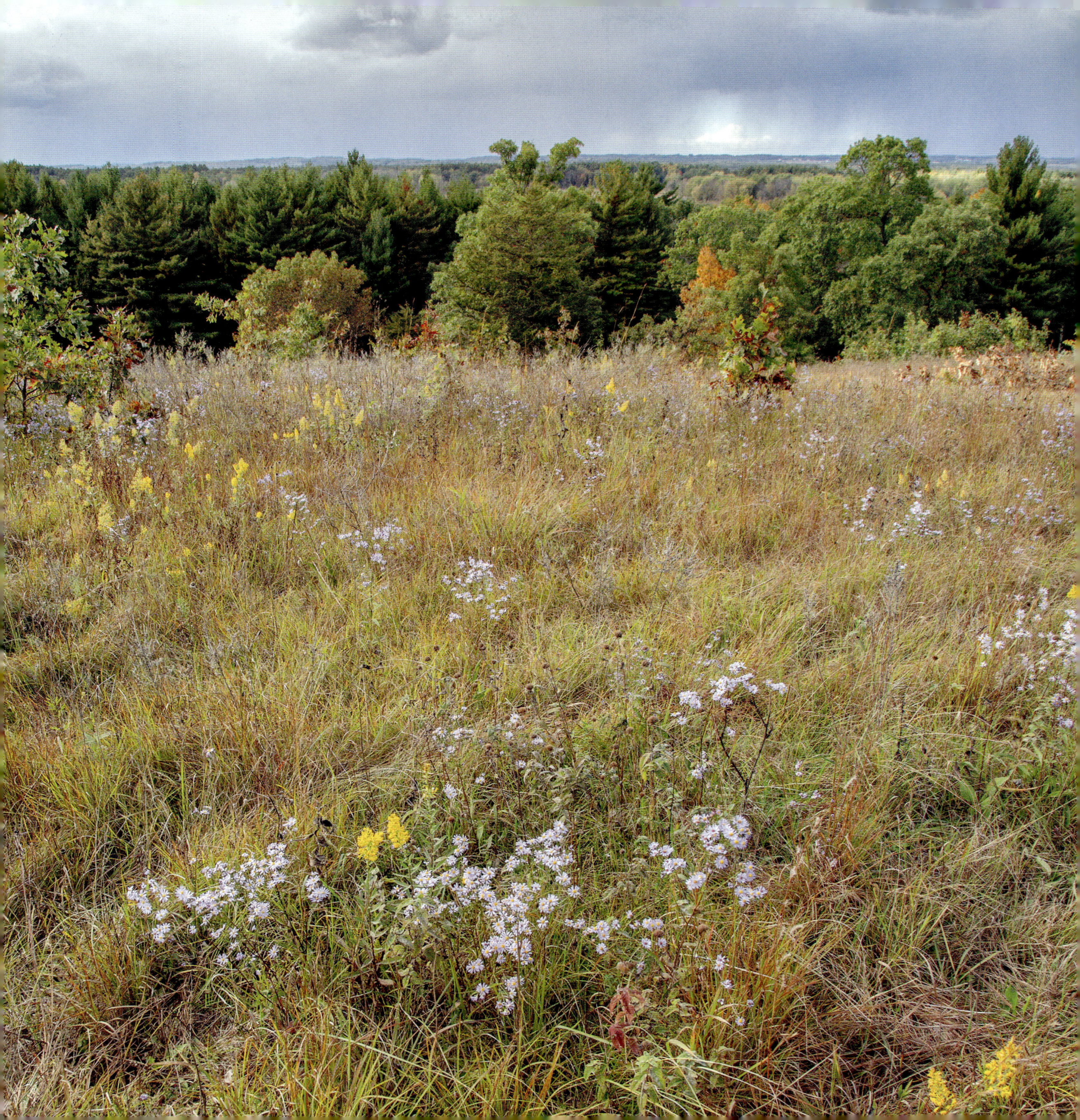

Ada Limón

KENTUCKY

"Look, we are not unspectacular things.

        We've come this far, survived this much. What

would happen if we decided to survive more?

        To love harder?"

From the poem "Dead Stars,"
from *The Carrying: Poems*

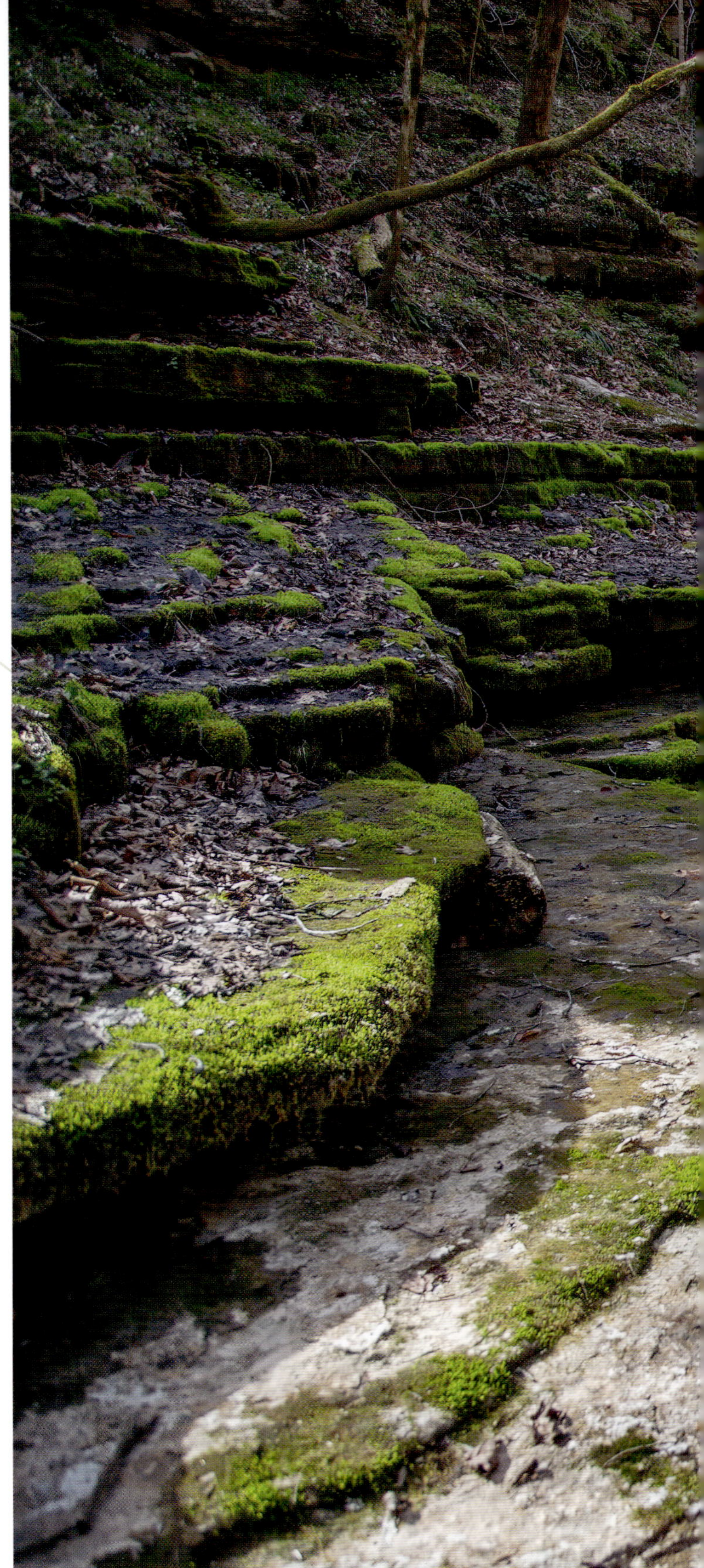

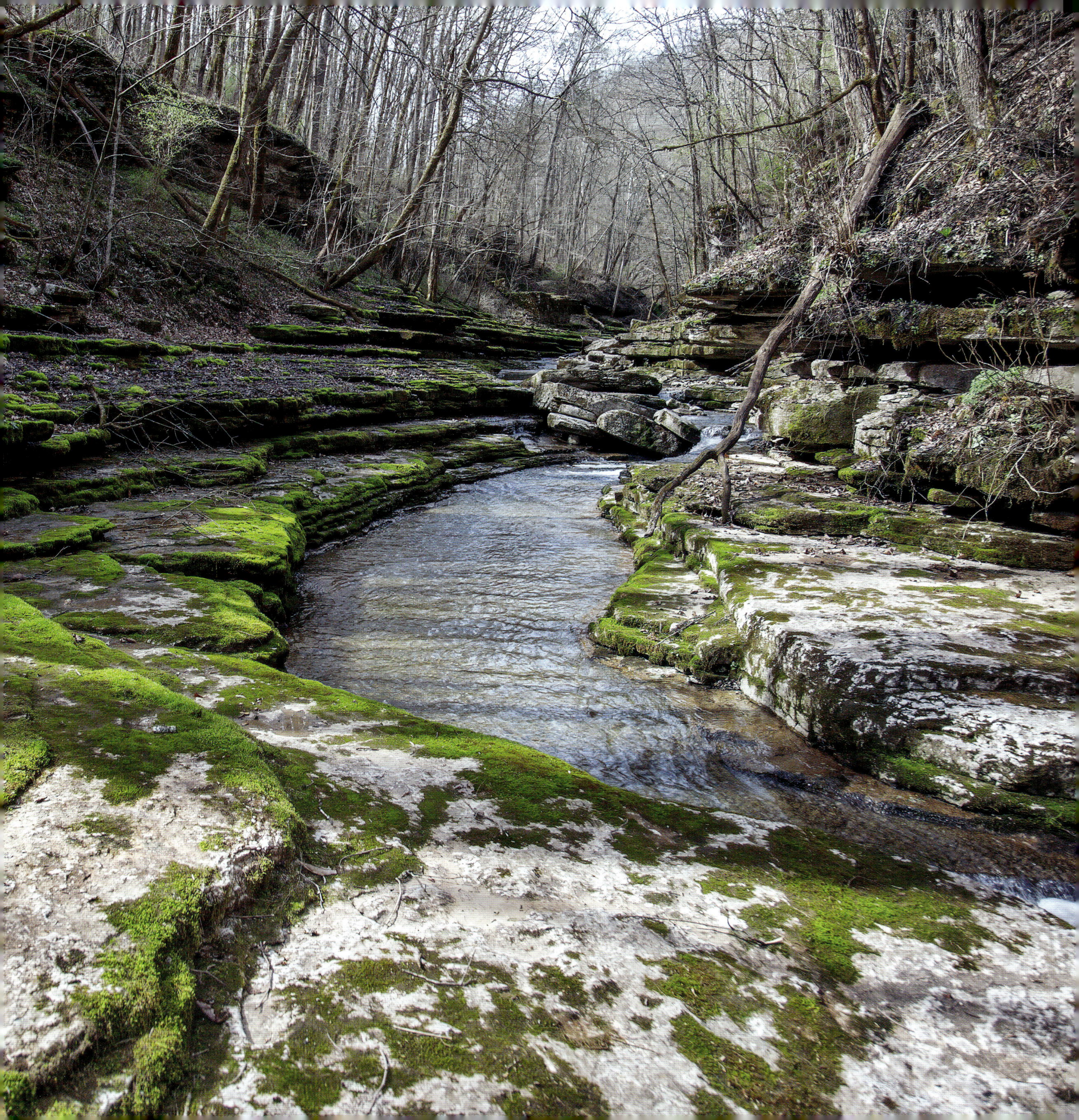

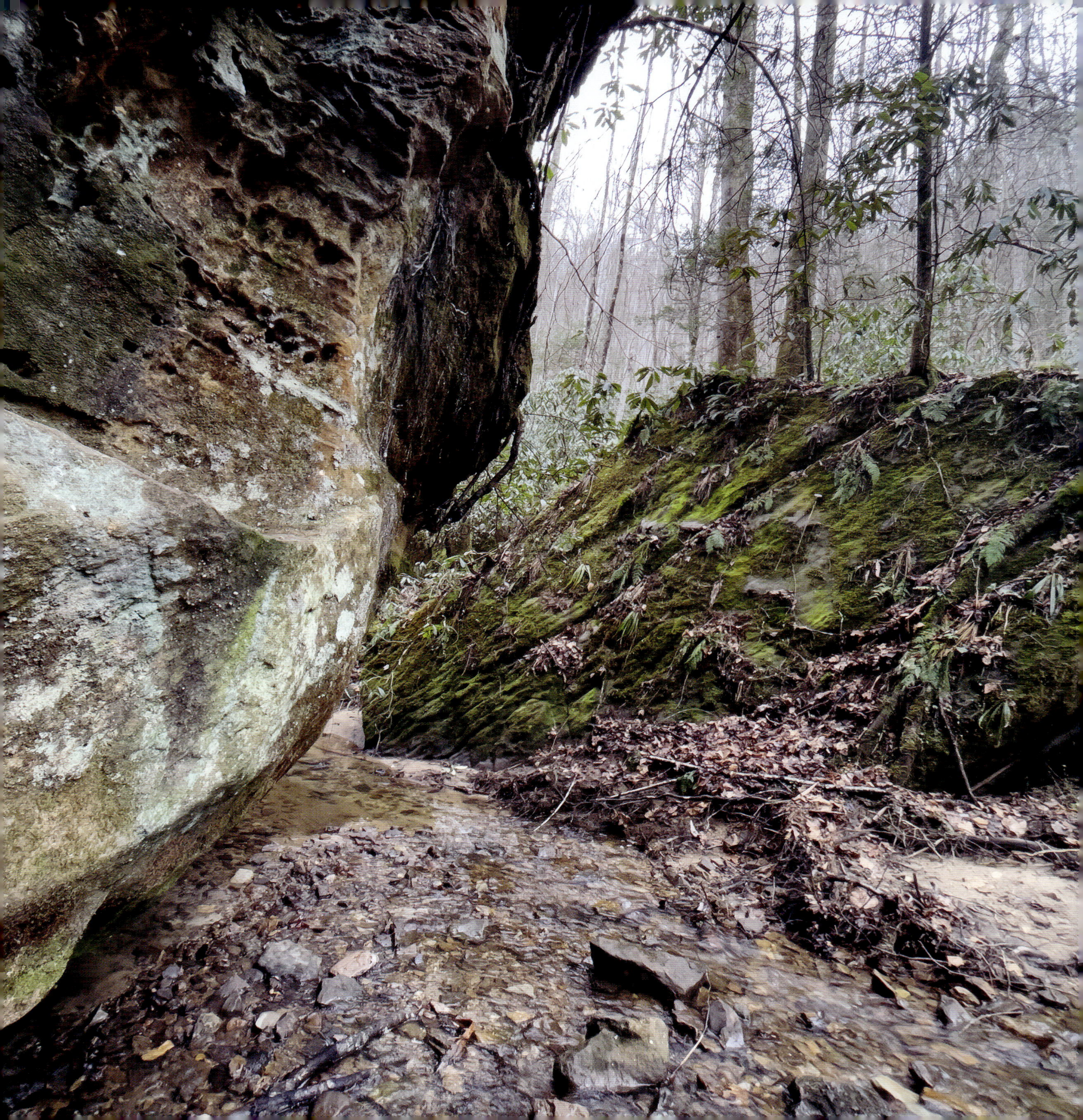

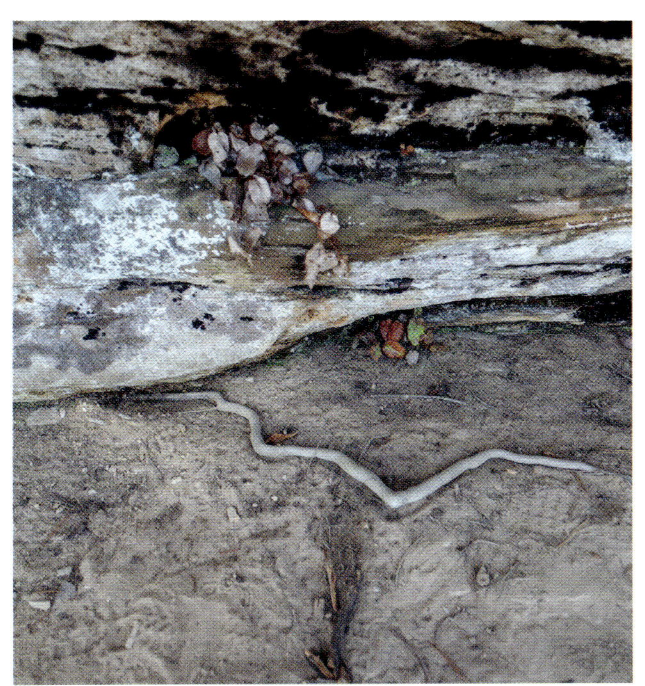
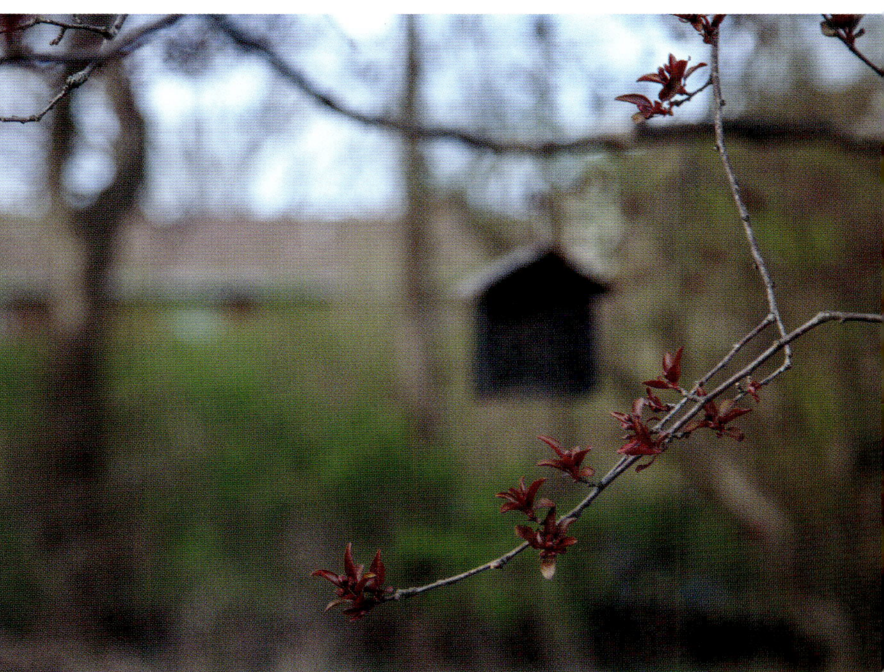

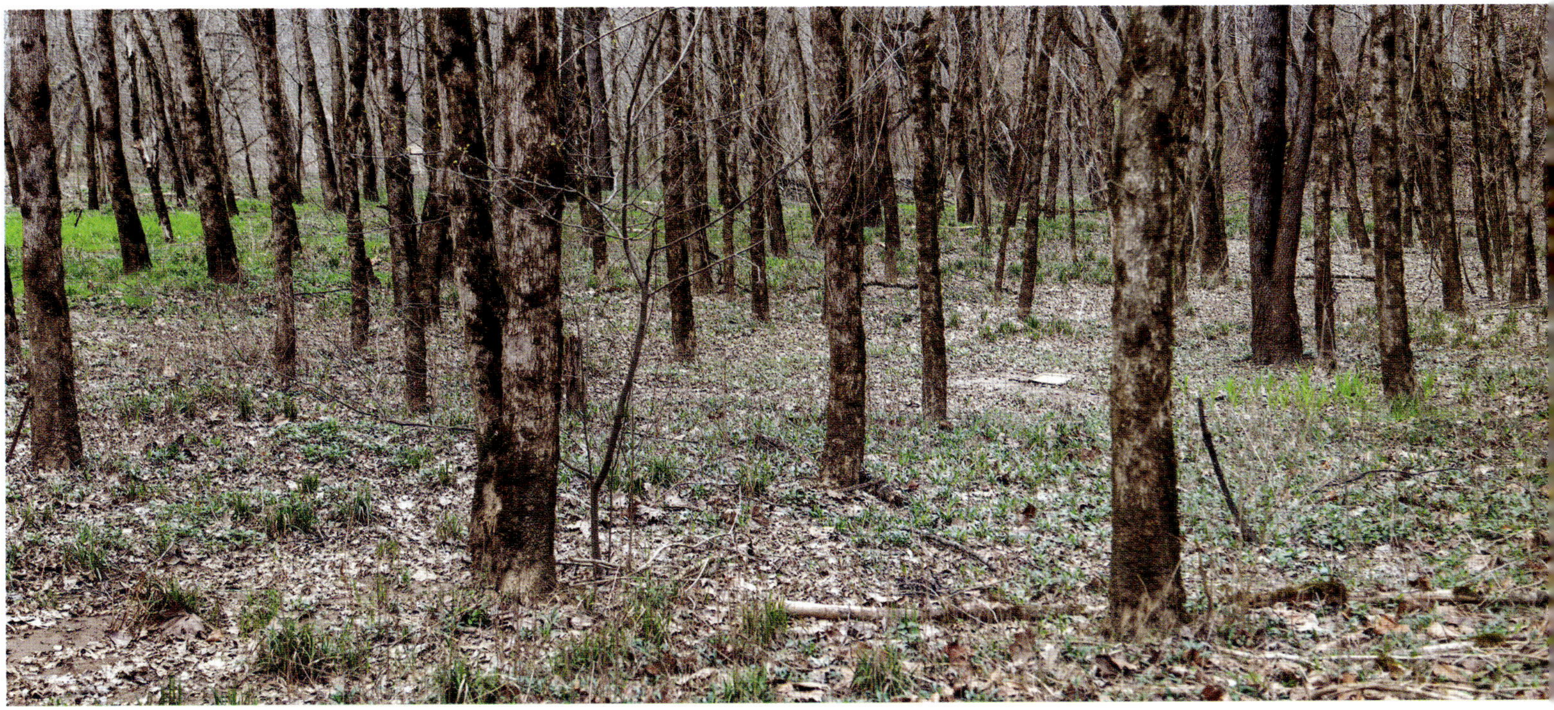

Barry Lopez

OREGON

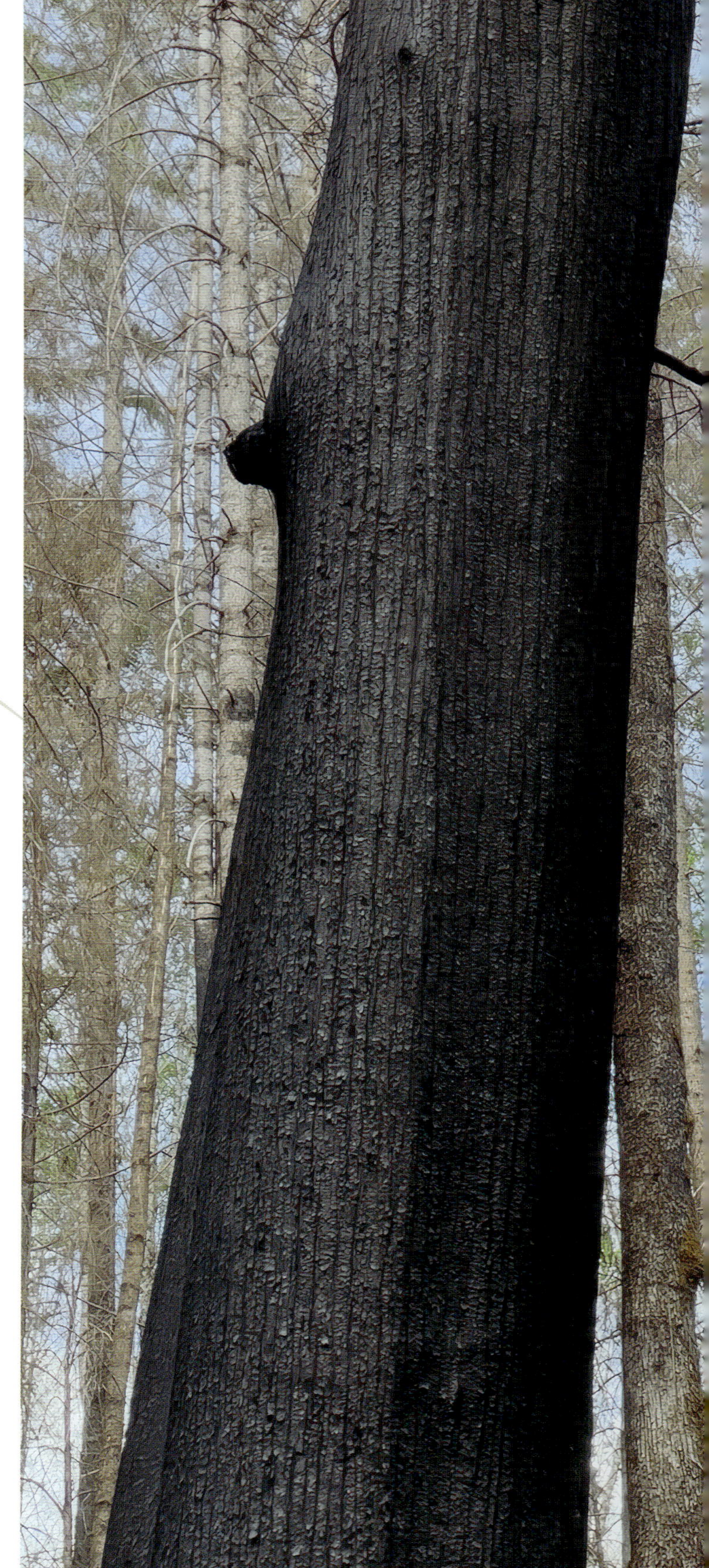

"Only the misled can insist that heaven awaits

the righteous while they watch the fires on Earth

consume the only heaven we have ever known."

From the essay "Love in a Time of Terror,"
from *Embrace Fearlessly the Burning World: Essays*

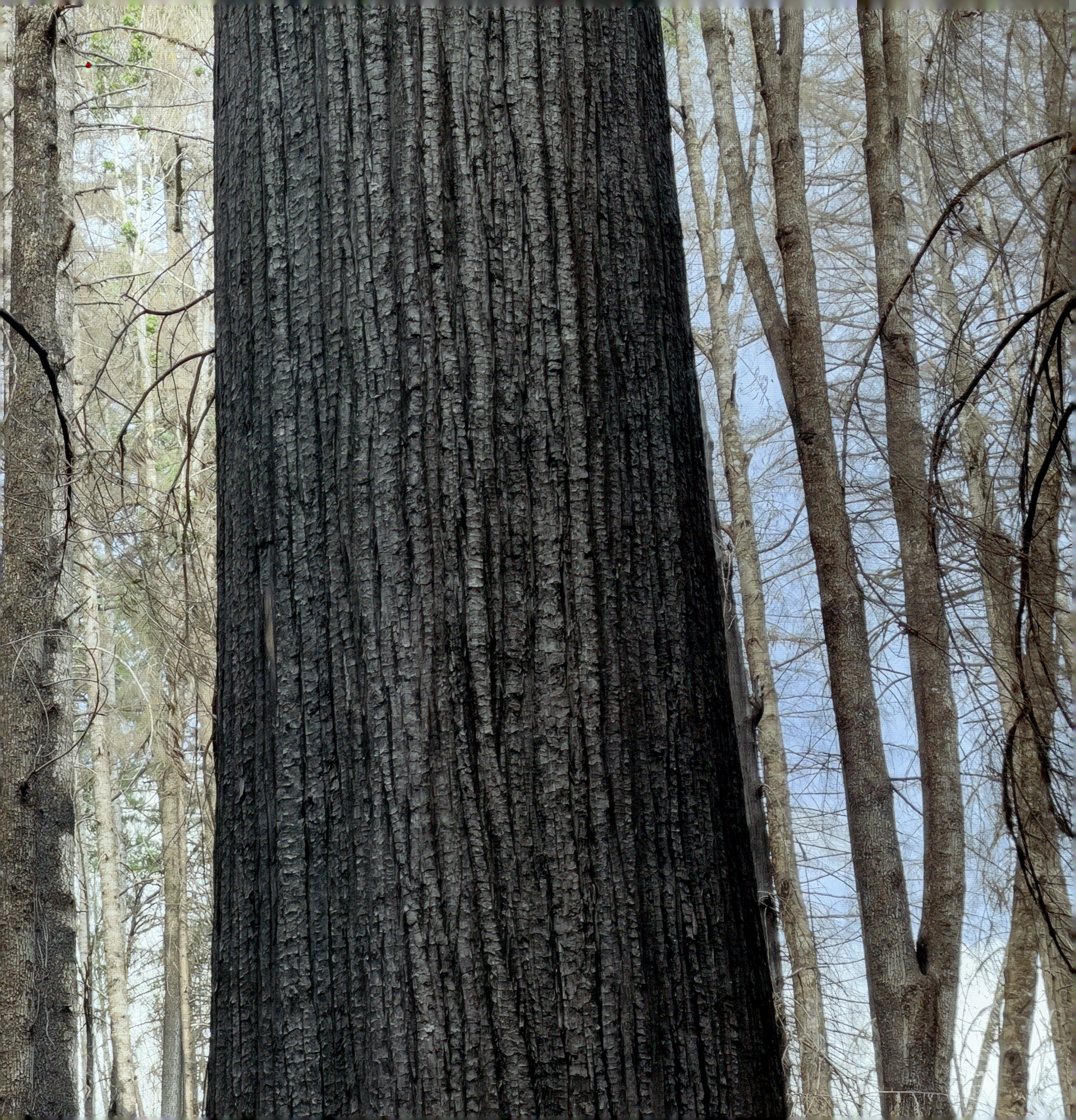

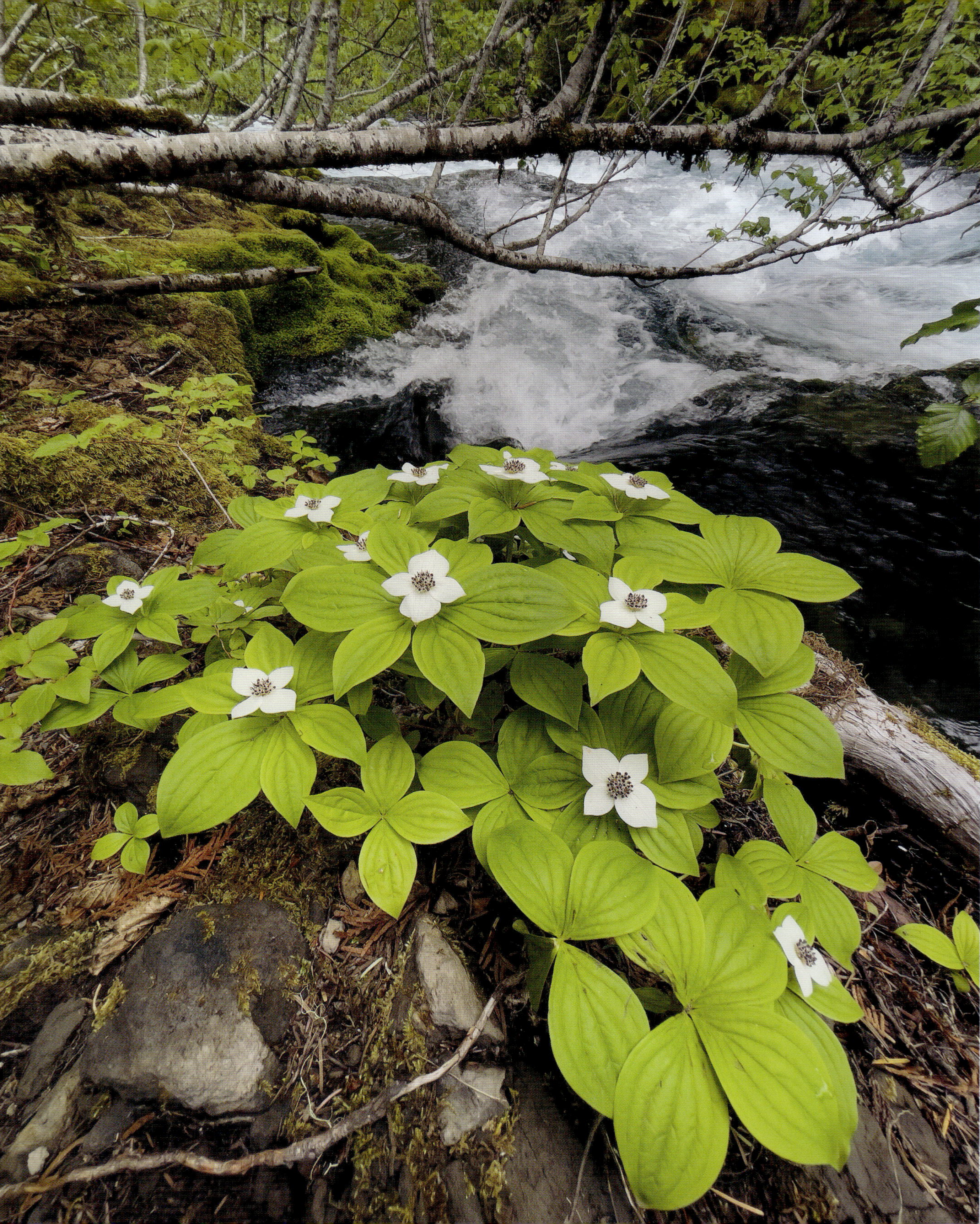

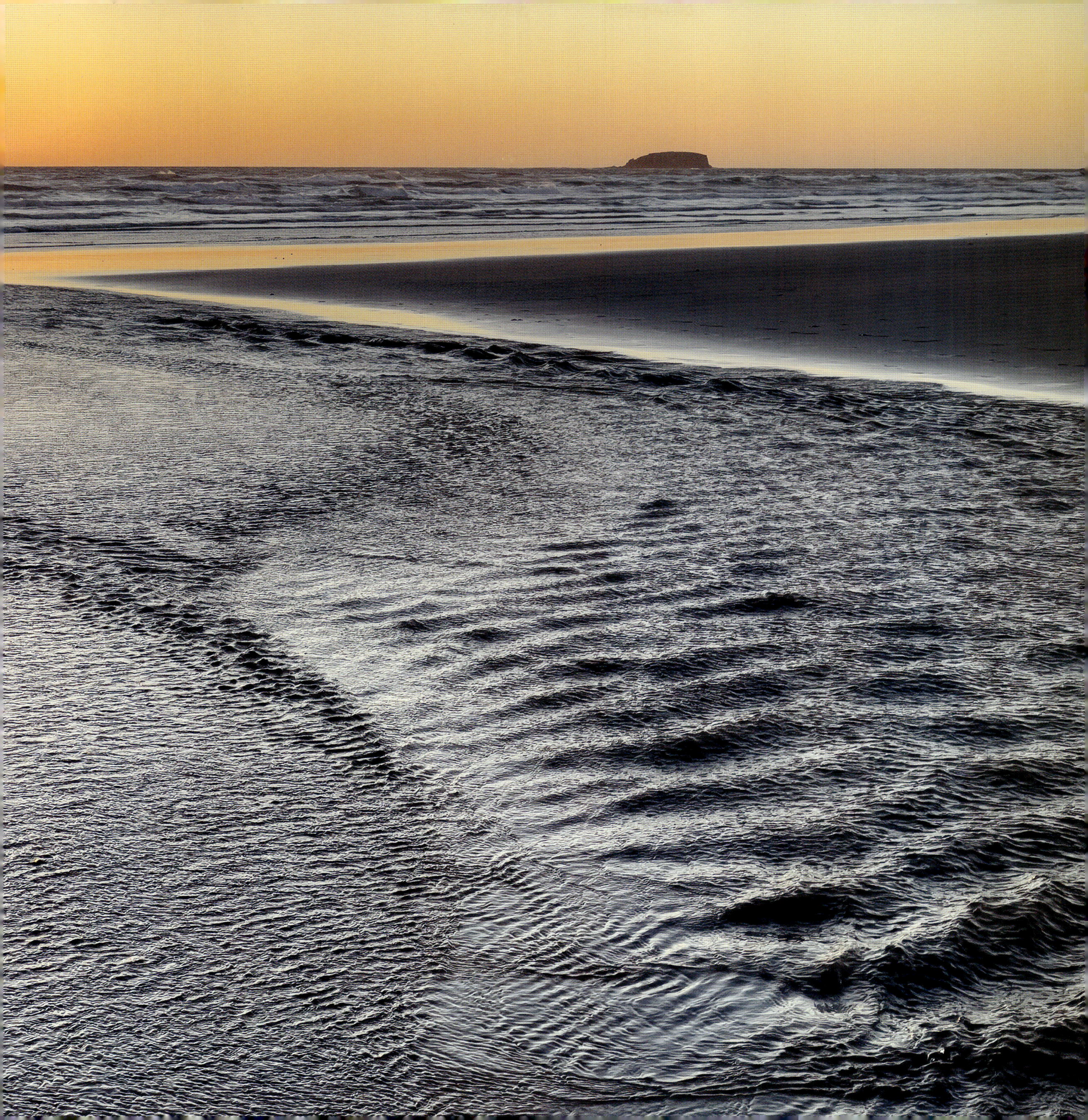

Peter Matthiessen

N E W   Y O R K

"The great stillness in these landscapes that once
made me restless seeps into me day by day, and
with it the unreasonable feeling that I have found
what I was searching for without ever having
discovered what it was."

From *The Tree Where Man Was Born*

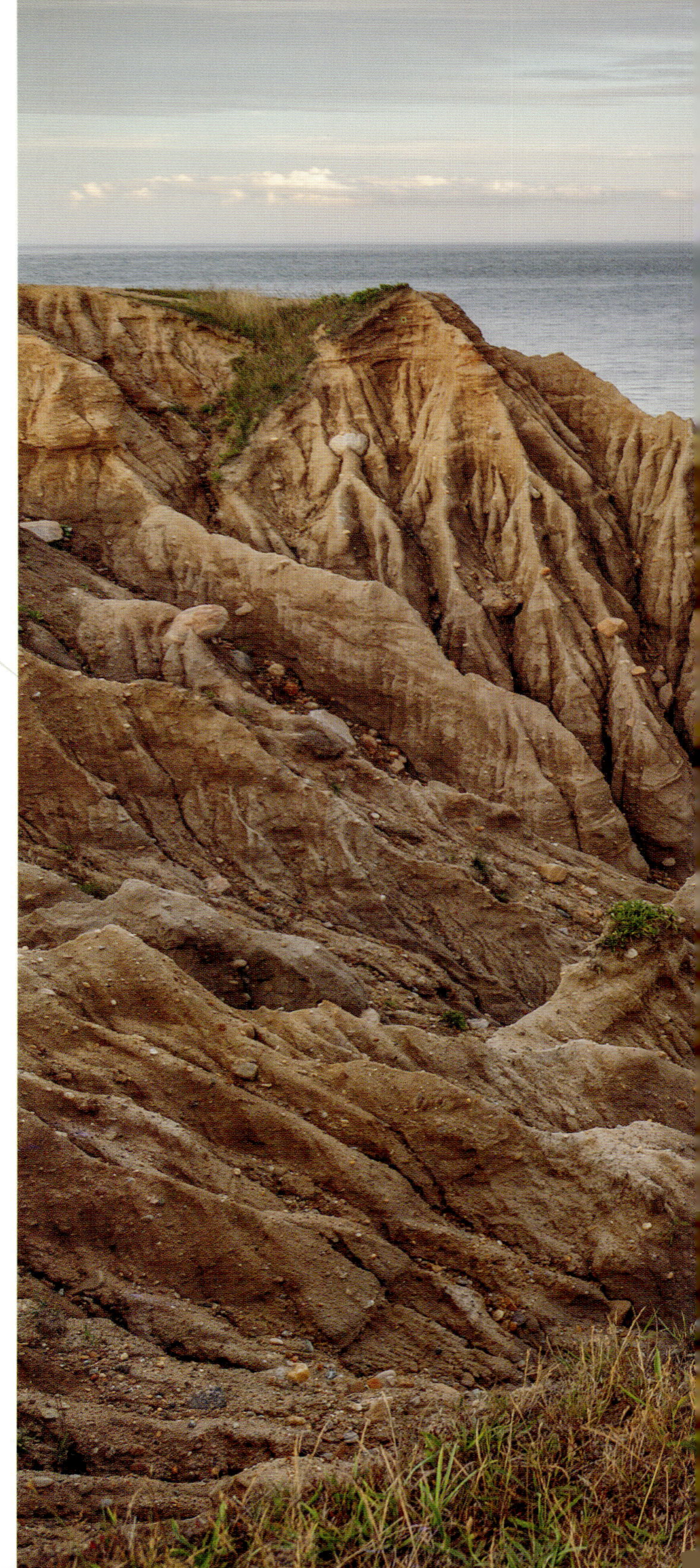

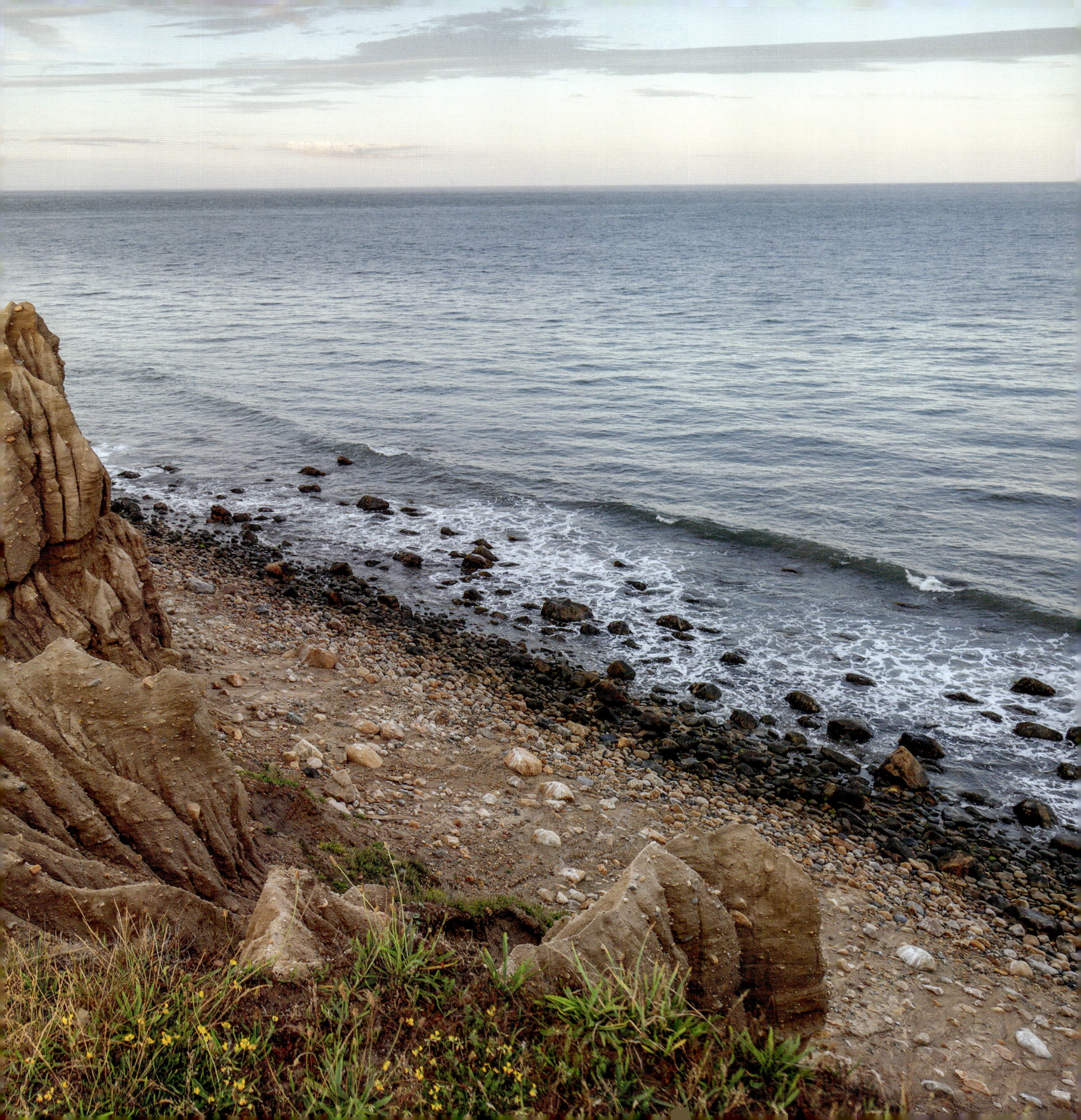

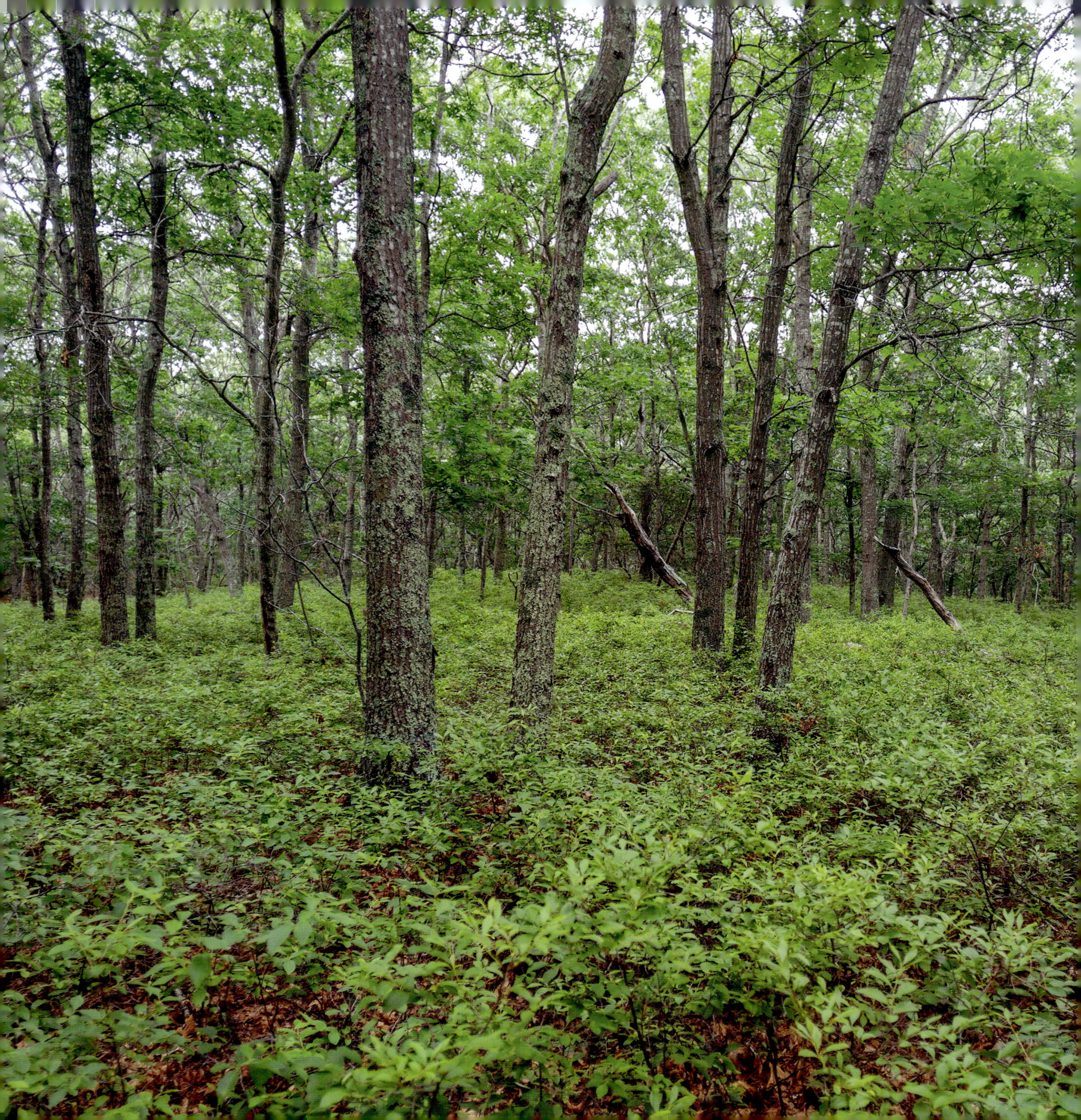

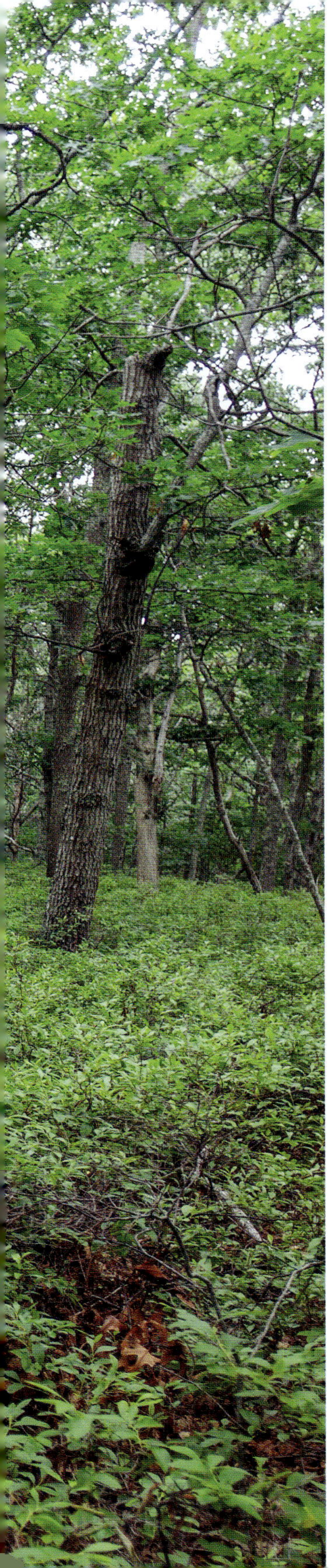

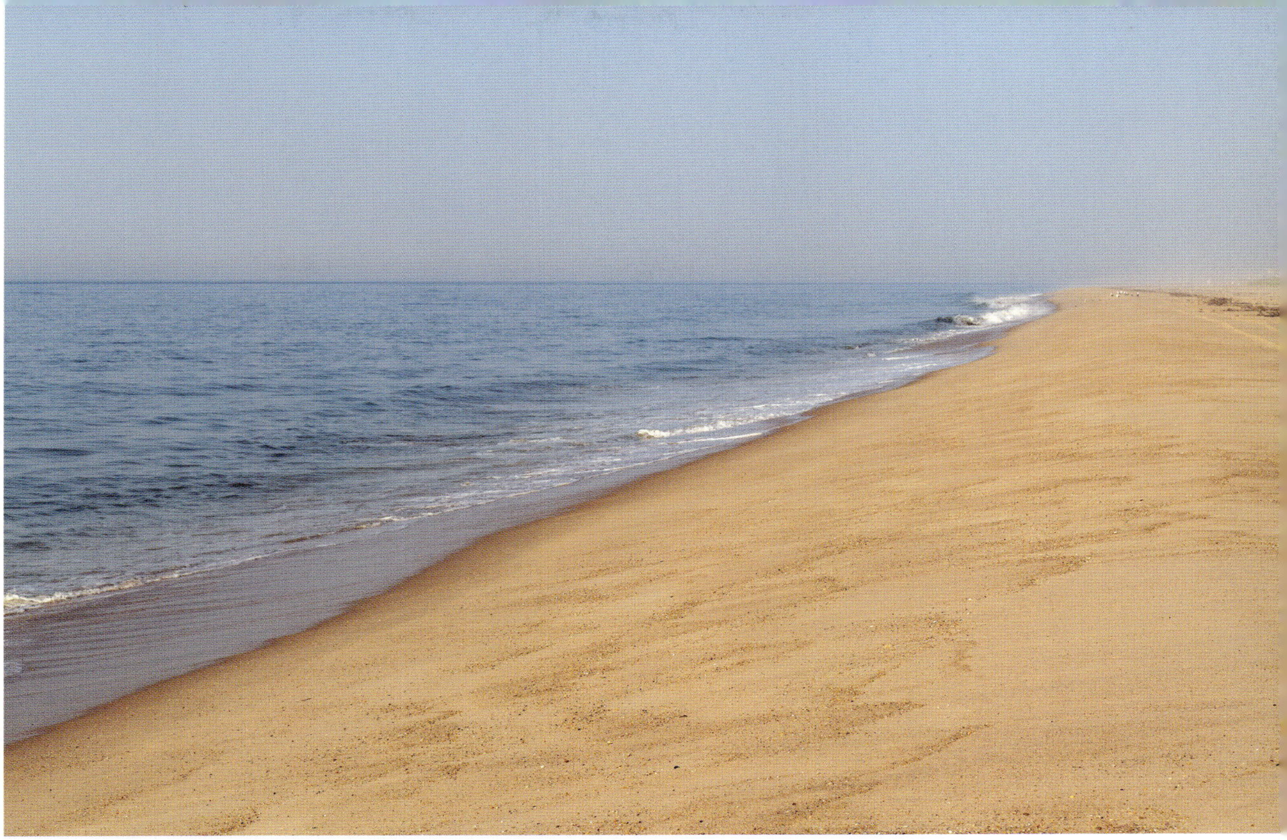

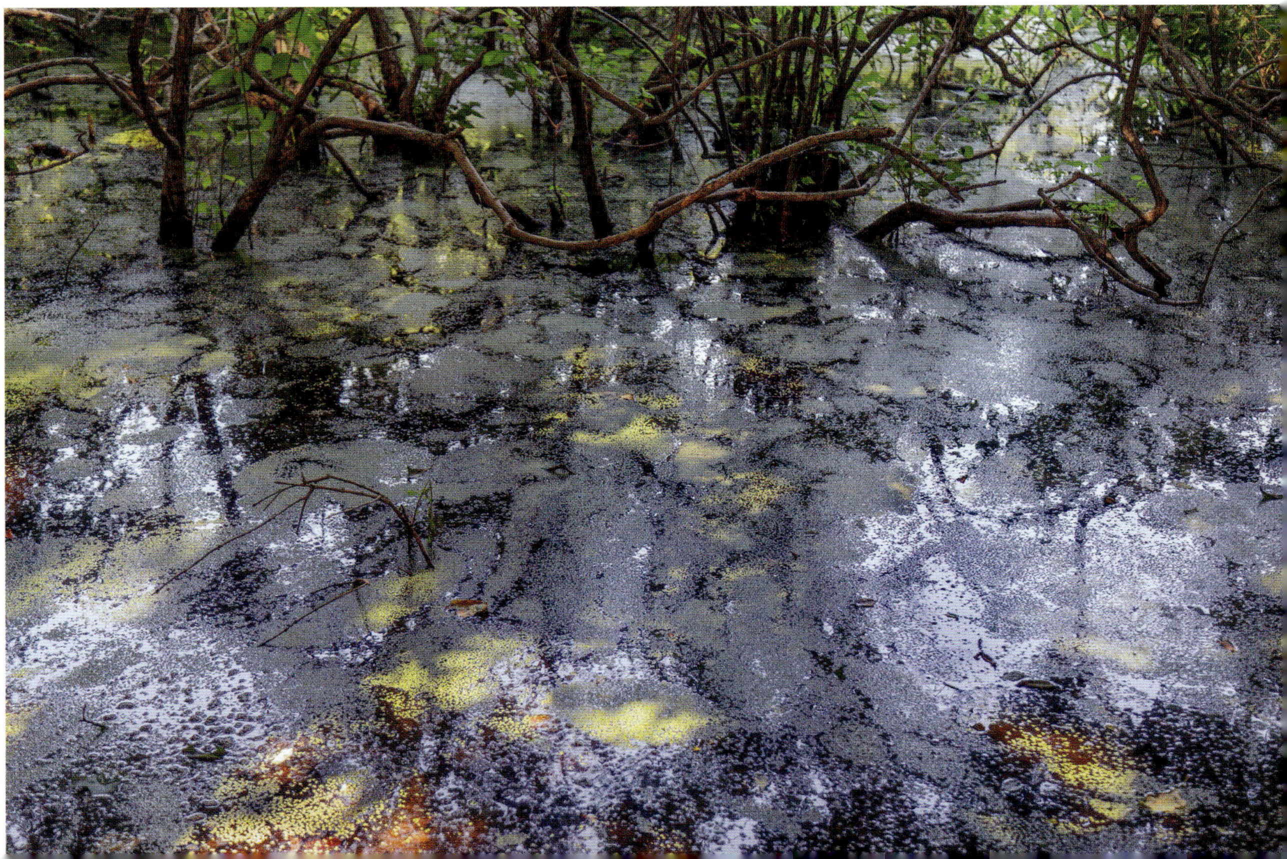

Bill McKibben

"But here's the point: what I've done, in my daily life and my political work and my writing, I've done because of these woods, these very woods we're walking through. They captured my imagination and taught me, in my twenties, that the suburban life I'd grown up in was not as engaging as life out here. I fell in love with these hemlocks, these steep slopes, these patches of rock, these streams lit by leaf-filtered sun. And having fallen in love, the usual braided combination of selfishness and selflessness led me to try to do what I could to protect them."

From *Wandering Home: A Long Walk
Across America's Most Hopeful Landscape*

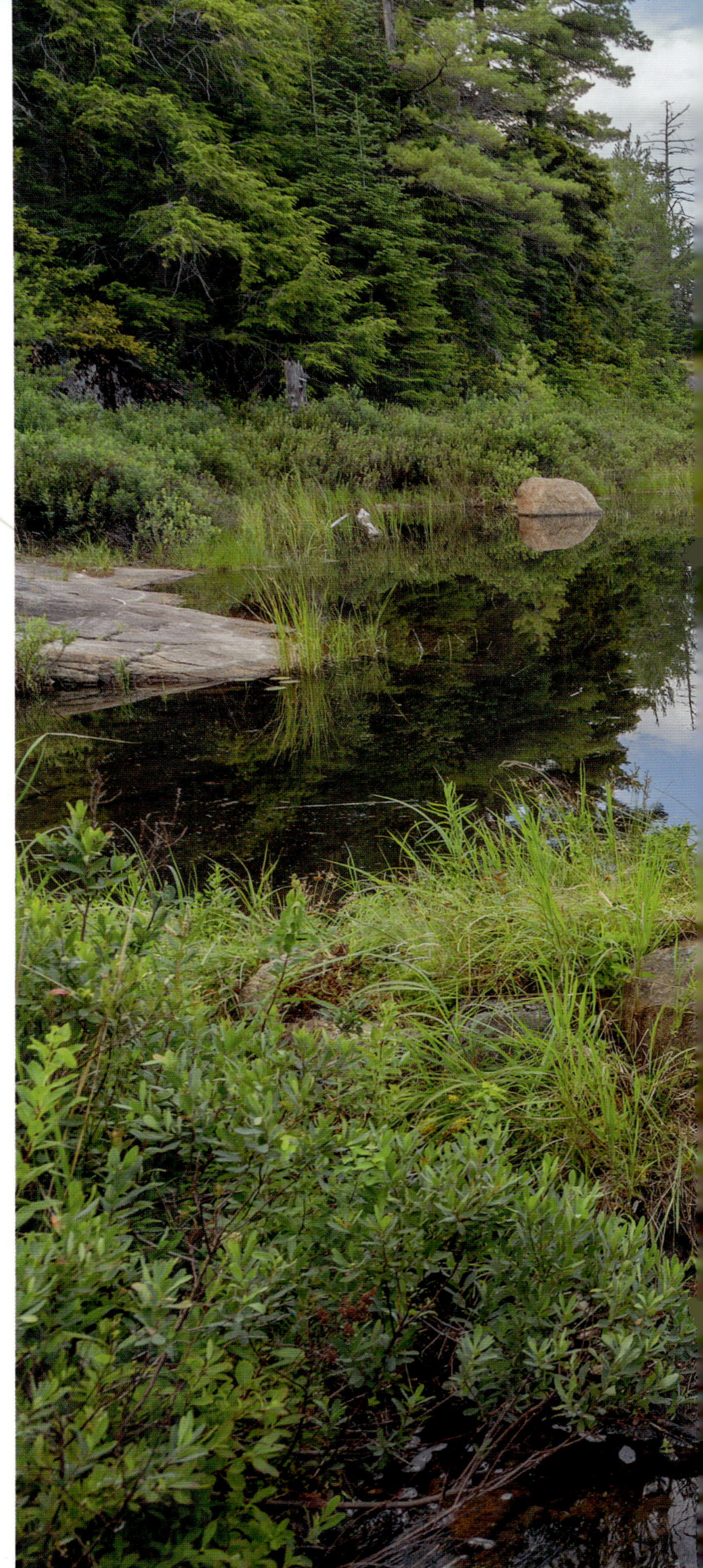

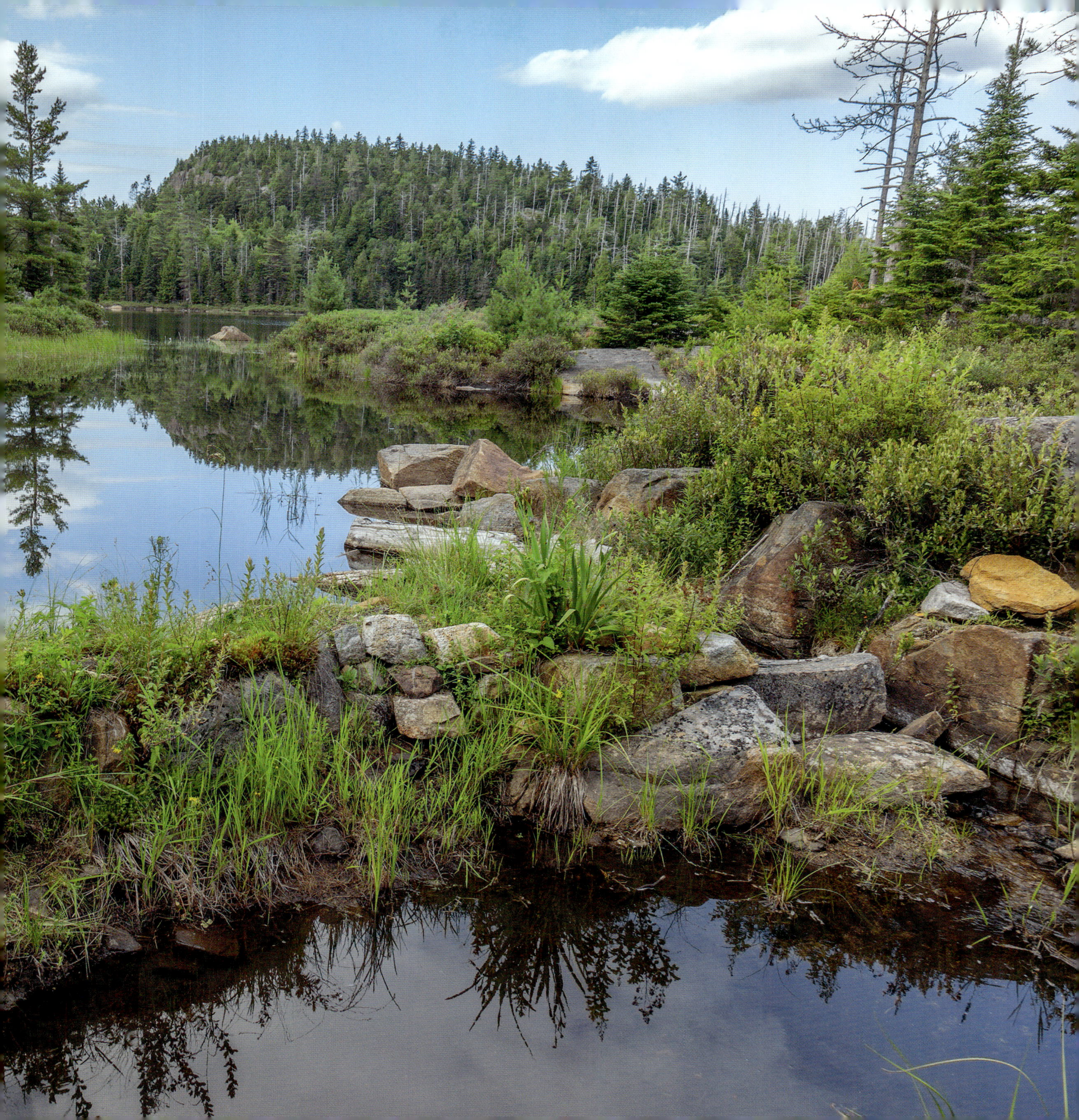

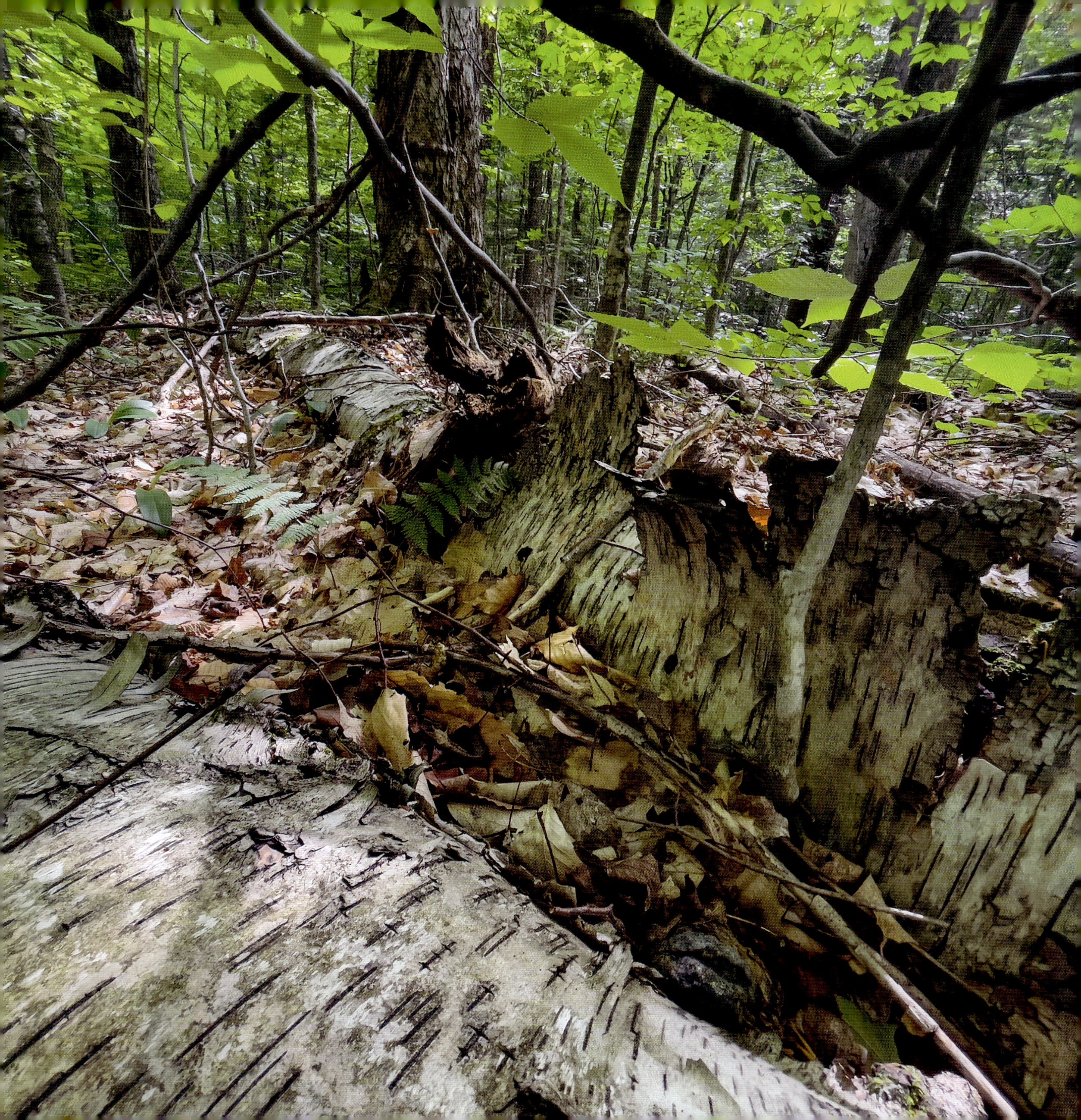

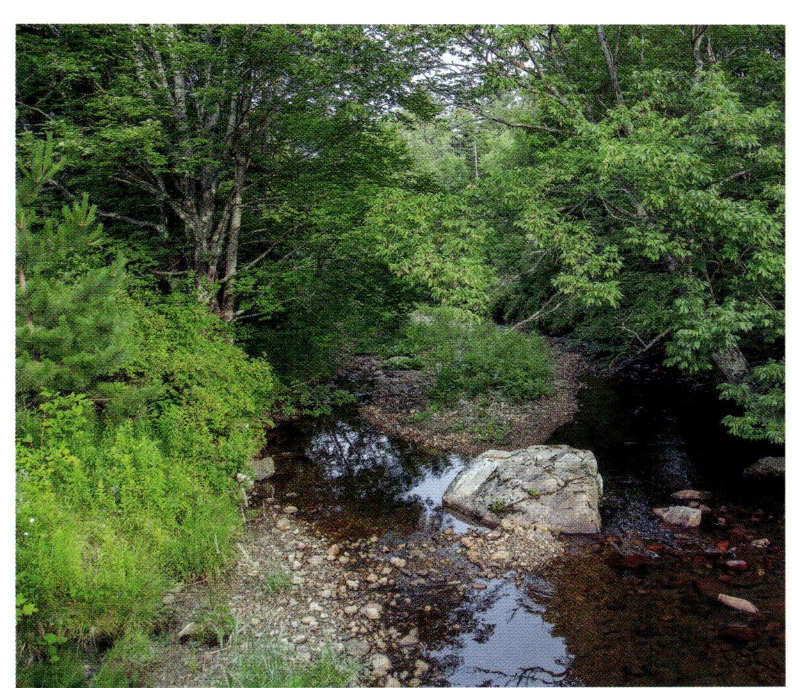
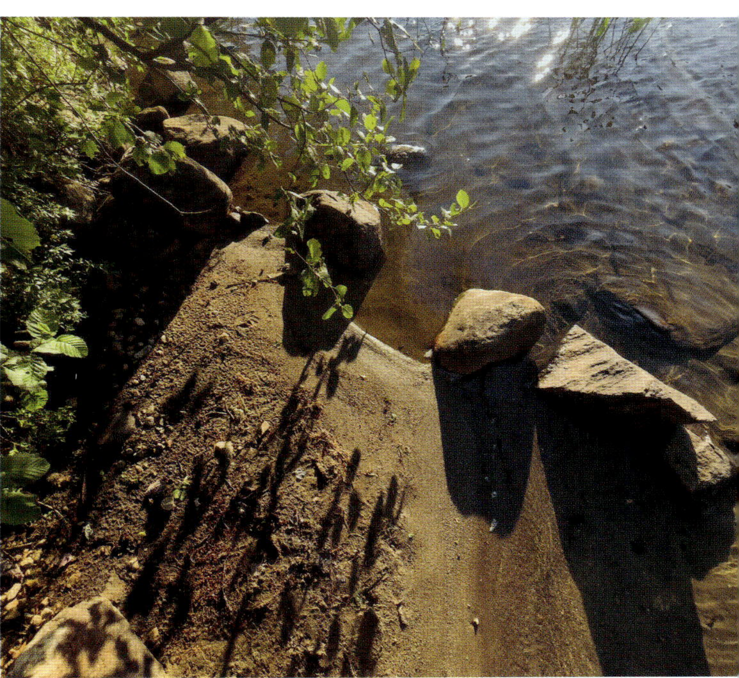

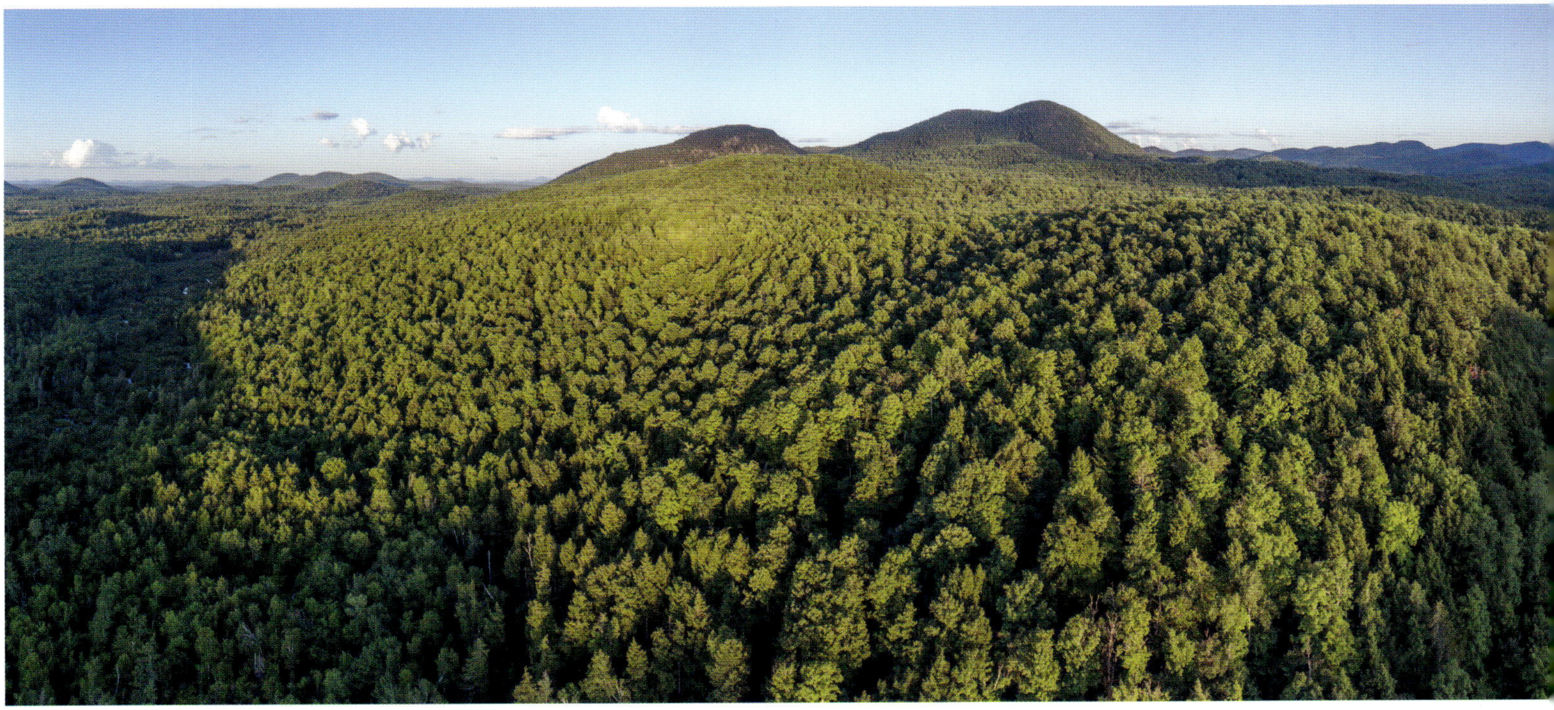

Ellen Meloy

"The West tutors us in native migration. It tells us to look for a home that can grasp the paradox of love and complication. It helps us decide what kind of men and women we want to be."

From *Seasons: Desert Sketches*

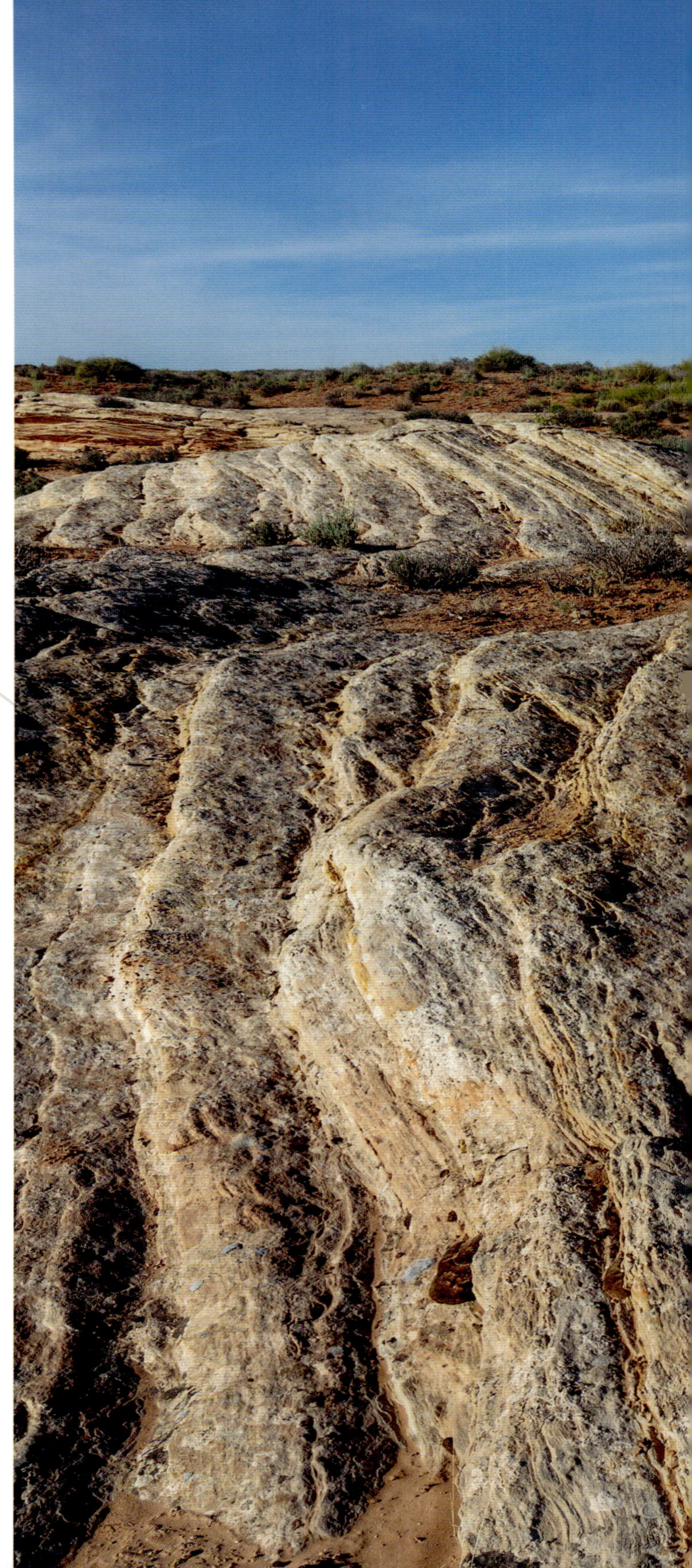

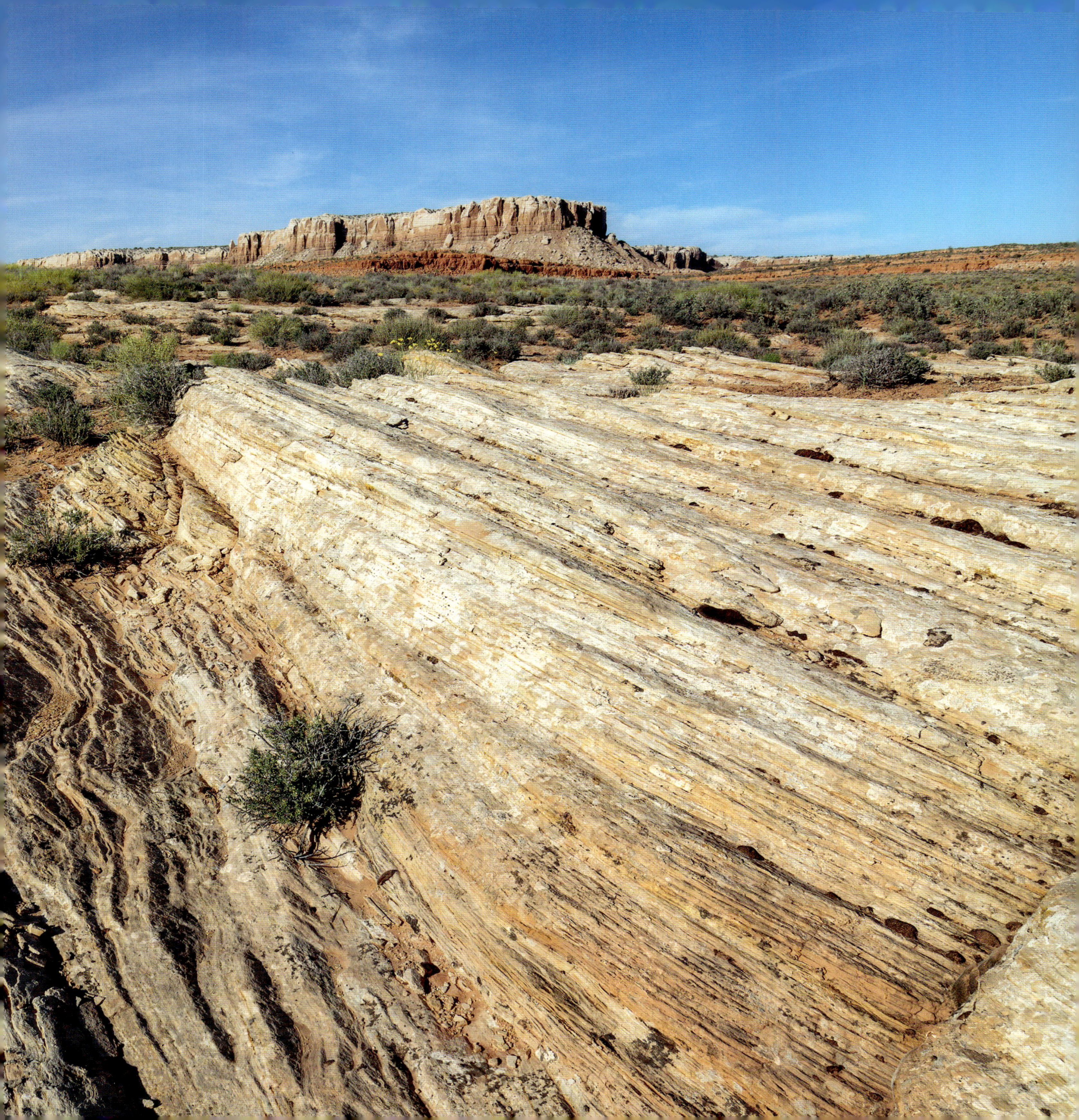

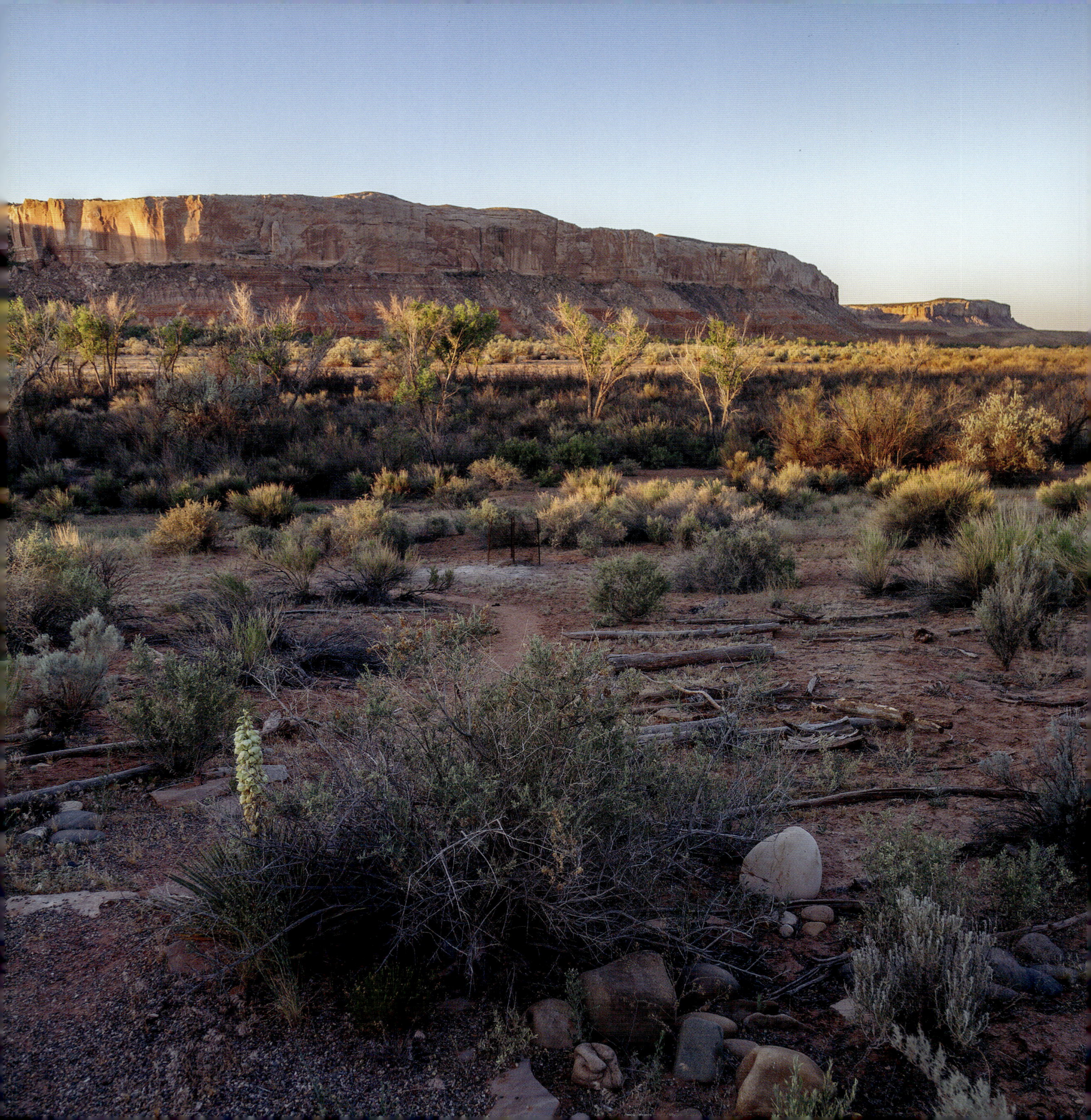

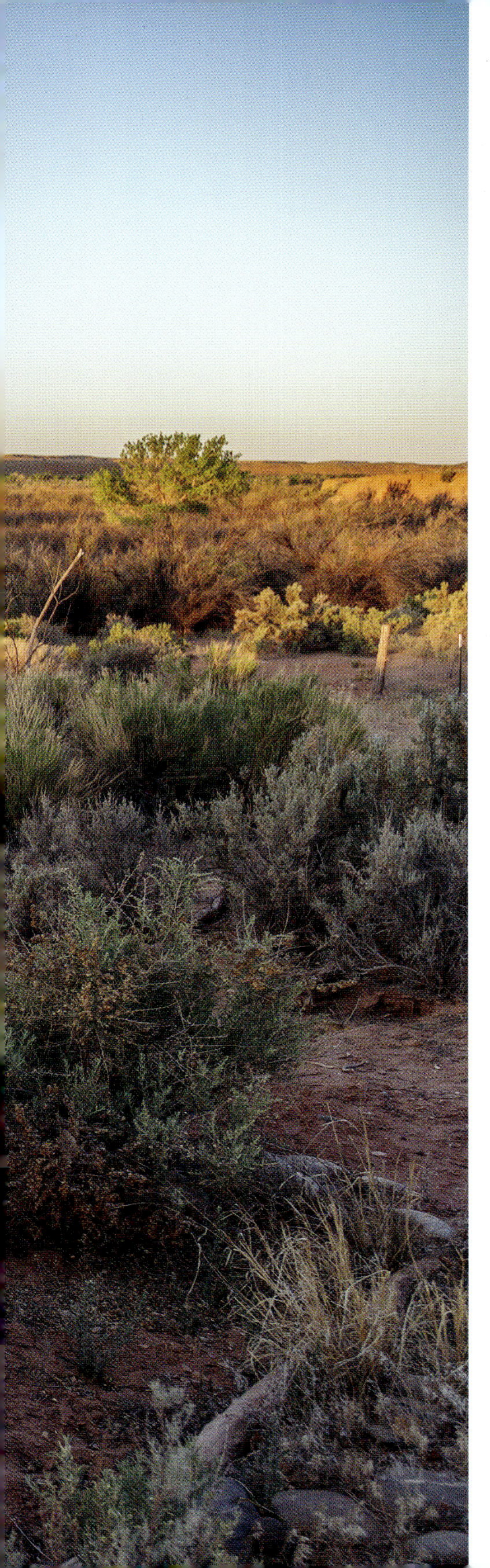
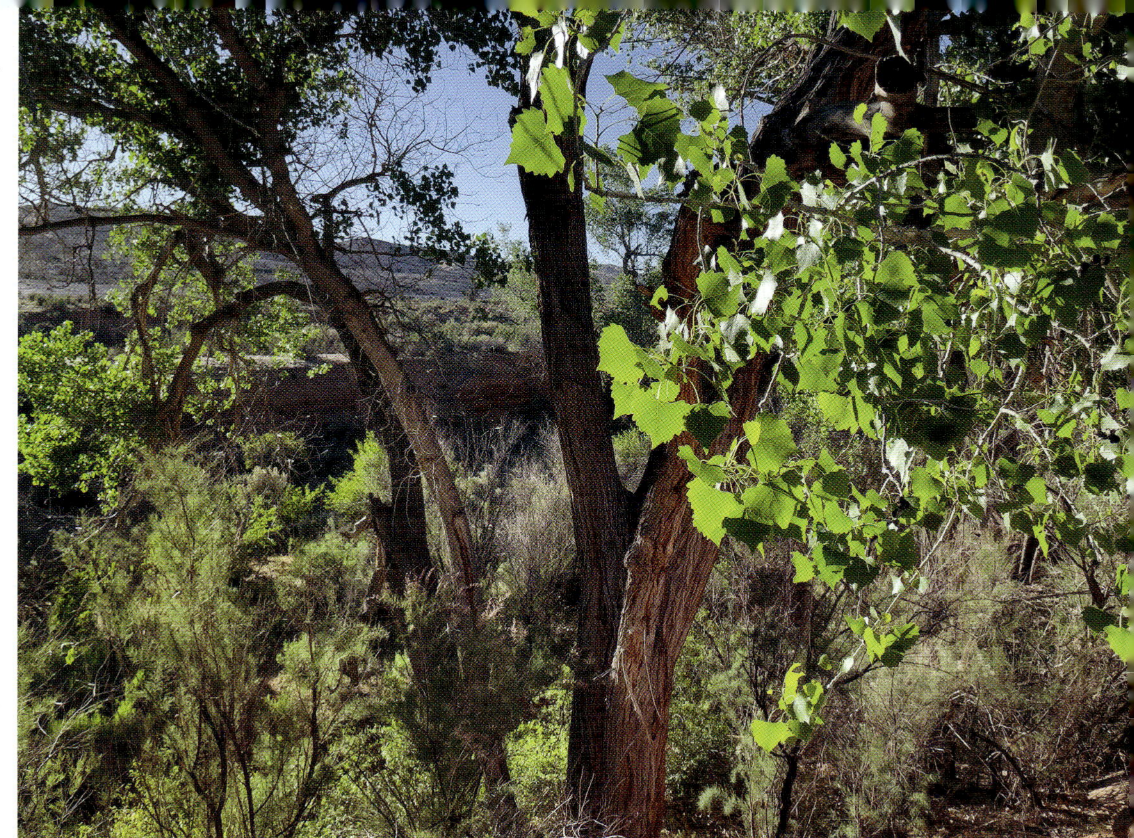
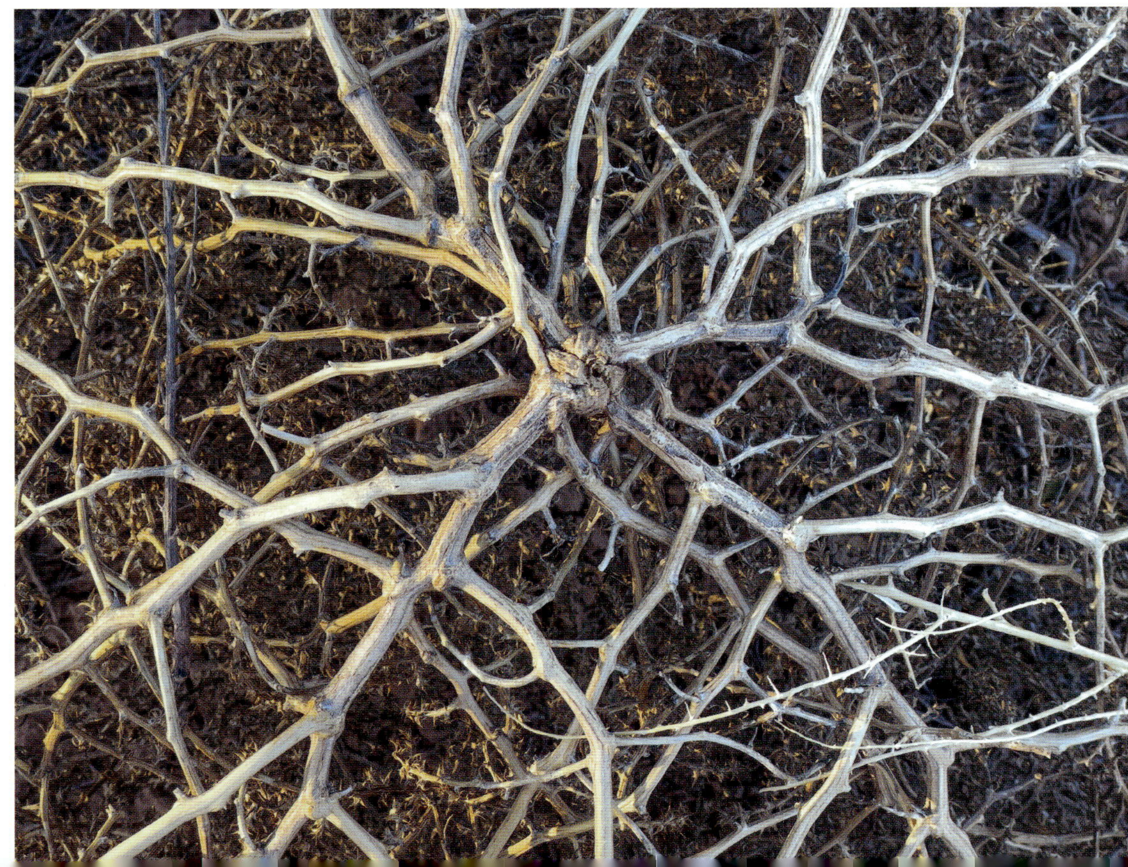

W. S. Merwin

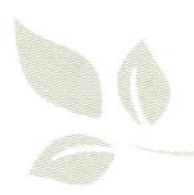

"Tell me what you see vanishing and I

Will tell you who you are"

From the poem "For Now,"
from *The Moving Target: Poems*

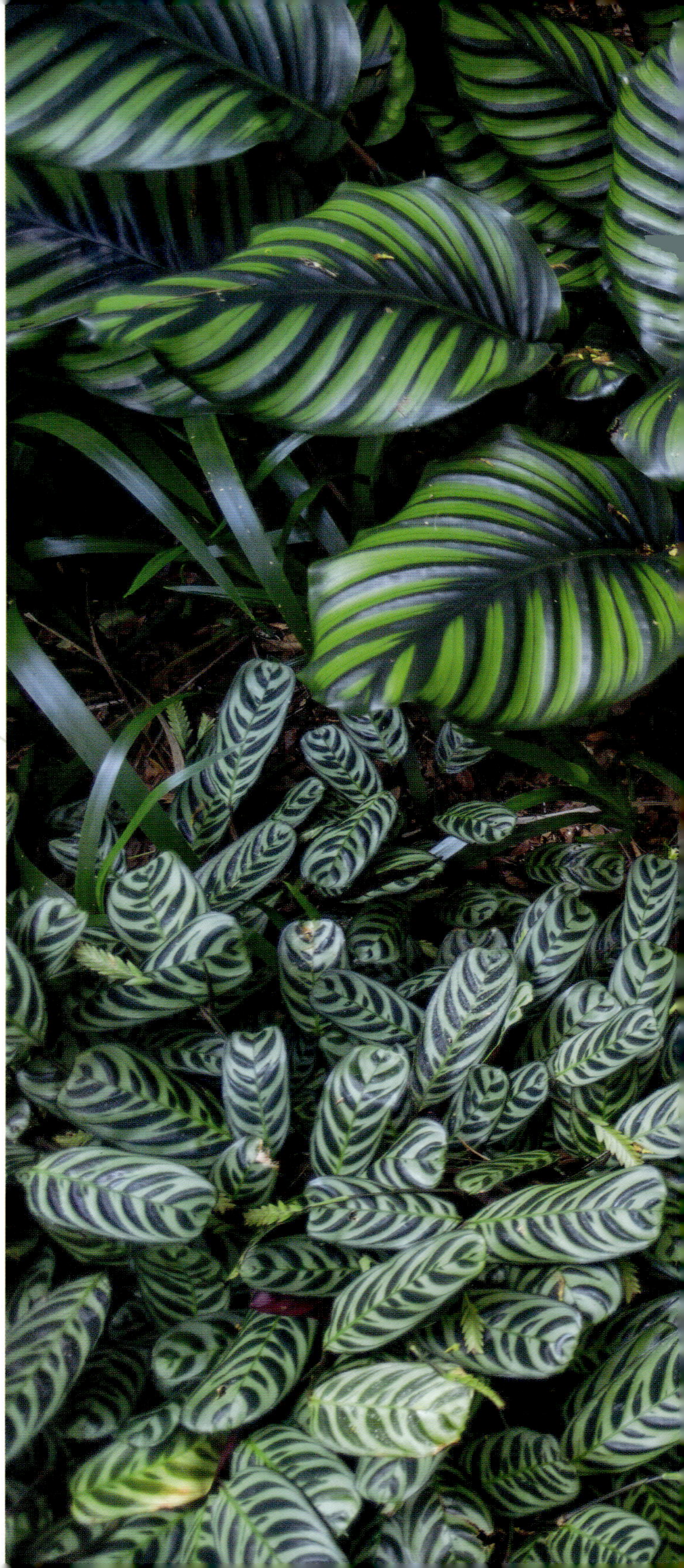

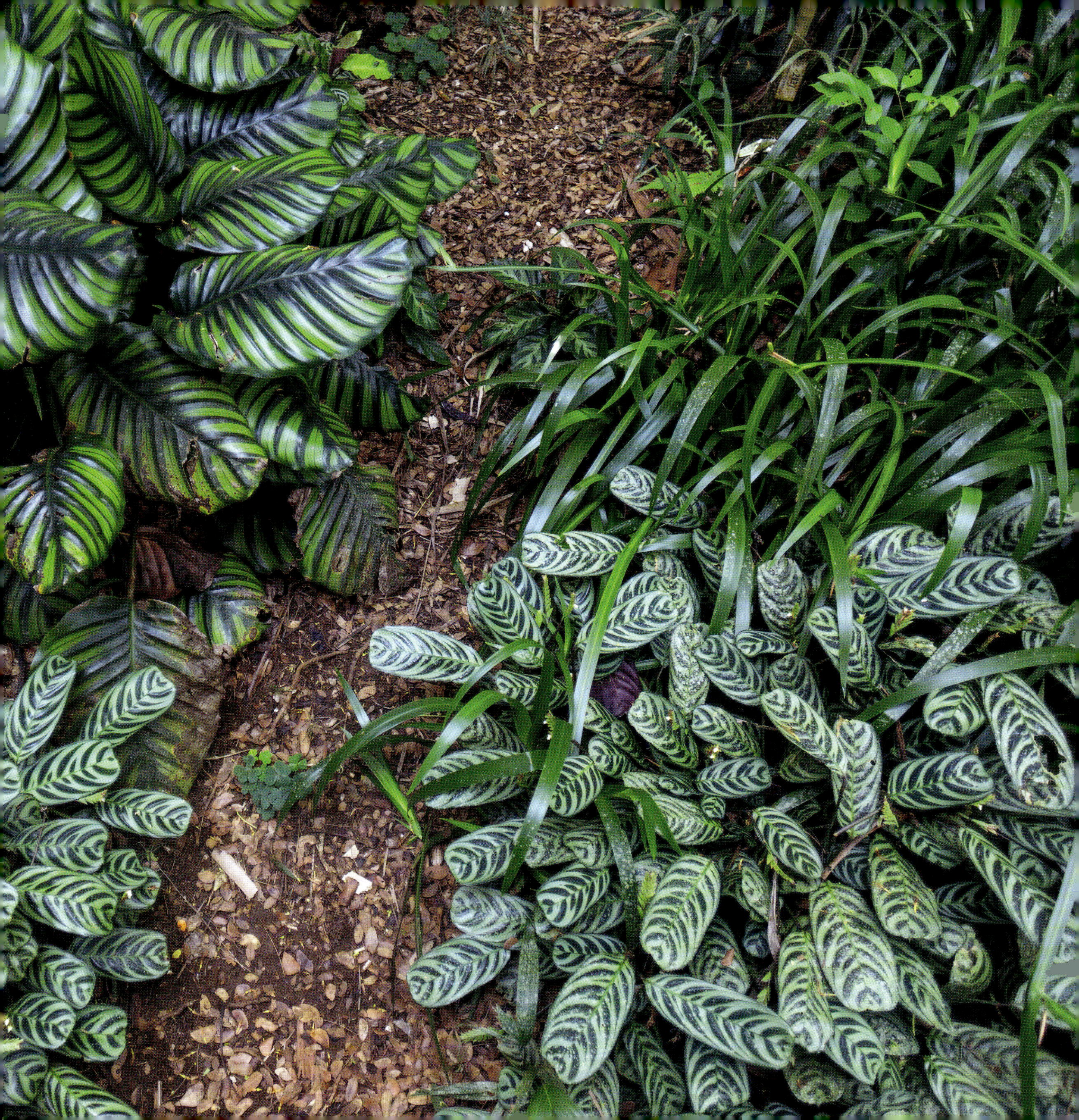

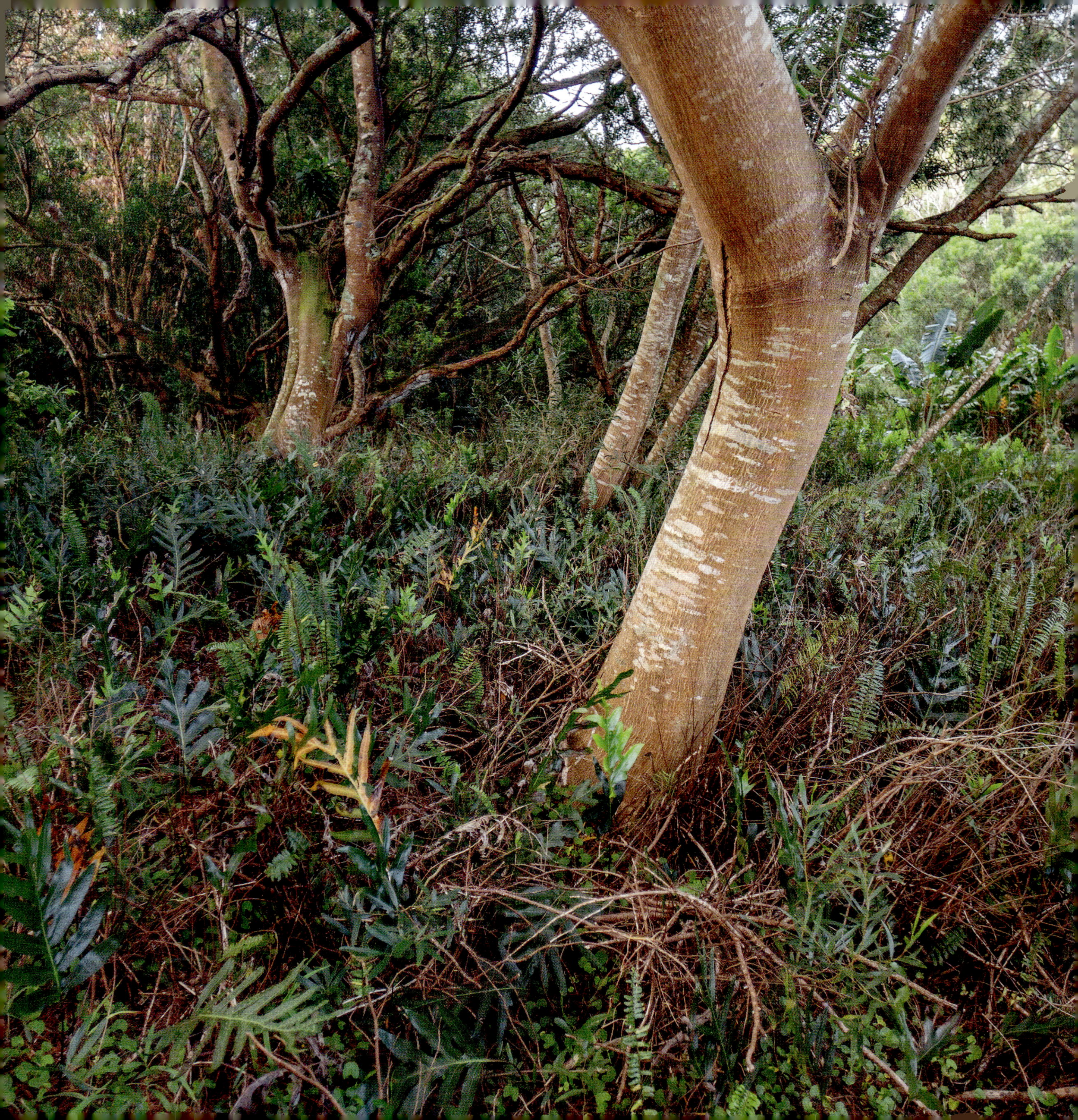

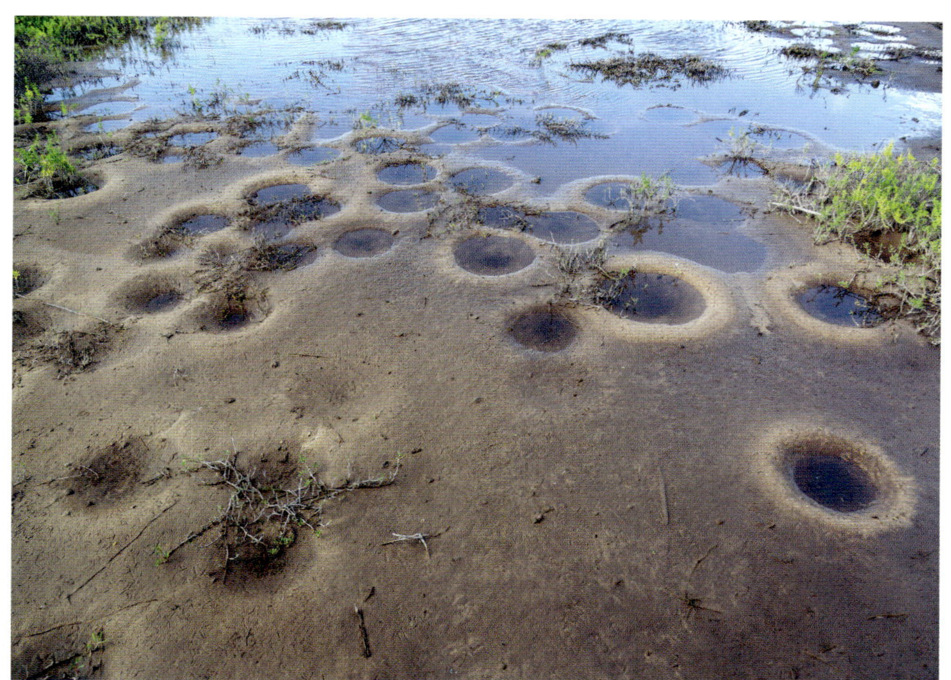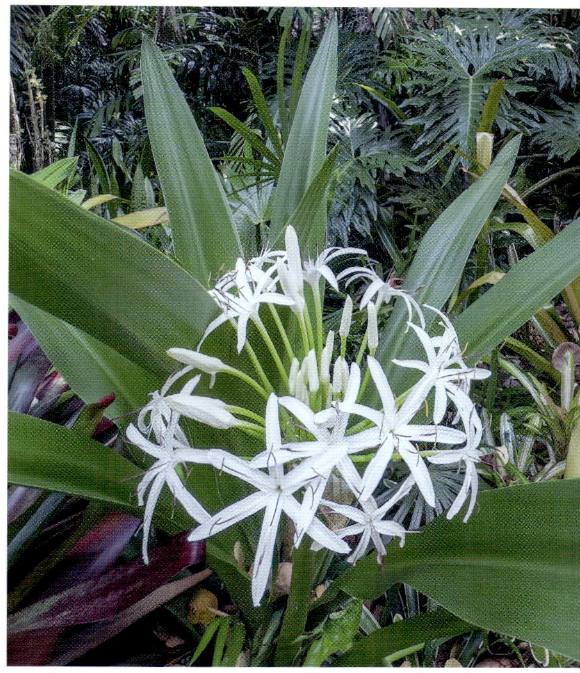

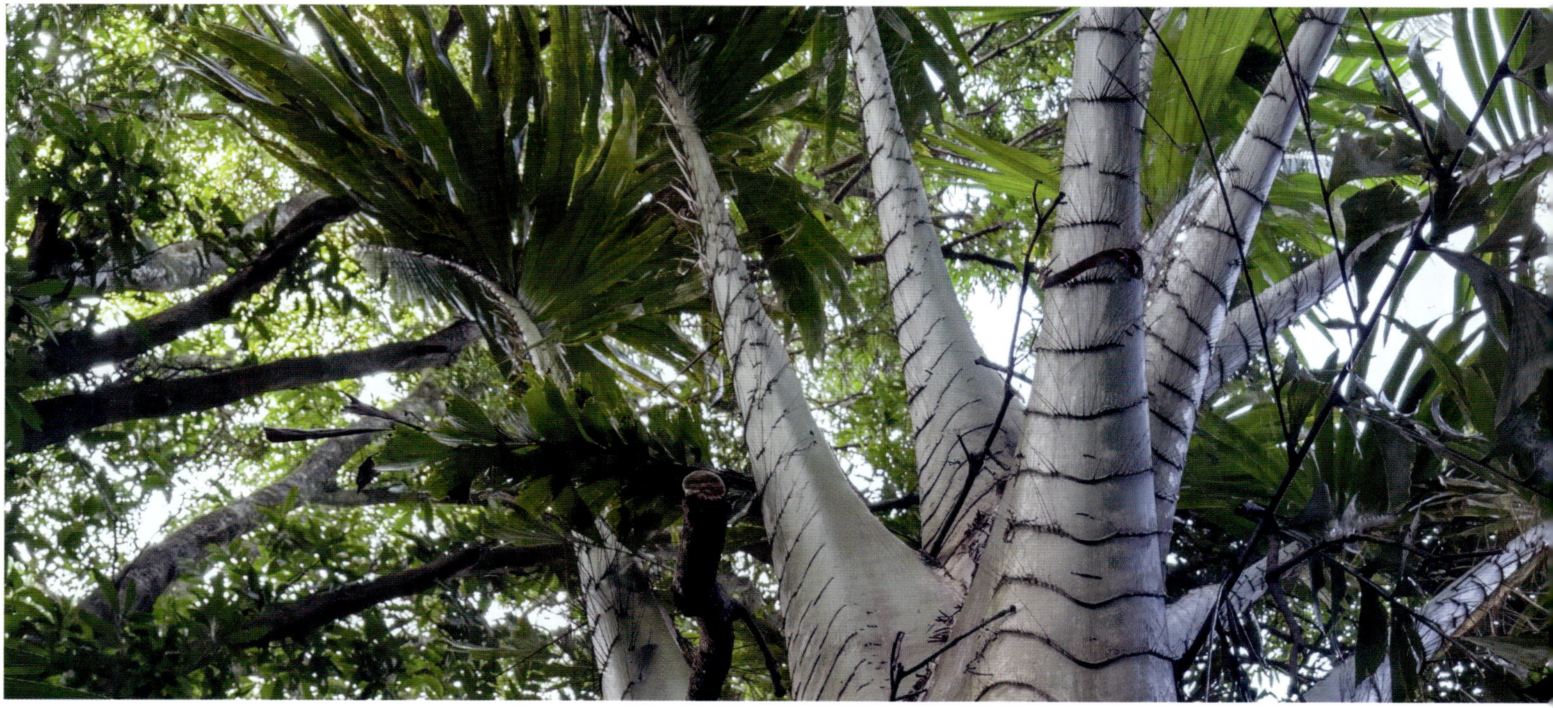

John Muir

"All the wild world is beautiful, and it matters but little
where we go, to highlands or lowlands, woods or
plains, on the sea or land or down among the crystals
of waves or high in a balloon in the sky; through all the
climates, hot or cold, storms and calms, everywhere
and always we are in God's eternal beauty and love.
So universally true is this, the spot where we chance
to be always seems the best …"

From *John of the Mountains:
The Unpublished Journals of John Muir*

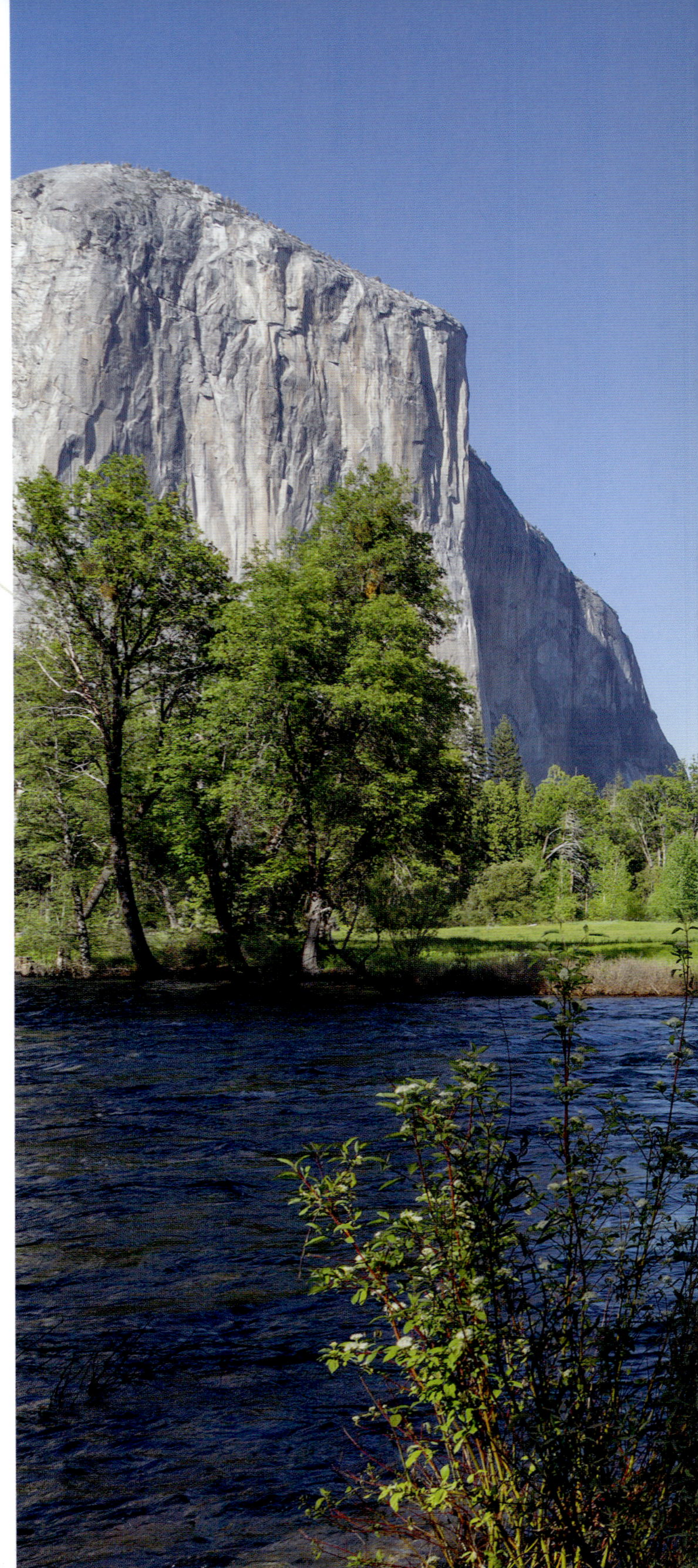

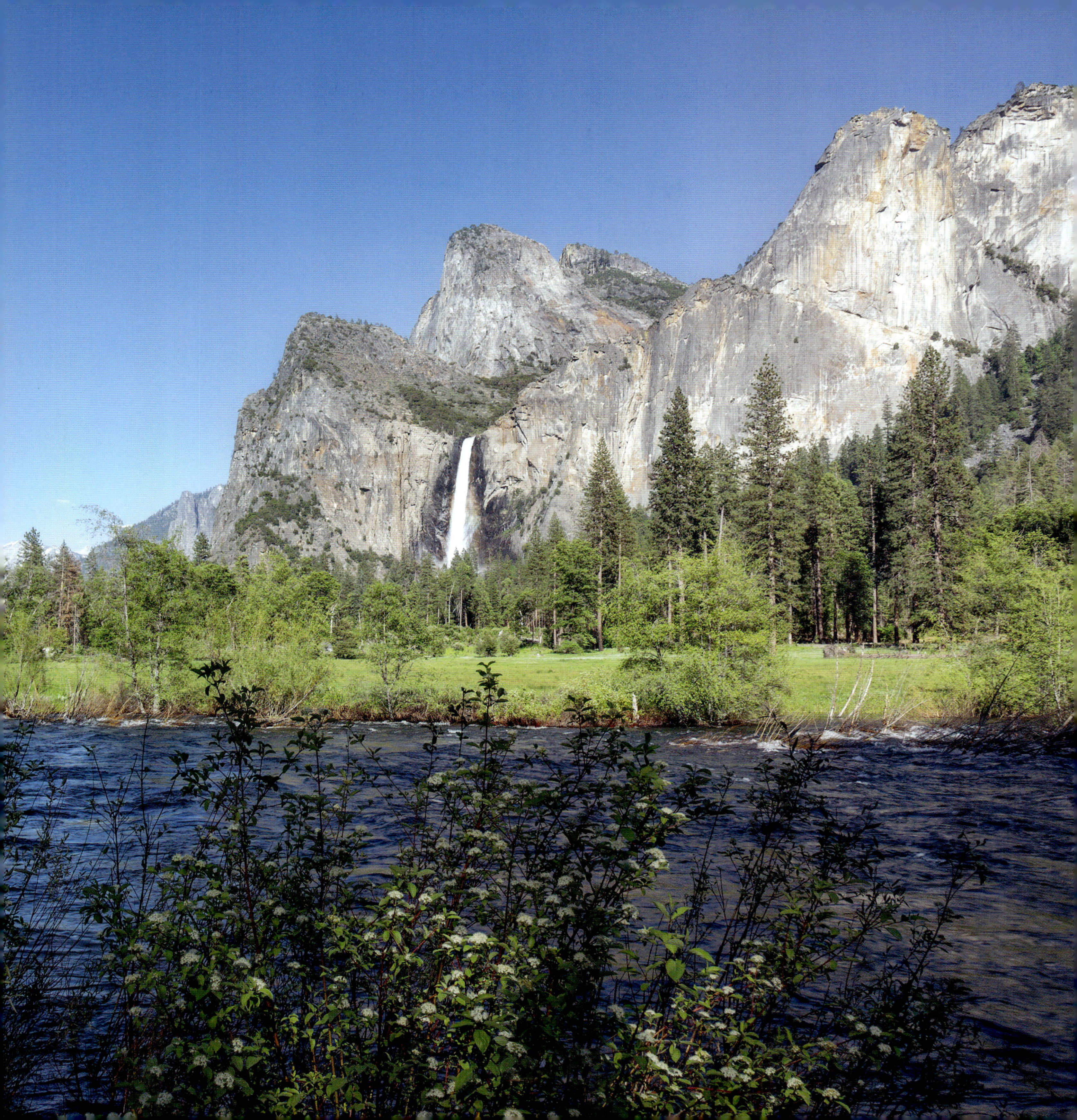

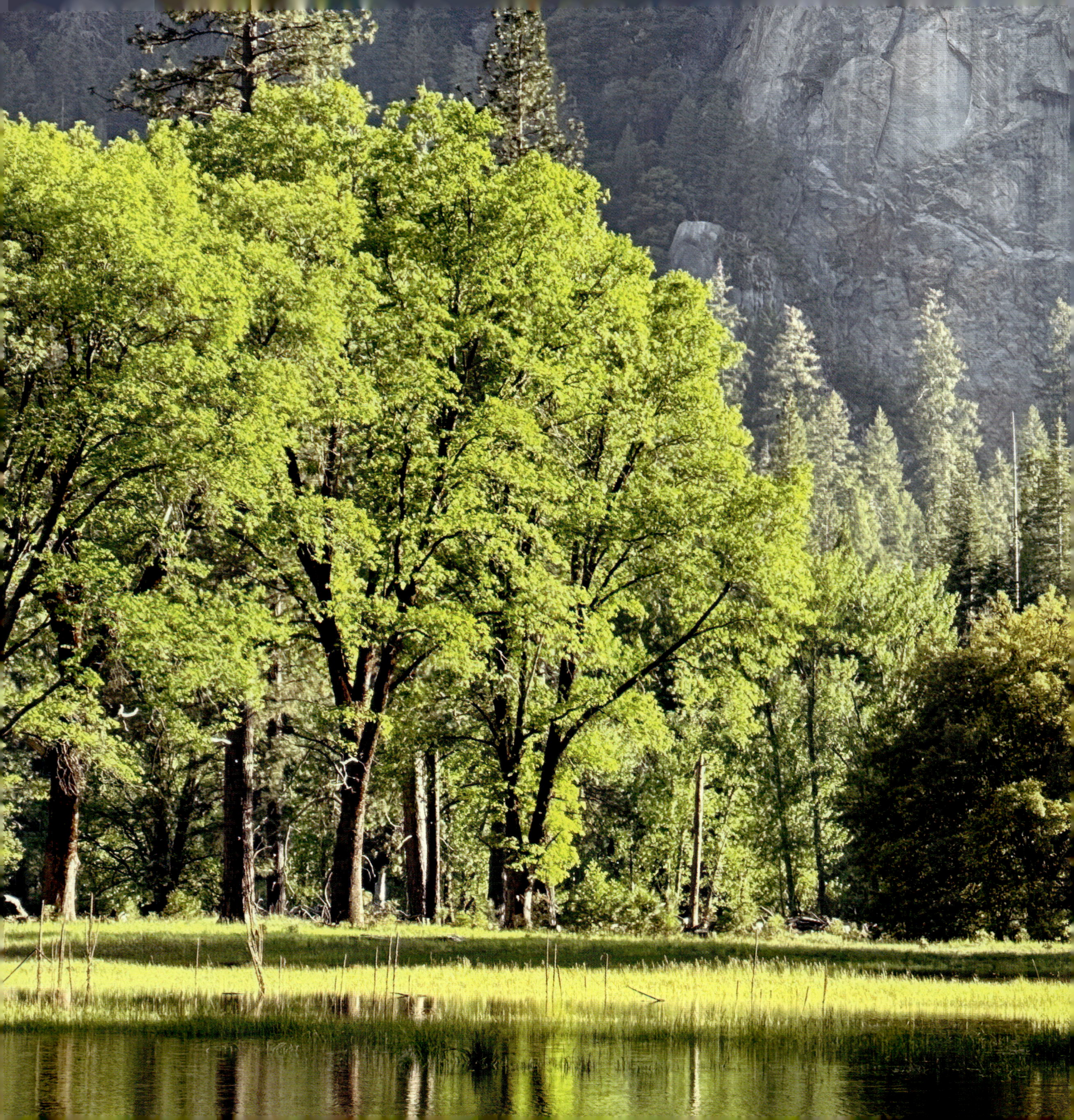

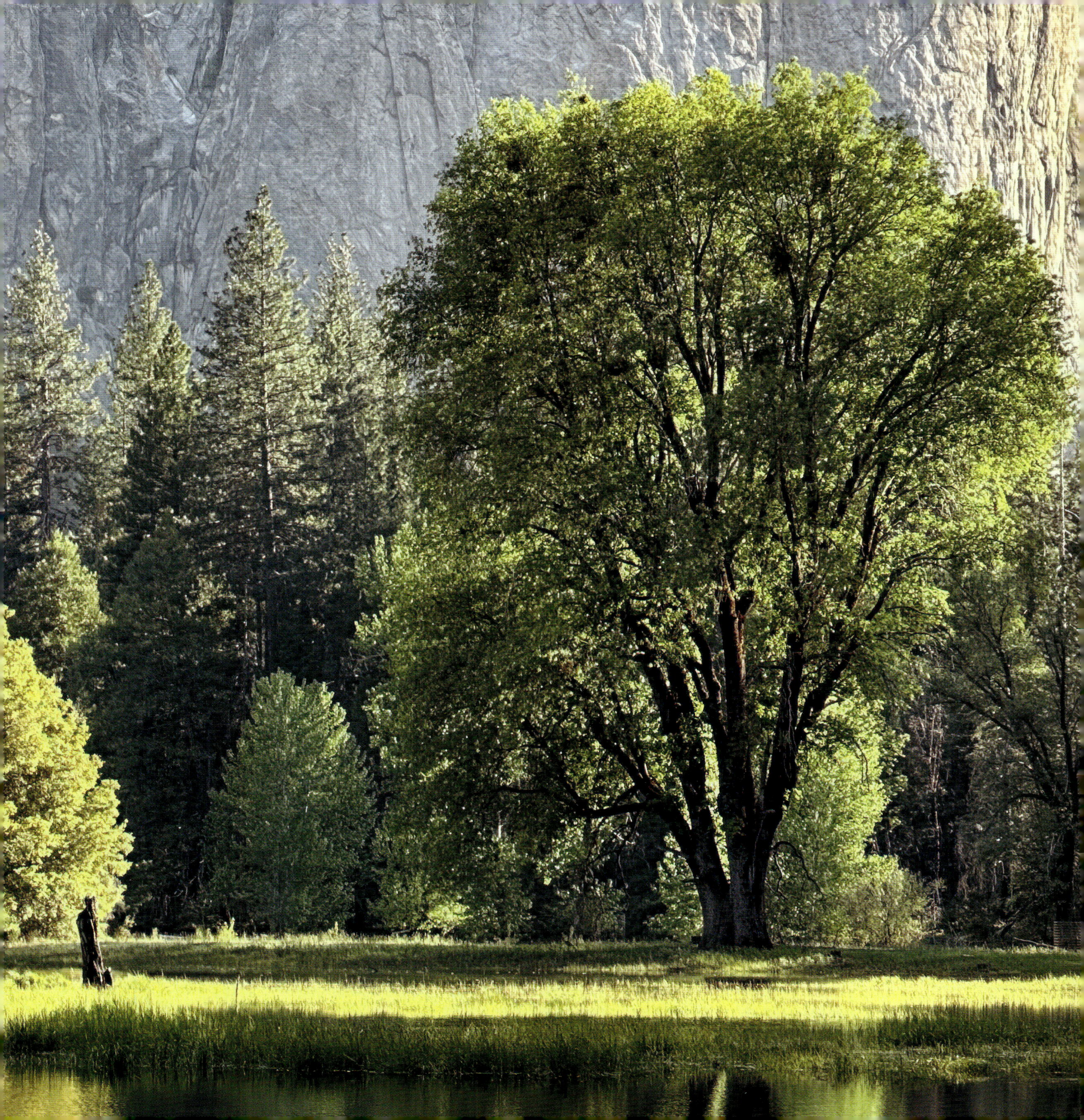

Sigurd F. Olson

"I named this place Listening Point because only when one comes to listen, only when one is aware and still, can things be seen and heard. Everyone has a listening-point somewhere. It does not have to be in the north or close to the wilderness, but some place of quiet where the universe can be contemplated with awe."

From *Listening Point*

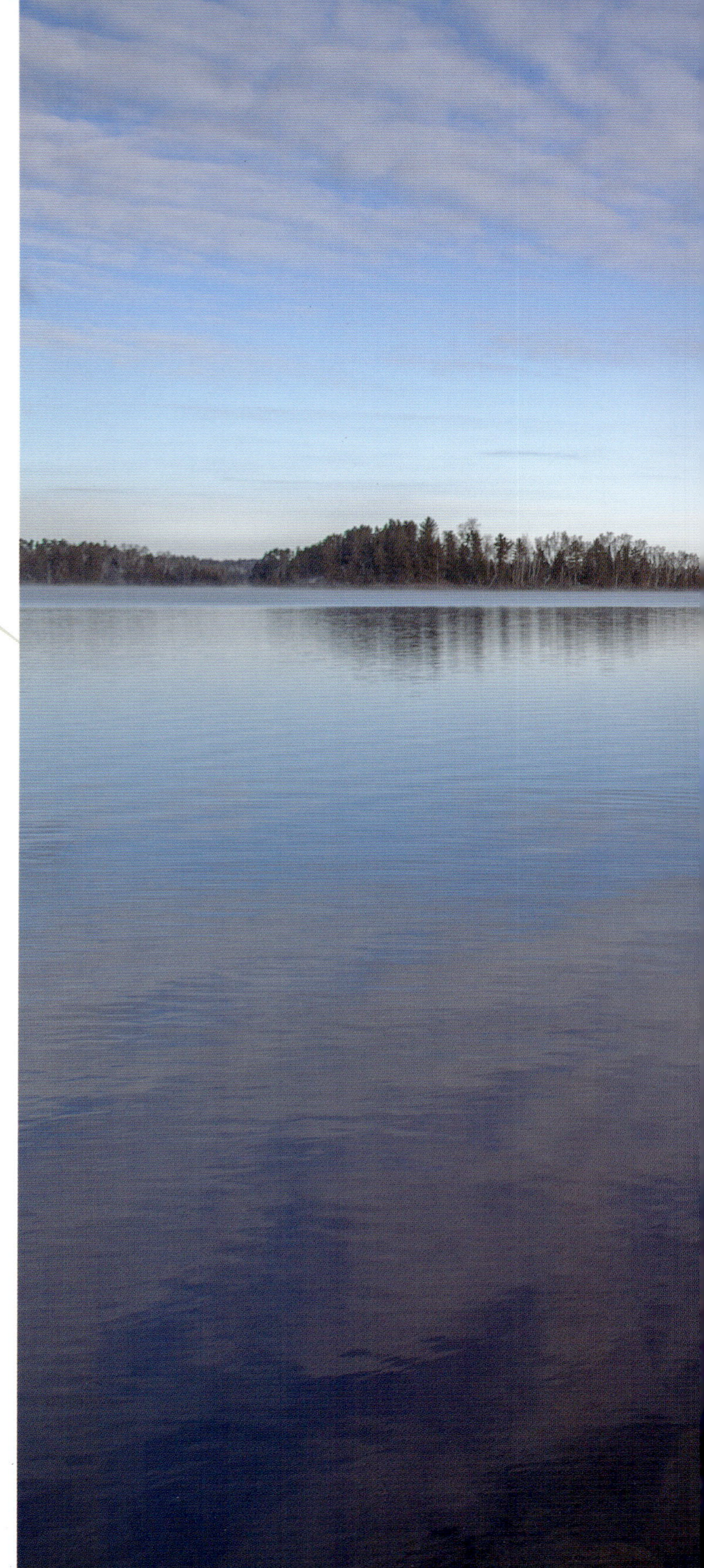

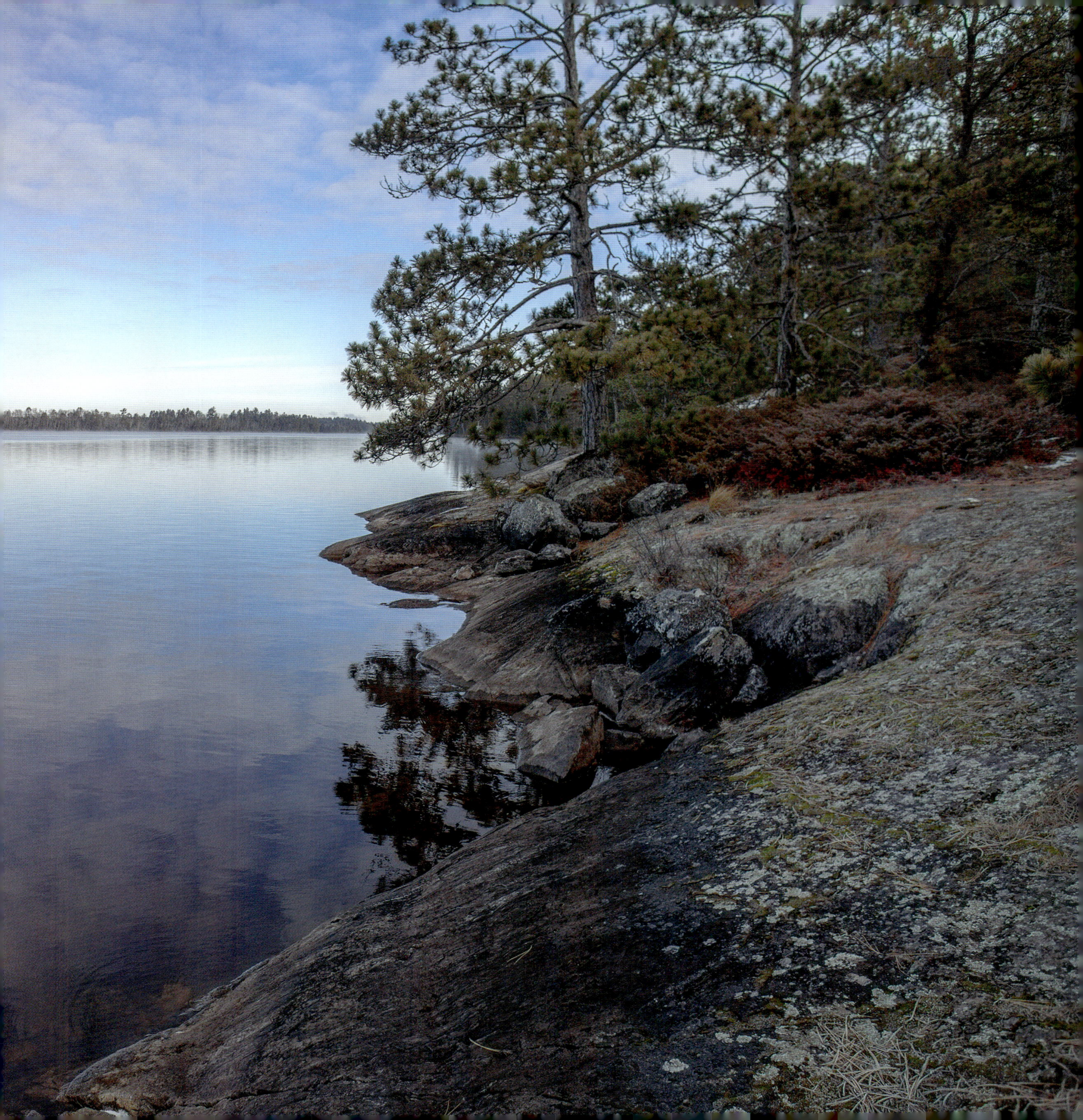

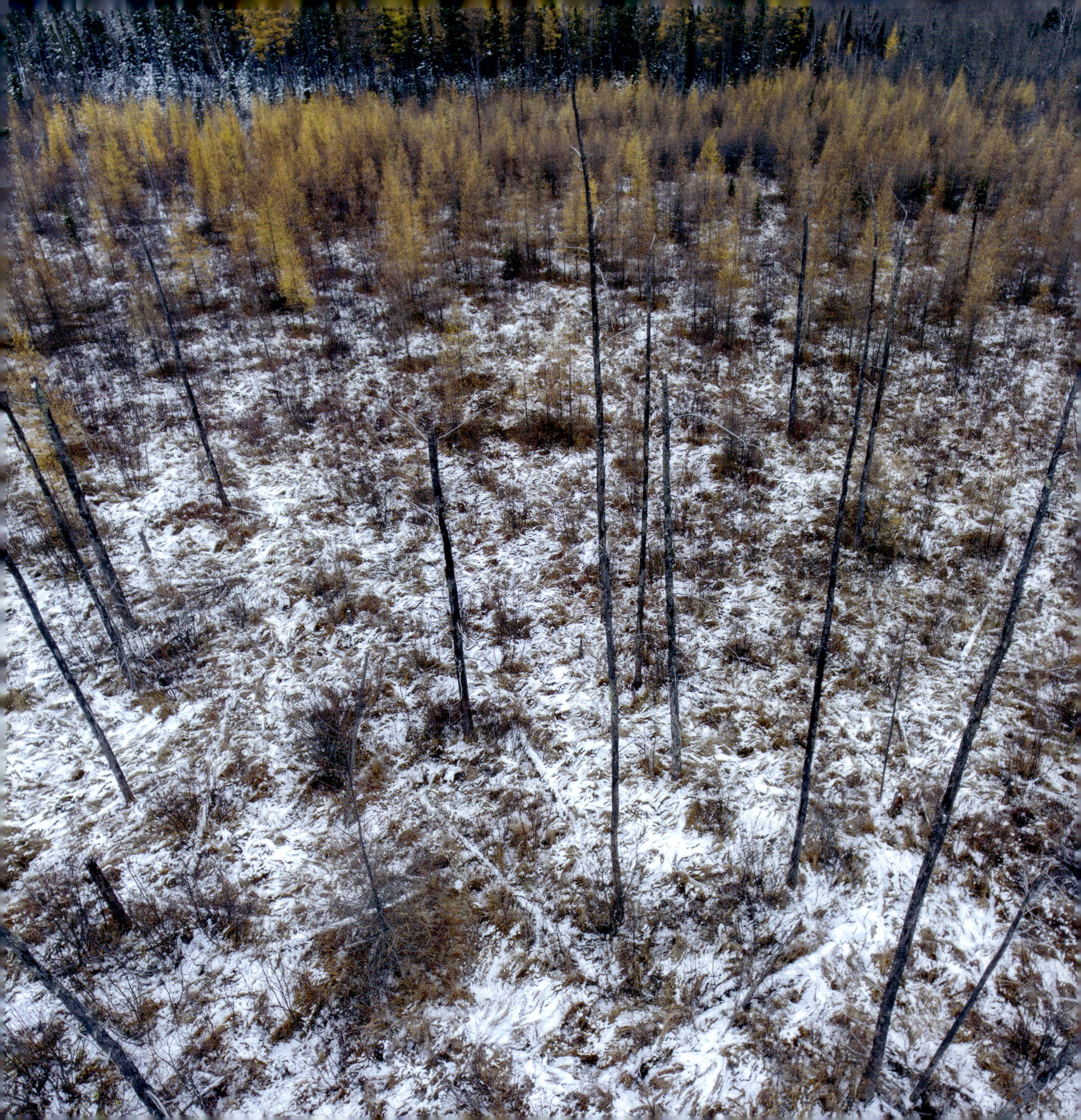

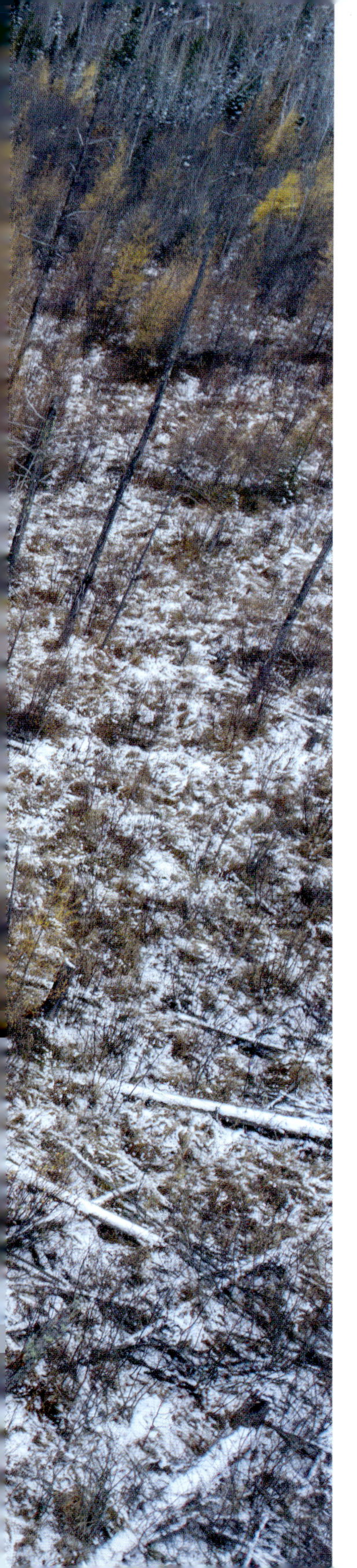

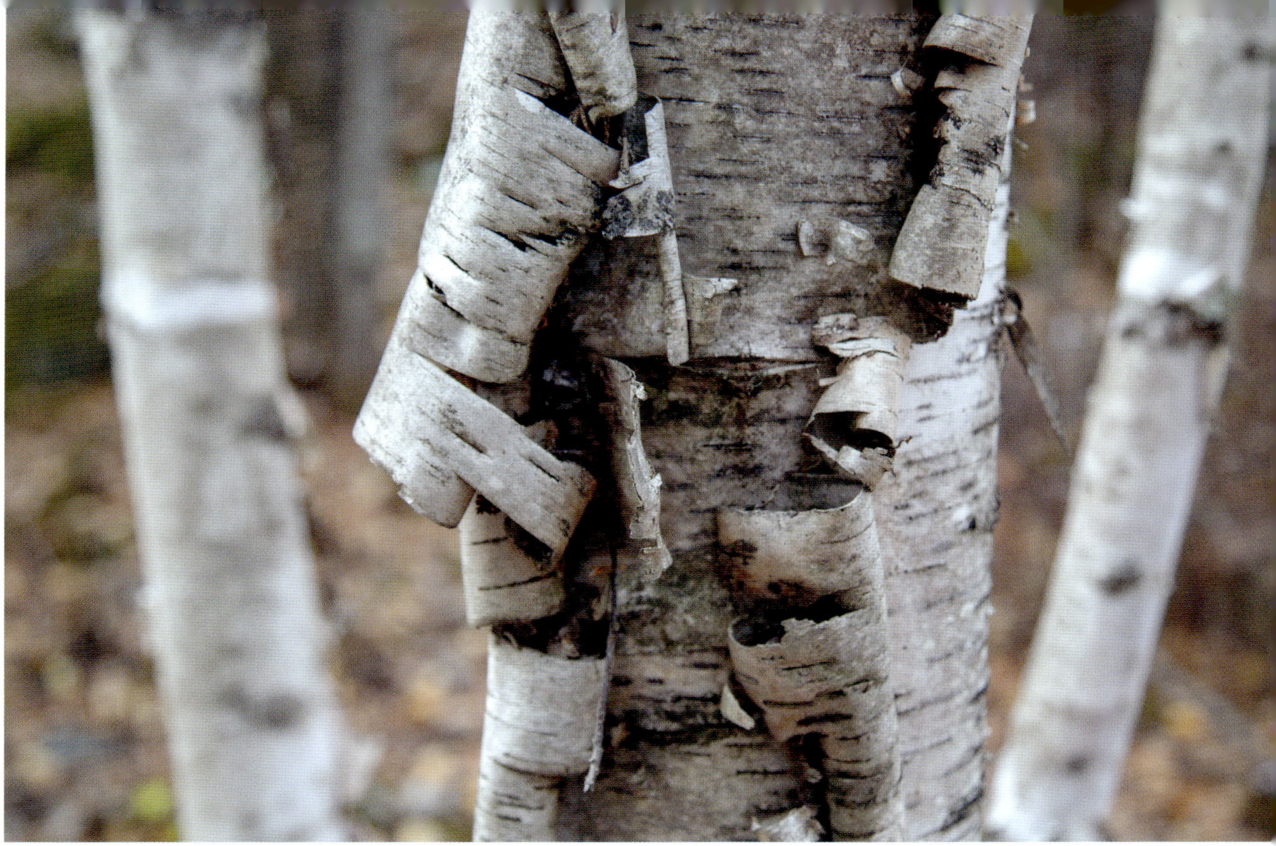

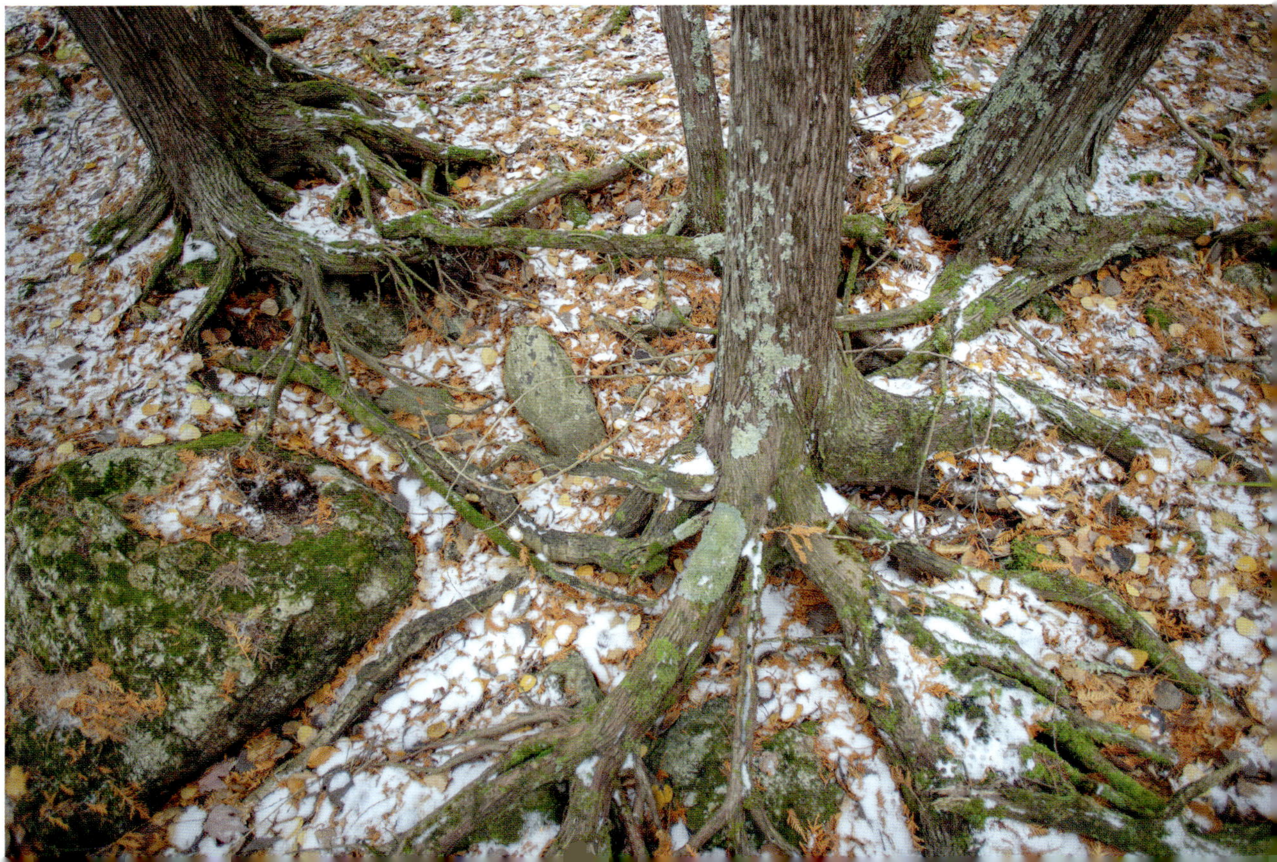

Craig Santos Perez

HAWAII

"It was summer all winter.

It was melting

and it was going to melt.

The last glacier fits

in our warm hands."

From the poem "Thirteen Ways of Looking at a Glacier,"
from *Habitat Threshold*

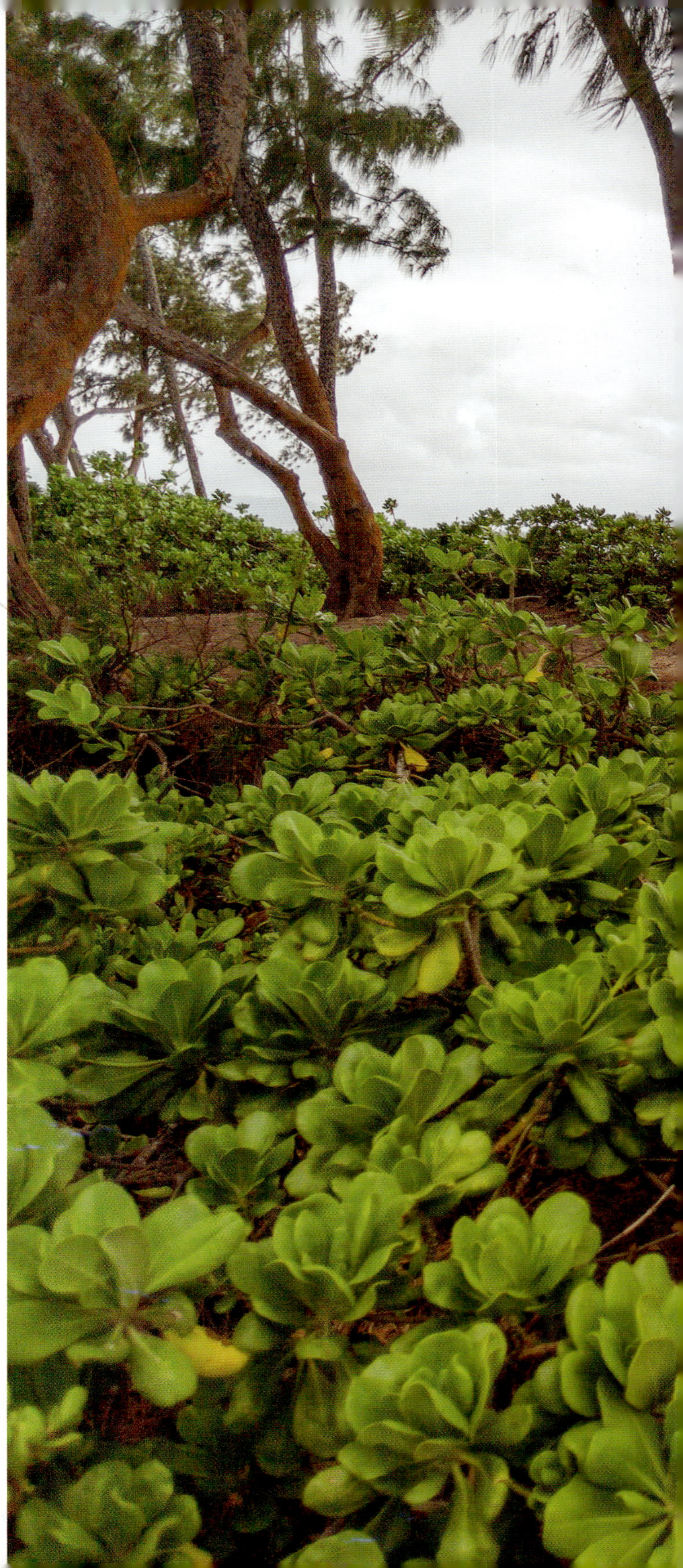

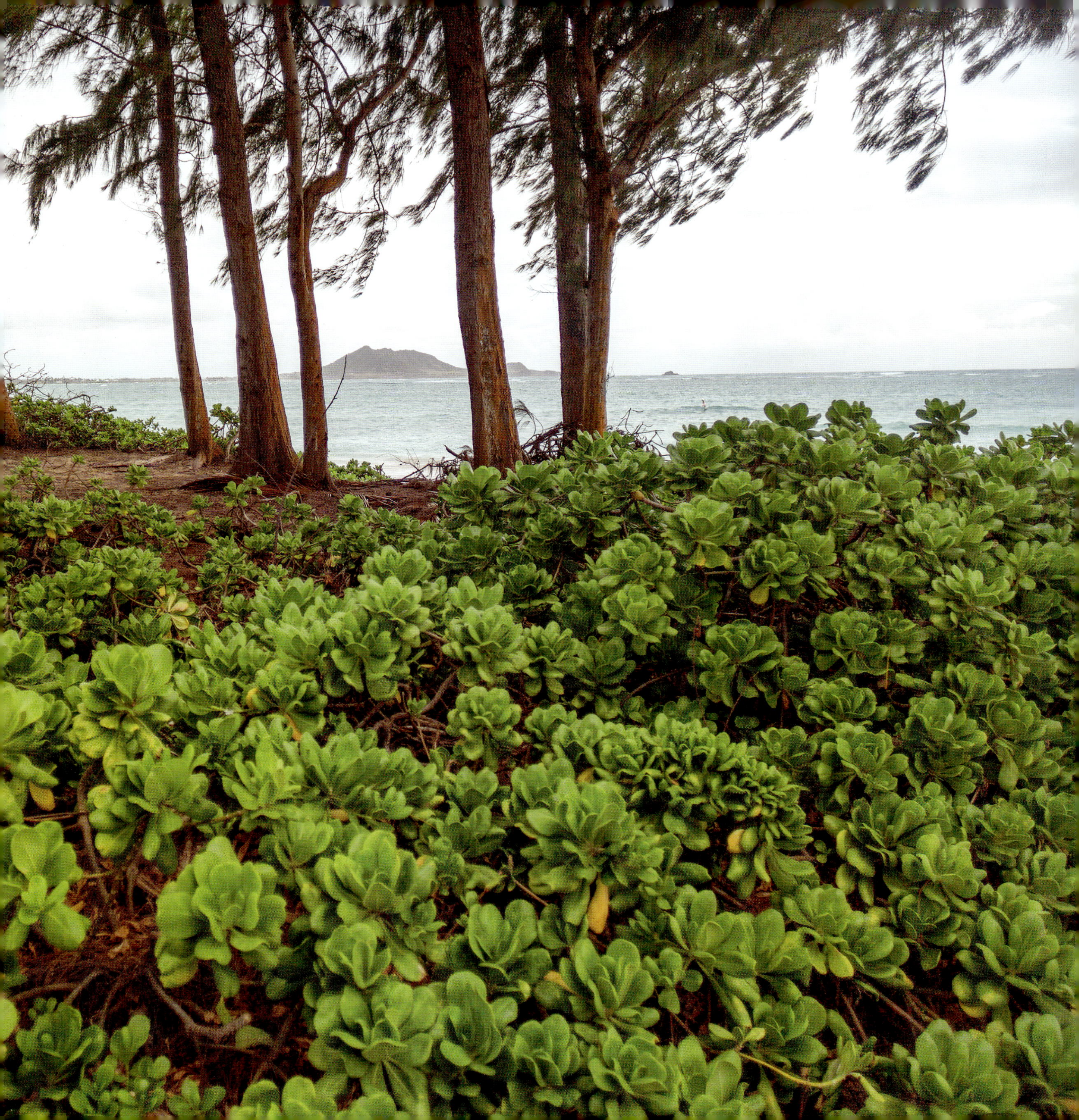

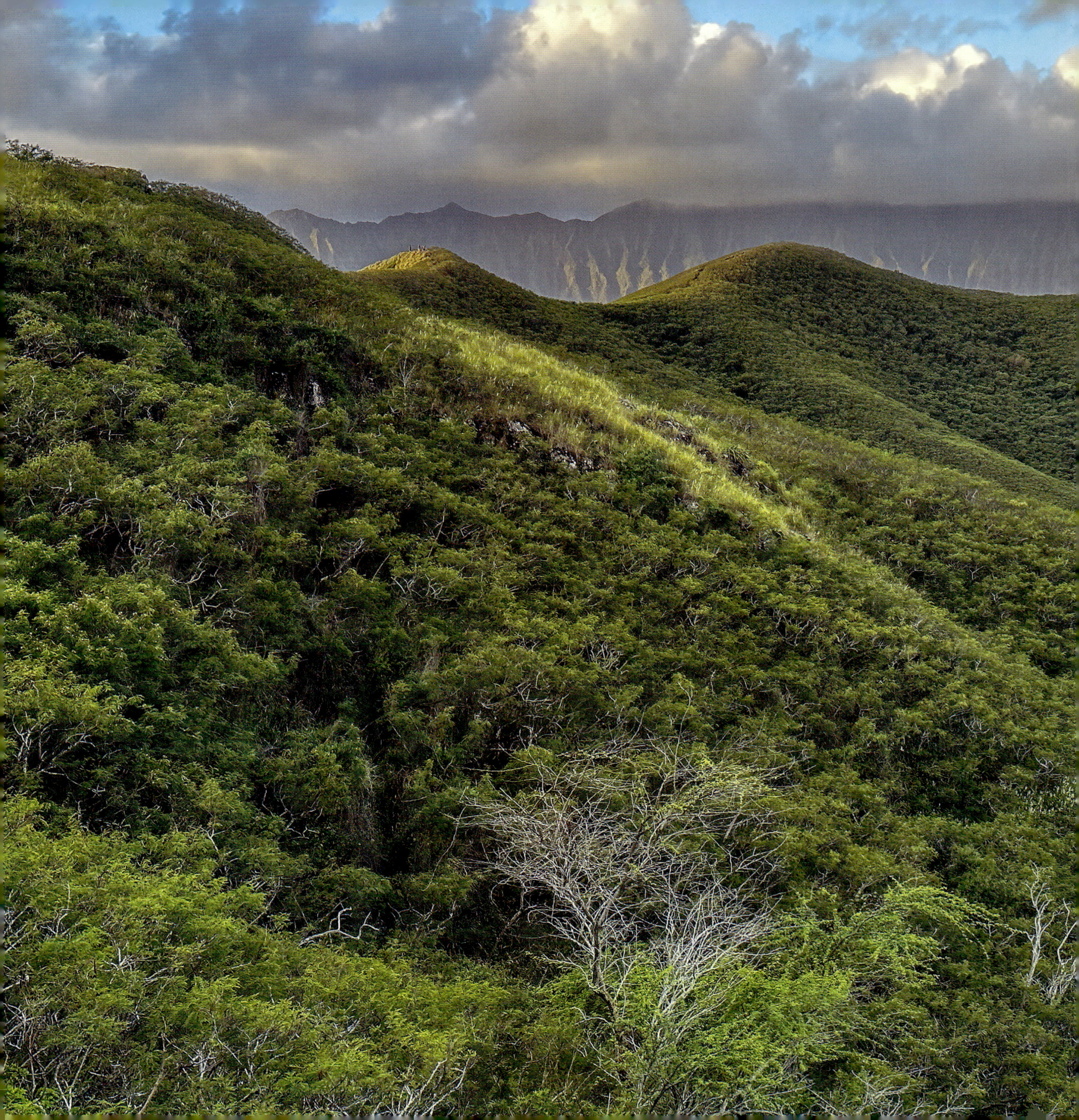

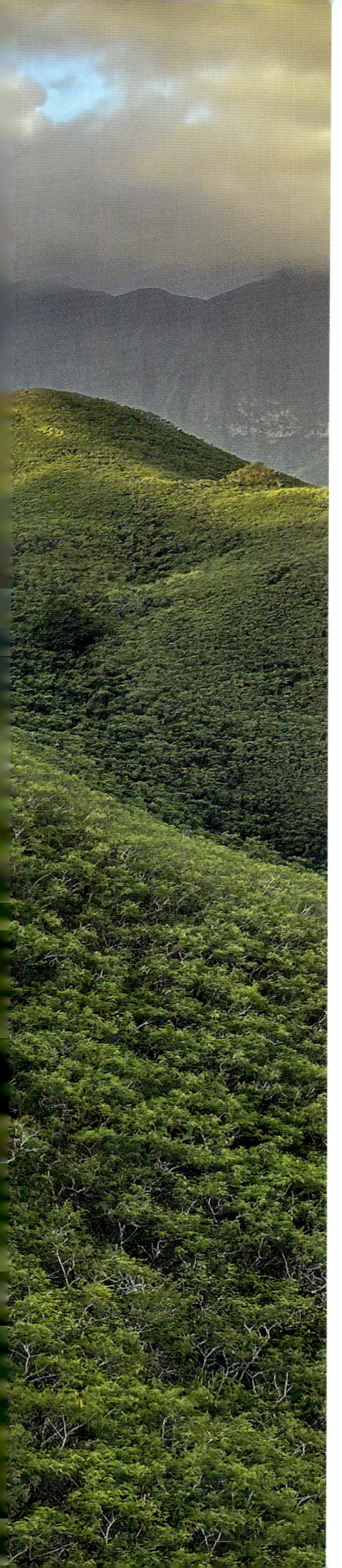

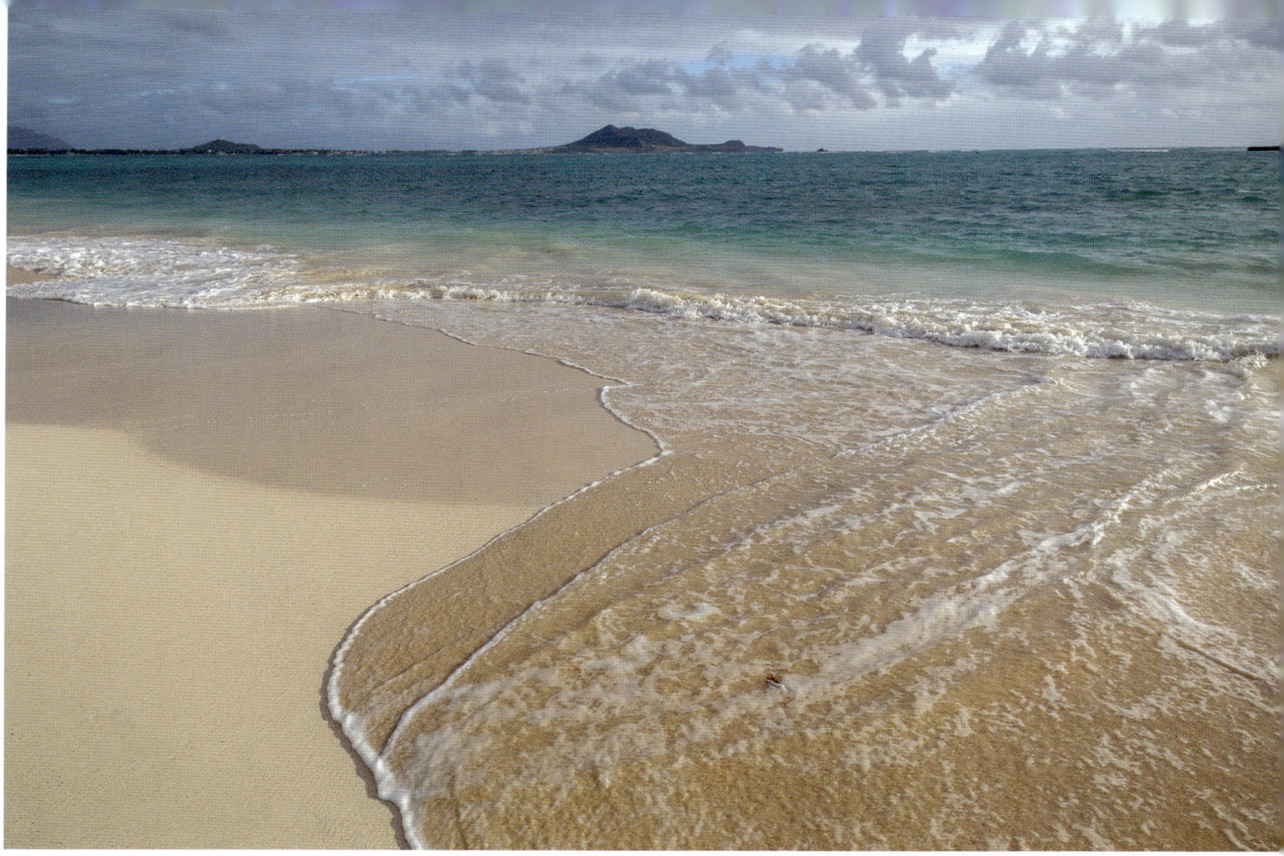

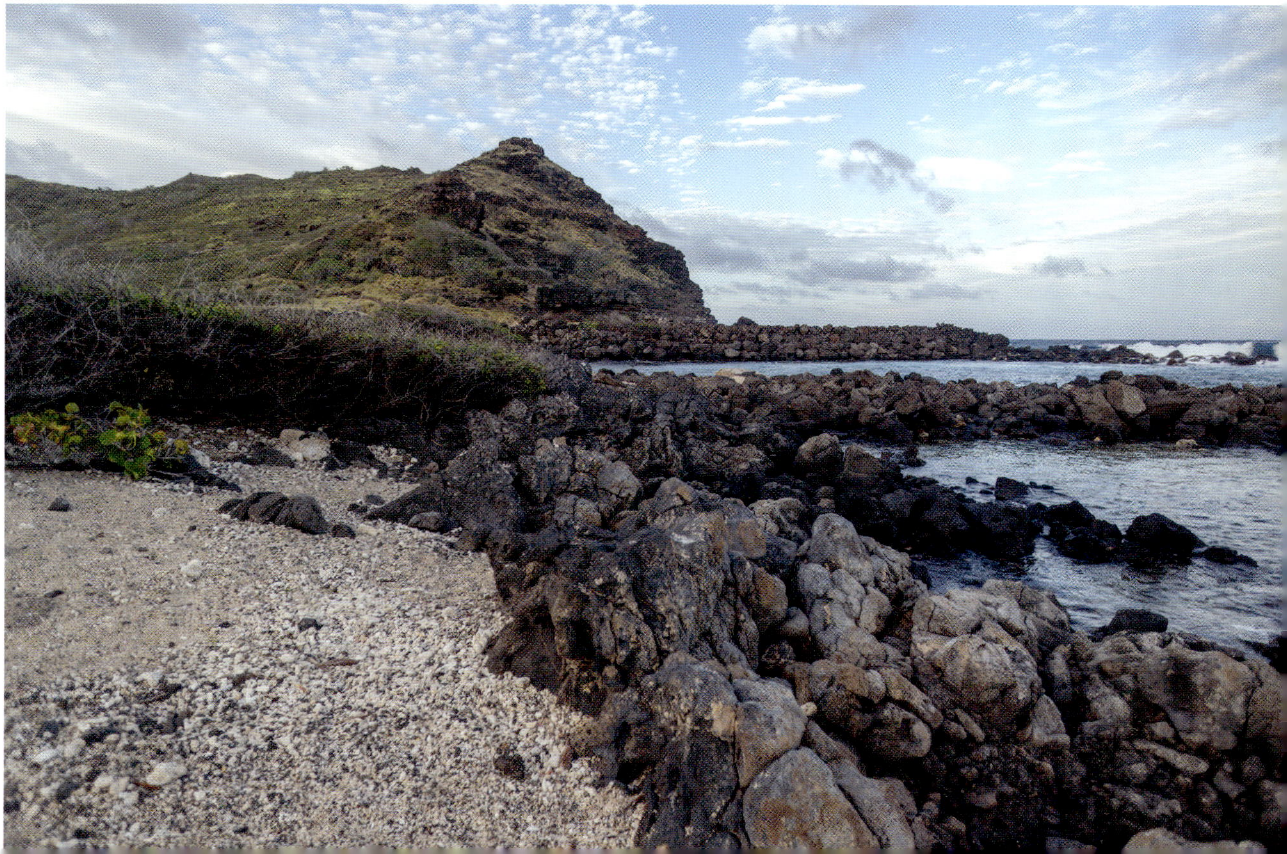

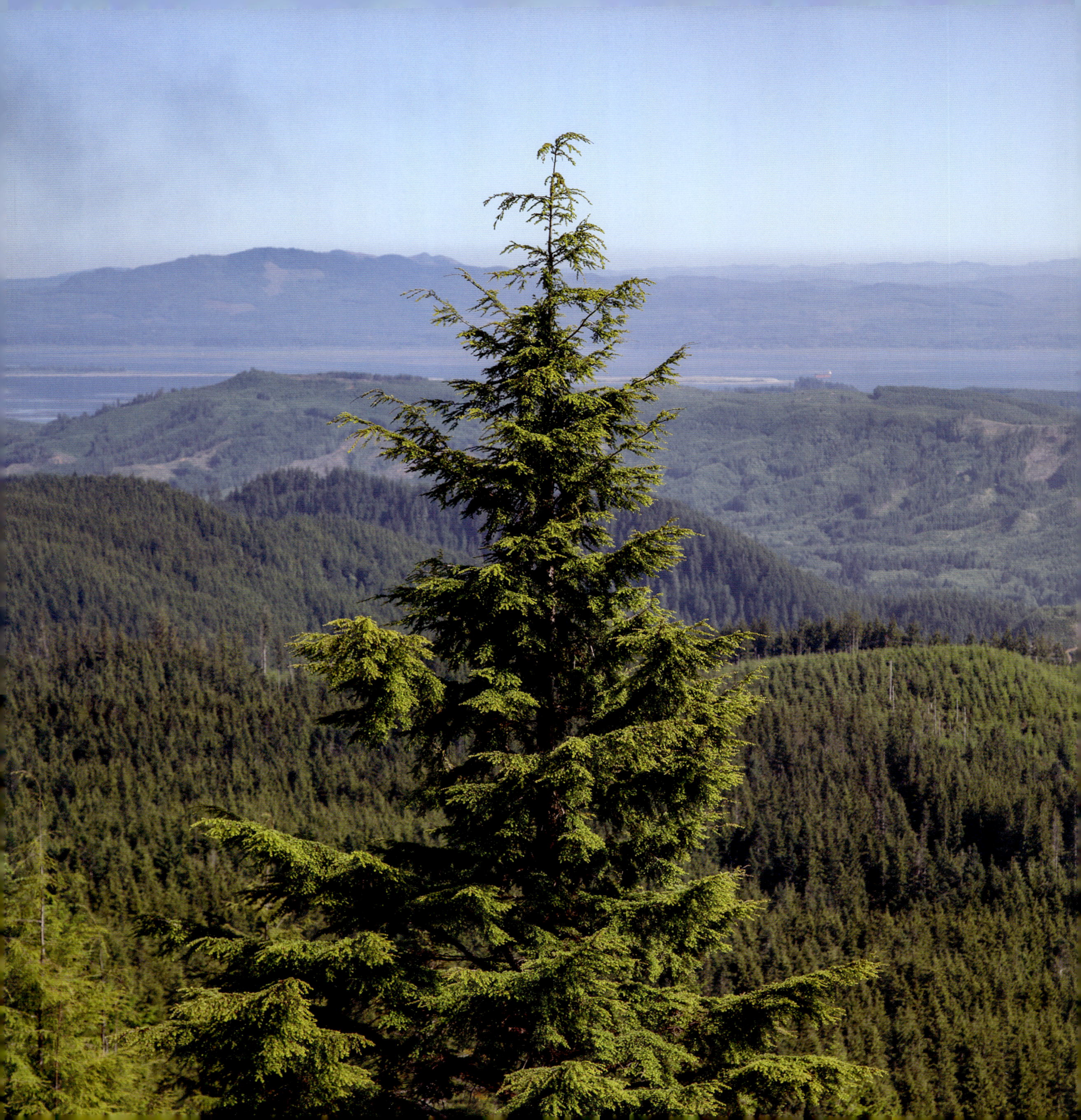

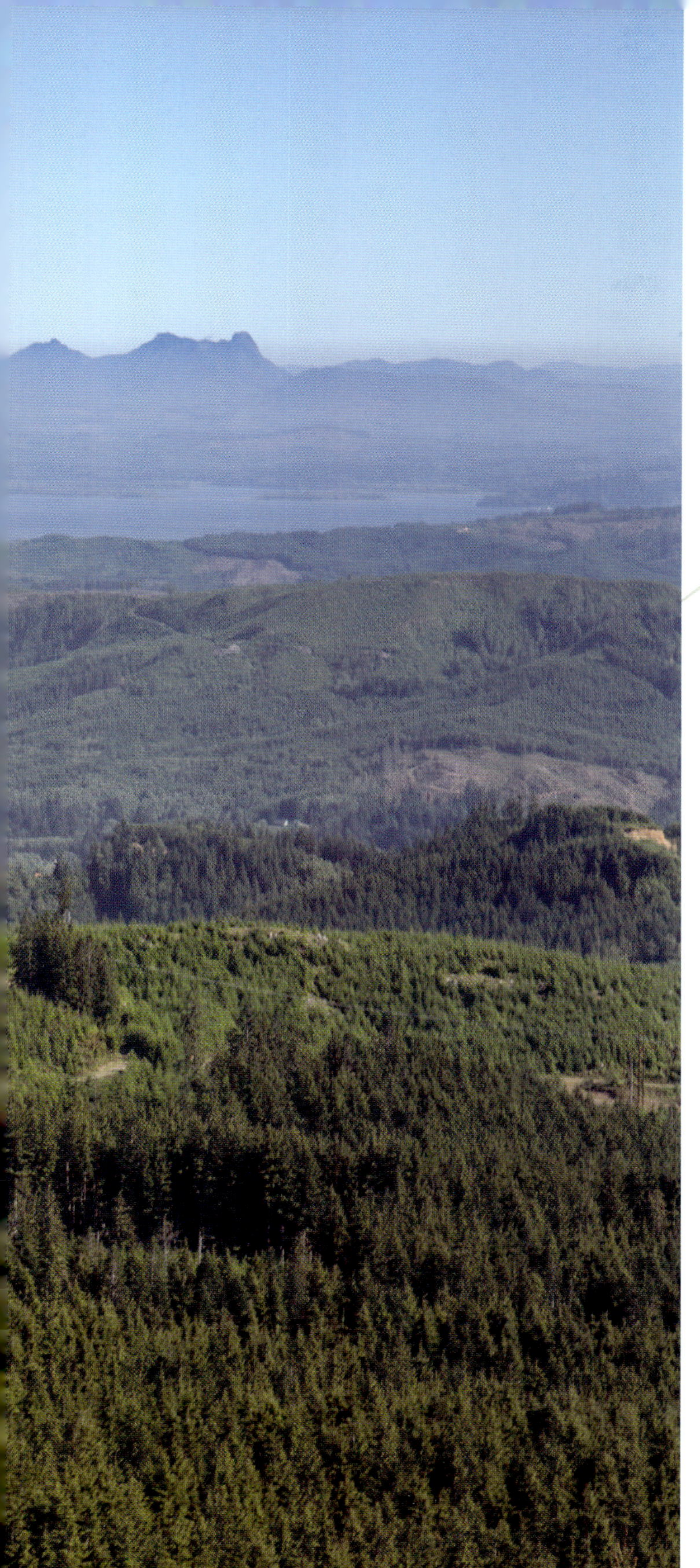

Robert Michael Pyle

"To allow the leaves to speak: that is the task. I often tell
students that we should aspire to be amanuenses to
the land: to let the land speak (in all its voices, human
and otherwise), then take dictation, and try to get some
of the words right. 'How do you know when you get
the words right?' they ask. 'You know,' I reply. When we
do, the leaves not only speak; they positively sing."

From the essay "Secrets of the Talking Leaf,"
from *Nature Matrix: New and Selected Essays*

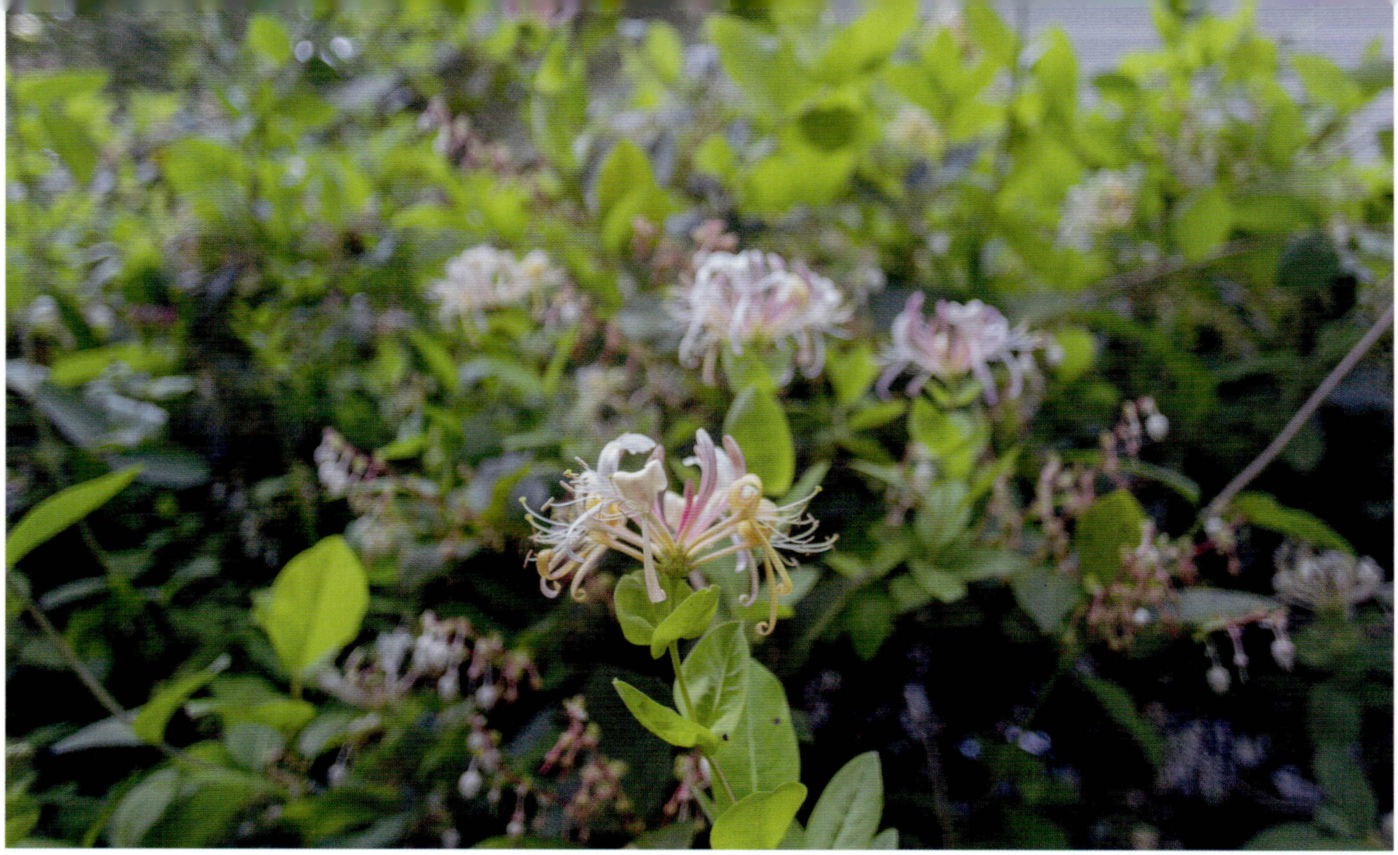

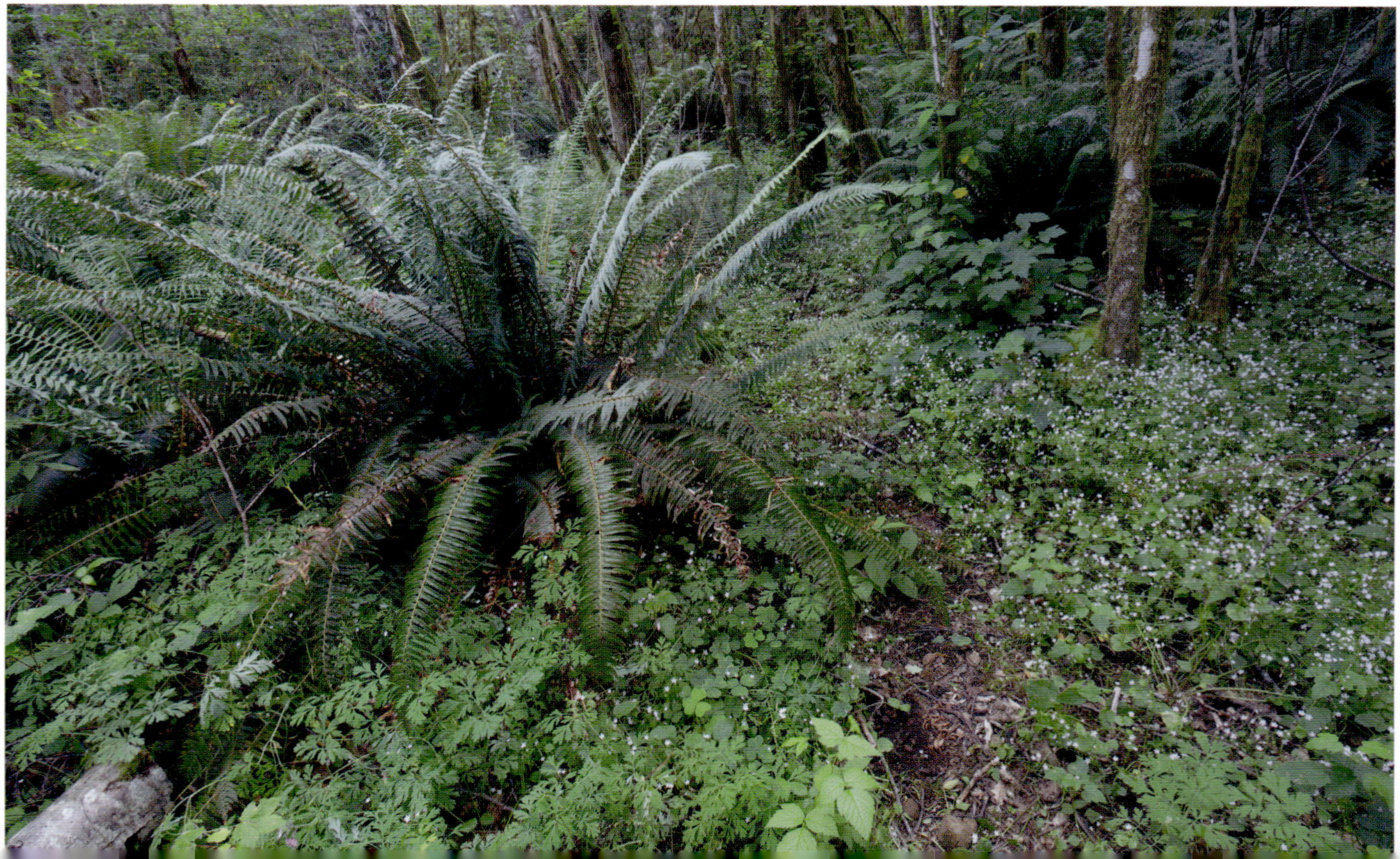

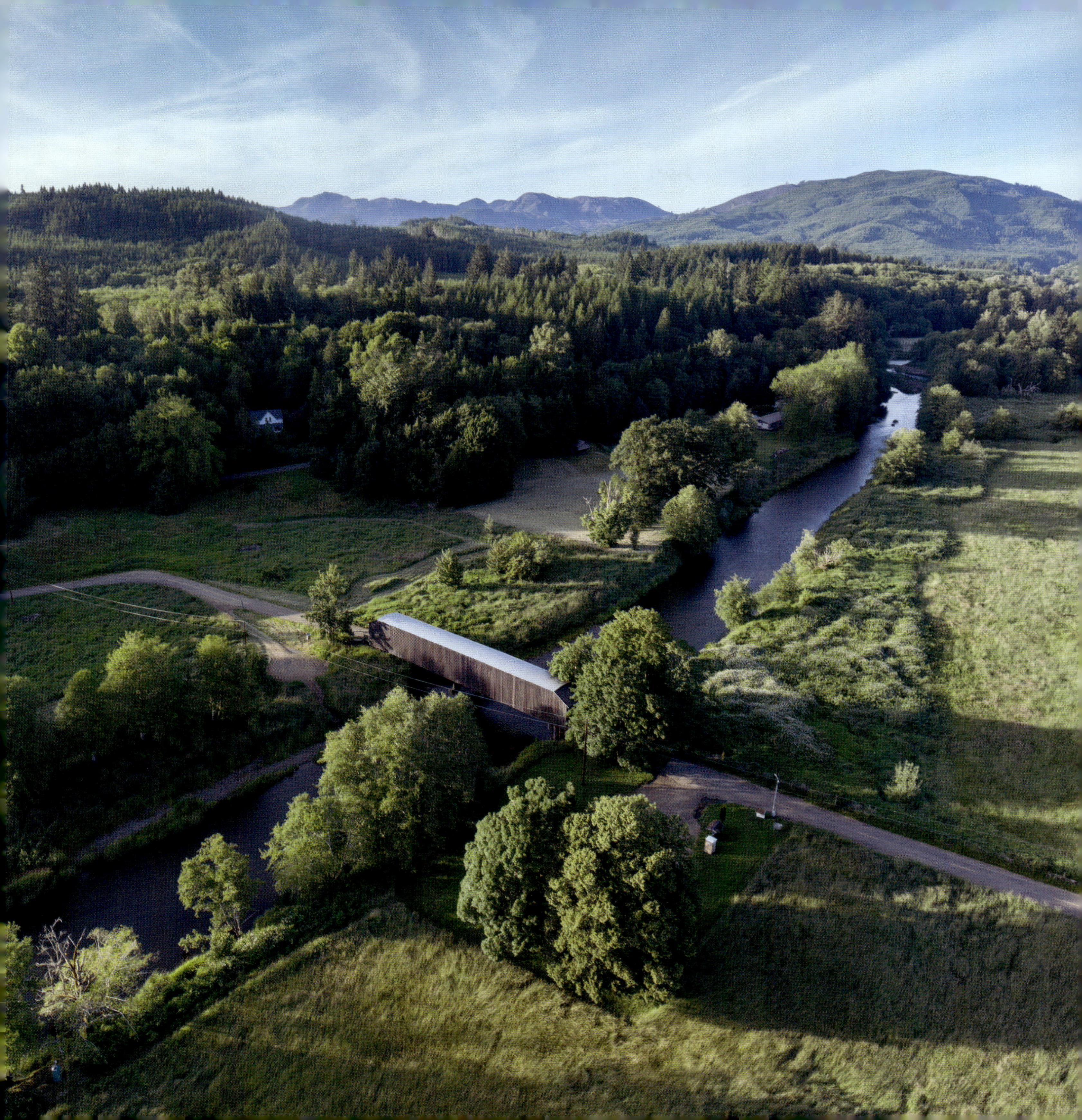

Janisse Ray

GEORGIA

"Not long ago I dreamed of actually cradling a place,
as if something so amorphous and vague as a region,
existing mostly in imagination and idea, suddenly
took form. I held its sunken relief in my arms, a baby
smelted from a plastic topography map, and when I
gazed down into its face, as my father had gazed into
mine, I saw the pine flatwoods of my homeland."

From *Ecology of a Cracker Childhood*

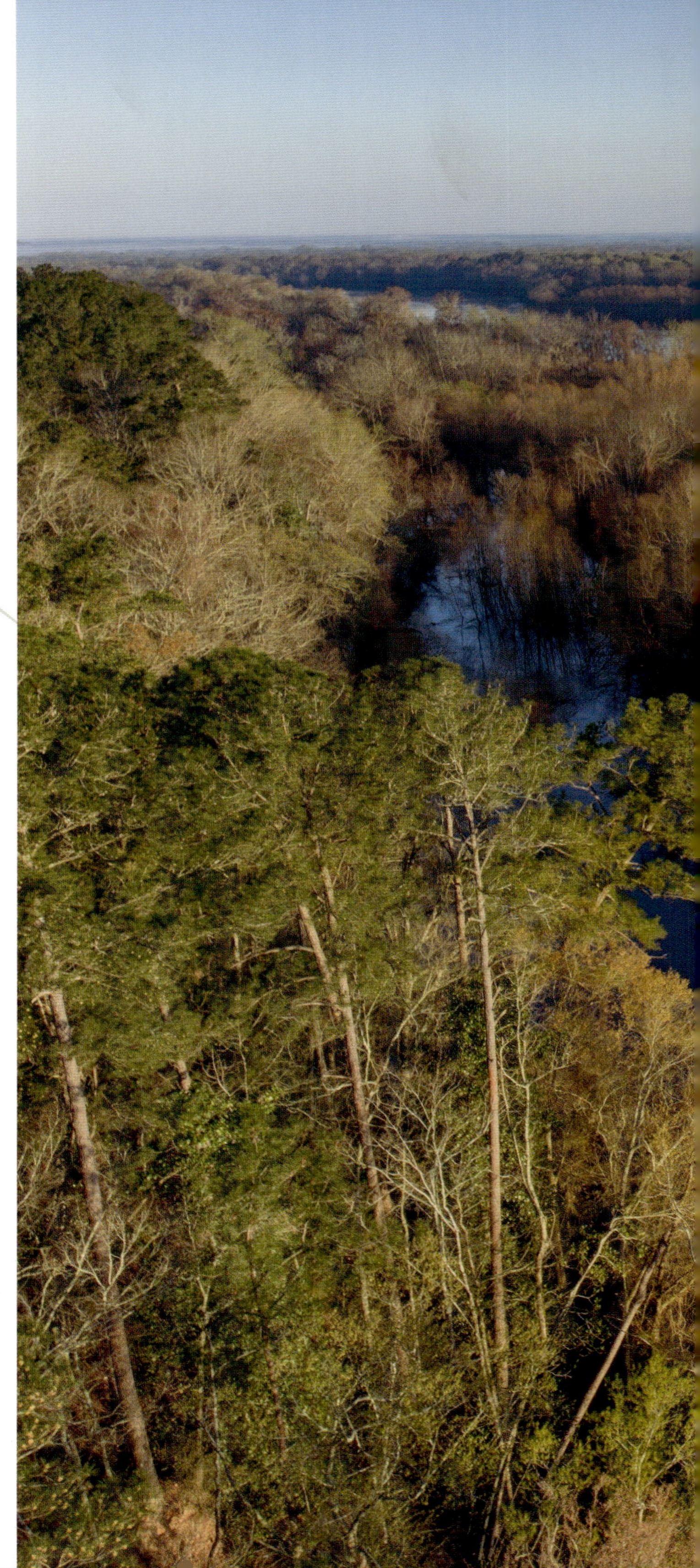

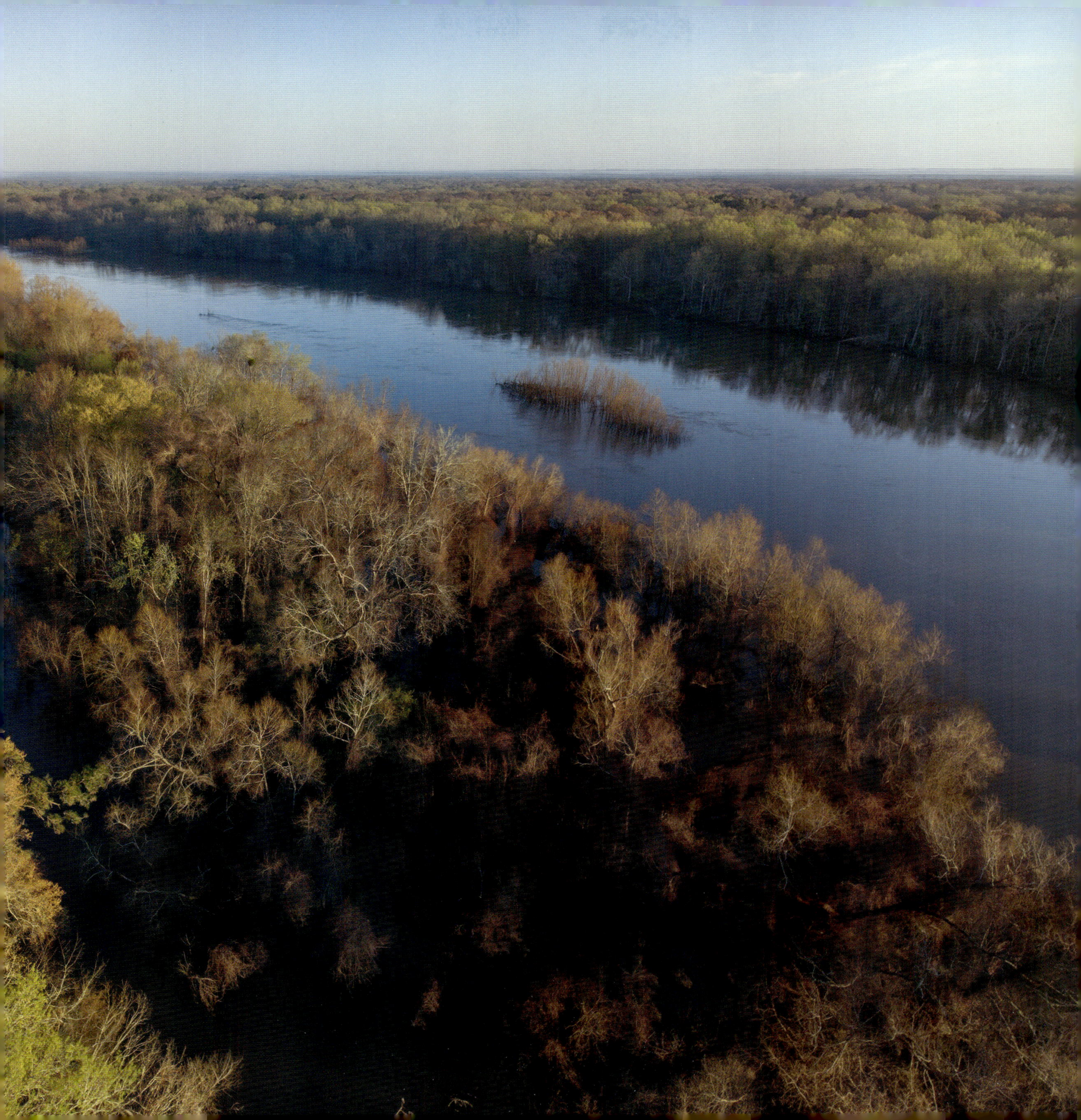

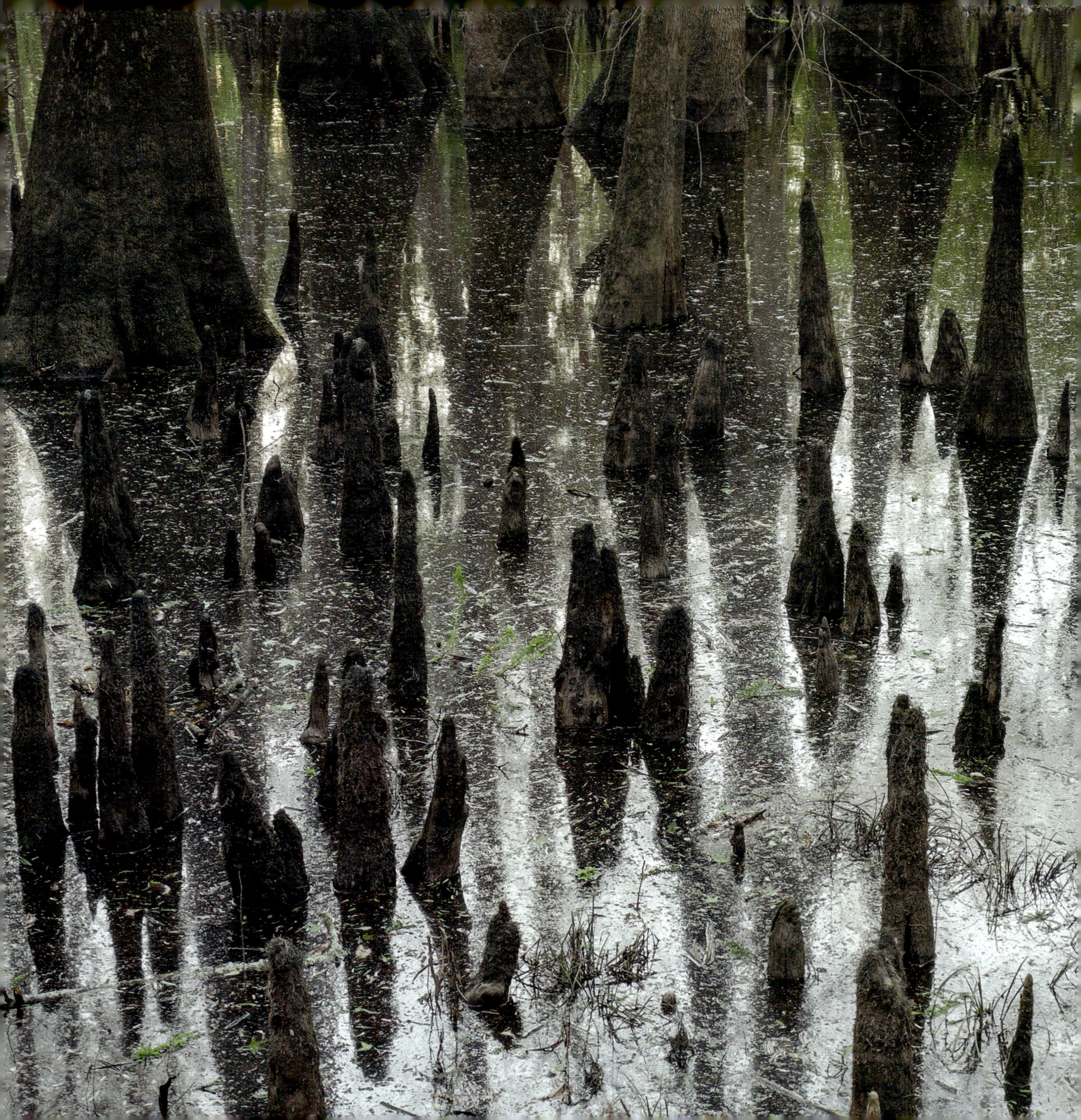

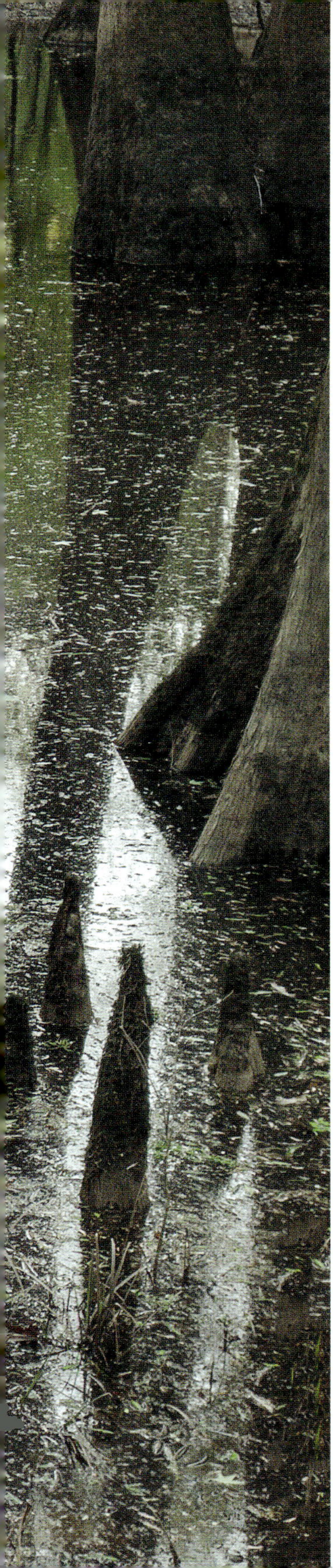

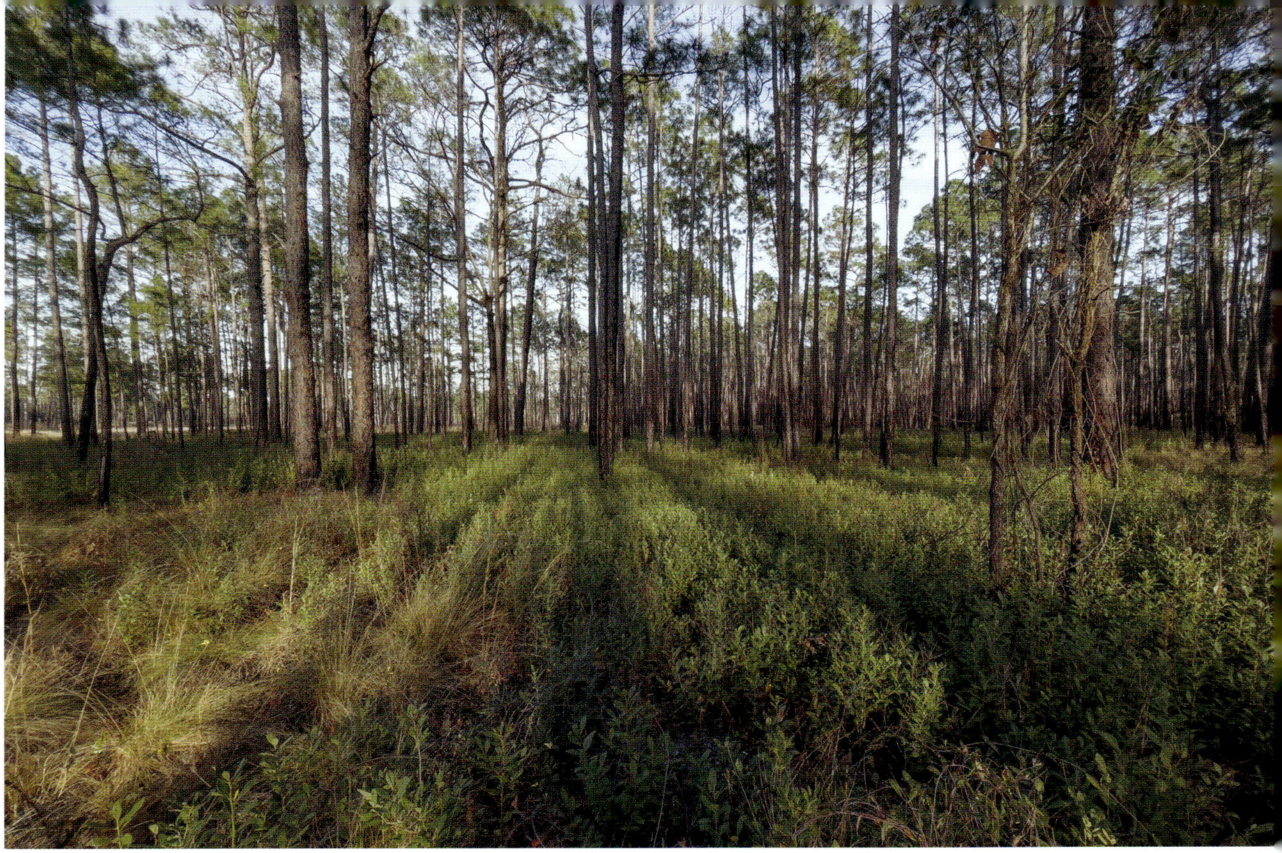

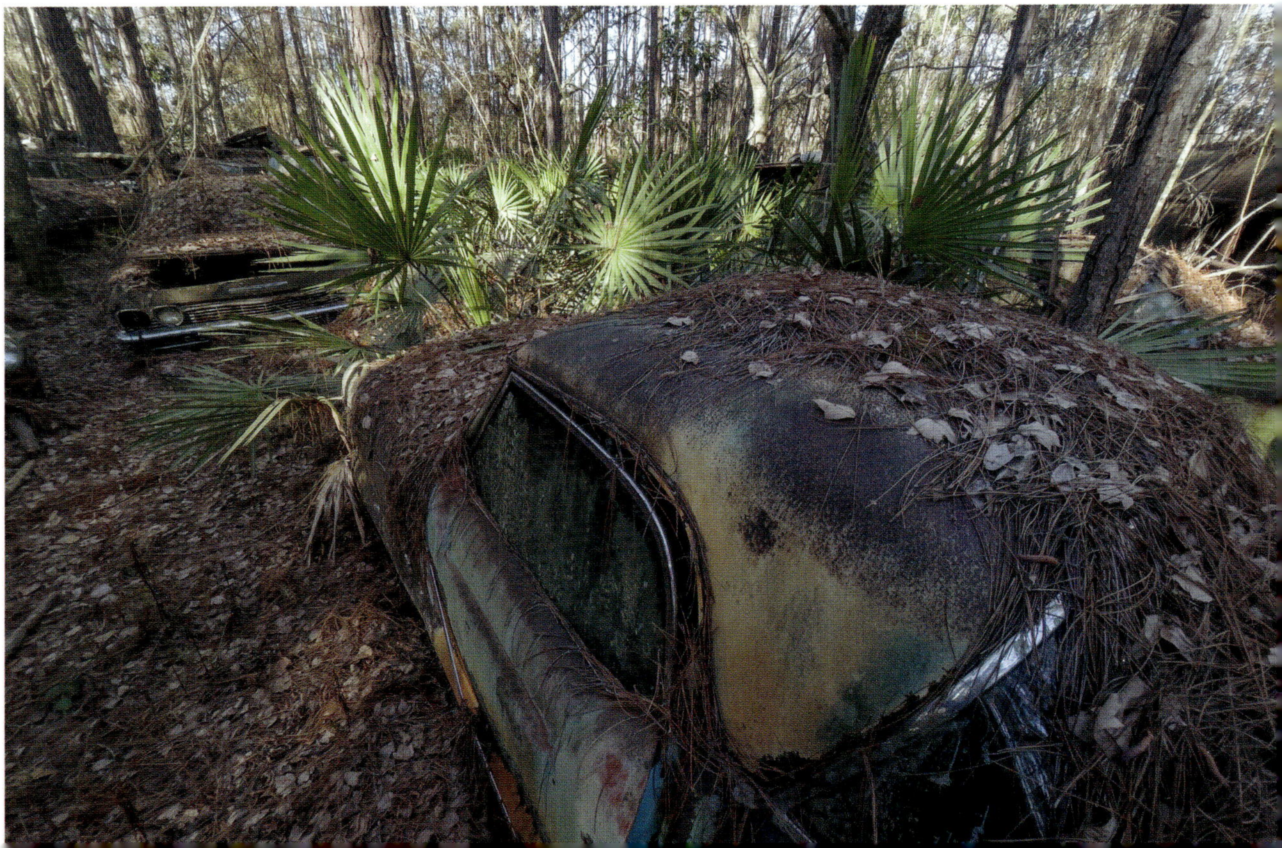

Theodore Roosevelt

"I grow very fond of this place, and it certainly has
a desolate, grim beauty of its own, that has a curious
fascination for me."

From *Letters from Theodore Roosevelt
to Anna Roosevelt Cowles, 1870–1918*

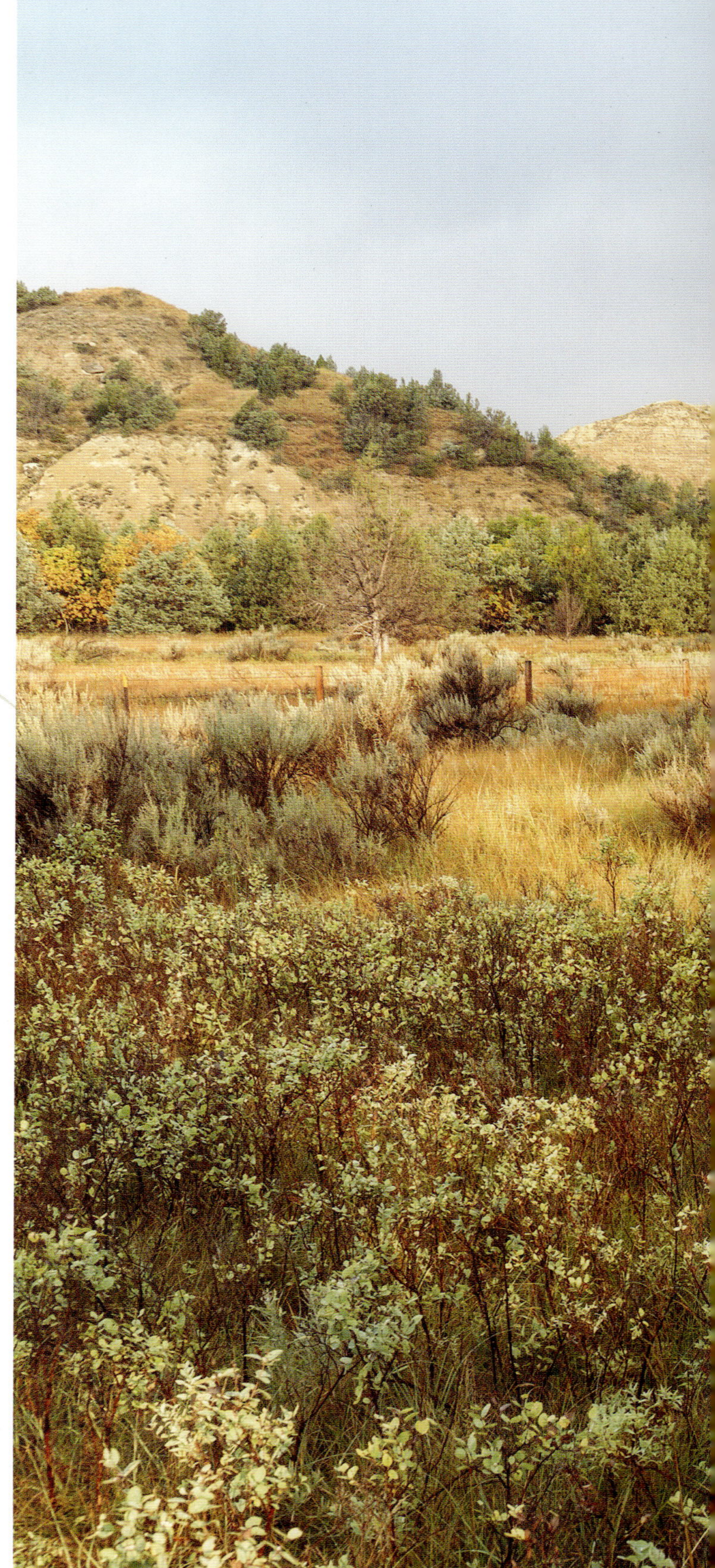

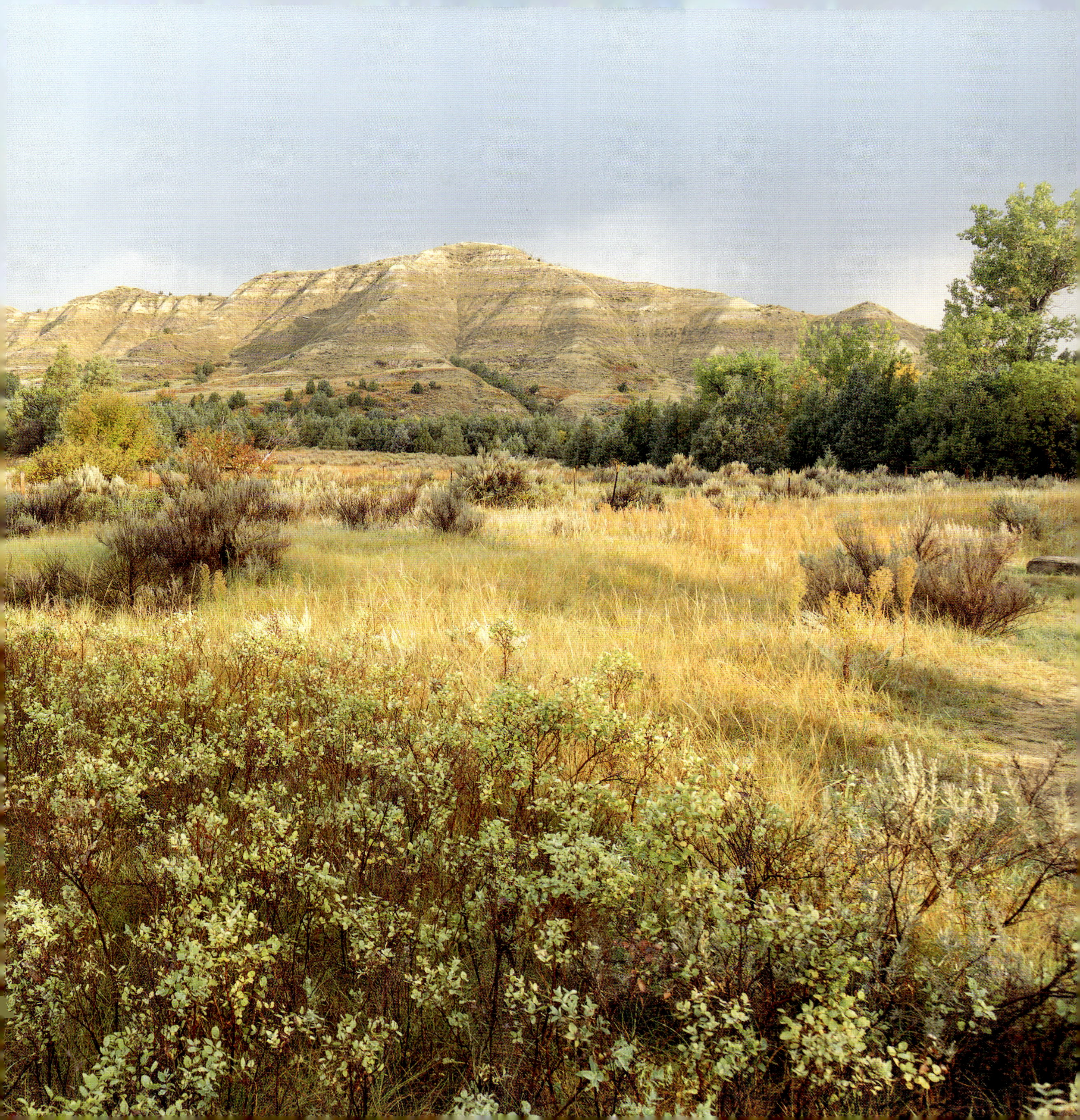

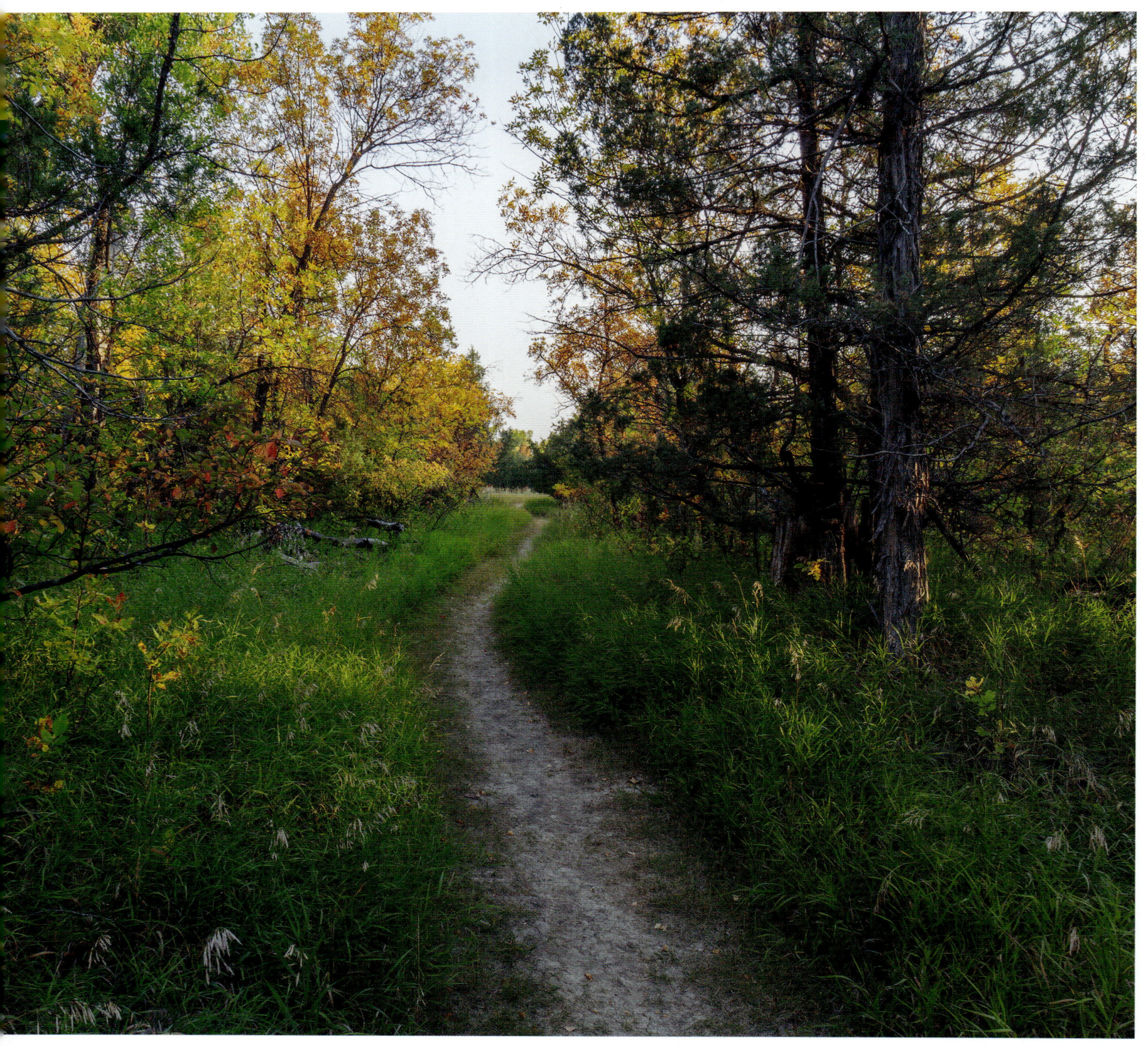

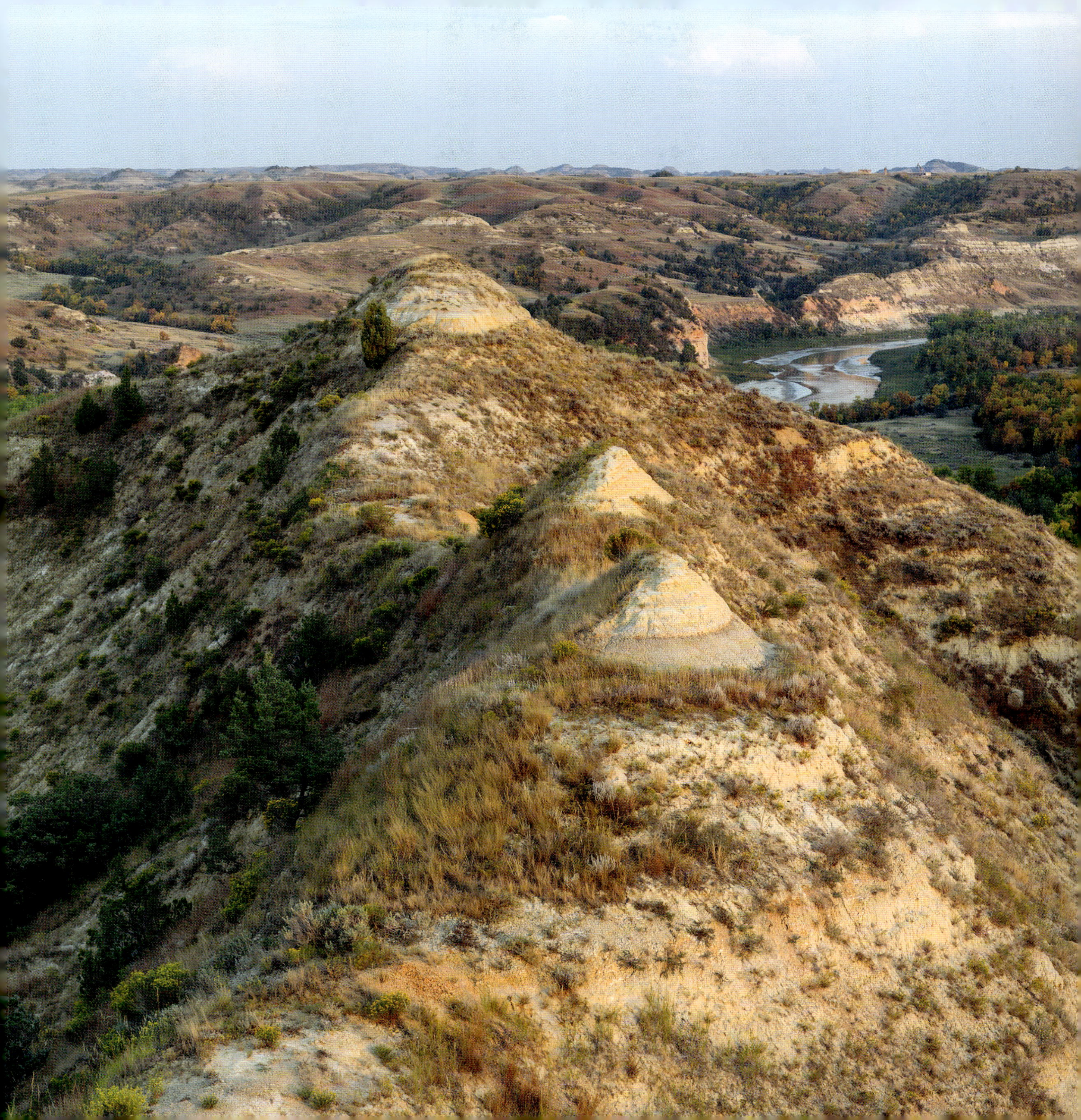

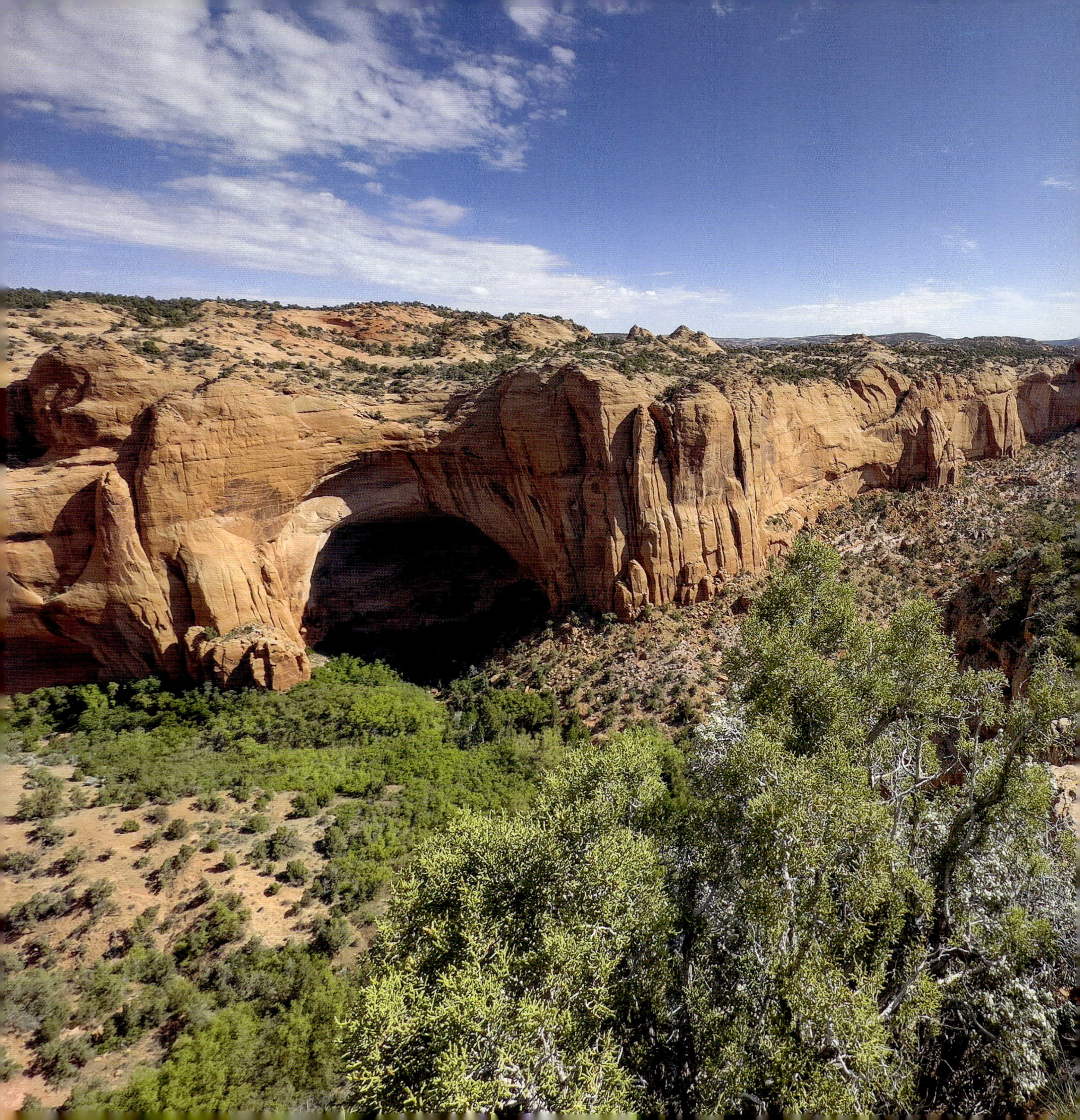

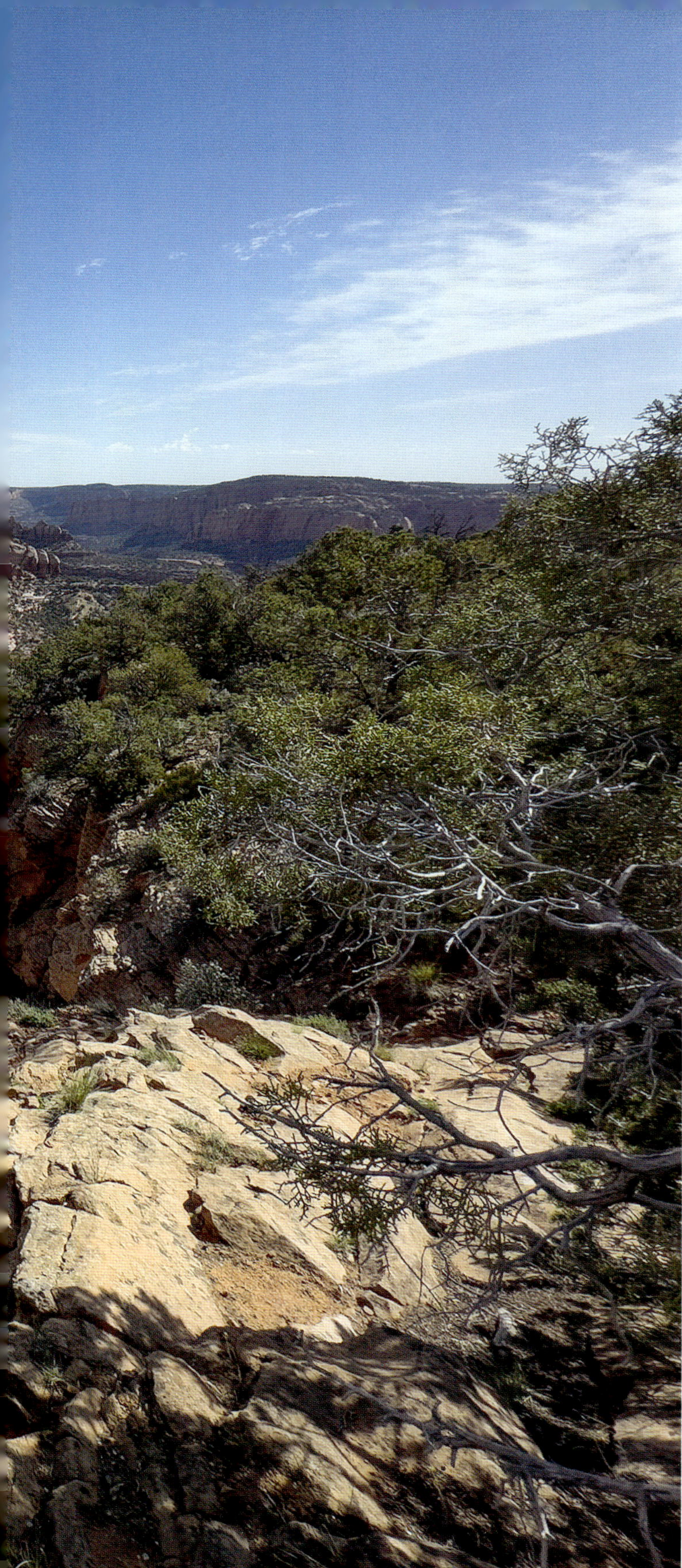

Enrique Salmón

ARIZONA

"In a worldview based on iwígara, humans are no more important to the natural world than any other form of life. This notion influences how I lead my own life and guides many of my decisions. Knowing that I am related to everything around me and share breath with all living things helps me to focus on my responsibility to honor all forms of life. I carefully consider all living and non-living things when making choices or weighing actions I might take. In short, I see myself as one of many stewards of the land and natural world. I share breath with it, so I endeavor to minister to it with appropriate ritual, thought, and ceremony."

From *Iwígara: The Kinship of Plants and People;*
American Indian Ethnobotanical Traditions and Science

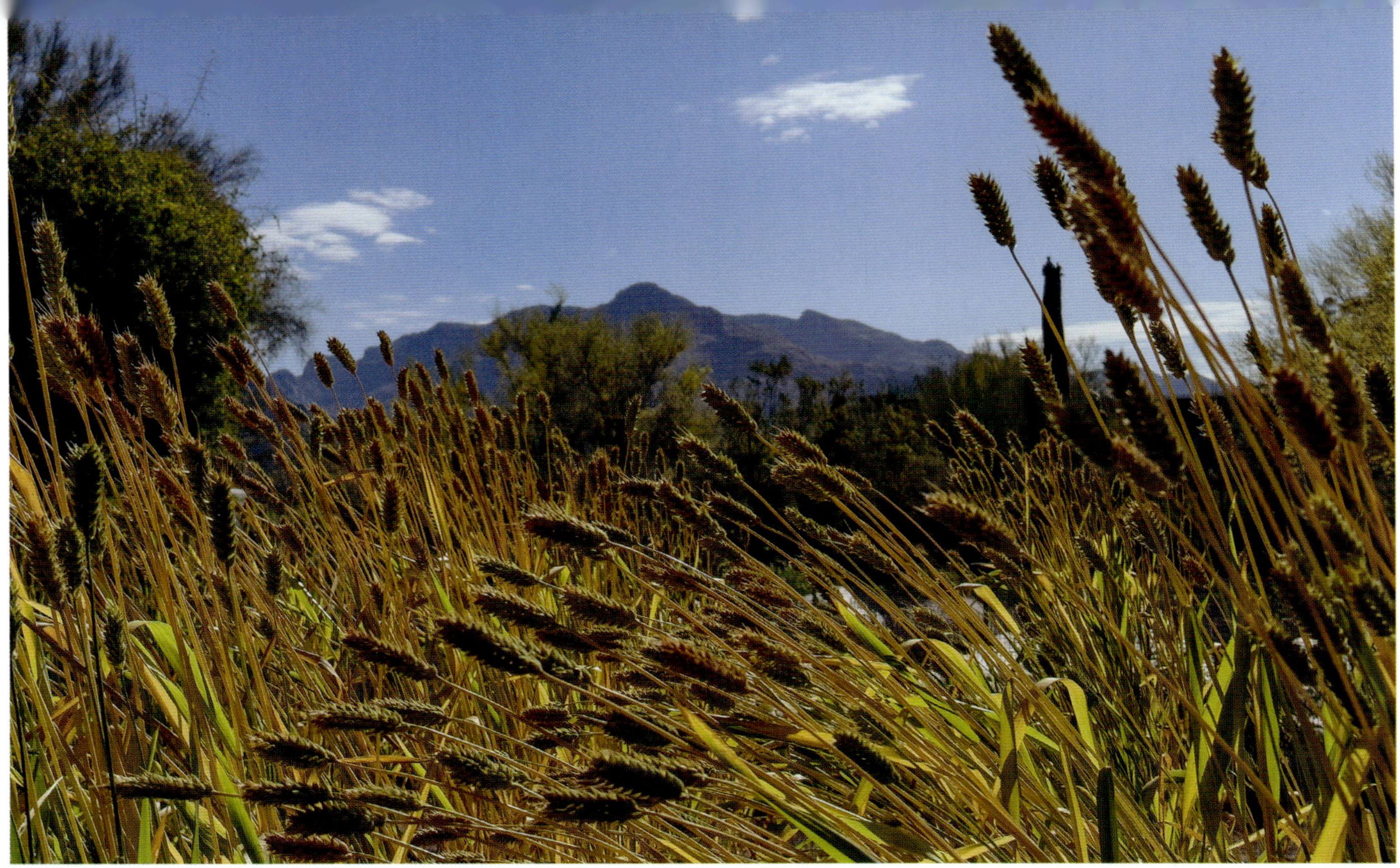

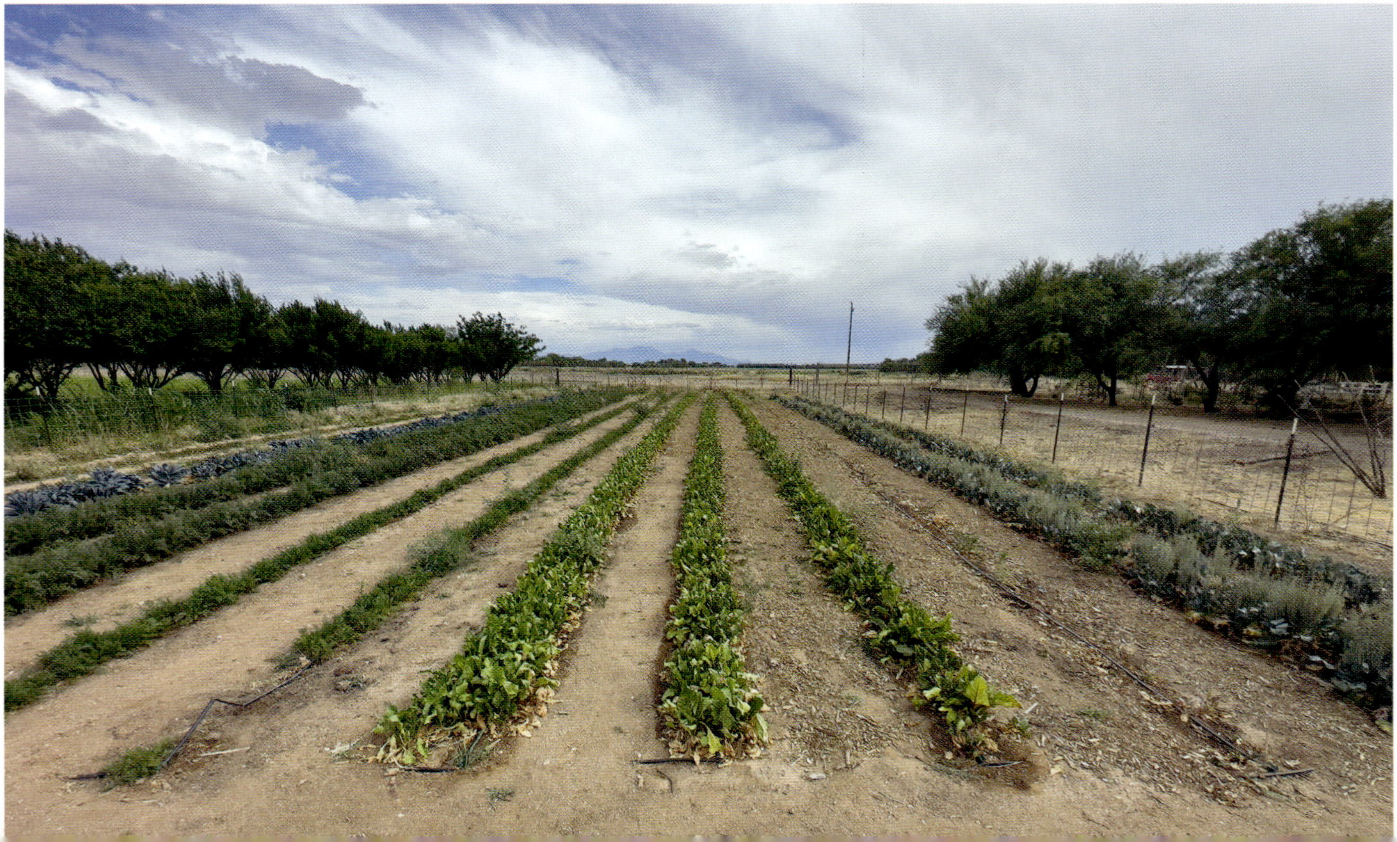

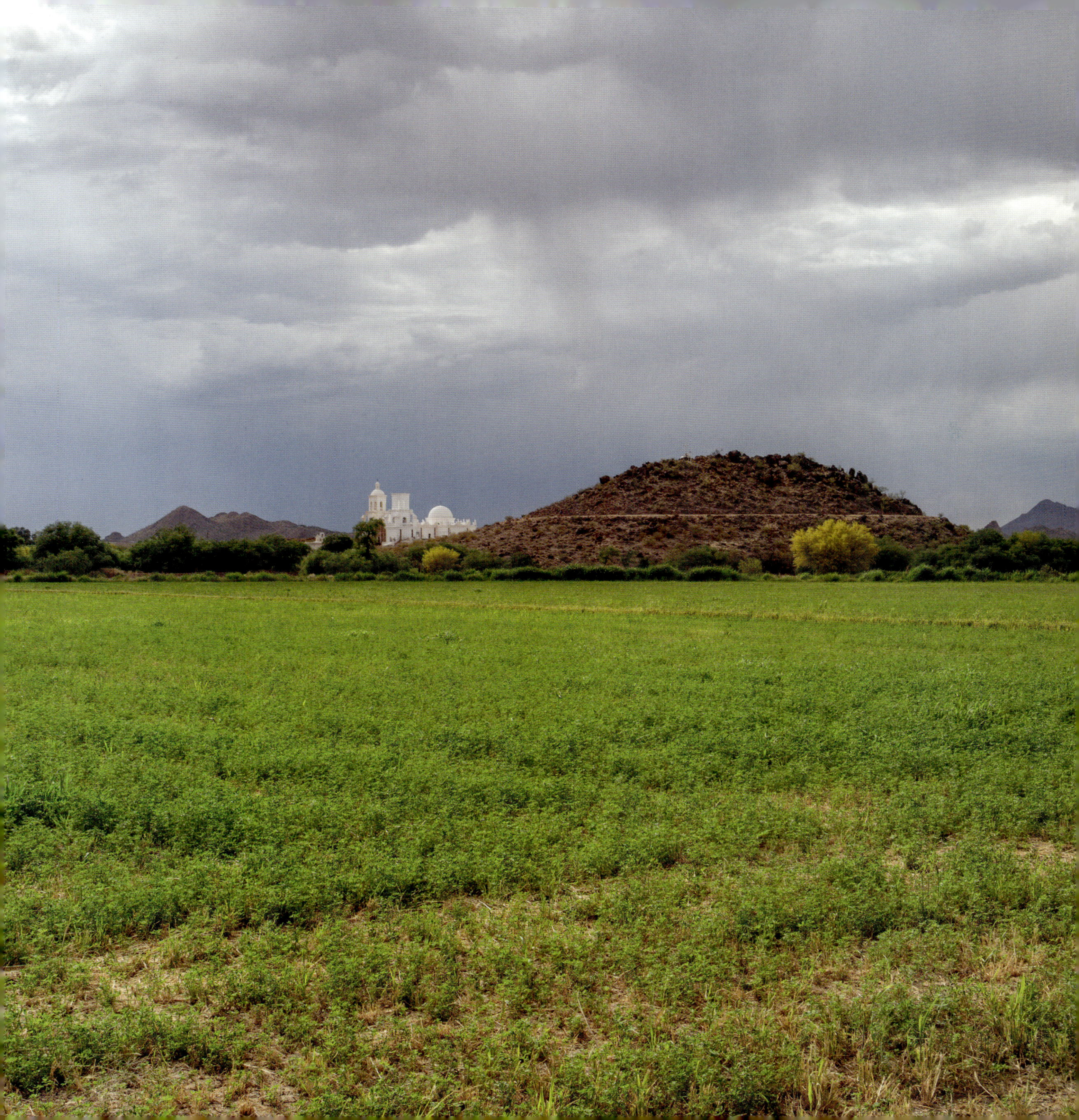

Gene Stratton-Porter

INDIANA

"Turn her loose out of doors; give her good books, and leave her alone. You won't be disappointed in the woman who evolves."

From *Laddie: A True Blue Story*

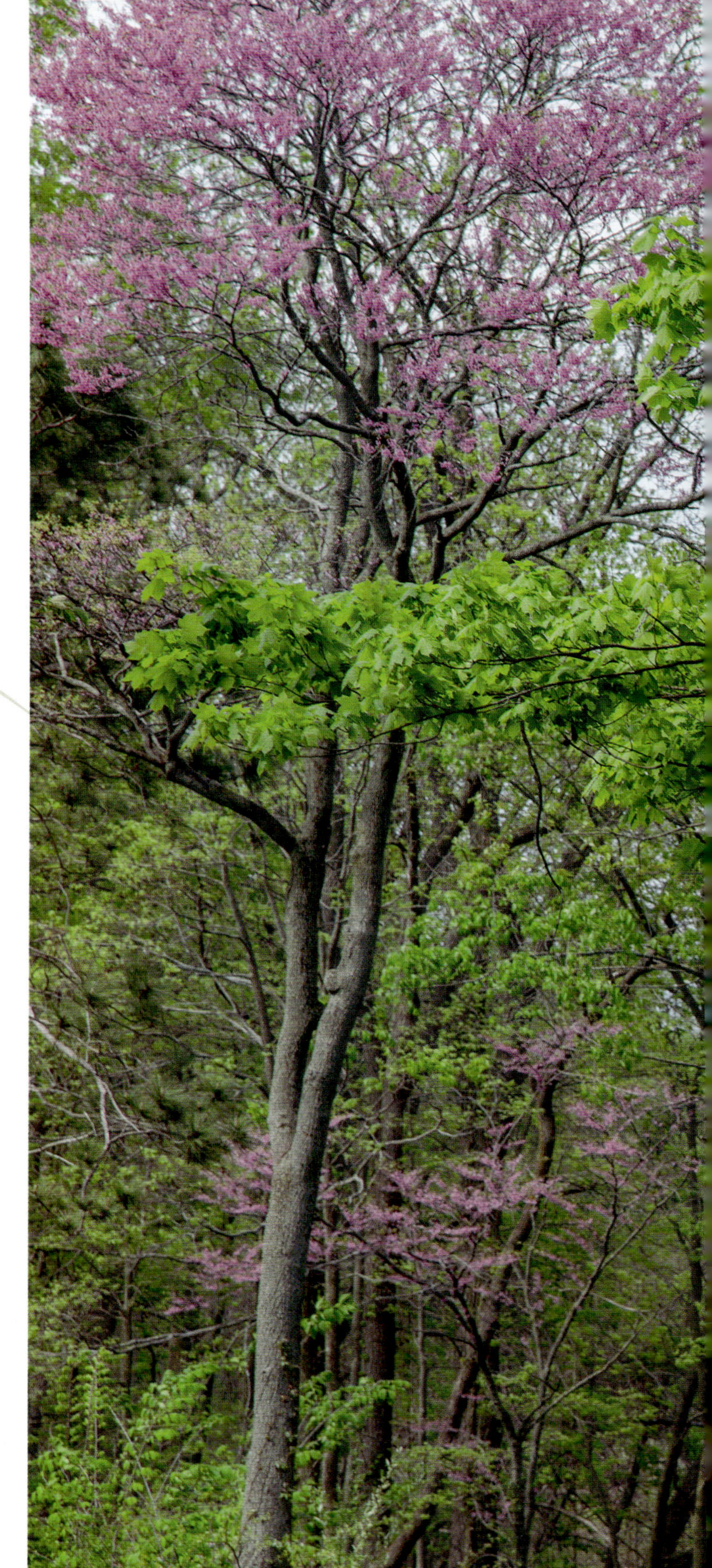

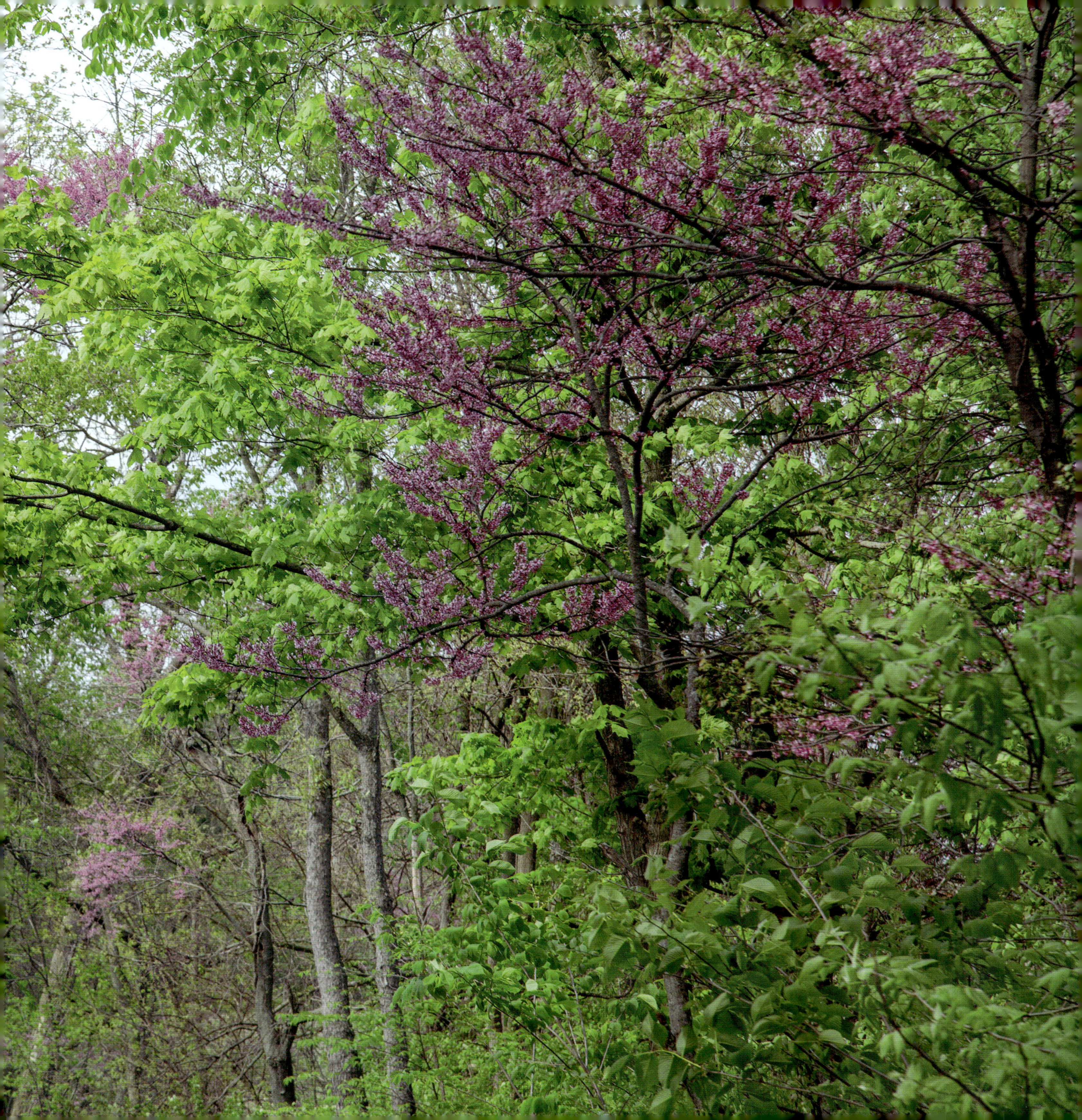

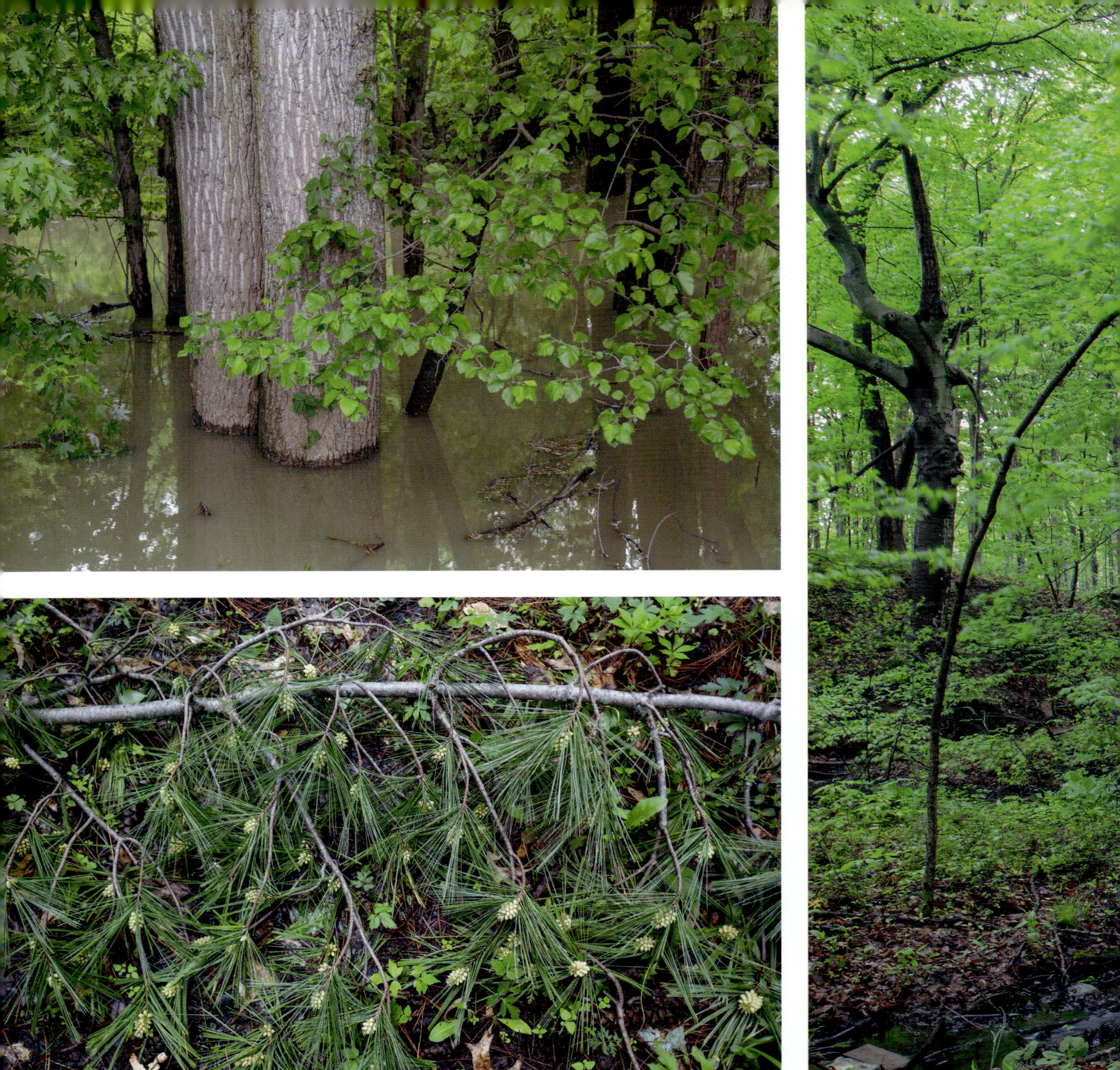

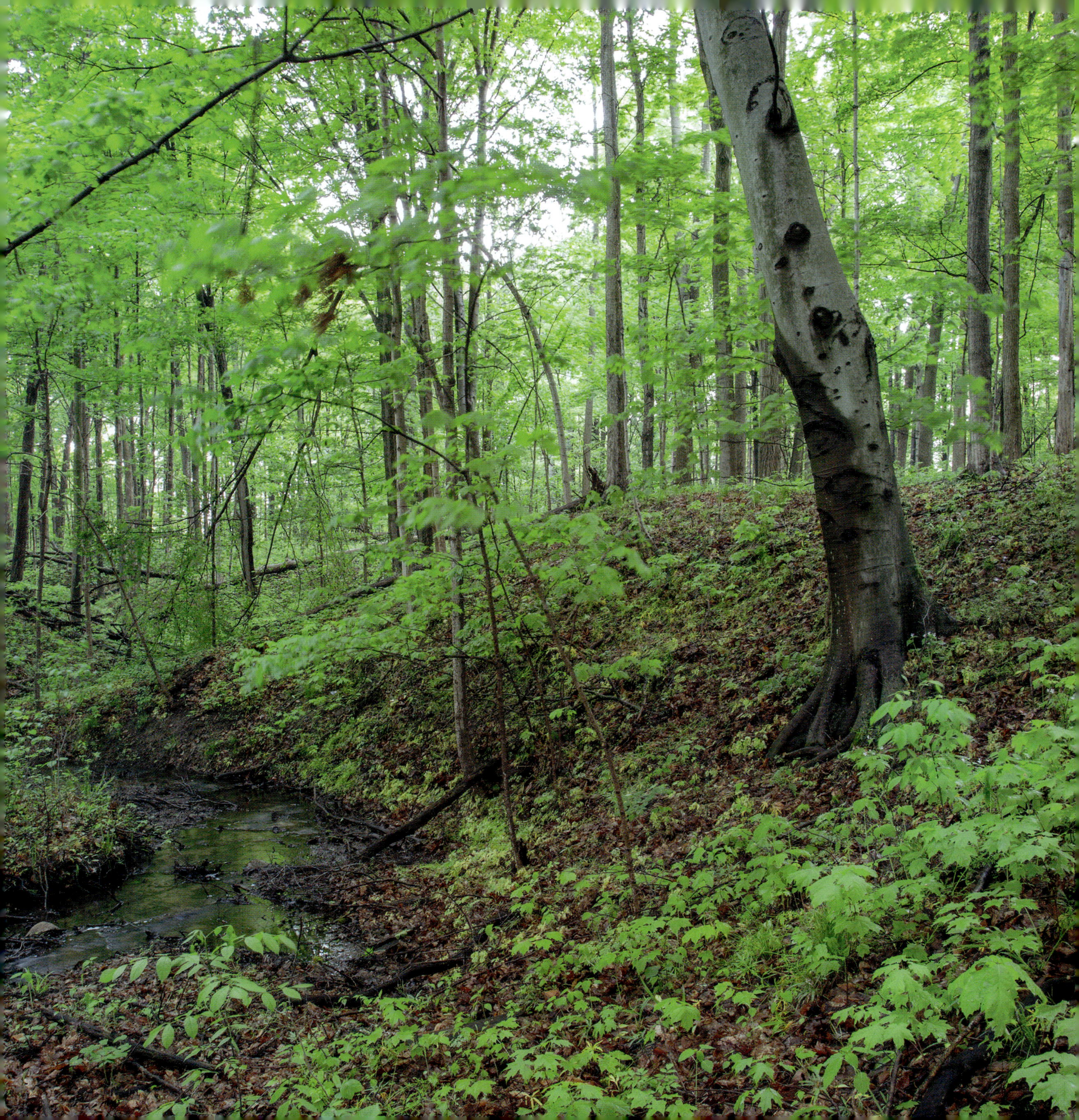

Henry David Thoreau

MASSACHUSETTS

"I love Nature partly *because* she is not man, but a retreat from him. None of his institutions control or pervade her. There a different kind of right prevails. In her midst I can be glad with an entire gladness. If this world were all man, I could not stretch myself, I should lose all hope. He is constraint; she is freedom to me. He makes me wish for another world. She makes me content with this."

From *The Writings of Henry D. Thoreau,*
Journal, Volume 5: 1852–1853

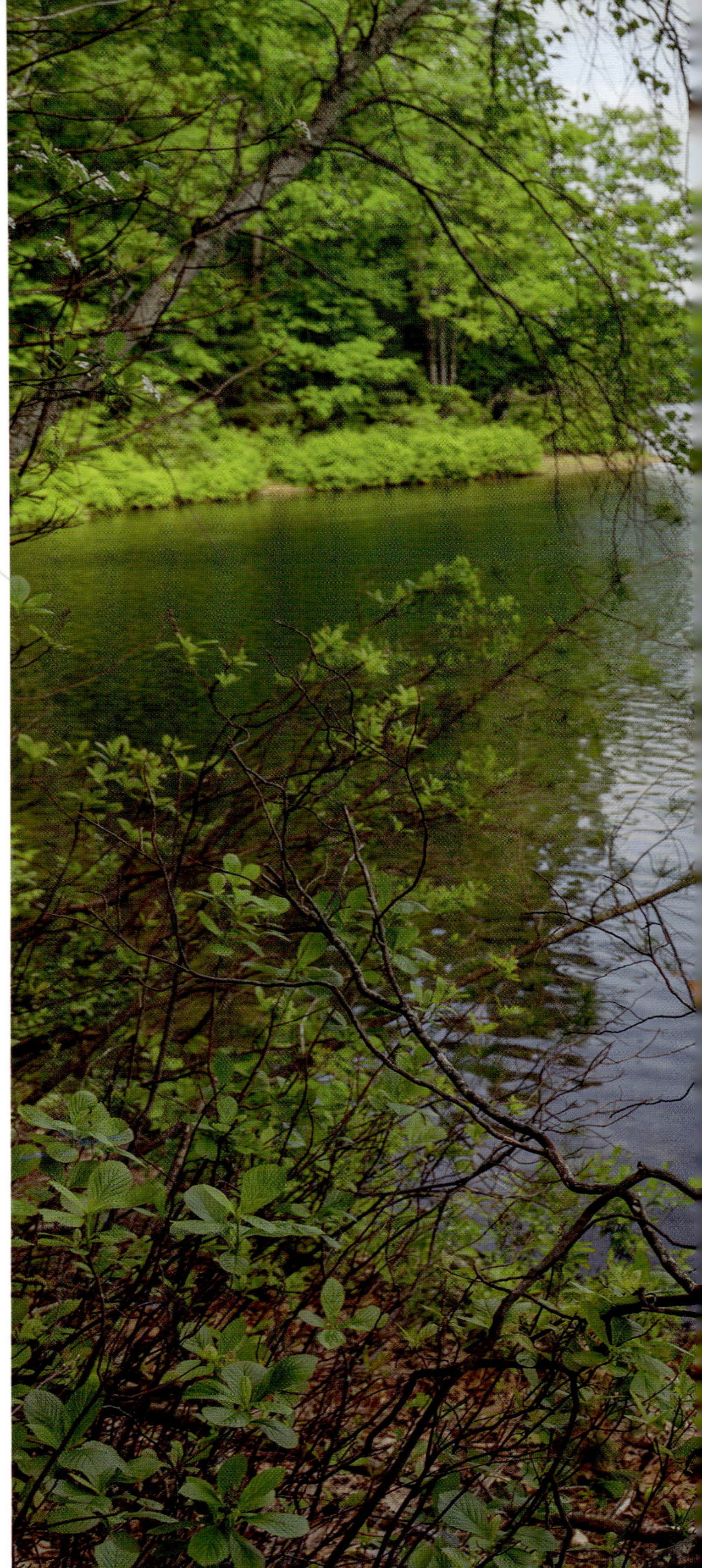

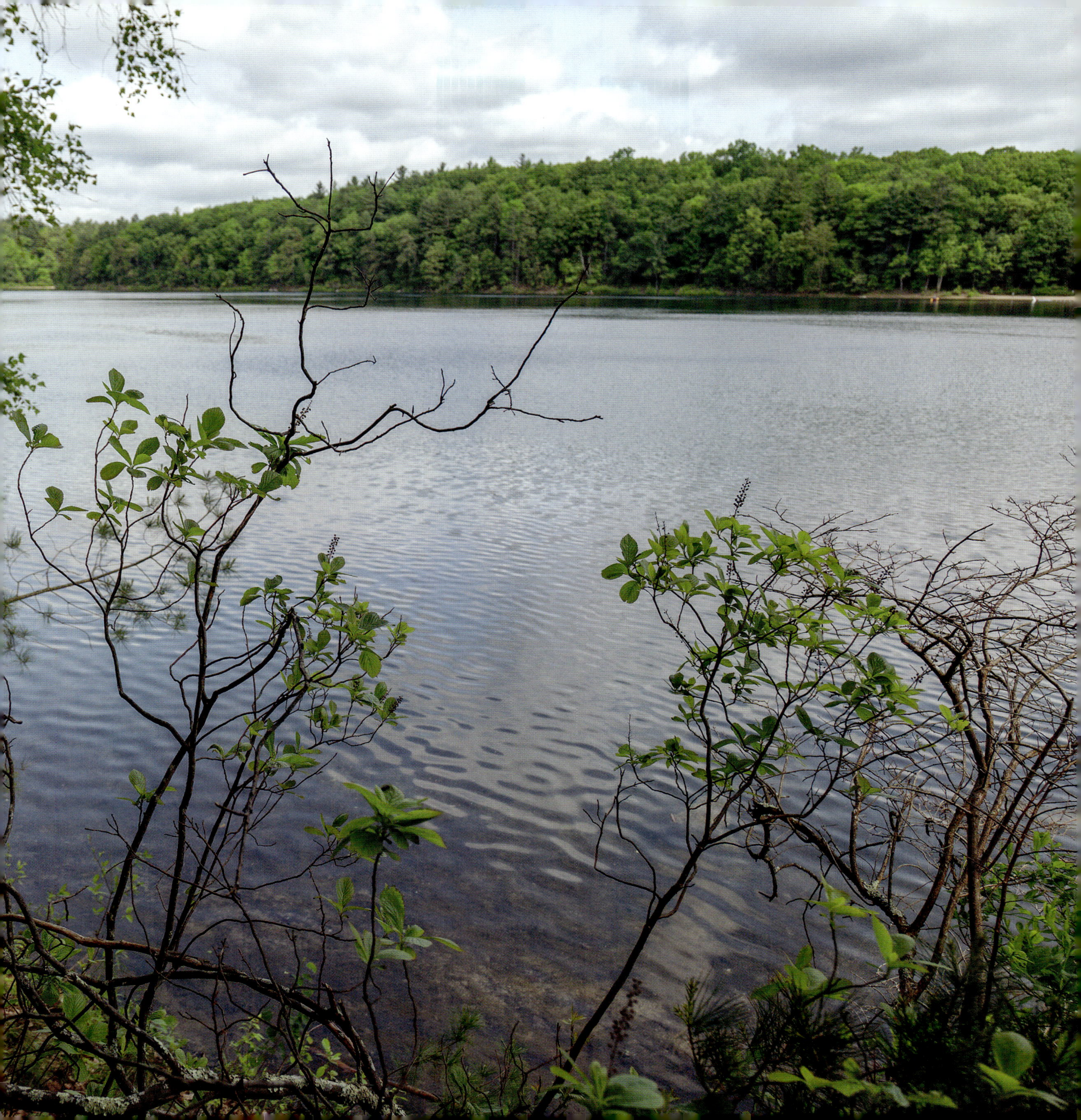

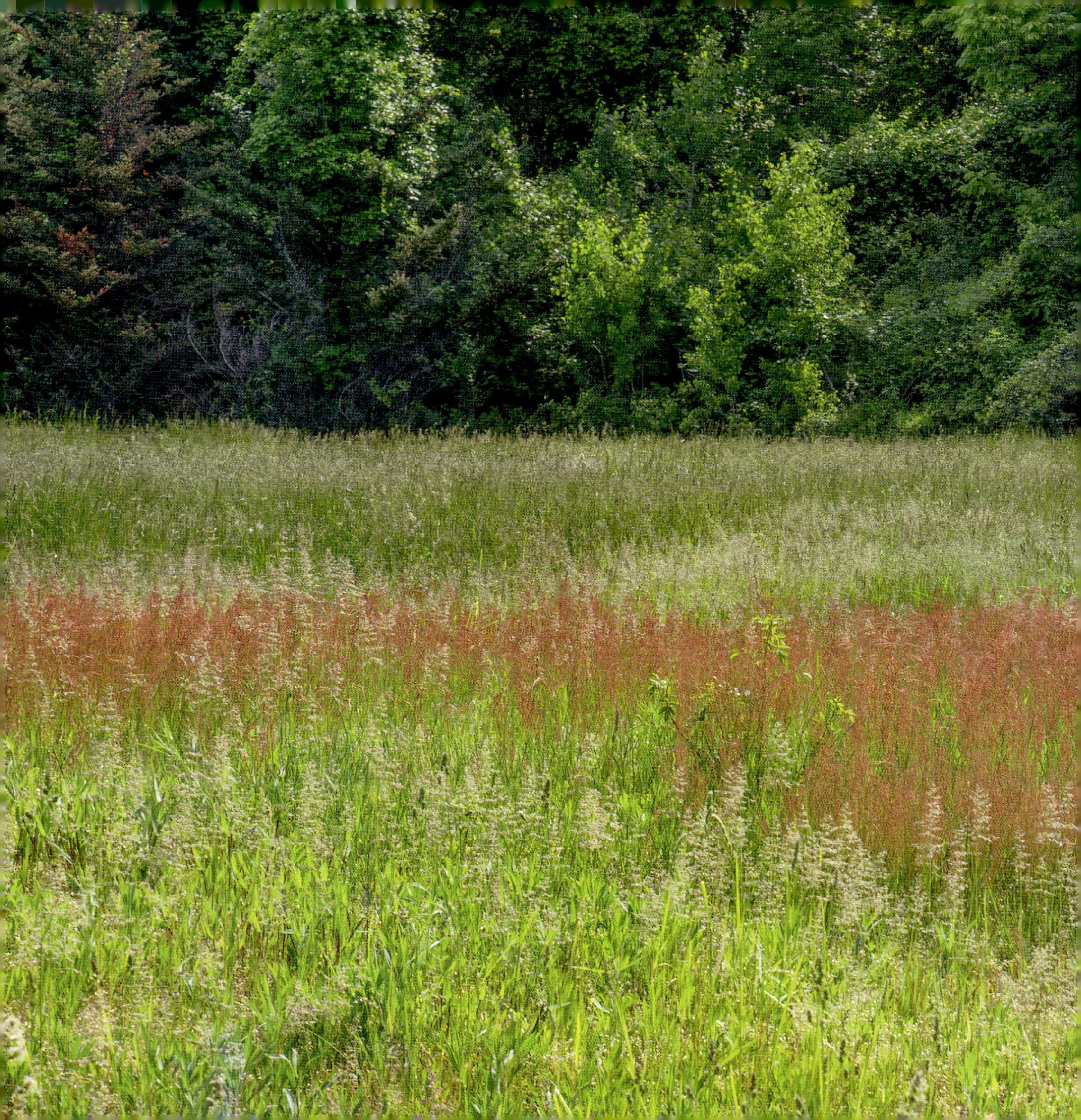

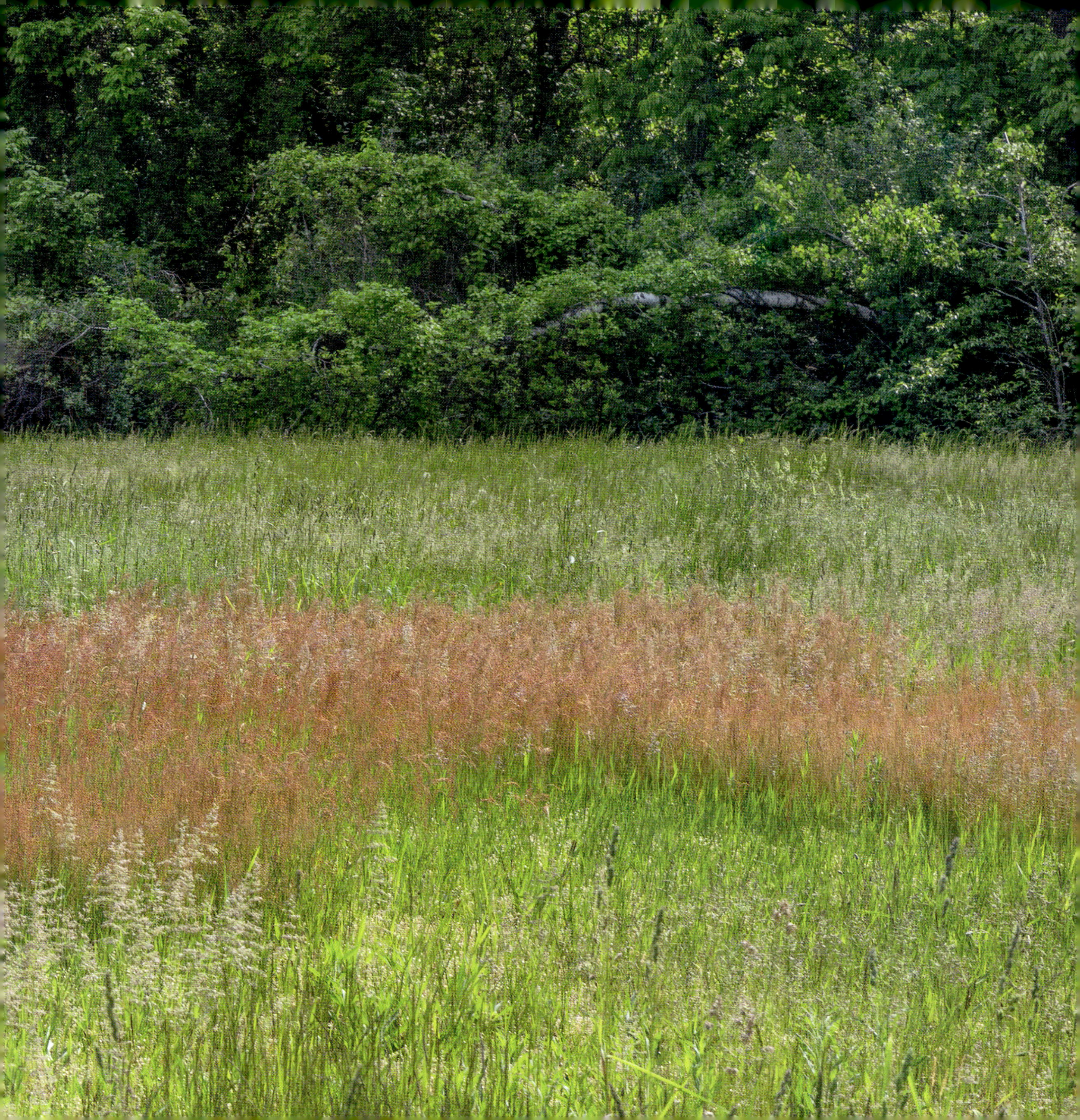

Terry Tempest Williams

UTAH & WYOMING

"It's strange how deserts turn us into believers.
I believe in walking in a landscape of mirages because
you learn humility. I believe in living in a land of little
water because life is drawn together. And I believe
in the gathering of bones as a testament to spirits that
have moved on. If the desert is holy, it is because it is
a forgotten place that allows us to remember the
sacred. Perhaps that is why every pilgrimage to the
desert is a pilgrimage to the self. There is no place
to hide, and so we are found."

From *Refuge: An Unnatural History of Family and Place*

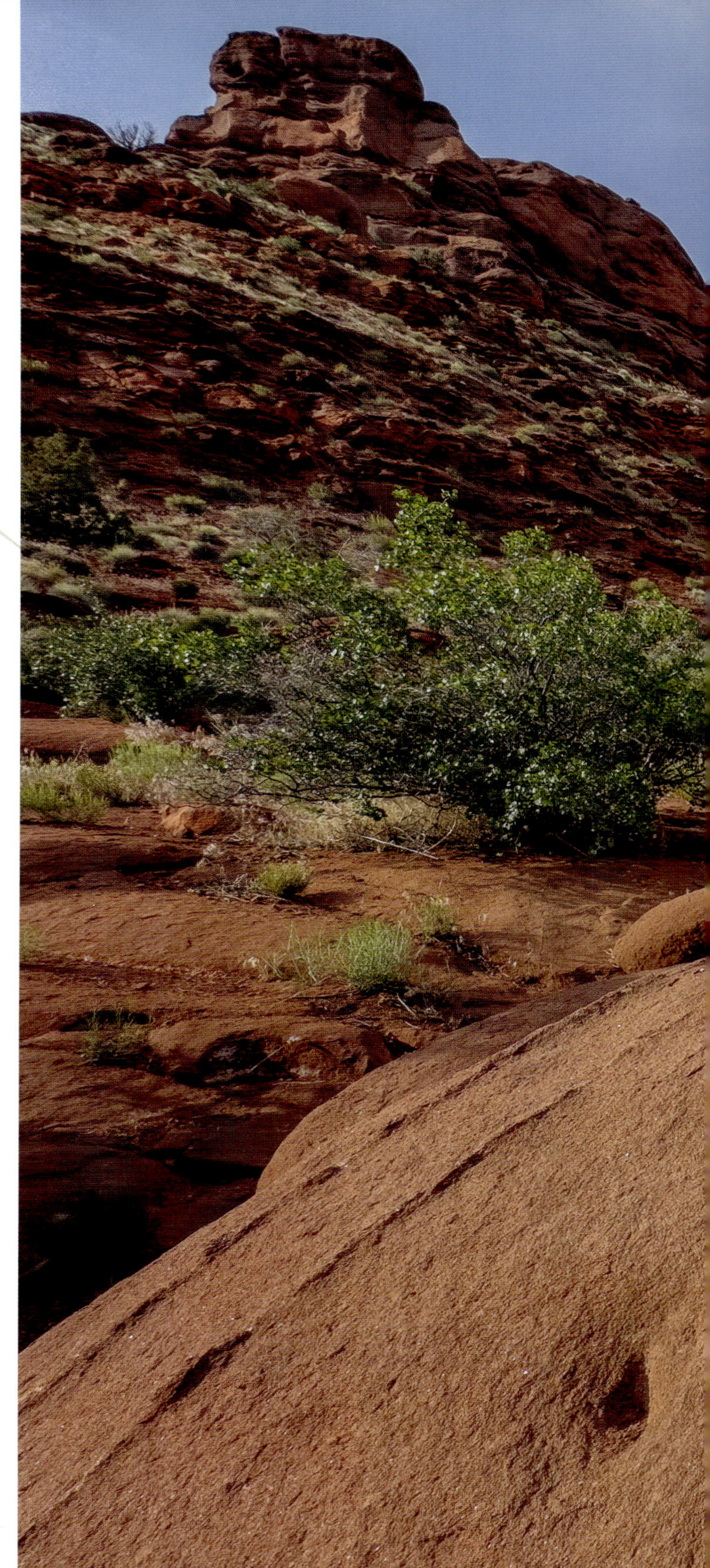

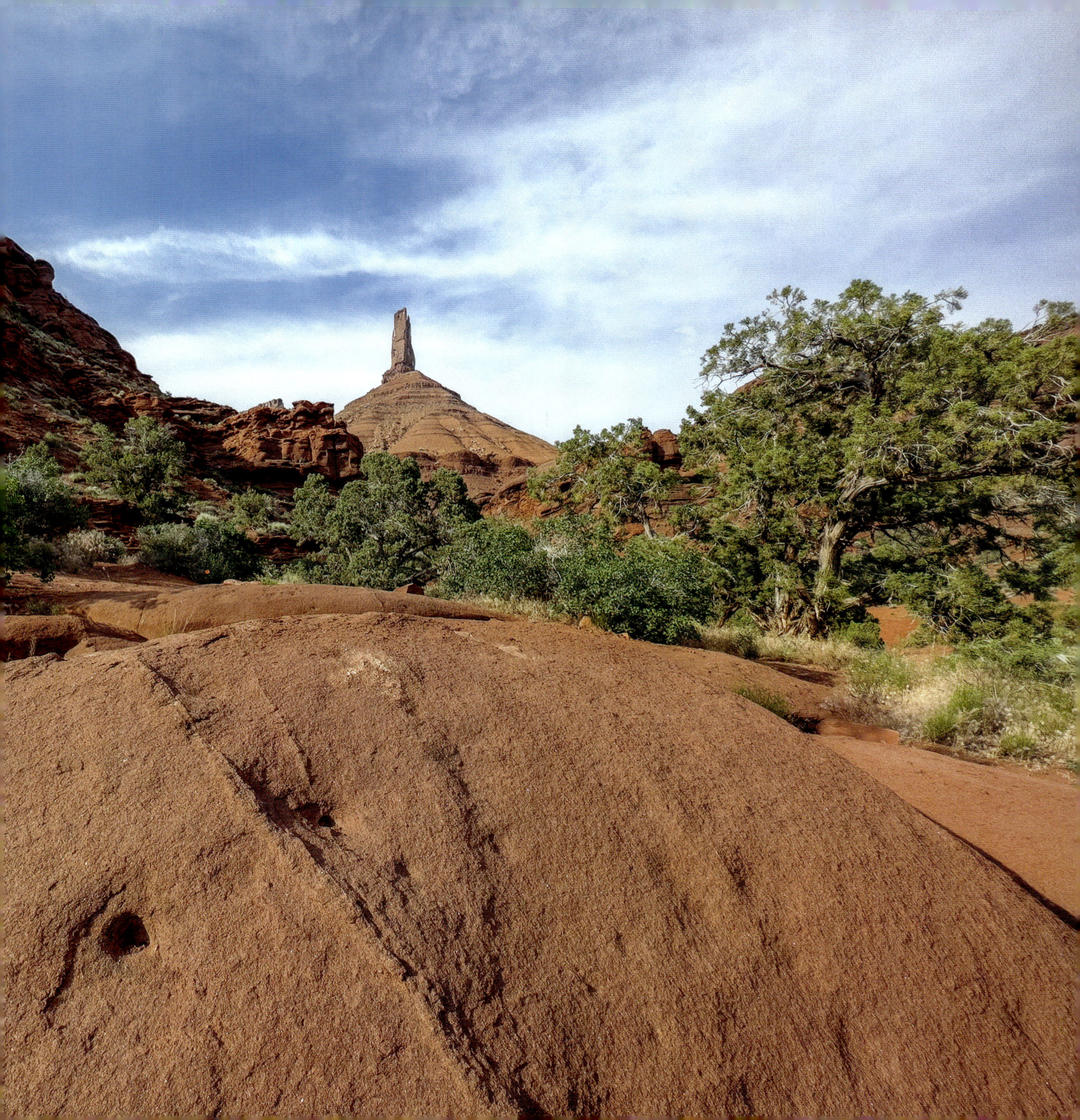

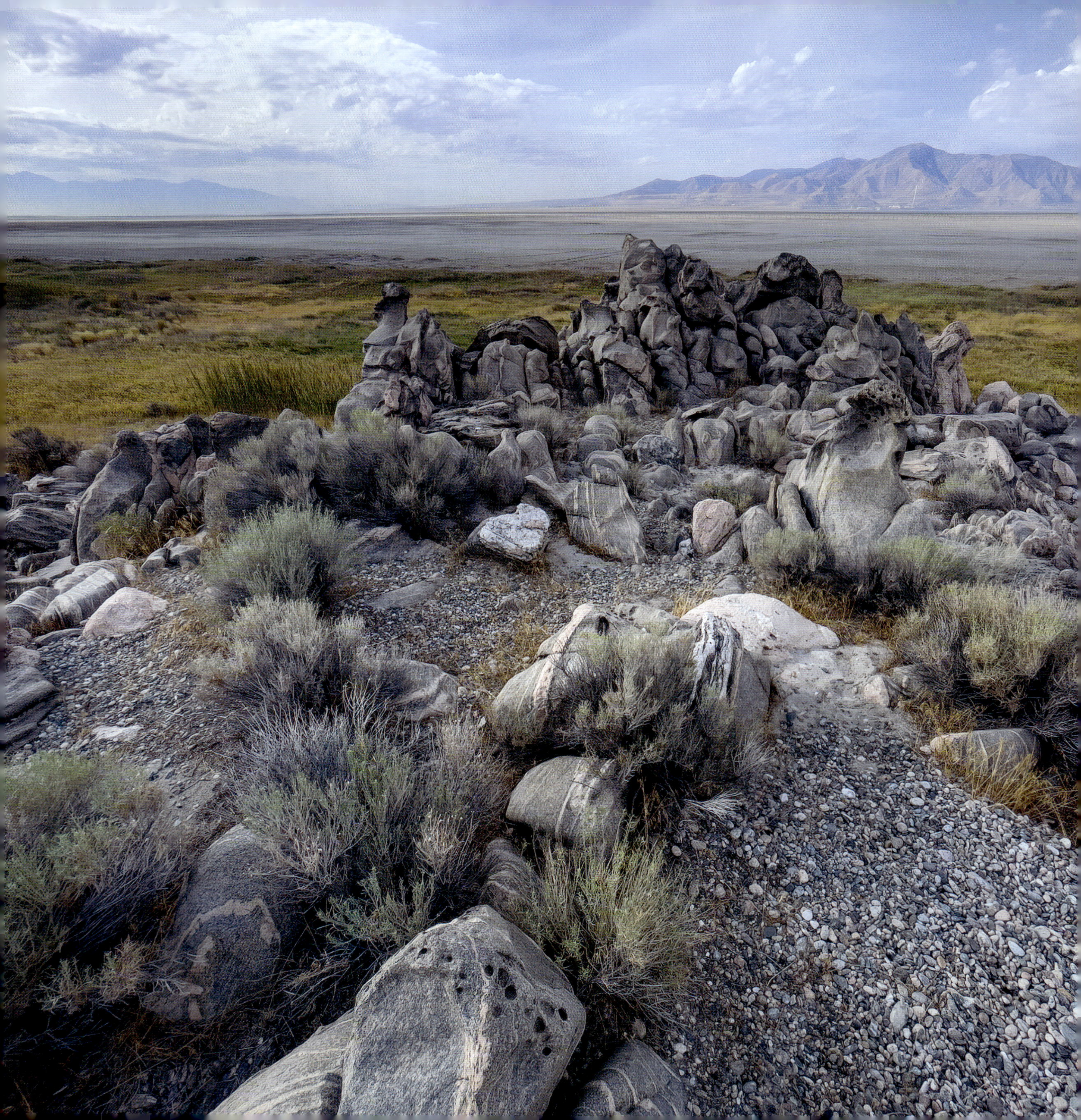

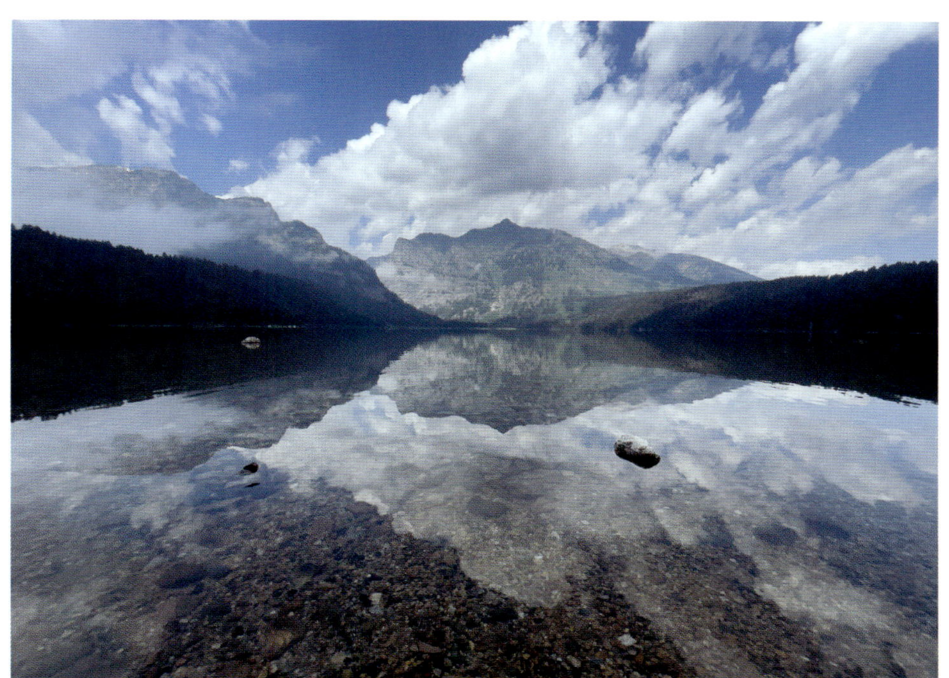
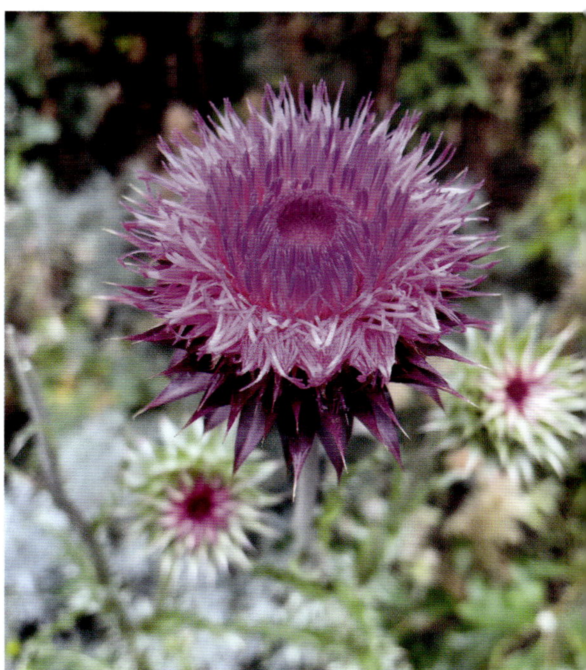

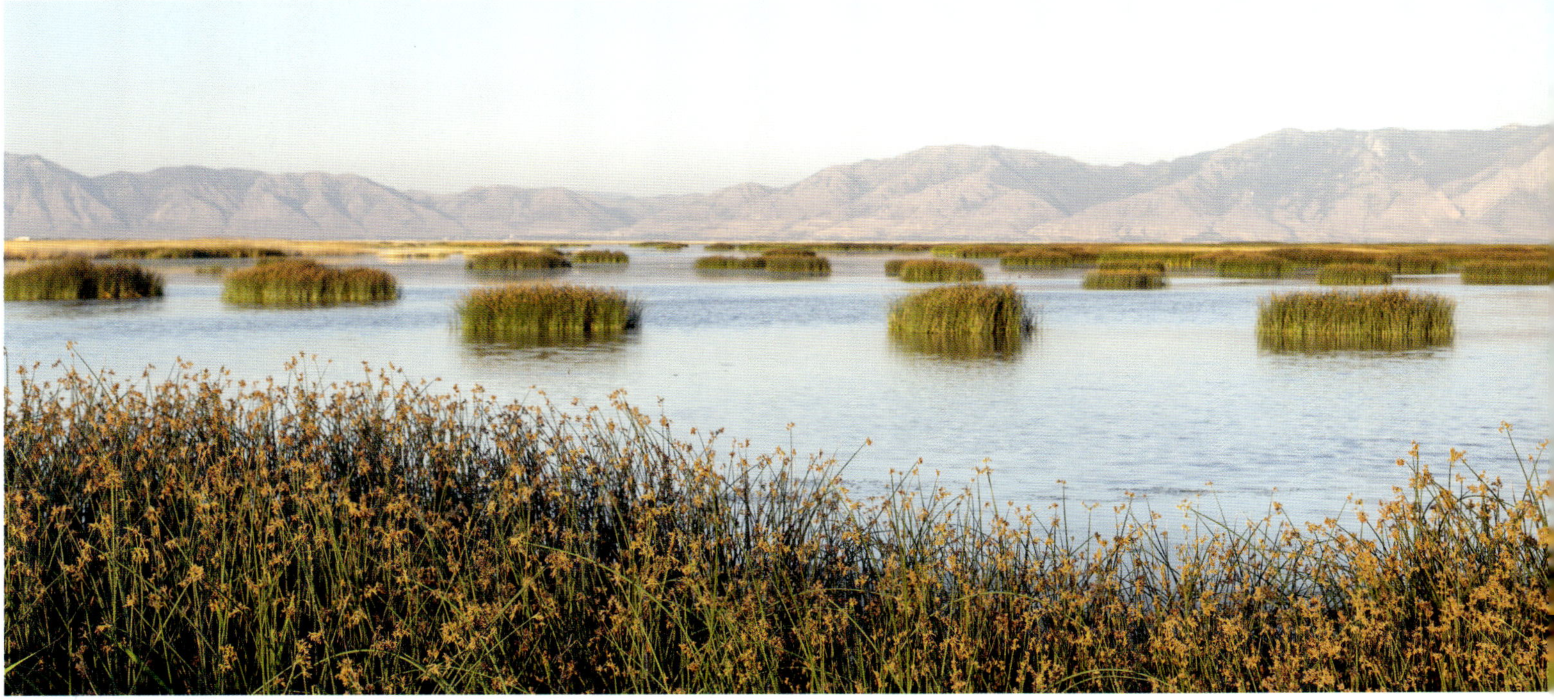

SOURCES

The quotations and excerpts featured in this book are from the following editions, which I encourage you to read in their entirety.

Abbey, Edward, *Desert Solitaire: A Season in the Wilderness* (New York: Ballantine Books, 2018), 208.

Austin, Mary Hunter, *The Land of Little Rain* (New York: Warbler Press, 2020), 55.

Bass, Rick, *Wild to the Heart*, Authors Guild backinprint.com edition (Bloomington, IN: iUniverse, 2012), 158.

Belleville, Bill, *Losing It All to Sprawl: How Progress Ate My Cracker Landscape* (Gainesville: University Press of Florida, 2006), 151.

Burroughs, John, *Signs and Seasons* (Syracuse, NY: Syracuse University Press, 2006), 6.

Busch, Akiko, *Nine Ways to Cross a River: Midstream Reflections on Swimming and Getting There from Here* (New York: Bloomsbury/Holtzbrinck, 2007), 185.

Carson, Rachel, *Silent Spring* (Boston: Houghton Mifflin, 1962), 277.

Cerulean, Susan, *I Have Been Assigned the Single Bird: A Daughter's Memoir* (Athens: University of Georgia Press, 2020), 42.

Connors, Philip, *A Song for the River* (El Paso, TX: Cinco Puntos Press, 2018), 118.

Deming, Alison Hawthorne, *Writing the Sacred into the Real* (Minneapolis, MN: Milkweed Editions, 2001), 92.

Douglas, Marjory Stoneman, *The Everglades: River of Grass* (New York: Rinehart & Co., 1947), 1.

Dungy, Camille T., *Soil: The Story of a Black Mother's Garden* (New York: Simon & Schuster, 2023), 10.

Ehrlich, Gretel, *Unsolaced: Along the Way to All That Is* (New York: Pantheon Books, 2021), 7.

Finch, Robert, *The Outer Beach: A Thousand-Mile Walk on Cape Cod's Atlantic Shore* (New York: W. W. Norton & Co., 2017), 241.

Freeman, Scott, *Saving Tarboo Creek: One Family's Quest to Heal the Land* (Portland, OR: Timber Press, 2018), 177.

Gessner, David, *All the Wild That Remains: Edward Abbey, Wallace Stegner, and the American West* (New York: W. W. Norton & Co., 2015), 164.

Graves, John, *Goodbye to a River: A Narrative* (New York: Vintage Books, 2002), 83.

Gruchow, Paul, *Journal of a Prairie Year* (Minneapolis, MN: Milkweed Editions, 2009), 2.

Haskell, David George, *The Forest Unseen: A Year's Watch in Nature* (New York: Viking, 2012), 158.

Hasselstrom, Linda M., *Between Grass and Sky: Where I Live and Work* (Reno: University of Nevada Press, 2002), 19.

Haupt, Lyanda Lynn, *Crow Planet: Essential Wisdom from the Urban Wilderness* (New York: Little, Brown & Co., 2009), 157.

Hoagland, Edward, *Balancing Acts: Essays* (New York: Simon & Schuster, 1993), 347.

Hogan, Linda, *Dwellings: A Spiritual History of the Living World* (New York: W. W. Norton & Co., 2007), 115.

Houston, Pam, *Deep Creek: Finding Hope in the High Country* (New York: W. W. Norton & Co., 2019), 298.

Jeffers, Robinson, *The Wild God of the World: An Anthology of Robinson Jeffers* (Stanford, CA: Stanford University Press, 2003), 151.

Kingsolver, Barbara, *Small Wonder: Essays* (New York: HarperCollins, 2002), 39.

Lanham, J. Drew, *The Home Place: Memoirs of a Colored Man's Love Affair with Nature* (Minneapolis, MN: Milkweed Editions, 2017), 157.

Leopold, Aldo, *A Sand County Almanac: And Sketches Here and There* (New York: Oxford University Press, 1949), 81.

Limón, Ada, *The Carrying: Poems* (Minneapolis, MN: Milkweed Editions, 2018), 22.

Lopez, Barry, *Embrace Fearlessly the Burning World: Essays* (New York: Random House, 2022), 122.

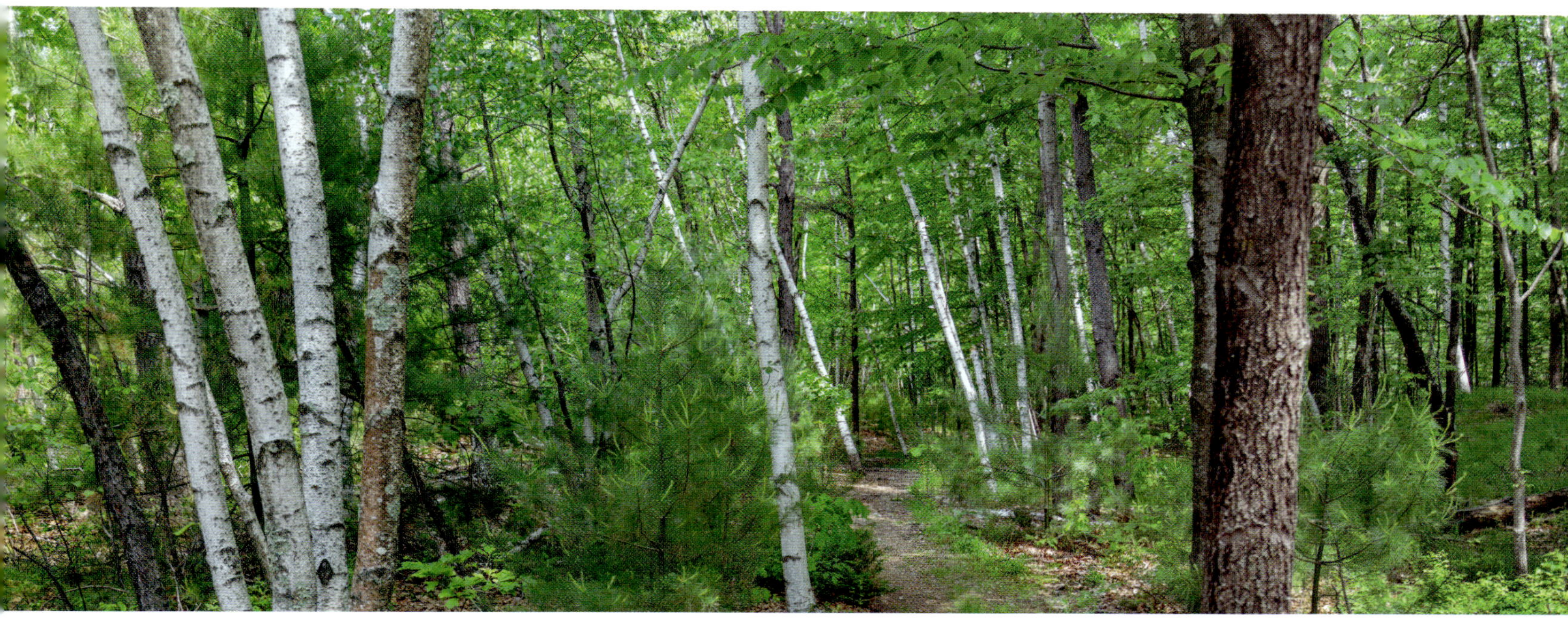

Matthiessen, Peter, *The Tree Where Man Was Born* (New York: Penguin Books, 2010), 201.

McKibben, Bill, *Wandering Home: A Long Walk Across America's Most Hopeful Landscape* (New York: Crown, 2005), 133.

Meloy, Ellen, *Seasons: Desert Sketches* (Salt Lake City, UT: Torrey House Press, 2019), 23.

Merwin, W. S., *The Moving Target: Poems* (New York: Atheneum, 1963), 93.

Muir, John, *John of the Mountains: The Unpublished Journals of John Muir*, ed. Linnie Marsh Wolfe (Boston: Houghton Mifflin, 1938), 299.

Olson, Sigurd F., *Listening Point* (Minneapolis: University of Minnesota Press, 2015), 8.

Perez, Craig Santos, *Habitat Threshold* (Oakland, CA: Omnidawn Publishing, 2020), 20.

Pyle, Robert Michael, *Nature Matrix: New and Selected Essays* (Berkeley, CA: Counterpoint Press, 2020), 5.

Ray, Janisse, *Ecology of a Cracker Childhood* (Minneapolis, MN: Milkweed Editions, 1999), 15.

Roosevelt, Theodore, *Letters from Theodore Roosevelt to Anna Roosevelt Cowles, 1870–1918* (New York: Charles Scribner's Sons, 1924), 63.

Salmón, Enrique, *Iwígara: The Kinship of Plants and People; American Indian Ethnobotanical Traditions and Science* (Portland, OR: Timber Press, 2020), 10.

Stratton-Porter, Gene, *Laddie: A True Blue Story* (New York: Doubleday, Page & Co., 1913), 109.

Thoreau, Henry David, *The Writings of Henry D. Thoreau, Journal, Volume 5: 1852–1853*, ed. Patrick F. O'Connell (Princeton, NJ: Princeton University Press, 1997), 422.

Williams, Terry Tempest, *Refuge: An Unnatural History of Family and Place*, 2nd ed. (New York: Vintage Books, 2001), 148.

FOR FURTHER READING

If you enjoyed the writings featured
in this book and cited in the
previous source list, here are some
more works by each author to
add to your reading list.

EDWARD ABBEY

Abbey's Road
The Brave Cowboy: An Old Tale in a New Time
The Fool's Progress: An Honest Novel
Hayduke Lives!
*The Journey Home: Some Words in Defense
    of the American West*
The Monkey Wrench Gang
One Life at a Time, Please

MARY HUNTER AUSTIN

Cactus Thorn: A Novella
Earth Horizon
The Land of Journeys' Ending
One-Smoke Stories

RICK BASS

The Book of Yaak
Colter: The True Story of the Best Dog I Ever Had
For a Little While
The Sky, the Stars, the Wilderness: Novellas
Why I Came West: A Memoir
*The Wild Marsh: Four Seasons at Home
    in Montana*
*With Every Great Breath: New and Selected
    Essays, 1995–2023*

BILL BELLEVILLE

The Peace of Blue: Water Journeys
*River of Lakes: A Journey on Florida's
    St. Johns River*
*Salvaging the Real Florida: Lost and Found
    in the State of Dreams*
*Sunken Cities, Sacred Cenotes, and Golden
    Sharks: Travels of a Water-Bound Adventurer*

JOHN BURROUGHS

Accepting the Universe: Essays in Naturalism
*The Art of Seeing Things: Essays by John
    Burroughs*
Camping and Tramping with Roosevelt
*In the Catskills: Selections from the Writings
    of John Burroughs*
Locusts and Wild Honey
Ways of Nature

AKIKO BUSCH

*Geography of Home: Writings on Where
    We Live*
*How to Disappear: Notes on Invisibility in a
    Time of Transparency*
*The Incidental Steward: Reflections on
    Citizen Science*
Patience: Taking Time in the Age of Acceleration

RACHEL CARSON

*Always, Rachel: The Letters of Rachel Carson
    and Dorothy Freeman, 1952–1964*
The Edge of the Sea
*Lost Woods: The Discovered Writing of
    Rachel Carson*
The Sea around Us

*The Sense of Wonder: A Celebration of
    Nature for Parents and Children*
Under the Sea-Wind

SUSAN CERULEAN

*Between Two Rivers: Stories from the Red
    Hills to the Gulf* (coedited with Janisse
    Ray and Laura Newton)
*Coming to Pass: Florida's Coastal Islands
    in a Gulf of Change*
*Florida Trails: A Guide to Florida's Natural
    Habitats*
*Tracking Desire: A Journey after Swallow-
    tailed Kites*

PHILIP CONNORS

All the Wrong Places: A Life Lost and Found
*Fire Season: Field Notes from a Wilderness
    Lookout*
*New West Reader: Essays on an Ever-Evolving
    Frontier*

ALISON HAWTHORNE DEMING

Blue Flax & Yellow Mustard Flower
    (forthcoming 2025)
*The Colors of Nature: Culture, Identity,
    and the Natural World* (coedited with
    Lauret E. Savoy)
*The Edges of the Civilized World: A Journey
    in Nature and Culture*
Stairway to Heaven: Poems
*Temporary Homelands: Essays on Nature,
    Spirit, and Place*
Zoologies: On Animals and the Human Spirit

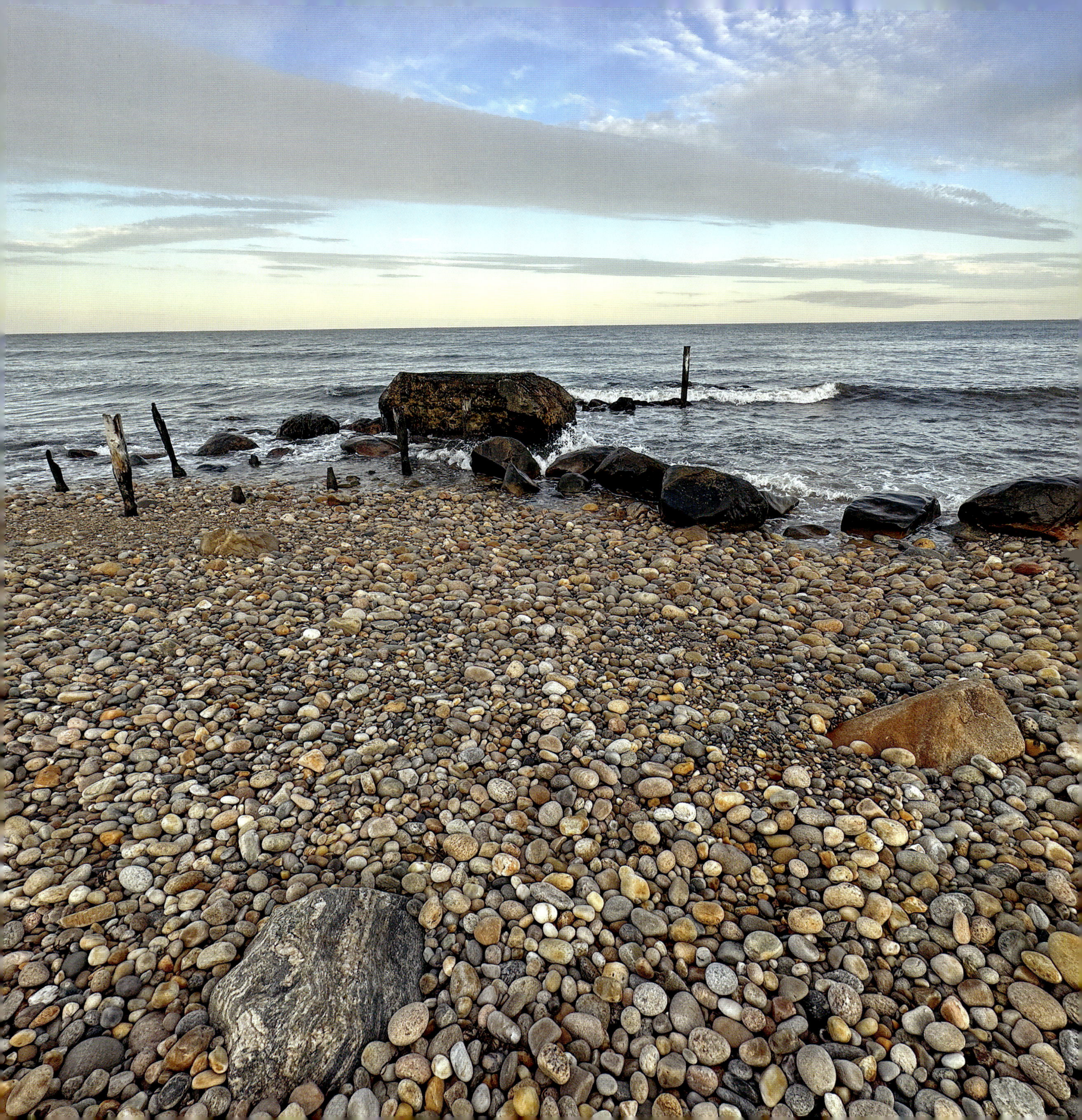

MARJORY STONEMAN DOUGLAS

Alligator Crossing

Florida: The Long Frontier

Hurricane

The Joys of Bird Watching in Florida

Nine Florida Stories by Marjory Stoneman Douglas (edited by Kevin M. McCarthy)

Road to the Sun

The Wide Brim: Early Poems and Ponderings of Marjory Stoneman Douglas (edited by Jack E. Davis)

CAMILLE T. DUNGY

Black Nature: Four Centuries of African American Nature Poetry (as editor)

Smith Blue: Poems by Camille T. Dungy

Trophic Cascade

GRETEL EHRLICH

Drinking Dry Clouds: Stories from Wyoming

The Future of Ice: A Journey into Cold

Islands, the Universe, Home

John Muir: Nature's Visionary

A Match to the Heart: One Woman's Story of Being Struck by Lightning

The Solace of Open Spaces

This Cold Heaven: Seven Seasons in Greenland

ROBERT FINCH

A Cape Cod Notebook

Common Ground: A Naturalist's Cape Cod

Death of a Hornet: And Other Cape Cod Essays

The Iambics of Newfoundland: Notes from an Unknown Shore

A Place Apart: A Cape Cod Reader (as editor)

The Primal Place

SCOTT FREEMAN

Biological Science, 7th edition

DAVID GESSNER

Leave It as It Is: A Journey through Theodore Roosevelt's American Wilderness

My Green Manifesto: Down the Charles River in Pursuit of a New Environmentalism

The Prophet of Dry Hill: Lessons from a Life in Nature

Quiet Desperation, Savage Delight: Sheltering with Thoreau in the Age of Crisis

Sick of Nature

A Traveler's Guide to the End of the World: Tales of Fire, Wind, and Water

Under the Devil's Thumb

JOHN GRAVES

From a Limestone Ledge: Some Essays and Other Ruminations about Country Life in Texas

Hard Scrabble: Observations on a Patch of Land

A John Graves Reader

Myself and Strangers: A Memoir of Apprenticeship

Texas Heartland: A Hill Country Year

PAUL GRUCHOW

Boundary Waters: The Grace of the Wild

Grass Roots: The Universe of Home

Letters to a Young Madman: A Memoir

The Necessity of Empty Places

Travels in Canoe Country (with photographer Gerald Brimacombe)

Worlds within a World: Reflections on Visits to Minnesota Scientific and Natural Area Preserves

DAVID GEORGE HASKELL

The Songs of Trees: Stories from Nature's Great Connectors

Sounds Wild and Broken: Sonic Marvels, Evolution's Creativity, and the Crisis of Sensory Extinction

Thirteen Ways to Smell a Tree: Getting to Know Trees through the Language of Scent

LINDA M. HASSELSTROM

Bitter Creek Junction: Poetry of the American West

Dakota: Bones, Grass, Sky

Feels Like Far: A Rancher's Life on the Great Plains

Gathering from the Grassland: A Plains Journal

No Place Like Home: Notes from a Western Life

Walking: The Changes (with photographer James W. Parker)

Windbreak: A Woman Rancher on the Northern Plains

LYANDA LYNN HAUPT

Mozart's Starling

Pilgrim on the Great Bird Continent: The Importance of Everything and Other Lessons from Darwin's Lost Notebooks

Rare Encounters with Ordinary Birds

Rooted: Life at the Crossroads of Science, Nature, and Spirit

The Urban Bestiary: Encountering the Everyday Wild

EDWARD HOAGLAND

African Calliope: A Journey to the Sudan

Alaskan Travels: Far-Flung Tales of Love and Adventure

Compass Points: How I Lived

The Devil's Tub: Collected Stories

In the Country of the Blind: A Novel

On Nature: Selected Essays

Tiger & Ice: Reflections on Nature and Life

LINDA HOGAN
Calling Myself Home
A History of Kindness
People of the Whale: A Novel
The Radiant Lives of Animals
Rounding the Human Corners: Poems
Solar Storms
The Woman Who Watches over the World:
    A Native Memoir

PAM HOUSTON
Contents May Have Shifted: A Novel
A Little More about Me
A Rough Guide to the Heart
Sight Hound: A Novel
Women on Hunting (as editor)

ROBINSON JEFFERS
The Collected Letters of Robinson Jeffers, with
    Selected Letters of Una Jeffers: Volume One,
    1890–1930 (edited by James Karman)
The Collected Letters of Robinson Jeffers, with
    Selected Letters of Una Jeffers: Volume Two,
    1931–1939 (edited by James Karman)
The Collected Poetry of Robinson Jeffers:
    Volume One, 1920–1928 (edited by Tim Hunt)
The Collected Poetry of Robinson Jeffers:
    Volume Two, 1928–1938 (edited by Tim Hunt)
The Collected Poetry of Robinson Jeffers:
    Volume Three, 1939–1962 (edited by Tim Hunt)
The Collected Poetry of Robinson Jeffers:
    Volume Four, Poetry 1903–1920, Prose, and
    Unpublished Writings (edited by Tim Hunt)
The Collected Poetry of Robinson Jeffers:
    Volume Five, Textual Evidence and
    Commentary (edited by Tim Hunt)

BARBARA KINGSOLVER
Animal, Vegetable, Miracle: A Year of Food Life

Flight Behavior: A Novel
Homeland and Other Stories
How to Fly (In Ten Thousand Easy Lessons):
    Poems
Last Stand: America's Virgin Lands (with
    photographer Annie Griffiths Belt)
Prodigal Summer: A Novel

J. DREW LANHAM
Joy Is the Justice We Give Ourselves
Sparrow Envy: Field Guide to Birds and Lesser
    Beasts

ALDO LEOPOLD
The Farmer as Conservationist
For the Health of the Land: Previously
    Unpublished Essays and Other Writings
    (edited by J. Baird Callicott and Eric T.
    Freyfogle)
Game Management
The River of the Mother of God and Other
    Essays by Aldo Leopold (edited by Susan L.
    Flader and J. Baird Callicott)
Round River: From the Journals of Aldo
    Leopold (edited by Luna B. Leopold)
Think Like a Mountain

ADA LIMÓN
Bright Dead Things: Poems
The Hurting Kind: Poems
Sharks in the Rivers
You Are Here: Poetry in the Natural World
    (as editor)

BARRY LOPEZ
About This Life: Journeys on the Threshold
    of Memory
Arctic Dreams
Crossing Open Ground

Desert Notes, River Notes: Stories
Field Notes: Stories
Horizon
Outside: Stories

PETER MATTHIESSEN
Cloud Forest: A Chronicle of South American
    Wilderness
End of the Earth: Voyages to Antarctica
Far Tortuga: A Novel
Men's Lives
Shadow Country
The Snow Leopard

BILL McKIBBEN
Eaarth: Making a Life on a Tough New Planet
The End of Nature
Falter: Has the Human Game Begun to Play
    Itself Out?
Fight Global Warming Now: The Handbook for
    Taking Action in Your Community
The Flag, the Cross, and the Station Wagon:
    A Graying American Looks Back at His
    Suburban Boyhood and Wonders What the
    Hell Happened
Hope, Human and Wild: True Stories of
    Living Lightly on the Earth
Oil and Honey: The Education of an
    Unlikely Activist

ELLEN MELOY
The Anthropology of Turquoise: Reflections
    on Desert, Sea, Stone, and Sky
Eating Stone: Imagination and the Loss of the
    Wild
The Last Cheater's Waltz: Beauty and Violence
    in the Desert Southwest
Raven's Exile: A Season on the Green River

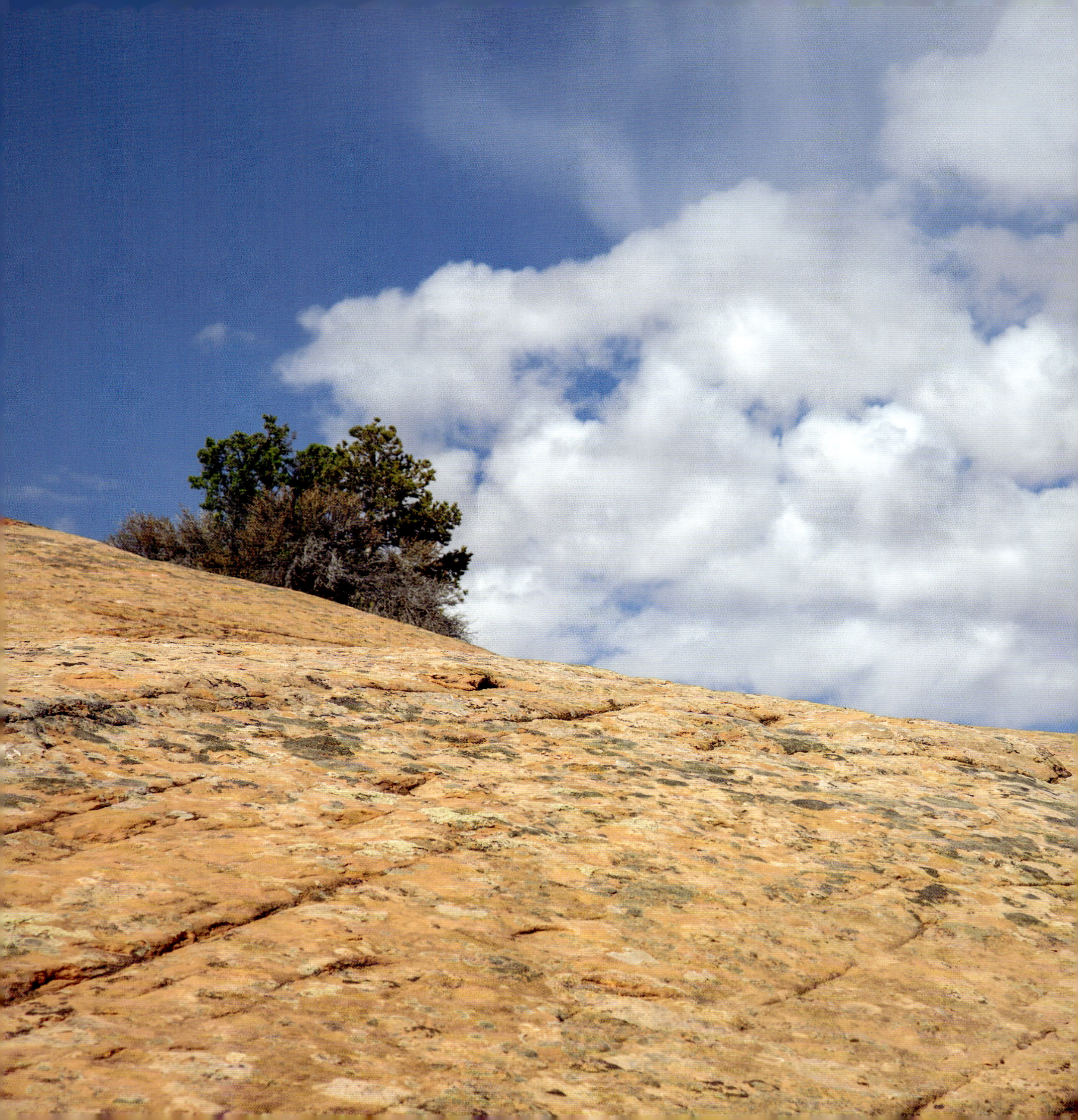

W. S. MERWIN

The Collected Poems of W. S. Merwin
 (edited by J. D. McClatchy)
The Folding Cliffs: A Narrative of
 19th-Century Hawaii
Garden Time
Migration: New & Selected Poems
The Moon before Morning
The Rain in the Trees
Summer Doorways: A Memoir

JOHN MUIR

The Mountains of California
My First Summer in the Sierra
Our National Parks
Stickeen
The Story of My Boyhood and Youth
A Thousand-Mile Walk to the Gulf
The Yosemite

SIGURD F. OLSON

The Lonely Land
The Meaning of Wilderness: Essential
 Articles and Speeches
Of Time and Place
Open Horizons
Reflections from the North Country
Runes of the North
The Singing Wilderness

CRAIG SANTOS PEREZ

From Unincorporated Territory [åmot]
From Unincorporated Territory [guma']
From Unincorporated Territory [hacha]
From Unincorporated Territory [lukao]
From Unincorporated Territory [saina]
Navigating Chamoru Poetry: Indigeneity,
 Aesthetics, and Decolonization

ROBERT MICHAEL PYLE

Magdalena Mountain: A Novel
Mariposa Road: The First Butterfly Big Year
Sky Time in Gray's River: Living for Keeps
 in a Forgotten Place
Through a Green Lens: Fifty Years of Writing
 for Nature
The Thunder Tree: Lessons from an Urban
 Wildland
Where Bigfoot Walks: Crossing the Dark Divide
Wintergreen: Listening to the Land's Heart

JANISSE RAY

Drifting into Darien: A Personal and
 Natural History of the Altamaha River
A House of Branches
Pinhook: Finding Wholeness in a
 Fragmented Land
Red Lanterns: Poems
The Seed Underground: A Growing
 Revolution to Save Food
Wild Card Quilt: Taking a Chance on Home
Wild Spectacle: Seeking Wonders in a World
 beyond Humans

THEODORE ROOSEVELT

Hunting Trips of a Ranchman: Sketches
 of Sport on the Northern Cattle Plains
Ranch Life and the Hunting Trail
Theodore Roosevelt: An Autobiography
Through the Brazilian Wilderness
Wilderness Writings

ENRIQUE SALMÓN

Eating the Landscape: American Indian Stories
 of Food, Identity, and Resilience

GENE STRATTON-PORTER

A Daughter of the Land
Freckles
A Girl of the Limberlost
Moths of the Limberlost
Music of the Wild
The Song of the Cardinal
What I Have Done with Birds

HENRY DAVID THOREAU

Cape Cod
Excursions
The Journal 1837–1861
Maine Woods
Walden, or Life in the Woods
A Week on the Concord and Merrimack Rivers
Where I Lived, and What I Lived For

TERRY TEMPEST WILLIAMS

Erosions: Essays of Undoing
Finding Beauty in a Broken World
The Hour of Land: A Personal Topography
 of America's National Parks
Leap
Red: Passion and Patience in the Desert
An Unspoken Hunger: Stories from the Field
When Women Were Birds: Fifty-Four
 Variations on Voice

ACKNOWLEDGMENTS 

First and foremost, to all the writers involved in this endeavor, thank you for seeing the value of this project and being willing to participate in such an undertaking. You, and often your partners, welcomed me into your lives and willingly gave your time to help me better understand the places that have influenced your writings and lives.

Thanks to Camille T. Dungy and Bill McKibben for adding your voices to this book. Your words and insights are greatly appreciated. Thank you to Terry Tempest Williams for allowing me to use the phrase "mentored by the land" from her book *An Unspoken Hunger* as the subtitle of my book. I believe this phrase captures perfectly what this project is all about.

To the many individuals who dedicate their lives to promoting the work of those writers who are no longer with us, your commitment to preserving their efforts is admirable.

Thank you to Roger Christie and Wendy Sisson, Linda Hasselstrom, and Elliot Ruchowitz-Roberts for opening up your homes and offering me a chance to get out of my tent or camper and have a comfortable bed and warm shower, and to Steffi Huberty and the Listening Point Foundation for offering me the first artist residency at Sigurd Olson's home.

At Rizzoli, thanks to Jim Muschett for recognizing the significance of this project and taking a chance on me and my work; Candice Fehrman for your attention to detail and ensuring I have my ducks in a row; and Susi Oberhelman for your vision and design expertise.

Thank you to the College of Arts and Humanities faculty grant committee members at Minnesota State University Moorhead and the grant committee members and staff at The Arts Partnership in Fargo, North Dakota. Without your financial assistance and support, this project would have been difficult to complete.

And last, thank you to friends and family members who have offered their moral support over the past five years. Your encouragement helped fuel my drive to see this project through to fruition.

Terry Tempest Williams • Utah

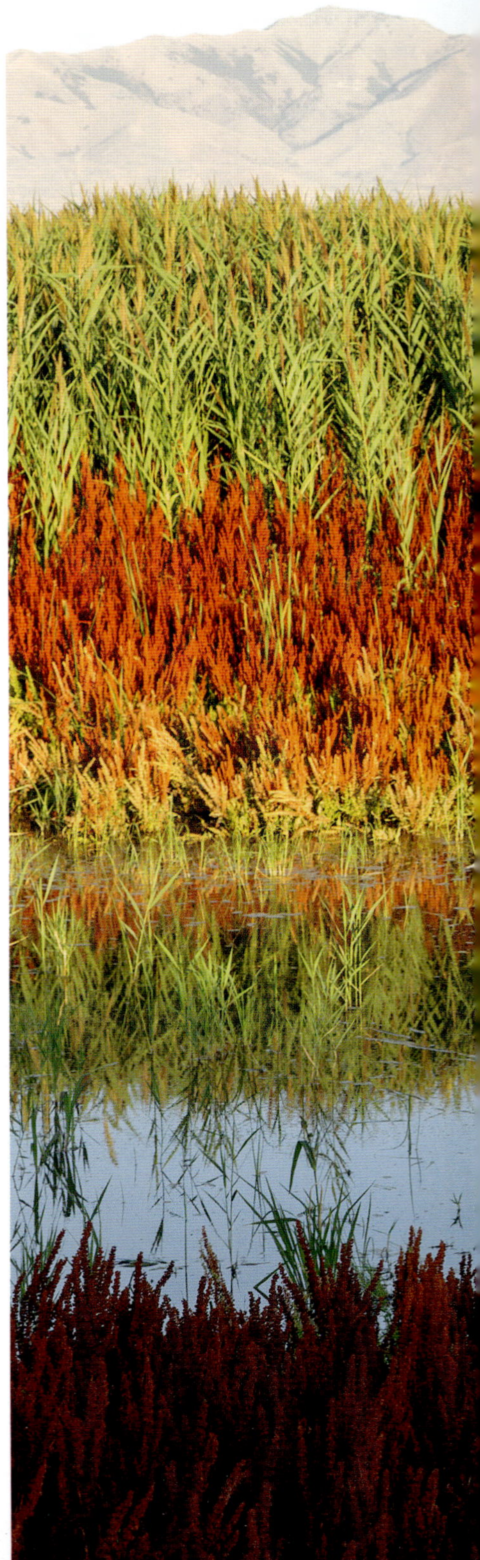

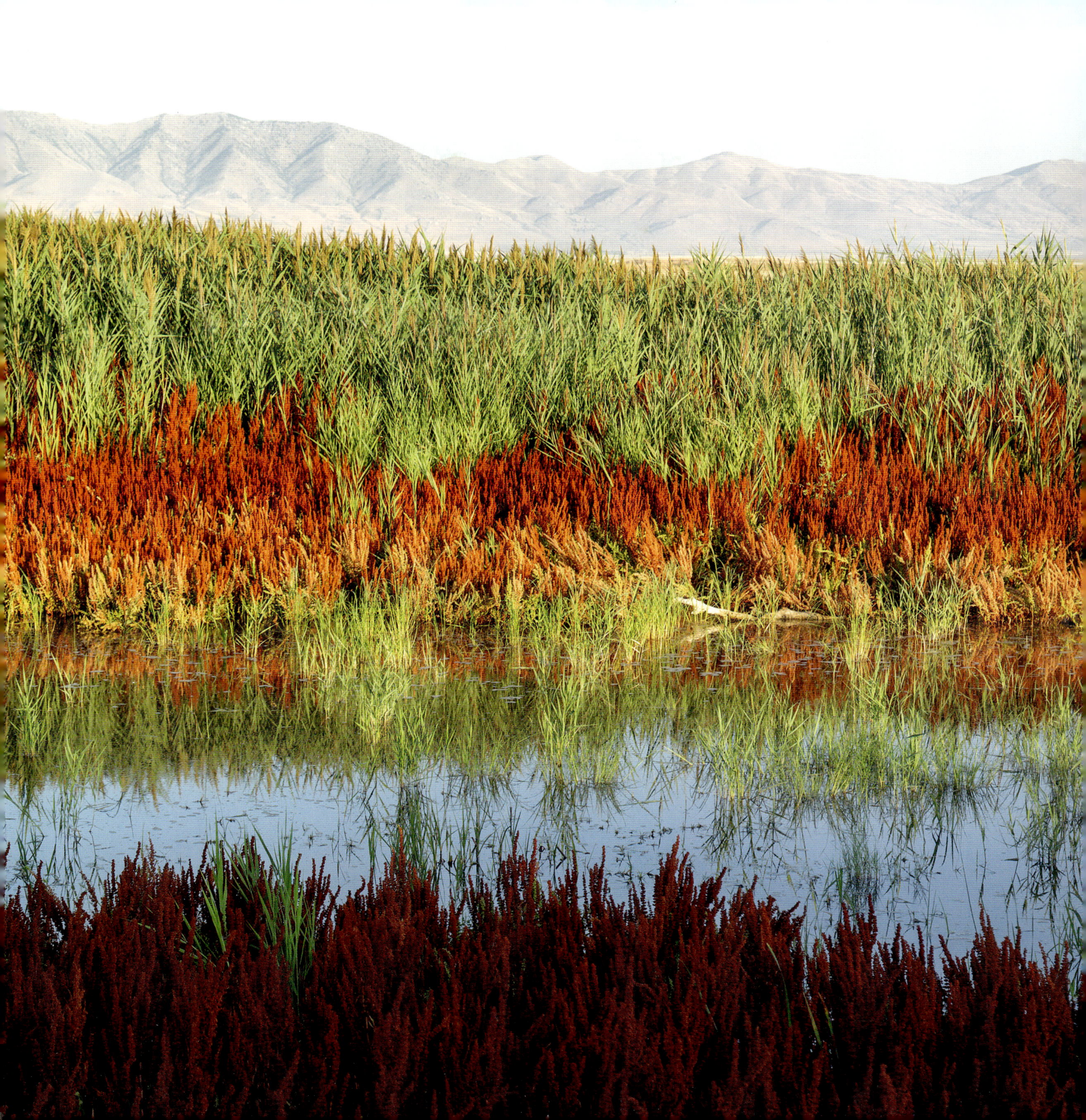

First published in the United States of America in 2024 by
Rizzoli International Publications, Inc.
300 Park Avenue South · New York, NY 10010 · www.rizzoliusa.com

Publisher: Charles Miers
Associate Publisher: James Muschett
Managing Editor: Lynn Scrabis
Editor: Candice Fehrman
Design: Susi Oberhelman

Printed in China

2024 2025 2026 2027 / 10 9 8 7 6 5 4 3 2 1

ISBN: 978-0-8478-3199-9

Library of Congress Control Number: 2024931345

Visit us online:
Facebook.com/RizzoliNewYork
Twitter: @Rizzoli_Books
Instagram.com/RizzoliBooks
Pinterest.com/RizzoliBooks
Youtube.com/user/RizzoliNY
Issuu.com/Rizzoli

Page 1: Akiko Busch · New York
Pages 2–3: Aldo Leopold · Wisconson
Pages 4–5: Theodore Roosevelt · North Dakota
Pages 6–7: Alison Hawthorne Deming · Arizona
Pages 8–9: Linda Hogan · Oklahoma

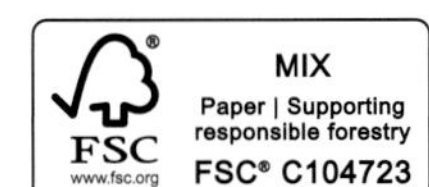